Communications in Computer and Information Science 1344

More information about this series at http://www.springer.com/series/7899

Laura Sara Agrati · Daniel Burgos ·
Pietro Ducange · Pierpaolo Limone ·
Loredana Perla · Pietro Picerno ·
Paolo Raviolo · Christian M. Stracke (Eds.)

Bridges and Mediation in Higher Distance Education

Second International Workshop, HELMeTO 2020
Bari, BA, Italy, September 17–18, 2020
Revised Selected Papers

Springer

Editors
Laura Sara Agrati
Giustino Fortunato University
Benevento, Italy

Daniel Burgos
Universidad Internacional de La Rioja
Logroño, La Rioja, Spain

Pietro Ducange
University of Pisa
Pisa, Italy

Pierpaolo Limone
University of Foggia
Foggia, Italy

Loredana Perla
University of Bari Aldo Moro
Bari, Italy

Pietro Picerno
eCampus University
Novedrate, Como, Italy

Paolo Raviolo
eCampus University
Novedrate, Como, Italy

Christian M. Stracke
Open University in the Netherlands
Heerlen, The Netherlands

ISSN 1865-0929 ISSN 1865-0937 (electronic)
Communications in Computer and Information Science
ISBN 978-3-030-67434-2 ISBN 978-3-030-67435-9 (eBook)
https://doi.org/10.1007/978-3-030-67435-9

This Springer imprint is published by the registered company Springer Nature Switzerland AG
The registered company address is: Gewerbestrasse 11, 6330 Cham, Switzerland

Preface

This volume of Communications in Computer and Information Science (CCIS) contains the post-proceedings of HELMeTO 2020, the Second International Workshop on Higher Education Learning Methodologies and Technologies Online. The event was successfully held online, organized by the University of Bari Aldo Moro, Italy, during September 17–18, 2020. HELMeTO 2020 aimed to bring together researchers and practitioners working in Higher Distance Education Institutions or studying Online Learning Methodologies to present and share their research in a multidisciplinary context. The workshop provided a forum for the discussion of new research directions and applications in these fields, where different disciplines effectively met, divided into two main tracks – 'Methodologies of eLearning' and 'Information Technology for eLearning' – and a special track – 'Facing COVID-19 Emergency in Higher Education Teaching and Learning' – together with their applications.

Some examples of the discussed interdisciplinary topics are: pedagogical framework studies, learning models, learning outcomes, online learning communities, blended learning, online peer assessment, social learning, evaluation for online education, assessment methods in online and blended learning environments, assessment and accreditation of courses and institutions, computer-aided assessment, community building, context dependent learning, course design and e-learning curricula, digital libraries for e-learning, distance and e-learning in a global context, e-learning platforms and portals, e-testing and new test theories, distance education, immersive learning, learning organization, mobile learning (m-learning), simulated communities and online mentoring, supervising and managing student projects, teacher evaluation, security aspects, standards and interoperability, ontologies and metadata standards, theoretical bases of e-learning environments, Web-based learning, wikis and blogs, educational Big Data mining, learning analytics, prediction of students' performance, design of proper retention strategies exploiting learning analytics, and educational Big Data.

HELMeTO 2020 received a total of 59 submissions, 40 of which were selected for presentation at the workshop as either long or short talks. We accepted 26 high-quality papers (44% of the original submissions) for publication in an extended version in this post-proceedings volume (23 long papers of more than 12 pages and 3 short papers of more than 8 pages), after a single-blind review round performed by at least three Program Committee members.

Submissions and participants in HELMeTO 2020 came from eleven different countries, namely France, Germany, Hungary, Italy, Japan, Morocco, Nigeria, Norway, Russia, Spain, and the UK, immediately making HELMeTO an international event. Following this ever-increasing international spirit, future HELMeTO editions are also expected to be held outside Italy.

Many people contributed to this successful edition. We express our gratitude to the authors for submitting their works, to the members of the Program Committee, coming from nine different countries (China, Finland, France, Germany, India, Italy, Morocco,

Gaetano Tieri	University of Rome Unitelma Sapienza, Italy
Chih-Hsiung Tu	Northern Arizona University, USA
Gennaro Vessio	Università di Bari Aldo Moro, Italy
Viviana Vinci	Mediterranea University of Reggio Calabria, Italy

Sponsors

University of Bari Aldo Moro, Italy
SIREM, Società Italiana di Ricerca sull'Educazione Mediale

Contents

The Challenge of Implementing Emerging Technology Solution for Online

Exploiting Time in Adaptive Learning from Educational Data 3
Gabriella Casalino, Giovanna Castellano, and Gennaro Vessio

Recognizing Cognitive Emotions in E-Learning Environment 17
Berardina De Carolis, Francesca D'Errico, Nicola Macchiarulo, Marinella Paciello, and Giuseppe Palestra

Semi-automated Student Feedback and Theory-Driven Video-Analytics: An Exploratory Study on Educational Value of Videos 28
Maka Eradze, Anna Dipace, Bojan Fazlagic, and Anastasia Di Pietro

Learning-State-Estimation Method Using Browsing History and Electroencephalogram During Programming Language Learning and Its Evaluation 40
Katsuyuki Umezawa, Tomohiko Saito, Takashi Ishida, Makoto Nakazawa, and Shigeichi Hirasawa

Making Use of Virtual Reality for Artificial Intelligence Education 56
Sølve Robert Bø Hunvik and Frank Lindseth

Online Learning Pedagogical Frameworks: Models, Perspectives and Application

Professional Development with Digital Practices and Collective Intelligence 73
Muriel Frisch, Jean-Marc Paragot, Simon-Joseph Ndi, and Victoria Pfeffer-Meyer

Improvement of Art Creative Skills by the Means of Signature Pedagogy in Online Musical Education 86
Svetlana V. Karkina, Juan J. Mena Marcos, and Roza A. Valeeva

A Multiple Case Study on Blended and Online Educational Strategies 100
Chiara Panciroli, Laura Corazza, Anita Macauda, and Simona Nicolini

New Perspectives for Using the Model of the Use and Acceptance of Technology in Smart Teaching 115
Giusi Antonia Toto and Pierpaolo Limone

Learning Between Real and Virtual. Narrative and Cognitive Elaborations of University Teaching 126
Marco Piccinno

Facing COVID19 Emergency in Higher Education Teaching and Learning: Tools and Practices

Conducting a College Through COVID-19: The Evolving Leadership Challenge 141
Neil Mort and John Daniel

The Educational Relationship Between Teachers and Young Tennis Players Continued During the Covid-19 Outbreak: Is the Online Teaching a New Start also for the University? 151
Valerio Bonavolontà, Stefania Cataldi, Davide Maci, and Francesco Fischetti

University Students' Online Social Presence and Digital Competencies in the COVID-19 Virus Situation 158
Edit Kővári and Gerda Bak

Virtual Internship as Mediatized Experience. The Educator's Training During COVID19 Emergency 170
Laura Sara Agrati and Viviana Vinci

Facing COVID19 Emergency in Higher Education Teaching and Learning: Frameworks and Overviews

Online Teaching in Higher Education with the Support of Start@Unito During Covid-19 Pandemic 187
Barbara Bruschi, Marina Marchisio, and Matteo Sacchet

Agility of the Post COVID-19 Strategic Plan on Distance Learning at Cadi Ayyad University. An Opportunity Towards a Total Digital Transformation of the University 199
Hana Ait Si Ahmad, Khadija El Kharki, and Khalid Berrada

Blended Learning and Transformative Processes: A Model for Didactic Development and Innovation 214
Loretta Fabbri, Mario Giampaolo, and Martina Capaccioli

Metamorphosis of Space into Digital Scholarship. A Research on Hybrid Mediation in a University Context 226
Loredana Perla, Alessia Scarinci, and Ilenia Amati

Online Learning Technologies in Practice

Experimentation of Flipped Learning in a University Course on Object-Oriented Programming Paradigm 243
Pasquale Ardimento and Michele Scalera

Leveraging Cloud Infrastructures for Teaching Advanced Computer Engineering Classes: Experiences at the University of Pisa. 256
Antonio Cisternino, Pietro Ducange, Nicola Tonellotto, and Carlo Vallati

Presente Digitale: An Online Education System for Teachers 271
Michela Fazzolari, Stefania Fabbri, Ilaria Matteucci, Marinella Petrocchi, and Anna Vaccarelli

Online Learning Strategies and Resources: e-Tutoring, Communities, Webinar and Tools

E-Tutoring in Higher Education: A Case Study. 289
Paolo Raviolo, Salvatore Messina, Irene Mauro, and Marco Rondonotti

The Strategic Role of the E-Tutor in New Learning Contexts 300
Simona Ferrari and Serena Triacca

Improving Student Progression in Distance Learning Using Synchronous Webinars. 315
Georgina Stebbings, Chris Mackintosh, Adrian Burden, and Dave Sims

The Differential Effects of Distance Learning and Presential Classroom Instructions on Performance of Male and Female Students of Science Education in Undergraduate Introductory Biology Course 324
Ebere Ibe, Joseph Aneke, and Joy Abamuche

The Flipped Inclusion Model: Eco-Sustainable and Inclusive Accessibility in the Era Covid-19. 337
De Giuseppe Tonia, Annalisa Ianniello, and Felice Corona

Author Index 353

COVID-19 pandemic has dramatically changed education, with the distinctive increase in e-learning environments. These environments are web-based platforms where educational content is provided, along with interactive and multimedia tools (such as wiki, forums, file exchange folders, video lessons, synchronous and asynchronous messages) to improve and support the individual training process. While these technologies break the boundaries of time and space, thus facilitating student enrollment, on the other hand they present the major problem of high dropout rates [1,11,27].

In traditional classrooms, teachers and students interact directly, so that student assessments can be easily monitored, and timely interventions can be implemented to improve students' learning gain. In online learning, students interact with the learning platform, so different approaches are needed to evaluate their performance. Student activities and their interactions with the VLE are continuously monitored and collected through logs, which represent a *digital footprint* for each student. Such data constitute a great and valuable source of information on student learning and behavior, which can be exploited to optimize the learning process [10].

The increased availability of this type of data has led to the birth of a new research area, referred to as *Educational Data Mining* (EDM), in which machine learning is used to analyze educational data. Predictive models for student assessment are one of the main applications of EDM. All stakeholders involved in VLEs, including teachers, students, tutors, system designers and administrators, can benefit from the information contained in these data and the predictive models based on them. Students may want to improve their grades. Teachers can be supported in evaluating the effectiveness of their courses and adapt them to particular needs. Administrators can identify at-risk students in order to reduce student retention and increase graduation rates. Useful information can also be extracted to support recruiting policies, course planning and hiring needs.

Several approaches have proved useful for predicting student outcomes based on demographic and click-stream data [27]. However, most of the existing works in the literature treat educational data as a monolithic block of static elements, while a small body of literature has investigated the evolving nature of these data which is intrinsically related to the evolution of student behavior [7,8,24,26]. Much attention has been paid to address the problem of huge amounts of data [12,15,16,23], thus handling these data from a spatial point of view but ignoring the time factor. This can lead to non-negligible implications. For example, although two students may appear to behave similarly when their data are aggregated over time, they can differ significantly when taking into account the time dimension. Also, the educational path of a student is inherently an evolving process, so incremental analysis of semantic partitions of educational data that take time into account (e.g., semesters) can provide more insight in outlining the student's profile. The data coming from subsequent semesters, in fact, are not independent and cannot be treated as static data, thus ignoring their time sequence. Students who have passed all courses in the previous semester will likely succeed those in the current semester. Conversely, when the student's performance declines over time, timely intervention would be required. In other words, the time factor is the key to a better understanding and analysis of educational data.

To this end, stream data mining algorithms could be used effectively to analyze educational data. They are in fact able to analyze data incrementally, creating models capable of adapting their internal structure, i.e. their embedded parameters, to the new incoming data [21]. In addition, these methods are able to summarize the data previously seen, so that the actual data can be injected into the process in near real-time, saving memory and computational costs. In this paper, we report the findings of an empirical study whose goal is to evaluate the effectiveness of the *adaptive* stream data mining approach to predict student outcomes, based on the educational data produced by the interaction of students with a VLE. Specifically, to assess the importance of exploiting the temporal factor in educational data, we fairly compared the Adaptive Random Forest classification algorithm to the same algorithm in batch mode. For this purpose, a subset of the Open University Learning Analytics Dataset (OULAD) [20], specifically designed for this study, has been extracted and used. The systematization of this subset represents an additional contribution of this work.

The rest of the paper is structured as follows. Section 2 describes in detail the considered subset of the OULAD dataset and the pre-processing steps aimed at obtaining the most useful information for the purpose of this study. Section 3 describes the methods used. The results obtained are discussed in Sect. 4. Section 5 concludes the paper and depicts future developments of our research.

2 Materials

A subset of the Open University Learning Analytics Dataset[1] (OULAD) was employed in the present study [20]. The Open University (OU) is one of the biggest distance learning universities in the world offering open data related to on-line courses.[2] The available data are organized in several csv files (assessments.csv, courses.csv, studentInfo.csv, and so on). They contain anonymous information extracted from the OU database. This contains demographic data, along with aggregated click-stream data of student interactions with the VLE, collected on a daily basis. In particular, the data express the students' interactions with the teaching material for the academic years 2013 and 2014, grouped into two semesters (*B* for February and *J* for October). Seven different courses are considered, four for STEM and three for Social Sciences. They are represented with the categorical labels "CCC", "DDD", "EEE", "FFF" and "AAA", "BBB", "GGG", respectively.

---

[1] Open University website: http://www.open.ac.uk.

[2] Freely available data from Open University: https://analyse.kmi.open.ac.uk/open_dataset#data.

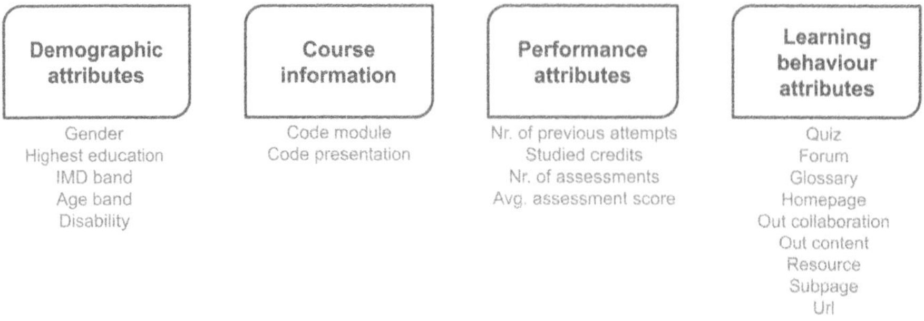

Fig. 1. Data description.

Our goal was to predict the student's outcome; to this end, a student-oriented dataset was extracted. In particular, to obtain the final features, a subset of the original data was considered, focusing only on information about the students.

The dataset collects data from 25,819 students described by 19 attributes grouped into demographic data, performance and learning behaviour. Since each entry of the data refers to a specific course, year and semester, course information is also recorded. As summarized in Fig. 1, each student is characterized by the following features:

- *Demographic attributes.* General information about the student and his social condition:
  - *Gender*: male or female (M/F);
  - *Highest education*: the highest level of education of the student in the UK at the time of enrollment (five levels are considered: level A or equivalent, High Education Qualification, Lower than A level, No Formal qualifications, Post graduate qualification);
  - *IMD band*: the Index of Multiple Deprivation band value of the place where the student lived at the time of enrollment. This is a UK government measure to assess deprived areas in UK local councils. It can take percentage values representing risk levels (0 for low, 100 for high). In particular, ten separate ranges were considered: $[0\%, 10\%]$, $[10\%, 20\%]$, $[20\%, 30\%]$, etc., and unknown value);
  - *Age band*: three age groups were considered: $[0-35]$, $[35-55]$, greater than 55;
  - *Disability*: yes or no (Y/N).

- *Course information.* Since data relates to student behavior for a specific course and semester, this information is needed to identify each entry. In fact, the data contains information about the same student in different courses and/or semesters.
  - *Code module*: code of the specific course ("AAA", "BBB","CCC", "DDD", "EEE", "FFF", and "GGG");
  - *Code presentation*: code of the year and semester in which the exam took place (2013B, 2013J, 2014B, 2014J).

- *Performance attributes.* Information on student performance for a specific course and semester. While the attributes *Number of previous attempts* and *Number of assessments* are already present in the original data, the two aggregated features *Number of assessments* and *Average assessment score* have been computed by us. Indeed, each student, for each course, could have been optionally collected several intermediate scores from intermediate assignments, plus a final (mandatory) score. Since the number of intermediate scores can vary considering different students, courses and semesters, aggregated features collect both the number of the assessments and the average score obtained. These features are relevant for analyzing student commitment to the course. In fact, the number of assessments could be strictly related to the final score, and therefore to the student outcome. On the other hand, these features could provide some insights into the quality of planned learning activities. In fact, they could not reflect course contents and extra information, resulting in low final scores.
  - *Number of previous attempts*: the number of student's failures in the final exam of the current module;
  - *Studied credits*: the number of credits the student was interacting with;
  - *Number of assessments*: number of assessments the student has submitted for the current module;
  - *Average assessments score*: the average assessment score for the current module.

- *Learning behaviour attributes.* These attributes store student interaction with the platform (click/visualization counts) using nine different educational aids. These aggregate data were obtained for each student by counting his activities. Additionally, as some tools were very specific to a particular course, the most used tools across all six courses were selected to avoid data sparsity:
  - *Quiz*: questionnaires on the contents of the module;
  - *Forum*: questions and answers on specific interactive platforms that connect students and teachers;
  - *Glossary*: hyper-link dictionary explaining some particular words in the module;
  - *Homepage*: module homepage visualizations;
  - *Out collaboration*: interactive activities carried out together by groups of students;
  - *Out content*: material, suggested by the professor, which is not stored in the VLE;
  - *Resource*: material provided by the professor which is stored in the VLE;
  - *Subpage*: subpages of the course focusing on particular topics;
  - *Url*: websites, related to the course topics, linked by the professor.

All categorical features have been converted to numbers for automatic processing. For example, we have 11 different ranges for IMD band, [0%, 10%], [10%, 20%], [20%, 30%], etc., corresponding to the numerical values 0, 1, 2, etc., respectively. In particular, only the ordinal features have been considered for

Table 1. Statistics of the created dataset.

Semester	*Pass*	*Fail*	Total
2013B	2,095	1,708	3,803
2013J	4,474	2,611	7,085
2014B	3,358	2,635	5,993
2014J	5,453	3,484	8,937

the numerical conversion, since the order must be preserved. For this reason, the original *Region* feature, representing the geographical information about where students lived during the course, has been ignored. In fact, defining a ranking of the geographical areas was not possible. Binary features are an exception; in these cases, 0 and 1 have been used.

The target output, i.e. the final result attribute, takes four values corresponding to different outcomes: *fail*, *pass*, *distinction* and *withdrawn*. However, experiments in [7] showed that low performance values are obtained for the multi-class classification problem over the entire dataset. This suggests that even with the availability of the entire dataset, it is difficult to discriminate correctly the four classes. In particular, the original classes *pass* and *distinction*, and *fail* and *withdrawn* were confused. For this reason, the original classes have been condensed into two single classes, respectively named *fail* and *pass*. In this way the student outcome prediction problem was converted into a binary classification task. Table 1 outlines the data class distribution. It is worth noting that the *fail* class is under-represented in all semesters. However, the number of failures per semester is quite high (a one-to-two ratio of successes), so analyses are needed to reduce the failure rate and to detect the most discriminating factors for the two classes. The created dataset is available on Zenodo[3] [9].

3 Methods

To evaluate the impact of the temporal factor in building prediction models from the dataset described above, a "batch" and an "incremental" classification algorithm were fairly compared. Particularly, the Random Forest (RF) algorithm and its incremental variant Adaptive Random Forest (ARF) were adopted.

RF represents a supervised tree-based method: it relies on the concept of *bagging* to build a "forest" of decision trees during the training stage and provides the majority vote of the single classes predicted by each decision tree during the testing stage [6]. Bagging consists of two phases: a random sample with replacement is iteratively selected from the training set and a decision tree based on this sample is then built. It is worth noting that RF does not take the entire feature set into account when building a single decision tree, but uses a randomly

[3] Student oriented subset of the Open University Learning Analytics dataset: https://zenodo.org/record/4264397#.X60DEkJKj8E.

chosen subset of features. This is to avoid the growth of highly related trees. As a splitting criterion for the construction of the trees, the well-known Gini index was used. In short, this index measures the likelihood of a particular variable being misclassified when chosen at random. Its formula is:

$$Gini = \sum_{k=1}^{K} \hat{p}_{mk}(1 - \hat{p}_{mk})$$

where $k = 1, \ldots, K$ are the different classes and $\hat{p}_{mk}$ is the subset of examples labeled with the class k at node m. We preferred this criterion over others, such as information gain, as it is computationally easy to calculate. The RF algorithm has proven very effective in a number of machine learning tasks (e.g., [14,19,22]).

Adaptive Random Forest is a variant of the Random Forest algorithm [17], specifically designed to work in an evolving and streaming environment. ARF was intended to include an effective re-sampling method and adaptive operators capable of coping with different types of concept drifts, without further optimization of the hyper-parameters. *Concept drift* refers to hard-to-predict changes in data distribution over time. Particularly, ARF implements an adaptive strategy based on using a drift monitor per tree to track warnings and drifts and to train additional trees in background. Training of these trees begins when a warning occurs and active trees are only replaced when a drift has taken place. However, concept drift detection is beyond the scope of this work. This technique is used by ARF to effectively adapt the model structure to the new incoming data.

It is worth noting that the relative depth of an attribute used as a splitting node in a tree can be employed to judge its importance in relation to the predictability of the output class. Features located at the higher levels of the tree contribute most to the final output prediction, as they involve splitting a larger fraction of the training samples. The proportion of training instances a node contributes to is combined with the reduction in impurity resulting from their division to create a normalized estimate of that node's discriminating power. By averaging these normalized estimates across multiple trees, it is possible to reduce the variance of the estimate and use it to select the most discriminating features in the dataset. This technique is known as "average decrease in impurity."

4 Results

Two different series of experiments were conducted. The first experiment was dedicated to comparing the predictive power of batch and incremental models. Subsequently, a second experiment was carried out to perform a semantic analysis aimed at highlighting the hidden relationships underlying the data and the differences between the two algorithms. To this end, a feature importance analysis was conducted by analyzing the ten most discriminating features for the binary classification task, which were returned by the two algorithms. In fact, selecting the most relevant features can help better design courses and prevent student failure.

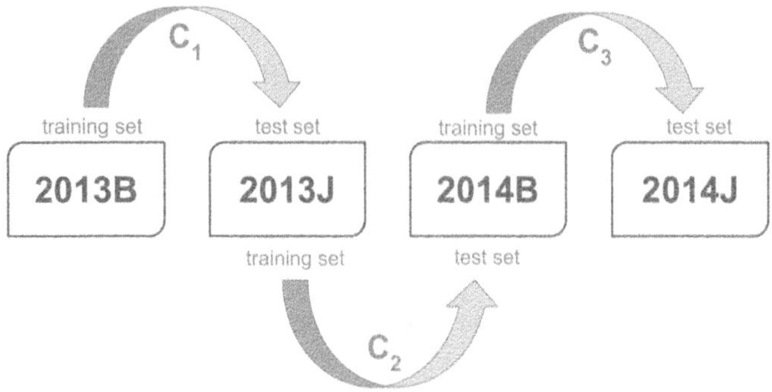

Fig. 2. Training-testing configurations (C_1, C_2 and C_3).

4.1 Classification Results

The purpose of this study was to assess the system's ability to predict student outcome based on stored history. Standard classification metrics, namely accuracy, precision and recall, were used. Each algorithm was incrementally trained and tested. The four semesters were used as units of time. Each algorithm was trained on the current semester and tested on the successive one. Figure 2 shows the considered training-testing configurations, namely C_1, C_2 and C_3.

Note that at each time t, only data belonging to a single semester were used to train the model. Previous data were not considered. However, while RF needs all the data to be stored, ARF learns incrementally, so the data history no longer needs to be stored, as it is "summarized" in its internal parameters.

Tables 2 and 3 report the classification results obtained by the two systems (RF and ARF, respectively). It can be observed that both algorithms are very accurate in predicting the third and fourth semester (2014B and 2014J), while lower accuracy values are returned for the second semester (2013J). Indeed, for this semester the two models are quite good at recognizing the *fail* class (high recall values), but have had some difficulties in discriminating the *pass* class. It is worth noting that while the *fail* class collects high recall values across chunks, the *pass* class exhibits different behaviors for different chunks. This could be justified by the presence of discriminating features that do not depend on courses or semesters (which change from one chunk to the next), but that characterize student failure. Conversely, students' success may be highly dependent on the actual course they are taking. For this reason, low recall values are returned in the first semester, while very high values are collected in the following semesters. There is usually a trade-off between recall and precision, so getting high values for both at the same time, while desirable, is often difficult.

ARF returned higher accuracy values for the three semesters considered. This result suggests that information about the history of student behaviors, embedded into the model, can improve its classification performance, at each time t. Therefore, stream data mining algorithms are suitable for incrementally analyzing educational data. Furthermore, we want to emphasize that the learn-

Table 2. Classification results obtained on the test sets with Random Forest.

Configuration	C_1		C_2		C_3	
Accuracy	Acc. = 57.08%		Acc. = 87.69%		Acc. = 87.45%	
Class	Prec.	Rec.	Prec.	Rec.	Prec.	Rec.
Pass	0.92	0.34	0,93	0.87	0.93	0.85
Fail	0.46	0.95	0.81	0.89	0.80	0.90

Table 3. Classification results obtained on the test sets with Adaptive Random Forest.

Configuration	C_1		C_2		C_3	
Accuracy	Acc. = 65.59%		Acc. = 89.92%		Acc. = 89.63%	
Class	Prec.	Rec.	Prec.	Rec.	Prec.	Rec.
Pass	0.91	0.51	0.85	0.99	0.87	0.97
Fail	0.52	0.91	0.98	0.78	0.94	0.78

ing process is inherently evolving and adaptive, because human beings react to external stimuli by adapting and evolving their neurons and therefore their knowledge. Hence, considering each semester in a static way, without taking into account the evolving history of the student, we could not reflect the way the human brain works. Conversely, adaptive and evolving algorithms, which are able to preserve the historical data in the created model, and use this information for predictions on previously unseen data, are better suited for analyzing data from students' daily interactions with Virtual Learning Environments.

4.2 Feature Importance Analysis

An analysis of the importance of the features used was carried out to ascertain the most discriminating attributes for the student outcome predictive task. To decrease the complexity of the algorithms, both RF and ARF select a subset of the most discriminating features to train the model. A ranking of all the features is then returned by the algorithms after the training phase. Figures 3 and 4 report a graphical representation of the ten most discriminating features for the binary prediction task, which were selected by RF and ARF, respectively, for each training semester (i.e., 2013B, 2013J, 2014B). The same colors were used to identify the same attributes, in order to improve the visualization of patterns in the results.

It can be observed that for both RF and ARF the two most discriminating features are *quiz* and *out collaboration* (more than 50% of all ten most relevant features). This suggests that a large number of interactions with the learning material helps to pass the exam. This is a predictable result, but it also suggests that the interactive materials provided to the students were designed properly: in fact, the students using them successfully complete the exam. Furthermore,

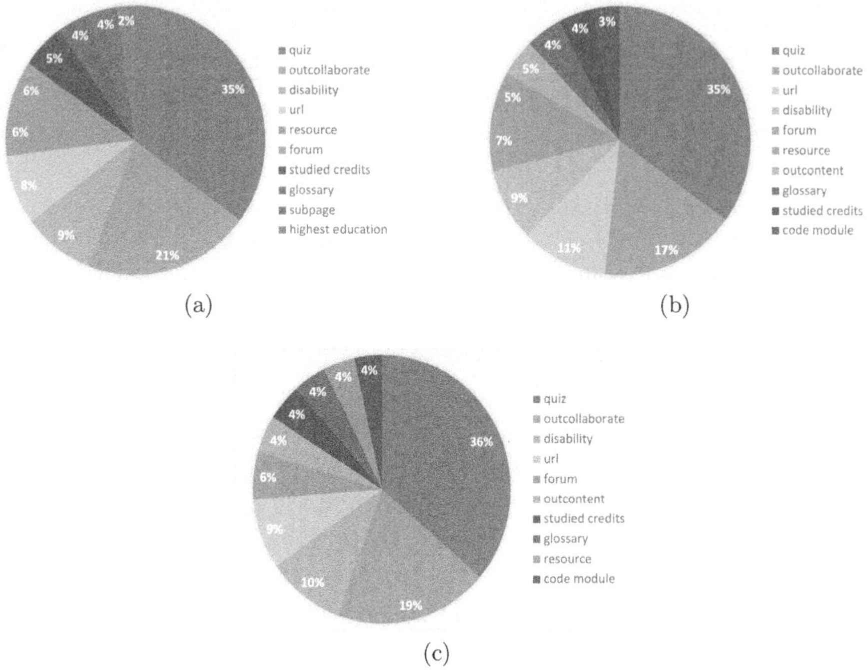

Fig. 3. Top ten most relevant features used by Random Forest to train the model on configurations C_1 (a), C_2 (b) and C_3 (c).

it is worth noting that both algorithms return *disability* as a discriminant factor for passing the exam. Unlike the previous features, this may suggest the need for interventions to support people with disabilities, as current facilities are not sufficient. Moreover, another interesting result is the lack of the demographic attributes (except for disability and higher education level, which has a very low influence for the training phase of the first semester) among the ten top discriminating features. Therefore, future investigations may ignore this type of information, focusing on student behavior. In fact, most of the selected attributes relate to behavioral information. Previous analyses partially confirm these results [7]. In fact, three different feature selection algorithms were applied to the entire dataset, and two of them suggested that the general information characterizing students are not discriminant for the classification problem, while a third method considered them.

There are some differences between the different semesters. This is also a predictable outcome, as different subjects were studied in different semesters, so it makes sense that different resources were used. However, we want to point out that the features returned by RF and ARF are different. Although low, there is variability in the features returned by RF. This is due to the fact that the algorithm learns from the actual semester and "forgets" past data. On the contrary, ARF incorporates historical data into its parameters, so we can observe from Fig. 4 that the graphs are more stable and there is less variability, because the model evolves and adapts its structure to the new incoming data. On the other hand, similar results, obtained from the feature importance analysis of RF and ARF, suggest that there are some features (factors) which influence the personal and pedagogical growth of students. They are independent of external factors, such as time (semesters) or specific courses, but are intrinsically related to the student's learning process. For this reason, they can be used effectively as predictors of student outcome in both batch and incremental analyses.

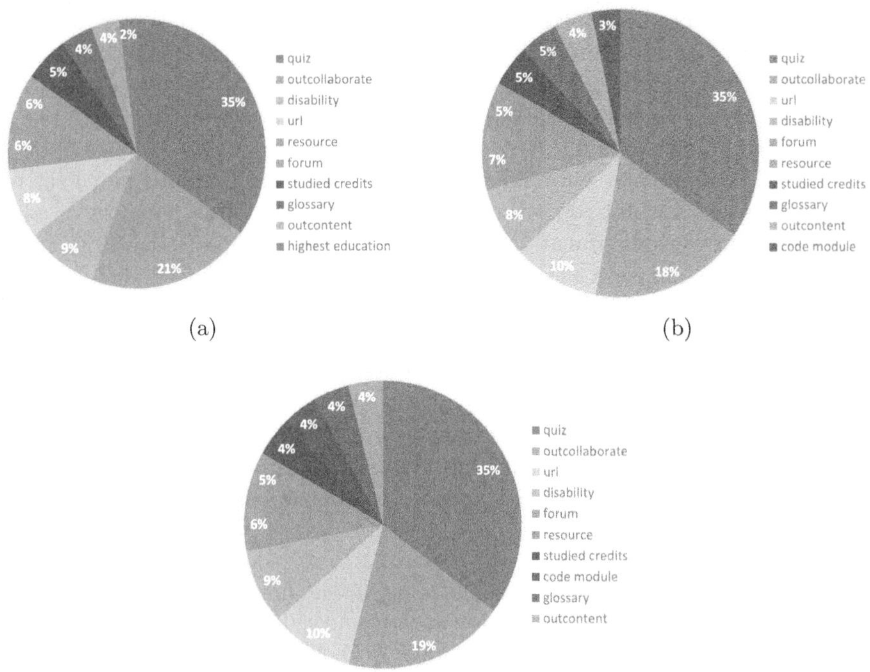

Fig. 4. Top ten most relevant features used by Adaptive Random Forest to train the model on configurations C_1 (a), C_2 (b) and C_3 (c).

5 Conclusion

In this paper, we studied the influence of the time factor on the classification of educational data for student outcome prediction. In particular, a subset of the Open University dataset was analyzed using the Random Forest algorithm in both its batch and incremental variant. The purpose of the analysis was to predict student results based on data belonging to semantically relevant time units such as semesters. Adaptive Random Forest has proven to be able to adaptively adjust its parameters to the new incoming data, while preserving historical information. Additionally, it returned better results than its batch version, suggesting that the information injected into the model is actually useful in improving its classification performance. Therefore, we can conclude that adaptive models are better suited than batch models for learning from VLE data, as they embed historical student data, which are needed to properly model student learning activities. Another contribution of this paper is a feature importance analysis that was carried out to highlight the top discriminating attributes for the predictive task. The results obtained suggest that behavioral attributes are more relevant to the classification problem than the demographic ones. In particular, the results obtained suggest that among the interactive tools available, the two most discriminating are *quiz* and *out collaboration*. This suggests that in a distance learning context, where a direct contact between the teacher and the students is absent, it is necessary to be in continuous contact with the students by monitoring their learning.

Future developments will be devoted to investigating in depth the effectiveness of adaptive learning algorithms when dealing with large amounts of complex and heterogeneous educational data. To this end, comparisons will be made with state-of-the-art evolving and adaptive algorithms. Moreover, the detection of changes in data distribution over time (concept drift detection) will be studied, as it could be effectively used for real-time detection of changes in student behavior, thus suggesting immediate intervention. Furthermore, qualitative studies will be carried out, relating to the influence of different categories of features on the prediction results. Finally, since the stakeholders involved in the Virtual Learning Environments are not necessarily technicians, we intend to experiment with some explainability strategies in order to improve the interpretation of the results achieved by different learning algorithms [3].

Acknowledgements. Gabriella Casalino acknowledges funding from the Italian Ministry of Education, University and Research through the European PON project AIM (Attraction and International Mobility), nr. 1852414, activity 2, line 1. All authors are members of the INdAM GNCS research group.

References

1. Al-Shabandar, R., Hussain, A.J., Liatsis, P., Keight, R.: Detecting at-risk students with early interventions using machine learning techniques. IEEE Access **7**, 149464–149478 (2019)
2. Aljohani, T., Pereira, F.D., Cristea, A.I., Oliveira, E.: Prediction of users' professional profile in MOOCs Only by utilising learners' written texts. In: Kumar, V., Troussas, C. (eds.) ITS 2020. LNCS, vol. 12149, pp. 163–173. Springer, Cham (2020). https://doi.org/10.1007/978-3-030-49663-0_20
3. Alonso, J.M., Casalino, G.: Explainable artificial intelligence for human-centric data analysis in virtual learning environments. In: Burgos, D., et al. (eds.) HELMeTO 2019. CCIS, vol. 1091, pp. 125–138. Springer, Cham (2019). https://doi.org/10.1007/978-3-030-31284-8_10

4. Ardimento, P., Bernardi, M.L., Cimitile, M.: Software analytics to support students in object-oriented programming tasks: an empirical study. IEEE Access **8**, 132171–132187 (2020)
5. Arrigo, M., et al.: HeARt mobile learning. In: 10th Annual International Conference on Education and New Learning Technologies (EDULEARN 2018), pp. 10899–10905. IATED Academy (2018)
6. Breiman, L.: Random forests. Mach. Learn. **45**(1), 5–32 (2001). https://doi.org/10.1023/A:1010933404324
7. Casalino, G., Castellano, G., Mannavola, A., Vessio, G.: Educational stream data analysis: a case study. In: IEEE Mediterranean Eletrotechnical Conference (MELECON 2020) (2020)
8. Casalino, G., Castellano, G., Mencar, C.: Incremental and adaptive fuzzy clustering for virtual learning environments data analysis. In: 23rd International Conference on Information Visualisation, pp. 382–387. IEEE (2019)
9. Casalino, G., Castellano, G., Vessio, G.: Student oriented subset of the Open University Learning Analytics dataset (2020). https://doi.org/10.5281/zenodo.4264397
10. Casalino, G., Castiello, C., Del Buono, N., Esposito, F., Mencar, C.: Q-matrix extraction from real response data using nonnegative matrix factorizations. In: Gervasi, O., et al. (eds.) ICCSA 2017. LNCS, vol. 10404, pp. 203–216. Springer, Cham (2017). https://doi.org/10.1007/978-3-319-62392-4_15
11. Castellano, G., Fanelli, A., Roselli, T.: Mining categories of learners by a competitive neural network. In: IJCNN 2001. International Joint Conference on Neural Networks. Proceedings (Cat. No. 01CH37222), vol. 2, pp. 945–950. IEEE (2001)
12. Coussement, K., Phan, M., De Caigny, A., Benoit, D.F., Raes, A.: Predicting student dropout in subscription-based online learning environments: the beneficial impact of the logit leaf model. Decis. Supp. Syst. **135**, 113325 (2020)
13. De Carolis, B., D'Errico, F., Macchiarulo, N., Palestra, G.: Engaged faces: measuring and monitoring student engagement from face and gaze behavior. In: IEEE/WIC/ACM International Conference on Web Intelligence-Companion Volume, pp. 80–85 (2019)
14. Diaz, M., Ferrer, M.A., Impedovo, D., Pirlo, G., Vessio, G.: Dynamically enhanced static handwriting representation for Parkinson's disease detection. Pattern Recogn. Lett. **128**, 204–210 (2019)
15. Ducange, P., Pecori, R., Sarti, L., Vecchio, M.: Educational big data mining: how to enhance virtual learning environments. In: Graña, M., López-Guede, J.M., Etxaniz, O., Herrero, Á., Quintián, H., Corchado, E. (eds.) SOCO/CISIS/ICEUTE -2016. AISC, vol. 527, pp. 681–690. Springer, Cham (2017). https://doi.org/10.1007/978-3-319-47364-2_66
16. Fischer, C., et al.: Mining big data in education: affordances and challenges. Rev. Res. Educ. **44**(1), 130–160 (2020)
17. Gomes, H.M., et al.: Adaptive random forests for evolving data stream classification. Mach. Learn. **106**(9–10), 1469–1495 (2017)
18. Guest, W., Wild, F., Di Mitri, D., Klemke, R., Karjalainen, J., Helin, K.: Architecture and design patterns for distributed, scalable augmented reality and wearable technology systems. In: IEEE International Conference on Engineering, Technology and Education, IEEE TALE 2019: Creative & Innovative Education to Enhance the Quality of Life (2019)
19. Impedovo, D., Pirlo, G., Vessio, G., Angelillo, M.T.: A handwriting-based protocol for assessing neurodegenerative dementia. Cogn. Comput. **11**(4), 576–586 (2019). https://doi.org/10.1007/s12559-019-09642-2

20. Kuzilek, J., Hlosta, M., Zdrahal, Z.: Open university learning analytics dataset. Sci. Data **4**, 170171 (2017)
21. Leite, D., Škrjanc, I., Gomide, F.: An overview on evolving systems and learning from stream data. Evol. Syst. **11**, 1–18 (2020). https://doi.org/10.1007/s12530-020-09334-5
22. Maggipinto, T., et al.: DTI measurements for Alzheimer's classification. Phys. Med. Biol. **62**(6), 2361 (2017)
23. Nakayama, M., Sciarrone, F., Uto, M., Temperini, M.: Estimating student's performance based on item response theory in a MOOC environment with peer assessment. In: Kubincová, Z., Lancia, L., Popescu, E., Nakayama, M., Scarano, V., Gil, A.B. (eds.) MIS4TEL 2020. AISC, vol. 1236, pp. 25–35. Springer, Cham (2021). https://doi.org/10.1007/978-3-030-52287-2_3
24. Pecori, R.: A virtual learning architecture enhanced by fog computing and big data streams. Future Internet **10**(1), 4 (2018)
25. Picerno, P., Pecori, R., Raviolo, P., Ducange, P.: Smartphones and exergame controllers as byod solutions for the e-tivities of an online sport and exercise sciences university program. In: Burgos, D., et al. (eds.) HELMeTO 2019. CCIS, vol. 1091, pp. 217–227. Springer, Cham (2019). https://doi.org/10.1007/978-3-030-31284-8_17
26. Qu, S., Li, K., Wu, B., Zhang, S., Wang, Y.: Predicting student achievement based on temporal learning behavior in MOOCs. Appl. Sci. **9**(24), 5539 (2019)
27. Romero, C., Ventura, S.: Educational data mining and learning analytics: an updated survey. Wiley Interdisc. Rev.: Data Min. Knowl. Discov. **10**(3), e1355 (2020)
28. Rooein, D.: Data-driven EDU chatbots. In: Companion Proceedings of the 2019 World Wide Web Conference, pp. 46–49 (2019)
29. Rossano, V., Lanzilotti, R., Cazzolla, A., Roselli, T.: Augmented reality to support geometry learning. IEEE Access **8**, 107772–107780 (2020)
30. Scalera, M., Gentile, E., Plantamura, P., Dimauro, G.: A systematic mapping study in cloud for educational innovation. Appl. Sci. **10**(13), 4531 (2020)
31. Tripathi, G., Ahad, M.A.: IoT in education: an integration of educator community to promote holistic teaching and learning. In: Nayak, J., Abraham, A., Krishna, B.M., Chandra Sekhar, G.T., Das, A.K. (eds.) Soft Computing in Data Analytics. AISC, vol. 758, pp. 675–683. Springer, Singapore (2019). https://doi.org/10.1007/978-981-13-0514-6_64
32. Vitanza, A., Rossetti, P., Mondada, F., Trianni, V.: Robot swarms as an educational tool: the Thymio's way. Int. J. Adv. Rob. Syst. **16**(1), 1729881418825186 (2019)

Recognizing Cognitive Emotions in E-Learning Environment

Berardina De Carolis[1], Francesca D'Errico[2], Nicola Macchiarulo[1(✉)], Marinella Paciello[3], and Giuseppe Palestra[4]

[1] Department of Computer Science, University of Bari, Bari, Italy
{berardina.decarolis,nicola.macchiarulo}@uniba.it
[2] Department For.Psi.Com, University of Bari, Bari, Italy
francesca.derrico@uniba.it
[3] Psychology Faculty, Uninettuno University, Rome, Italy
[4] Hero Srl, Salmour, Italy
giuseppepalestra@gmail.com

Abstract. In the present work, we describe the development of a Facial Expressions Recognition (FER) system able to recognize cognitive emotions in a distance education context. In this case, many research works show that the recognition of basic emotions is not enough and that recognizing emotions more related to the presence/lack of engagement and flow would be more appropriate. Therefore, we developed a FER system able to classify the following cognitive emotions: enthusiasm, interest, surprise, boredom, perplexity, frustration, and the neutral one. After several experiments, we tested which was the best combination of features and the best algorithm for our classification problem. Results show that the combination of Action Units and gaze and a Multiclass Support Vector Machine achieves the best accuracy on the dataset. Results are encouraging and we plan to integrate the system into an e-learning platform to create a more personalized educational environment.

Keywords: Cognitive emotion recognition · E-learning · Computer vision

1 Introduction

Emotions play a critical role in the learning process that may influence in a critical way the student's performance. Emotions have an influence on cognitive processes by affecting student learning and achievements [1, 4]. Recently, especially due to the need of taking advantage of distance education because of the COVID-19 emergency, there has been a lot of interest in detecting emotions during learning in distance education contexts where the automatic assessment and monitoring of students' emotions may provide information about their wellbeing and help in understanding problems and difficulties. This information can then be used for providing personalized support through appropriate interventions [41].

Emotional processes are directly linked to the learning process [2, 3], in particular, Pekrun et al. [3] highlighted that positive emotions are related to reflection and

L. S. Agrati et al. (Eds.): HELMeTO 2020, CCIS 1344, pp. 17–27, 2021.
https://doi.org/10.1007/978-3-030-67435-9_2

creative thinking, whereas negative emotions are more associated with lower levels of performance. The hypothesis underpinning our work is that the detection of emotions in distance education can be used to develop an emotional profile of the students not only to detect a specific emotional issue in a particular moment during the lecture, but also to monitor the evolving of the situation over time, and identify relevant changes.

Given the importance of detecting and monitoring emotions, advances in the field of computer vision made possible the recognition of emotions from facial expressions [5]. Many research works proposed to use facial expression analysis for detecting and interpreting students' emotions during e-learning [6, 7]. However, many of them focused on the recognition of basic emotions (anger, disgust, fear, happiness, sadness, and surprise) [8] that, in this application domain, is not sufficient since, basic emotions are quite infrequent during short e-learning sessions [27] Moreover, they do not allow to understand the user's mental state during the learning process [9]. Instead, affective states such as engagement, boredom, confusion, frustration, happiness, curiosity, and anxiety are much more frequent in this context since they are related to goals achievement, state of flow, the understanding of the learning material.

Since most software available for emotion recognition is trained to recognize only primary emotions, we developed a computer vision module for the recognition of the cognitive emotions that typically arise during the learning process. In the present work, we describe the development of a Facial Expressions Recognition (FER) system to recognize cognitive emotions in the context of distance education from facial expressions. Our FER system classifies the following cognitive emotions that were found to be more related to presence/lack of engagement and flow: enthusiasm, interest, surprise, boredom, perplexity, frustration, and the neutral one.

This module will be integrated into e-learning systems to create a more personalized educational environment in which the system detects and monitors, besides the evaluation of the students' performance based for instance on tests, also their emotional states allowing to reason on their wellbeing during the learning process.

2 E-Learning and Cognitive Emotions

Emotion and cognition are related, and these relations become even more important in the context of online education [9]. Several studies investigated the kind of emotions and experiences that are present in e-learning activities.

Loderer et al. [28] identified three kinds of emotions in technology-rich learning environments: positive activating emotions (i.e. enjoyment), negative activating emotions (i.e. anxiety), and negative deactivating emotions (i.e. boredom). Duffy et al. [29] indicated that, in particular, positive emotions such as enjoyment and negative activating emotions such as anxiety as the most strongly experienced ones in e-learning contexts. Recently, D'Errico et al. [17] found a positive correlation between academic self-efficacy and the experience of positive emotions during e-learning activities, and that self-efficacy was negatively associated with negative emotions. In other words, when students experience positive emotions in e-learning contexts, can be interpreted as a positive experience of self-efficacy since they can feel the fact that they live a positive experience in interaction with the class. The focus of the present paper is to automatically recognize the cognitive emotions that in Scheffler work [38] can be considered as the "emotional filters through which we view the world, interpret its objects and evaluate its critical features. They involve seeing things as beneficial or harmful, promising or threatening, fulfilling or thwarting" (p.45). In addition, the acquisition of new knowledge/skills elicit cognitive emotions that usually monitor incoming content [30] and thus they can operate a central role in the learning process. Cognitive emotions can be also associated with the student' "flow state", that is a positive mental state associated to enjoyment and concentration during a stimulating activity [43]. In our perspective thus, observing the cognitive emotions can be a way to monitoring a more general state of the students, including his/her sense of control or enjoyment, toward the learning process. In this sense, the recognition of cognitive factors, at the basis of the emotional processes, can be a way to understand learner's beliefs, expectations and goals [31] that are strictly linked to learning and content delivery. For instance, in terms of real time appraisal process, the emotional state of excitement can be strongly linked to a new acquired information (relevant for the student); or a state of frustration and confusion can be interpreted as negative feedback that the new information is in contrast with the previous ones. Speaking about psychological factors implied in the learning process, recent works showed the relevance of the self-efficacy in the academic adjustment, particularly considering the performance and the well-being (for a review see [17]).

The psychological features of the self-efficacy concern the students' beliefs of being able to plan, control, and direct their learning activities. Thus, it implies cognitive strategies of (a) planning learning actions, (b) assessing learning activities, and (c) reflecting in order to modulate learning actions even in case of difficulties.

In particular, in e-learning environments, the cited study showed a different the cognitive emotions considering younger adults and adult students when they interact with teacher (chat or video activities). Results indicated that in the case of younger adults' self-efficacy was linked to positive emotions, as in the case of interest, and also to academic adjustment and well-being. In parallel, in older adult students' feeling negative cognitive emotions like, frustration and boredom, can be also an emotional signal of lower levels of self-efficacy and also low levels of academic adjustment [32]. On the contrary, for older students, weak academic self-efficacy could increase personal distress resulting in negative emotional states during online learning processes. This could probably be related to their low levels of self-control in returning to study and feeling difficulties as an impossible situation to face during online learning processes, for example. In other words, during e-learning activities, on one hand, young adult students with high self-efficacy could reach the 'state of flow' in which cognitive effort can be most likely promoted by the willingness to develop and to build one's own professional pathway. On the other hand, older students with low self-efficacy could feel states of frustration and boredom, probably related to the awareness of the difficulties that need to be overcome to manage the academic tasks that they have to perform and to face. Indeed, these older students expressed emotions such as boredom, which could attest that an academic task is perceived as too simple for them or not interesting given their past experiences and knowledge. Another possible emotion could be frustration. In this case, frustration could indicate the presence of a task perceived too difficult for them. The co-presence of these negative states highlighted that for the older students the state of 'flow' is more difficult to achieve. This difficulty seems related to their low perceptions of efficacy in controlling academic tasks and self-regulate in academic online setting.

We also detected by face the relation between cognitive emotions and personality traits [18]. This previous study partially confirms findings in classical literature of emotional expressions since results show that for young students' emotions like perplexity during the video lectures are negatively associated with energy and openness to experience. In the case of adults instead the energy trait and the emotional stability were associated with boredom and frustration. Moreover, the extroversion of young students is positively associated with positive emotions in the chat interaction with a tutor. In adult students, instead, energy and emotional stability are related to less presence of negative emotions like boredom and frustration, during the interaction in the online chat with the teacher. Instead, adult learners with low levels of emotional stability can easily lose the state of flow during the learning process.

In addition, for adult students, neuroticism can be related to more vulnerability with respect to negative emotions. For adult students with high levels of neuroticism, negative emotions could be provoked by an absence of new stimulus, when they feel boredom, or by a presence of problematic and complex information, when they feel frustration. Moreover, adult students with high levels of neuroticism show more negative emotions in all e-learning settings that have been examined. Finally, it is interesting to note that for adult students another significant personality trait to consider is conscientiousness. More Conscientious adult students feel low negative emotions, such as frustration, perplexity, and boredom, when they interact by chatting with peers.

3 Emotion Detection from Facial Expressions in E-Learning Context

To assess students' emotional state, most of the times, self-report measures are used. In this case, the emotional state is usually collected with specific questionnaires in which students report their own perception of what they felt during the learning session. However, even if questionnaires are useful to collect subjective evaluation of the student's state and to relate automatic measurements to self-assessment of being in a particular affective state, they have some limitations. First of all, they do not link the actual, expressed emotions of students to the particular moment of the learning task. Moreover, answering a questionnaire may take time and may result boring and disturbing for students.

Since in this context learning is performed using a digital environment, it is feasible to adopt an approach based on automatic analysis of the student behavior during the learning process. Emotions can be detected automatically from the analysis of a student's behavior from multiple communication channels. For instance, in [38, 39] facial expressions have been used to detect the student affective state. In [40], besides facial expressions, other data have been used for the same purpose. However, facial expressions are the most commonly used communicative channel to display emotions and facial features are also the most commonly used for automatic emotion recognition since their detection does not require the adoption of expensive or intrusive hardware since webcams are present on many devices and the user does not have to wear sensors or particular devices. Then, we focus on facial features to detect affective states.

Several research studies recognize the emotional state of students in e-learning environments by analyzing facial expressions [19–21, 44]. Ashwin et al. [19], in their multi-user face detection-based e-learning system, used a SVM (Support Vector Machine) to classify emotions. Al-Alwani et al. [20] classify moods from facial features using a neural network for improving students' involvement in e-learning platforms. Neural networks have been used in Magdin et al. [22] to evaluate in real-time the emotional state of the user through a webcam with a good accuracy. An approach based on a deep learning Convolutional Neural Network model for identifying students' attentiveness from facial expressions is proposed in Tabassum et al. [26]. However, much of the work on emotion detection from facial expressions has focused on the emotions of anger, fear, sadness, happiness, disgust, and surprise. However, the results of the analysis reported in [27] indicate that basic emotions are quite infrequent during learning sessions with technology. In particular, they analyzed five studies concerning automatic monitoring and detection while users were performing conceptually difficult tasks. The analysis of results indicates that, in this context, emotions such as anxiety, boredom, confusion, curiosity, engagement, frustration, and happiness were much more frequent than basic ones.

In the proposed work we aim at developing a new FER system which recognizes in real-time the cognitive-emotional states of students in e-learning systems.

4 The FER System for Cognitive Emotion Recognition

Recognizing facial expressions from images requires the implementation of a pipeline involving different modules. Figure 1 illustrates the schema of the one used in our work in which, after a pre-processing phase, the faces present in the input image are detected and then they are cropped and registered [5]. These preliminary operations are necessary to get a similar position for the components of the face. Then, the feature extraction task is performed and the extracted features can then be used to classify facial emotions.

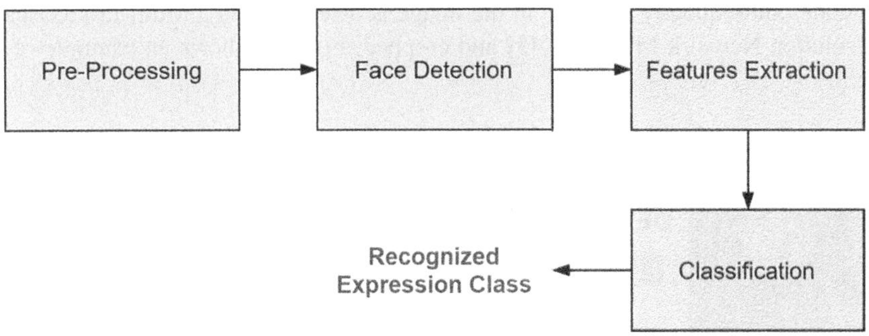

Fig. 1. A schema of a typical pipeline of a FER system.

4.1 Dataset

To train the classifier a dataset is needed with examples of the target emotions. As far as our knowledge goes there are not available validated datasets for the above-mentioned cognitive emotions with enough examples for each class to properly train a classifier. For this reason, we mixed up examples in the existing dataset with a set of images found on the web.

The first portion of the dataset was collected by taking images from different datasets:

- EU-Emotion Stimulus Set [10],
- Yale Face dataset of the UC San Diego,
- Japanese Female Facial Expression (JAFFE) of the University of Kyushu [11],
- Senthil IRTT database [12].

In particular, we selected a set of 200 images whose distribution is the following: enthusiasm (34), interest (28), surprise (32), boredom (32), perplexity (24), frustration (18), and neutral (32).

Then we selected by searching on the web other images for these emotions. We excluded images containing very exaggerated expressions. The selected images (210 in total) of facial expressions were clear and as frontal as possible, moreover, we excluded images of elderly people and without a beard to be as close as possible to the images taken by the validated dataset.

This new set of images was validated by three expert human raters and we considered the inter-annotator agreement by evaluating the Fleiss' kappa [13]. The average value of the kappa calculated for all the images examined was equal to 0.81, then there was an almost perfect agreement among the raters.

Then the obtained final dataset was made up of 410 images in total with the following distribution: enthusiasm (60), interest (66), surprise (56), boredom (58), perplexity (58), frustration (58), and neutral (54).

4.2 Preprocessing, Face Detection and Cropping

The input of the implemented pipeline is a single facial image that it is converted in grayscale. Subsequently, the face in the image is detected with a Multi-task Cascaded Convolution Network MTCNN [45] and cropped. Figure 2 shows an example of this face.

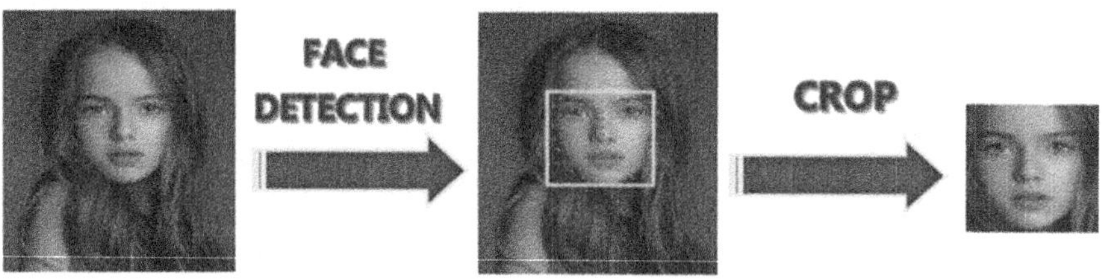

Fig. 2. Face detection and cropping.

4.3 Classifying Facial Expressions

The emotion recognition system is based on machine learning, specifically on the classification task. The input of the classifier is a set of features extracted from the face. These sets of features should be created to characterize the facial expression. Due to the low numbers of examples for each class in the dataset, we did not consider approaches based on deep learning.

To decide which type of features to use to train a classifier for facial expressions we considered HOG (Histogram of Oriented Gradients, [14]) descriptors, AUs (Action Units [15]) and AU plus gaze direction.

HOG features have been considered since facial expressions result from muscle movements that generate a kind of deformation. Considering that HOG features are sensitive to object deformations and have been used widely as features in FER systems, they have been selected for our experiment.

As features, besides HOG (we considered 4464 HOG descriptors), we considered the presence and intensity (expressed as a float from 0 to 5) of 17 facial AUs (AU01r, AU02r, AU04r, AU05r, AU06r, AU07r, AU09r, AU10r, AU12r, AU14r, AU15r, AU17r, AU20r, AU23r, AU25r, AU26r, AU45r and the presence of the facial action unit AU28c) and estimated orientation of the subject's gaze (x, y and z coordinates of the left and right eye gaze directions). Even, if the gaze is not part of facial expressions, the direction of the gaze may help in improving the recognition of certain affective states since they are related to cognitive processes and not necessarily to an answer to a stimulus [33].

To extract these features, we used OpenFace 2.0 [16] a freely available tool capable of accurate facial landmark detection, recognize a subset of Action Units (AUs), and gaze tracking and head pose estimation. The selected AU are those that are possible to estimate with the OpenFace software.

Figure 3 illustrates an example of a facial analysis made with the Openface software. It is possible to notice that on the left side of the figure the visualization of the extracted facial landmarks, gaze direction and head pose is shown. In the middle of the figure, it is possible to visualize the cropped face and its HOG representation. On the right side, the presence of AUs and their intensity is shown.

For selecting the most accurate classification model we tested the performance of three classification algorithms (Multi-SVM [23], Random Forest [24], MultiLayer Perceptron [25]) on three different sets of features: HOG, AUs, and AUs + Gaze.

To test the performance of the proposed approach we used the k-fold cross-validation with $\mathbf{k} = 10$. In Table 1 the results of the testing phase are reported.

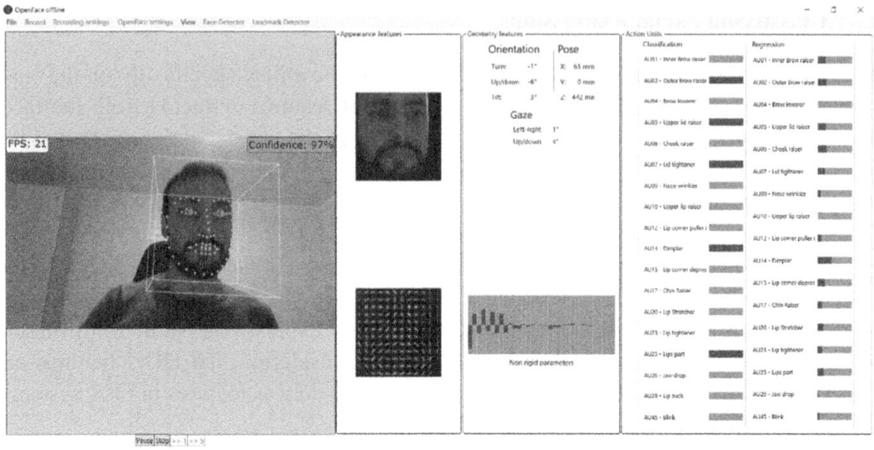

Fig. 3. Face analysis with OpenFace.

Table 1. A summary of precision rate and F1 scores of each feature set (HOG, AUs, AUs + GAZE) for the three algorithms (Multi-SVM, Random Forest, MLP).

Features	Algorithm	Precision	F1
HOG	Multiclass SVM	0.558	0.561
	Random Forest	0.485	0.491
	MLP	–	–
AUs	Multiclass SVM	0.764	0.764
	Random Forest	0.867	0.864
	MLP	0.754	0.753
AUs + GAZE	Multiclass SVM	**0.916**	**0.914**
	Random Forest	0.787	0.778
	MLP	0.885	0.884

We can notice that the Multi-SVM classifier (cost = 1000 e gamma = 0.001) reached the best precision rate using AUs + Gaze features. Random Forest classifiers on AUs and MultiLayer Perceptron (MLP) on AUs + Gaze have achieved a slightly lower precision than the Multi-SVM but it was still quite high.

Figure 4 shows an example of emotion recognition of a student's facial expression as boredom during an e-learning session.

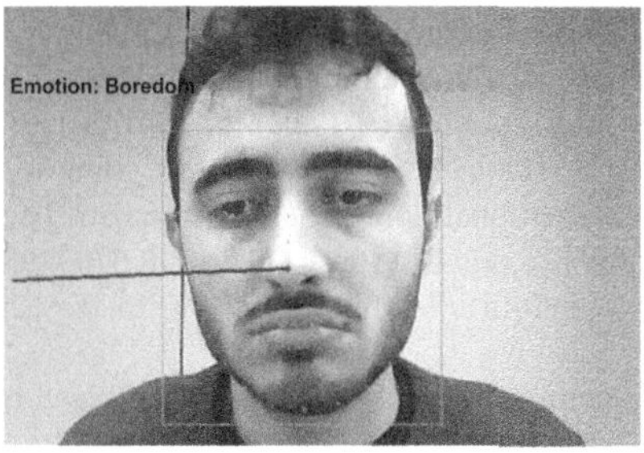

Fig. 4. Recognition of a facial expression as "boredom" during an e-learning class.

5 Conclusions

This paper presented our research in the context of emotions and their relation to the learning process in distance education contexts. In particular, we developed a FER system able to recognize cognitive emotions from facial expressions in real-time.

In previous studies, we obtained results that indicate that emotions can be used as indicators of the quality of the student's learning process [17, 18]. We plan to use the cognitive emotion recognition module for analyzing the emotional profiles during distance education courses (MOOCs, e-learning) and to reason on the possible causes of positive and negative experiences during learning, so moving from recognition to the interpretation of the student's mental state. In particular, we are planning a user study for monitoring the student's mental state during the learning process and enhancing the student's learning experience in real-time through the use of gamification strategies [34], a virtual tutor [35] or a robot [36].

References

1. Damasio, A.R.: Descartes Error: Emotion, Reason and the Human Brain. G.P. Putnam Sons, New York (1994)
2. Pekrun, R.: The control-value theory of achievement emotions: assumptions, corollaries, and implications for educational research and practice. Educ. Psychol. Rev. **18**(4), 315–341 (2006). https://doi.org/10.1007/s10648-006-9029-9
3. Pekrun, R., Goetz, T., Frenzel, A.C., Barchfeld, P., Perry, R.P.: Measuring emotions in students' learning and performance: the achievement emotions questionnaire (AEQ). Contemp. Educ. Psychol. **36**(1), 36–48 (2011)
4. Picard, R.W.: Affective Computing. MIT Press, Cambridge (1997)
5. Del Coco, M., Carcagnì, P., Palestra, G., Leo, M., Distante, C.: Analysis of HOG suitability for facial traits description in FER problems. In: Murino, V., Puppo, E. (eds.) ICIAP 2015. LNCS, vol. 9280, pp. 460–471. Springer, Cham (2015). https://doi.org/10.1007/978-3-319-23234-8_43
6. Khalfallah, J., Slama, B.H.: Facial expression recognition for intelligent tutoring systems in remote laboratories platform. Procedia Comput. Sci. **73**, 274–281 (2015)
7. Shen, L., Wang, M., Shen, R.: Affective e-learning: "using emotional" data to improve learning in pervasive learning environment. J. Educ. Technol. Soc. **12**(2), 176 (2009)
8. Ekman, P.: Basic emotions. In: Dalgleish, T., Power, M.J. (eds.) Handbook of Cognition and Emotion, pp. 45–60. Wiley, Hoboken (1999). https://doi.org/10.1002/0470013494.ch3

9. O'regan, K.: Emotion and e-learning. J. Asynchronous Learn. Netw. **7**(3), 78–92 (2003)
10. O'Reilly, H., et al.: The EU-emotion stimulus set: a validation study. Behav. Res. Methods **48**(2), 567–576 (2016). https://doi.org/10.3758/s13428-015-0601-4
11. Lyons, M.J., Akamatsu, S., Kamachi, M., Gyoba, J.: Coding facial expressions with gabor wavelets. In: 3rd IEEE International Conference on Automatic Face and Gesture Recognition, pp. 200–205 (1998). http://doi.org/10.1109/AFGR.1998.670949
12. http://www.geocities.ws/senthilirtt/Senthil%20IRTT%20Face%20Database%20Version%201.1
13. Fleiss, J.L.: Measuring nominal scale agreement among many raters. Psychol. Bull. **76**(5), 378–382 (1971)
14. Dalal, N., Triggs, B.: Histograms of oriented gradients for human detection. In: IEEE Computer Society Conference on Computer Vision and Pattern Recognition, CVPR 2005, vol. 1, pp. 886–893. IEEE (2005)
15. Ekman, P., Friesen, W.: Facial Action Coding System: A Technique for the Measurement of Facial Movement. Consulting Psychologists Press, Palo Alto (1978)
16. https://github.com/TadasBaltrusaitis/OpenFace
17. D'Errico, F., Paciello, M., De Carolis, B., Vattani, A., Palestra, G., Anzivino, G.: Cognitive emotions in e-learning processes and their potential relationship with students' academic adjustment. Int. J. Emot. Educ. **10**(1), 89–111 (2018)
18. De Carolis, B., D'Errico, F., Paciello, M., Palestra, G.: Cognitive emotions recognition in e-learning: exploring the role of age differences and personality traits. In: Gennari, R., Vittorini, P., De la Prieta, F., Di Mascio, T., Temperini, M., Azambuja Silveira, R., Ovalle Carranza, D.A. (eds.) MIS4TEL 2019. AISC, vol. 1007, pp. 97–104. Springer, Cham (2020). https://doi.org/10.1007/978-3-030-23990-9_12
19. Ashwin, T.S., Jose, J., Raghu, G., Reddy, G.R.: An E-learning system with multifacial emotion recognition using supervised machine learning. In: IEEE Seventh International Conference on Technology for Education (2015)
20. Al-Awni, A.: Mood extraction using facial features to improve learning curves of students in elearning systems. Int. J. Adv. Comput. Sci. Appl. **7**(11), 444–453 (2016)
21. Krithika, L.B., Lakshmi Priyya, G.G.: Student emotion recognition system (SERS) for e-learning. Procedia Comput. Sci. **85**, 767–776 (2016)
22. Magdin, M., Turcani, M., Hudec, L.: Evaluating the Emotional State of a User Using a Webcam. Special Issue Artif. Intell. Underpinn. **4**(1), 61–68 (2016)
23. Roli, F.: Multiple classifier systems. In: Li, S.Z., Jain, A. (eds.) Encyclopedia of Biometrics, p. 1843. Springer, Boston (2009). https://doi.org/10.1007/978-0-387-39940-9
24. Ho, T.K.: Random decision forests. In: Proceedings of 3rd International Conference on Document Analysis and Recognition, Montreal, Quebec, Canada, vol. 1, pp. 278–282 (1995). https://doi.org/10.1109/icdar.1995.598994
25. Rumelhart, D., Hinton, G., Williams, R.: Learning representations by back-propagating errors. Nature **323**, 533–536 (1986). https://doi.org/10.1038/323533a0
26. Tabassum, T., Allen, A.A., De, P.: Non-intrusive identification of student attentiveness and finding their correlation with detectable facial emotions. In: Proceedings of the 2020 ACM Southeast Conference (ACM SE 2020), pp. 127–134. Association for Computing Machinery, New York (2020)
27. D'Mello, S.K., Calvo, R.A.: Beyond the basic emotions: what should affective computing compute? In: Brewster, S., Bødker, S., Mackay, W. (eds.) Extended Abstracts of the ACM SIGCHI Conference on Human Factors in Computing Systems (CHI 2013), pp. 2287–2294. ACM, New York (2013)
28. Loderer, K., Pekrun, R., Lester, J.C.: Beyond cold technology: a systematic review and meta-analysis on emotions in technology-based learning environments. Learn. Instruct. 101162 (2018)

29. Duffy, M.C., Lajoie, S.P., Pekrun, R., Lachapelle, K.: Emotions in medical education: examining the validity of the medical emotion scale (MES) across authentic medical learning environments. Learn. Instruct. 101150 (2018)
30. Castelfranchi, C.: Affective Appraisal *versus* Cognitive Evaluation in Social Emotions and Interactions. In: Paiva, A. (ed.) IWAI 1999. LNCS (LNAI), vol. 1814, pp. 76–106. Springer, Heidelberg (2000). https://doi.org/10.1007/10720296_7
31. Miceli, M., Castelfranchi, C.: Expectancy and Emotion. OUP, Oxford (2014)
32. Di Mele, L., D'Errico, F., Cerniglia, L., Cersosimo, M., Paciello, M.: Convinzioni di efficacia personale nella regolazione dell'apprendimento universitario mediato dalle tecnologie. Qwerty-Open Interdisc. J. Technol. Cult. Educ. **10**(2), 63–77 (2015)
33. Pecchinenda, A., Petrucci, M.: Emotion unchained: facial expression modulates gaze cueing under cognitive load. PLoS ONE **11**, e0168111 (2016)
34. Cassano, F., Piccinno, A., Roselli, T., Rossano, V.: Gamification and learning analytics to improve engagement in university courses. In: Di Mascio, T., et al. (eds.) MIS4TEL 2018. AISC, vol. 804, pp. 156–163. Springer, Cham (2019). https://doi.org/10.1007/978-3-319-98872-6_19
35. De Carolis, B., Ferilli, S., Novielli, N., Leuzzi, F., Rotella, F.: Social attitude recognition in multimodal interaction with a pedagogical agent. J. E-Learn. Knowl. Soc. **8**(3), 141–151 (2012). https://doi.org/10.20368/1971-8829/649
36. Malerba, D., et al.: Advanced programming of intelligent social robots. J. E-Learn. Knowl. Soc. **15**(2) (2019). https://doi.org/10.20368/1971-8829/1611
37. D'Errico, F., Paciello, M., Cerniglia, L.: When emotions enhance students' engagement in e-learning processes. J. e-Learn. Knowl. Soc. **12**(4) (2016)
38. Bosch, N., D'Mello, S.K., Ocumpaugh, J., Baker, R.S., Shute, V.: Using video to automatically detect learner affect in computer-enabled classrooms. ACM Trans. Interact. Intell. Syst. **6**(2), Article 17, 26 (2016). https://doi.org/10.1145/2946837
39. Whitehill, J., Serpell, Z., Lin, Y.-C., Foster, A., Movellan, J.R.: The faces of engagement: automatic recognition of student engagement from facial expressions. IEEE Trans. Affect. Comput. **5**(1), 86–98 (2014)
40. Zeng, Z., Pantic, M., Roisman, G.I., Huang, T.S.: A survey of affect recognition methods: audio, visual, and spontaneous expressions. IEEE Trans. Pattern Anal. Mach. Intell. **31**(1), 39–58 (2009)
41. Temdee, P.: Smart learning environment: paradigm shift for online learning (2020). https://doi.org/10.5772/intechopen.85787
42. Scheffler, I.: In Praise of the Cognitive Emotions. Routledge, New York (1991)
43. Bassi, M., Steca, P., Delle Fave, A., Caprara, G.V.: Academic self-efficacy beliefs and quality of experience in learning. J. Youth Adolesc. **36**(3), 301–312 (2007). https://doi.org/10.1007/s10964-006-9069-y
44. Chen, S., Dai, J., Yan, Y.: Classroom teaching feedback system based on emotion detection. In: 9th International Conference on Education and Social Science (ICESS 2019), pp. 940–946 (2019)
45. Zhang, K., Zhang, Z., Li, Z., Qiao, Y.: Joint face detection and alignment using multitask cascaded convolutional networks. IEEE Sig. Process. Lett. **23**(10), 1499–1503 (2016)

Semi-automated Student Feedback and Theory-Driven Video-Analytics: An Exploratory Study on Educational Value of Videos

Maka Eradze[1(✉)], Anna Dipace[1], Bojan Fazlagic[1], and Anastasia Di Pietro[2]

[1] Department of Education and Human Sciences, University of Modena and Reggio Emilia, Viale Antonio Allegri, 9, 42121 Reggio Emilia, Italy
{maka.eradze,anna.dipace,bojan.fazlagic}@unimore.it
[2] University of Foggia, Via Antonio Gramsci, 89, 71122 Foggia, Italy
anastasia.dipietro@unifg.it

Abstract. Learning Analytics (LA) is a relatively novel method for automated data collection and analysis with promising opportunities to improve teaching and learning processes, widely used in educational research and practice. Moreover, with the elevated use of videos in teaching and learning processes the importance of the analysis of video data increases. In turn, video analytics presents us with opportunities as well as challenges. However, to make full use of its potential often additional data is needed from multiple other sources. On the other hand, existing data also requires context and design-awareness for the analysis. Based on the existing landscape in LA, namely in video-analytics, this article presents a proof-of-concept study connecting cognitive theory-driven analysis of videos and semi-automated student feedback to enable further inclusion of interaction data and learning outcomes to inform video design but also to build teacher dashboards. This paper is an exploratory study analysing relationship between semi-automated student feedback (on several scales on the perceived educational value of videos), video engagement, video duration and theory-driven video annotations. Results did not indicate a significant relationship between different video designs and student feedback; however, findings show some correlation between the number of visualisations and video designs. The results can design implications as well as inform the researchers and practitioners in the field.

Keywords: Learning analytics · Video-analytics · Student feedback

1 Introduction

LA is a modern data-gathering technique that mainly relies on automatically aggregated learning traces. While it presents opportunities to gather insights into the teaching and learning practices, it is often difficult to analyse and interpret this data without additional context and multiple sources of data. With the emergence of the Massive Online Open Courses (MOOCs), we aggregate even more data, and since MOOCs are mainly

L. S. Agrati et al. (Eds.): HELMeTO 2020, CCIS 1344, pp. 28–39, 2021.
https://doi.org/10.1007/978-3-030-67435-9_3

video-driven, they become the main data source for analytics thus the analysis of video data becomes crucial. Also, the design of educational videos needs more evidence-based approaches by connecting different video designs with underlying factors such as learning outcomes, learner behaviour and learner perception on the educational value of the videos. Research indicates that the analysis of the video learning traces gives useful insights into the learning processes [1] but can also be beneficial for learning dashboards, however, the research into this direction is still its in infancy [2].

Based on the existing challenges in video-analytics, this paper offers a new approach to enrich video analytics with feedback data to understand the connection between the design of videos, student behaviour and student's perceptions on the educational value of the videos, which is done by introducing semi-automated student feedback on several scales directly in the videos. In the current paper, we present a proof-of-concept study connecting cognitive theory-driven [3] analysis of video designs and semi-automated student feedback to enable meaningful inclusion of interaction data and potentially learning outcomes to inform video design but also to build teacher dashboards.

2 Background and Related Literature

Learning Analytics (LA), as a field, has established itself as a ubiquitous method for analysis of large sets of digital footprints coming from the interactions between/with the learners, teacher or the learning environment. LA has many promises, one of which is the capability to contribute to the awareness and reflection on learning processes. However, among one of the critical issues with learning analytics are the dimension of data (mainly click-based) and the connection of the data with context: theory and design [4, 5]. For this reason, LA is rarely used on its own and it usually is combined with other types of data collection and analysis methods - such as self-report data, annotations for sense-making, observations, multimodal data etc. [6].

Video-based learning has been explored from different angles: mostly their effect on learning outcomes, attendance and academic performance, which yields mixed results [1]. There are also different types of videos for learning and depending on their affordances of interactions, we can have different types of data. This data can give us information on learning processes aligned with the data on other types of interactions and student profiles: *"combination of various learning analytics (e.g. content metadata, learners' profile) as well as the state-of-the-art statistical analysis techniques"* [7]. For instance, some studies investigated potential attitudinal differences among the diverse video lectures usage patterns and found that usage patterns affect students' attitudes to video lectures as a learning tool [8]. However, there remain many essential unexplored aspects of video-based learning and the related challenges and opportunities; such as, how to use all the data obtained from the learner, how to combine data from different sources, how to make sense heterogeneous learning analytics, how to synchronize and take the full advantage of learning analytics coming from different sources, how to use analytics to inform and tune smart learning etc. [7].

There are different properties of videos used as indicators for diverse reasons. One of the most highly cited studies in the area has investigated the relationship between the engagement of students and video properties [9] defining video properties with their length, speaking rate, video type, production style. A literature review found that most common measurements in video-analytics are *video watch time*, *video interactions* and *learning results*, reporting fine-grain measurement indicators for each [2]. According to the literature review by Poquet et al., the most common focus is the modality, and the most studied independent variable is the presentation style, while independent - recall test. Self-reports (feedback) are often used to evaluate different effect sizes [1].

Even though researchers and practitioners have been largely focused on the effects of video learning in higher education, the information on the impact of the videos on online students' learning perceptions and experiences has been scarce [10]. Some findings show that students' satisfaction with video learning has a strong relationship with a positive overall learning experience and perception of the impact of video on learning [11]. However, most of the studies investigate the overall perceptions of the general concept of a video as a learning tool but not the educational value of individual videos. Moreover, to the best of our knowledge, semi-automated student feedback on the educational value of the videos is one of the underexplored areas.

From an analytics perspective, video data can be useful to understand and improve learning processes [12]. Fine-grain video interaction data can bring valuable insights [1] and they can also be helpful to build learner or teacher dashboards, but this area is in an initial stage [2]. It is worth noting, that most of the video analysis is based on the interaction analysis of learning traces, for this reason, it is important to look beyond the click-stream data. Depending on the learning activity, meaningful interactions may not be tracked by digital learning platforms [13]. Thus, narrowing down the analysis to the data available in the digital platforms introduces the so-called issue of the "street light effect" bias [14, 15]. Moreover, to make sense of the learning data on one hand, and on the other, to have actionable learning dashboards the connection with theory [16], and human-centred design is needed, involving user feedback as in the data collection but also the development processes [17]. At the same time, only automated data is often superficial and not enough to create a hypothesis space and as educational processes and systems are highly contextual, different factors such as pedagogical design, actors, learning settings etc. come into play [18]. Human inference through annotations is often used to make sense of learning analytics data and contextualise automatically-collected learning traces. Moreover, since one of the challenges of learning analytics is the theory-driven analysis of data, we suggest using human inference and combining it with different sources of data [19].

In this paper, we argue that to understand the connection between student learning perceptions and experiences about the educational value of videos, we can collect semi-automated student feedback on the perceptions of the educational value of the videos, and combine with interaction (log data). To understand the objective value of the videos and their design i.e. to establish the ground truth, we can also relate them to the theory-driven properties of videos through human inference. Moreover, since the data is quantified and semi-automated later on, it can be used for different purposes: for real-time analytics and dashboards, or retrospective analysis to combine different sources of data and enrich the analysis.

In the following chapters, we will present the methodology of this exploratory, proof of concept study, present preliminary results and discuss them thoroughly with their limitations and potential areas to explore.

3 Methodology, Research Questions and Methods

3.1 Context of the Study, Research Design and Research Question

The context of the study is situated in higher education, blended learning setting. The study investigates and preliminarily evaluates the usefulness of semi-automated student feedback in the evaluation of the educational value of videos and inclusion of feedback in the learning dashboards with other data such as logs and learning outcomes. To this end, in this study we investigate the feasibility and usefulness of using semi-automated ratings on videos (Fig. 1) to gather feedback from the students based on three different scales: (a) quality of audio and video, (b) clarity of the teacher and (c) usefulness of the video to prepare for the exam. We hypothesise that this information later can be further aligned with different indicators to enrich the data coming from videos with structured user (student) feedback. The semi-automated student feedback is based on the 5-star ratings. This input can potentially be useful not only to inform better design of the videos but also to feed the data to learning dashboards.

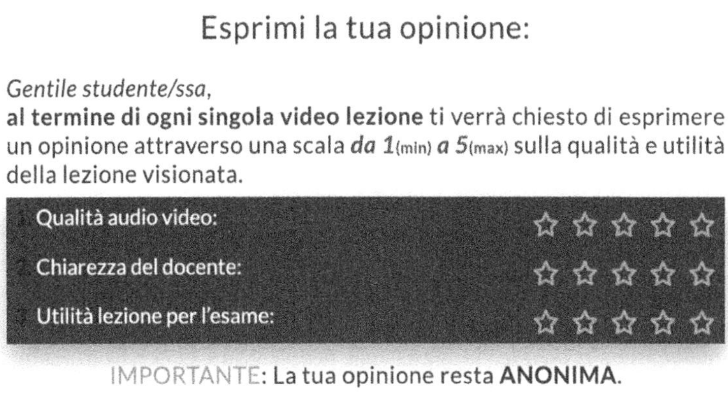

Fig. 1. The rating system based on 3 scales. (translation: 1. Quality of audio and video 2. Clarity of the lecturer 3. Usefulness of the lecture for the exam)

Therefore, this article answers to the following research question: *Can we use semi-automated video-ratings and theory-driven video annotations to understand what types of videos lead to learning satisfaction and perceived educational outcomes?*

To illustrate and evaluate our exploratory study and the proposal, and to operationalize theory-driven video properties, we have used a research-based cognitive theory of Multimedia Learning Principles (MLP). *"Multimedia instruction refers to presenting words and pictures that are intended to foster learning"* and consists of 12 principles aimed at providing effective and evidence-based tools for multimedia learning [3].

The theory of 12 principles of multimedia learning has been developed by Richard Mayer and is based on the cognitive theory of learning. Its three main assumptions are that:

- We have two separate channels for processing information, one is the visual/pictorial and the other one is the auditory/verbal;
- There is a limited channel capacity for processing;
- Learning is an active process of filtering, selecting, organizing and integrating information [20].

Multimedia learning is learning from words and pictures, it focuses on the assumption that "people learn more deeply from words and pictures than from words alone".

Of course, it is not enough to associate images with words but it is essential to understand how pictures and words can be used together to foster learning, avoiding overloading the learner's working memory capacity. Within this pedagogical framework, there are three fundamental goals for instructional design to improve the results of learning strategies:

- **Minimize extraneous processing,** cognitive processing that is not related to the instructional goal.
- **Manage essential processing**, understanding what kind of items are necessary to represent and summarize the complexity of the material.
- **Foster generative processing,** cognitive processing aimed at making sense of the incoming material, organizing and integrating it.

For each of these goals, Mayer provided to regroup the 12 principles of multimedia learning, explaining their indicators [21].

Five principles to **reduce extraneous processing** are:

1) The *coherence principle* implies to avoid extraneous, distracting material
2) The *signalling principle,* suggests that people learn better when essential words are shown on the screen and highlighted;
3) The *redundancy principle,* suggests that people learn better from animation and narration than animation, narration and text altogether;
4) The *spatial contiguity principle* implies that corresponding texts and pictures should be near and on the same page or screen;
5) The *temporal contiguity principle* implies that corresponding narration and animation should be presented together, at the same moment.

Three principles to **manage essential processing** are:

6) The *segmenting principle*, suggests that people learn better when information is presented in segments, rather than a long stream;
7) The *pre-training principle*, suggests that people learn better if they already know the basics of what they are learning, for instance, the meanings of essential components;

8) The *modality principle*, suggests that people learn better from graphics and spoken words rather than a printed text.

Four principles to **foster generative processing** are:

9) The *multimedia principle*, suggests that people learn better from words and pictures than from words alone;
10) The *personalization principle*, suggests that people learn better from an informal, conversational style;
11) The *voice principle*, suggests that people learn better from a human voice than a computer voice;
12) The *image principle*, suggests that people learn better from the animation on the screen than a talking head video of an instructor.

To evaluate the feasibility and usefulness of the approach, this study has used several sources of data: video annotations based on the 12 MLP principles; video ratings on several scales to gather semi-automated student feedback based on 5-scale ratings; engagement with videos (visualisations); the total number of ratings; video duration.

3.2 Data Collection and Sample

Videos were coded based on annotations according to the 12 MLP principles to denote whether and how many of the principles were followed. One expert coder coded the videos in discussion with another expert coder to establish the reliability; in case of doubt, the codes were agreed between the coders. At the same time, for reliability reasons, the codes were also reviewed on a random basis. The unit of analysis in this study is the video. We chose 6 different blended courses from the Department of Education and Human Sciences and we coded only the videos with ratings above 25 to account for the relative uniformity of data. The course information with the number of students is reported below:

1. Cognitive Psychology (N. of students 372);
2. Group Psychology (N. of students 388);
3. Environments and Technologies for Training (N. of students 116);
4. Digital Linguistics (N. of students 117);
5. Developmental and Educational Psychology (N. of students 113);
6. Society and Digital Educational Contexts (N. of students 122).

While the amount of the videos in each course varies (from a minimum of two videos for Developmental and Educational Psychology to a maximum of 20 videos for Group Psychology), we hypothesise that this is due to the video properties that videos in some courses are not rated above average.

As previously mentioned, aside from annotations, we have collected:

1) Semi-automated data:

- video ratings on several scales to gather semi-automated student feedback based on 5-scale ratings; this data has been collected in the period between February-May 2020.

2) Automated data:

- engagement with videos (visualisations);
- total number of ratings;
- video duration.

3.3 Data Analysis and Results

The first finding is that based on the analysed 44 videos students' average ratings do not significantly differ across the dataset: the average ratings are 4 and above, there was no rating below 4 (on a scale of 5). Initially, we run some analysis with Tableau software [22]. We plotted the average of N. Total ratings against the Total number of principles broken down by Course (total 6 courses). Preliminary results show there is some association between N° of MLP followed (above 10) on average per course and students' N° of ratings (Fig. 2) while different dimensions of the ratings (clarity, quality, usefulness) are not counted.

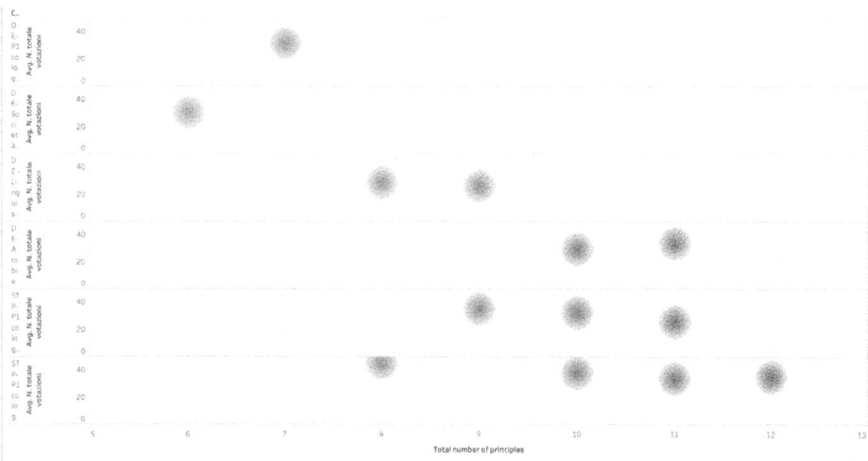

Fig. 2. Preliminary results: the plot of average of N. Total ratings for the total N. of principles broken down by Course (total 6 courses). The colour shows the average of Total N. of principles. Details are shown for Course. (Color figure online)

While this analysis mainly illustrates our sample, it also gives us some possible ideas on video-ratings: videos/courses that tend to have a lower number of principles preserved also get a lower number of ratings on average. However, this is a preliminary finding as the number of students in some courses were significantly higher than others and we chose videos for coding that had higher than 25 N. of ratings. This result is also associated with other finding reported further (association between the N. of visualisations and N. of principles followed). In a way, N. of ratings can be indicative of principles followed. One observation is that most of the time in our sample, N. of principles followed can be generalized to the whole course (the number and types of principles followed in the videos are almost invariable across courses). This analysis also illustrates that students tend not to rate some videos if the course contains videos with low N. of principles preserved (hence the selection of our sample).

From the visualisation (Fig. 3) we can see that the clarity and usefulness in some videos are associated with the N° of principles followed; we can notice that when the N° principles followed descend below 9, clarity and usefulness are rated lower.

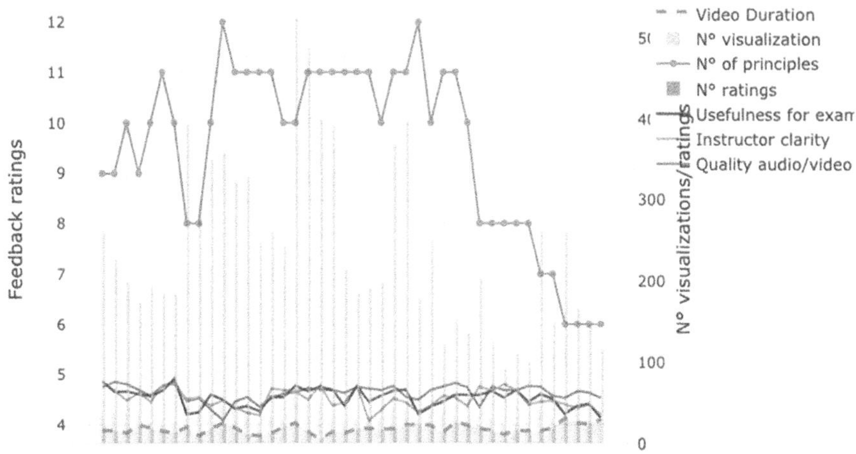

Fig. 3. The plot visualizing different data sources analysed together. In some cases, we can observe a slight tendency of decreasing ratings for *Usefulness for the Exam* and *Instructor Clarity* when the number of principles followed fall below 9.

To better understand the correlations between different indicators, we have also run a regression analysis on the dataset in R based on the following indicators:

1. N. of total principles followed and video duration;
2. N. of total principles followed and N. of total ratings;
3. N. of total principles followed and N video visualisations (engagement);
4. And finally, the correlations between different questions (quality of audio and video; clarity of the lecturer, usefulness of the lecture for the exam) and all the above indicators (video duration, N. of total ratings and N video visualisations (engagement) (Fig. 4).

The analysis showed that there is some correlation between the N° of principles and the N of visualisations (R = 0.37; P = 0.016) (Fig. 5). We could presume that the

cor_princ_duration	-0.305914233119041
cor_princ_total_rat	0.108523074171377
cor_princ_visual	0.370675064029024
cor_q1_duration	-0.193673278410796
cor_q1_princ	-0.0609351172907482
cor_q1_visual	-0.292335672809443
cor_q2_duration	-0.272164524135274
cor_q2_princ	-0.02045189467625
cor_q2_visual	-0.0124956958405718
cor_q3_duration	-0.263486105613218
cor_q3_princ	0.26463271871687
cor_q3_visual	0.148508719381604

Fig. 4. An overall analysis of different indicators: *princ* = N° of total principles, *duration* = duratioN. of the video; *visual* = N° of visualisations; *total_rat* = N° of total ratings; *q1, q2, q3* = three feedback questions

number of MPL followed should be at least 9 for the videos to have educational value for the students, however, given the size of the sample and insignificant variance between video ratings, we will need further studies. Also, to understand the relationship between different principles (out of 12) and the ratings, in future, we will need to analyse data according to each principle with a larger data-set.

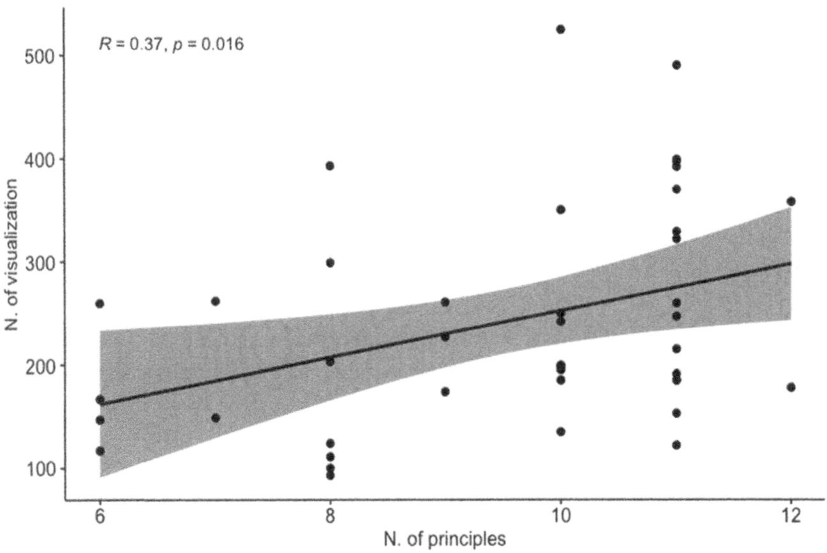

Fig. 5. Regression analysis based on N° of principles and the N° of visualisations.

4 Conclusions and Discussion

Generally, the most interesting preliminary finding in this exploratory, proof-of-concept study is the weak correlation between the research-based MLP and significant differences in the average student ratings (all above 4). So, our main question in a way remained open. It is also due to little differences in video ratings, we were not fully able to respond to our main question. However, we found that the N. of principles followed are somewhat correlated to the video visualisations. While this might mean that we need to reconsider the questions asked, it can also be by different factors, this finding needs further research with mixed methods approaches, as it can have design implications for the feedback system and respective dashboards. Aside from this, our study demonstrates the need for contextual, theory and design-driven data to solve validity issues of analytics data, and the need to examine the data-set closely before including them in the dashboards.

Aside from field-specific findings that are relevant to TEL and LA researchers, the results our study can potentially inform the research and practice in other contexts where student feedback is used for evaluation of the performance of the academic staff; while it is true that if we did analyse a big enough dataset, still, we found that average ratings across contexts and designs did not change, even if the video's properties did change. This potentially can mean that, first of all, careful consideration of the student evaluation questions is needed. Second, we need to think about the quality and dimension of the data: qualitative approaches, different data sources and triangulation, as well as careful formulation of questions to be asked are important. Furthermore, this study once again confirms previous research on the need for contextual data for learning analytics studies [23].

The limitations of the preliminary study include the sampling method of the coded videos, that was based on above 25 N. of ratings. Due to the lower N. of ratings, this might have introduced a selection bias in our data-set. At the same time, the overall data-set for this proof-of-concept study was quite small that naturally restrict the generalizability of the findings. However, since the nature of this research was exploratory, the indicators enabled by the results will be used to inform the research design of the next study as well as the design of semi-automated student feedback tool and the dashboard study. Potential scenarios are discussed in the following chapter.

5 Future Research

Following the study, we will first analyse larger data-set, after which will involve students to investigate the factors behind the ratings and the correct formulation of the rating questions. This will result in a redesign of the rating system, after which we will aggregate more data to re-evaluate it. Moreover, the outcomes of this research will be used to build learning analytics dashboards and evaluate the potential of our proposal for its actionability to understand whether our approach brings valuable insights to educators. To create a path for actionable dashboards we will also run a qualitative study involving a design session with participatory approaches to understanding what indicators teachers need for evidence-based teaching practice; the aggregated visualizations will be presented to the teachers to understand whether semi-automated student feedback is informative and actionable for them. We also plan to include different sources of data such as learner engagement, motivation and learning outcomes to answer our next research question: *What are the relationship between video design, student engagement and student perceived educational value and quality of the videos and the learning outcomes?*

Acknowledgements. The research has been made possible and funded under the European Union's Erasmus + grant 2019-1-ES01-KA203-065558.

References

1. Poquet, O., Lim, L., Mirriahi, N., Dawson, S.: Video and learning: a systematic review (2007–2017). In: Proceedings of the 8th International Conference on Learning Analytics and Knowledge, pp. 151–160 (2018)
2. Seidel, N.: Analytics on video-based learning. A literature review. In: CEUR Workshop Proceedings (2018)
3. Mayer, R.E.: Using multimedia for e-learning. J. Comput. Assist. Learn. **33**, 403–423 (2017)
4. Eradze, M., Rodriguez Triana, M.J., Laanpere, M.: Context-aware multimodal learning analytics taxonomy. In: Companion Proceedings 10th International Conference on Learning Analytics & Knowledge (LAK20), CEUR Workshop Proceedings (2020)
5. Mirriahi, N., Jovanovic, J., Dawson, S., Gašević, D., Pardo, A.: Identifying engagement patterns with video annotation activities: A case study in professional development. Aust. J. Educ. Technol. **34**, 57–72 (2018). https://doi.org/10.14742/ajet.3207
6. Eradze, M., Rodríguez-Triana, M.J., Milikic, N., Laanpere, M., Tammets, K.: Contextualising learning analytics with classroom observations: a case study. Interact. Des. Archit. J.-IxD&A. **44**, 71–95 (2020)
7. Giannakos, M.N., Sampson, D.G., Kidziński, Ł.: Introduction to smart learning analytics: foundations and developments in video-based learning. Smart Learn. Environ. **3**(1), 1–9 (2016). https://doi.org/10.1186/s40561-016-0034-2
8. Giannakos, M.N., Jaccheri, L., Krogstie, J.: Exploring the relationship between video lecture usage patterns and students' attitudes. Br. J. Educ. Technol. **47**, 1259–1275 (2016)
9. Guo, P.J., Kim, J., Rubin, R.: How video production affects student engagement: an empirical study of MOOC videos. In: Proceedings of the First ACM Conference on Learning@ Scale Conference, pp. 41–50 (2014)
10. Hsin, W.-J., Cigas, J.: Short videos improve student learning in online education. J. Comput. Sci. Coll. **28**, 253–259 (2013)
11. Scagnoli, N.I., Choo, J., Tian, J.: Students' insights on the use of video lectures in online classes. Br. J. Educ. Technol. **50**, 399–414 (2019)
12. Giannakos, M.N., Chorianopoulos, K., Ronchetti, M., Szegedi, P., Teasley, S.D.: Analytics on video-based learning. In: Proceedings of the Third International Conference on Learning Analytics and Knowledge - LAK 2013, p. 283. ACM Press, New York (2013). https://doi.org/10.1145/2460296.2460358
13. Ochoa, X., Worsley, M.: Augmenting Learning Analytics with Multimodal Sensory Data. J. Learn. Anal. **3**, 213–219 (2016)
14. Ochoa, X.: Multimodal learning analytics. In: Lang, C., Siemens, G., Wise, A.F., Gaševic, D. (eds.) The Handbook of Learning Analytics, pp. 129–141. Society for Learning Analytics Research (SoLAR), Alberta (2017)
15. Freedman, D.H.: Why scientific studies are so often wrong: the streetlight effect. Discov. Mag. **26** (2010). https://www.discovermagazine.com/the-sciences/why-scientific-studies-are-so-often-wrong-the-streetlight-effect. Accessed 06 Jan 2021

16. Jivet, I., Scheffel, M., Drachsler, H., Specht, M.: Awareness is not enough: pitfalls of learning analytics dashboards in the educational practice. In: Lavoué, É., Drachsler, H., Verbert, K., Broisin, J., Pérez-Sanagustín, M. (eds.) EC-TEL 2017. LNCS, vol. 10474, pp. 82–96. Springer, Cham (2017). https://doi.org/10.1007/978-3-319-66610-5_7
17. Buckingham Shum, S., Ferguson, R., Martinez-Maldonaldo, R.: Human-centred learning analytics. J. Learn. Anal. **6**, 1–9 (2019). https://doi.org/10.18608/jla.2019.62.1
18. Shibani, A., Knight, S., Shum, S.B.: Contextualizable learning analytics design: a generic model and writing analytics evaluations. In: ACM International Conference Proceeding Series (2019). https://doi.org/10.1145/3303772.3303785
19. Worsley, M., Abrahamson, D., Blikstein, P., Grover, S., Schneider, B., Tissenbaum, M.: Situating multimodal learning analytics. In: 12th International Conference of the Learning Sciences: Transforming Learning, Empowering Learners, ICLS 2016, pp. 1346–1349. International Society of the Learning Sciences (ISLS) (2016)
20. Mayer, R.E.: Cognitive theory of multimedia learning. Cambridge Handb. Multimed. Learn. **41**, 31–48 (2005)
21. Mayer, R.E.: Applying the science of learning: evidence-based principles for the design of multimedia instruction. Am. Psychol. **63**, 760 (2008)
22. Murray, D.G.: Tableau Your Data!: Fast and Easy Visual Analysis with Tableau Software. Wiley, Hoboken (2013)
23. Rodríguez-Medina, J., Rodríguez-Triana, M.J., Eradze, M., García-Sastre, S.: Observational scaffolding for learning analytics: a methodological proposal. In: Pammer-Schindler, V., Pérez-Sanagustín, M., Drachsler, H., Elferink, R., Scheffel, M. (eds.) EC-TEL 2018. LNCS, vol. 11082, pp. 617–621. Springer, Cham (2018). https://doi.org/10.1007/978-3-319-98572-5_58

Learning-State-Estimation Method Using Browsing History and Electroencephalogram During Programming Language Learning and Its Evaluation

Katsuyuki Umezawa[1(✉)], Tomohiko Saito[1], Takashi Ishida[2], Makoto Nakazawa[3], and Shigeichi Hirasawa[4]

[1] Shonan Institute of Technology, Fujisawa, Kanagawa 251–8511, Japan
umezawa@info.shonan-it.ac.jp
[2] Takasaki City University of Economics, Takasaki, Gunma 370–0801, Japan
[3] Junior College of Aizu, Aizuwakamatsu, Fukushima 965–8570, Japan
[4] Waseda University, Shinjuku, Tokyo 169–8555, Japan

Abstract. The failure of learners to obtain sufficient knowledge is caused by various factors, such as the difficulty level and quality of the learning materials and learner's prior knowledge. The use of the learner's learning log and biological information, such as the brain waves, heart rate, and eye movements during learning, makes it possible to detect the factors. If different brain waves can be measured according to the difficulty level of task execution, the difficulty level of e-learning materials can be adjusted so that the optimum learning effect can be obtained for each student. In this study, a system that obtains the learning logs during learning has been proposed. However, the learning time is insufficient to understand the learning state of the learners. For example, if the learning time is short, whether the learning materials were too easy or too difficult to abandon cannot be determined. Therefore, we propose a system and a method for estimating the learning state of the learners by comprehensively analyzing his/her learning history and brain wave. Moreover, we evaluate the learning state of high school students learning the C and Scratch programming languages using the proposed method. Also, by comparing the estimated results with those obtained from the questionnaire administered after the experiments, we evaluate the effectiveness of our proposed method.

Keywords: Simple EEG · Brain wave · Learning analytics · E-learning

1 Introduction

Currently, researches have been conducted to effectively apply web-based teaching materials to learning [1] and integrate digital textbooks and e-learning systems [2]. For a similar purpose, we developed a prototype of digital teaching

L. S. Agrati et al. (Eds.): HELMeTO 2020, CCIS 1344, pp. 40–55, 2021.
https://doi.org/10.1007/978-3-030-67435-9_4

materials and evaluated them in a classroom [3]. We also developed two systems that can extract the browsing history [4] and the editing history [5], respectively. We used these systems in both the English class [6] and programming class [7]. Numerous studies have been conducted to improve the coding skills of developers by analyzing the editing process of programming [8,9].

During intellectual work, the brain waves were measured, and the β waves were found to be strongly correlated with the person's mental state [10]. In previous studies [11,12], it has been reported that the ratio of α waves to β waves effectively estimated the state of the human mind. We have experimentally confirmed that the ratio of low-β/low-α, in which "low" indicates low frequency, increases during the execution of difficult tasks [15,16].

As previously mentioned, numerous researchers have proposed a system that can extract the browsing history, and they have used brain waves to estimate the state of the learner. However, just collecting the browsing history, such as the learner's browsing time, seems insufficient. For instance, when the browsing time is short, it is either that the learning materials are too easy for the learner or the learners have given up learning due to the difficulty level of the learning materials. Accordingly, we proposed a system to estimate the learning state of the learners through the integration and analysis of both the learning history and brain waves.

We evaluated the learning state of high school students who were learning the C [17] and the Scratch programming languages using our proposed method. Moreover, by comparing the estimated results with those obtained from the questionnaire administered after the experiments, we evaluated the effectiveness of our proposed method.

The remainder of this paper is organized as follows. In Sect. 2, we describe our previous work, and in Sect. 3, we discuss our proposed system and the method for estimating the learning state of the learners. In Sect. 4, we present the experimental methods and results. In Sect. 5, we analyze the estimation results obtained using our proposed method, as well as the questionnaire results. Finally, in Sect. 6, we summarize our study and discuss the future work.

2 Related Work

2.1 Web-Based Learning-Log-Collection System

When we read the educational content in the PDF format on the web, the information "someone downloaded the PDF" is recorded, whereas the information that "someone looked at the x page of the PDF" is not. Thus, knowing exactly "which page of the PDF was viewed and how many times" is difficult for us as the browsing action for the PDF content is not recorded. In our previous study, we proposed a web-based log-collection system to support learning [4]. This system stores log information, such as learner ID, content number, page number, open and closed times, and number of seconds the page was viewed.

We have also developed an editing history visualization system [5] that collects not only the browsing logs but also the programming editing logs. It is a web-based system capable of collecting all the program codes during coding and visualizing the changed part of the program code. We can use this system to identify programming structures that is easy to make mistakes for programming beginners. We applied this system in the analysis of English learning [6] and programming learning [7].

Numerous studies have been conducted to improve the coding skills of developers by analyzing the editing process of programming. In [8, 9], other researchers have analyzed the coding process of 40 students using event logs during programming using a cloud-based programming development environment. They argue that by analyzing our proposed method, how to improve the coding skills of developers may be well understood.

2.2 Brain Waves for Learning

In previous studies, the learning state of the learners was estimated by measuring the α and β waves through the discrete Fourier change on the brain waves. Giannitrapani found that the low-β wave increases during intellectual work [10].

Uwano et al. have found that the ratio of the α and β waves can effectively estimate the learning state of the learners [11]. Conversely, Yoshida et al. found that a learner's learning state can be estimated by measuring the ratio of the α and β waves [12].

Some researchers have studied memory performance using brain waves. They found that the low-γ wave is an effective index for the measurement of memory performance [13]. The analysis results of the relationship between the low-γ wave (which reflects the memory work) and θ wave [14] revealed that the $(\theta + \alpha)/10$ wave and low-γ have synchronous wavelengths and that the $(\theta + \alpha)/(10 \times \text{low-}\gamma)$ ratio is an effective index for the measurement of memory performance. In our previous experiment, we employed a typing software that is capable of changing the difficulty level of the learning materials. We found that the β/α ratio increases during the execution of difficult tasks [15] and that the ratio of low-β/low-α affects the difficulty level [16].

To completely understand the characteristics of learners, several studies have been conducted to measure the brain waves during programming learning. In [18], researchers used EEG to directly evaluate the expertise of programmers. They proposed an approach for investigating expert knowledge in understanding programming languages. Moreover, in [19], researchers employed EEG to determine the differences between the beginners and experts in programming, both of which were found to exhibit different abilities in understanding the program. According to the EEG data, programming experts are excellent in understanding the programs.

3 Proposed System and Method

Figure 1 presents our proposed system that can be used to analyze the learning state of the learners. This system extracts the browsing logs from an existing learning-log-collection system and brain waves from an existing brain-wave-collection system. First, the browsing history obtained from the learning-log-collection system is stored via the learning-log-collecting part. Figure 2 presents an example of the browsing history log. For example, as presented in Fig. 2, a user called "ma001" read the seventh page for 49.3 s. Conversely, the brain waves obtained from the brain-wave-collection system is stored via the brain-wave-collecting part. Figure 3 presents an example of the brain-wave-collection log. For example, as presented in Fig. 3, the 11:30:21 α_l value of a user called "ma001" is 1097. The analysis part analyzes the learning state of each learner using the stored browsing history and brain wave information as well as stores the analysis results.

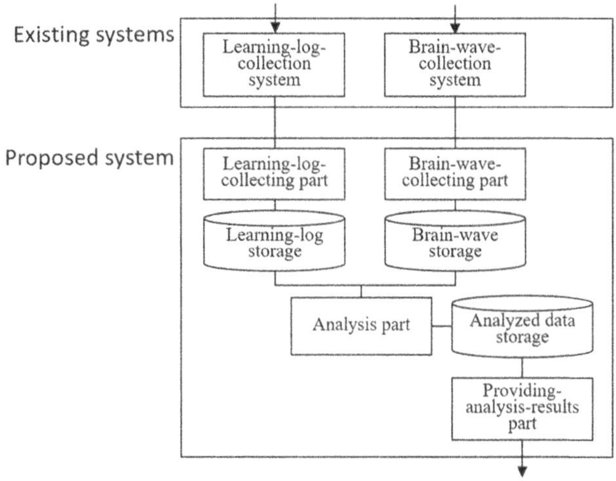

Fig. 1. Proposed system

```
userId=ma001 page=7 start=2016-06-12T11:05:53
end=2016-08-18T11:35:43 time=49.3
userId=ma001 page=8 start=2016-06-12T11:06:43
end=2016-08-18T11:36:06 time=22.9
userId=ma001 page=9 start=2016-06-12T11:07:06
end=2016-08-18T11:36:20 time=14.2
......
```

Fig. 2. Example of browsing history log

```
Date,userID,Page,Attention,Meditation,α1,β1
2016/08/18T11:30:21,ma001,3,56,41,1097,883
2016/08/18T11:30:22,ma001,3,70,23,138094,62256
2016/08/18T11:30:23,ma001,3,96,10,12529,22642
2016/08/18T11:30:24,ma001,4,100,1,3034,8763
2016/08/18T11:30:25,ma001,4,100,3,128468,7349
......
```

Fig. 3. Example of brain wave log

A conventional method [12] that estimates the learning state of the learners by using a simple EEG has been proposed. With this method, whether the learner is solving a difficult problem or not can be determined. However, we cannot identify whether they have given up solving the problem or the problem is just too easy. In some cases, it is desirable to determine whether the learner understands the entire learning material or just a part of it. To solve these problems, we proposed an estimation algorithm.

Figure 4 presents the proposed method for the analysis conducted in the "Analysis part" of Fig. 1. First, the data indicating the degree of attention obtained from the EEG is used to evaluate whether "a learner cannot concentrate on learning (NC)" (Condition 1). We describe "attention" in detail in Sect. 4.3.

Next, based on the relationship between the degree of contemplation defined from the EEG value and the time spent browsing the teaching material, it is estimated whether the "content of learning is too easy (TE)" (Condition 2). Furthermore, using the same data as Condition 2, it is determined whether the "content of learning is too difficult (TD)" (Condition 3). Finally, using the number of page returns, it is estimated whether "there is a part that cannot be partially understood (PU)" (Condition 4). If all of the above conditions are not true, the learning state of the learner is estimated to be "a standard understanding state (ST)."

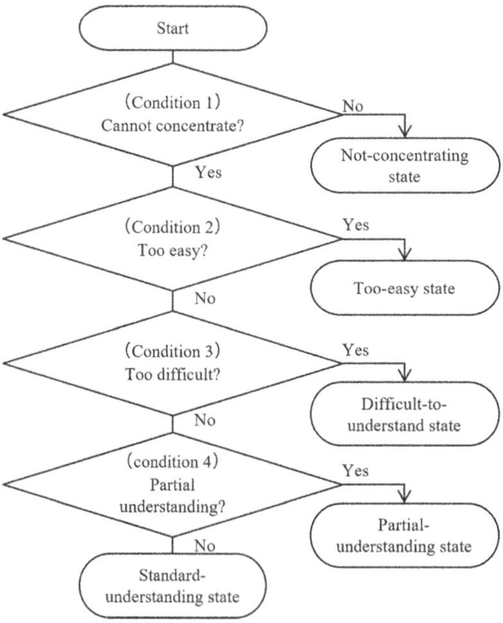

Fig. 4. Proposed method

Specifically, the algorithm works as follows. First, if the degree of attention of the learner is low, he/she is considered to have failed to concentrate using Condition 1. Next, using Conditions 2 and 3, it is determined whether the learners felt that the learning materials are too easy or too difficult. Although the difficulty level cannot be specified alone by the learning time, our proposed method adds brain wave information to the estimation formula to enable the estimation of the learner's condition. This makes it possible to distinguish between cases in which the learner needs time to think deeply (Condition 3) and cases in which taking time is not needed as the learning materials are easy to understand (Condition 2). If the learning materials are too difficult, the learner is considered to have lost concentration according to Condition 1. Finally, the learning state of the learner is estimated to be partially understood, depending on the number of times the page is returned in Condition 4. If Conditions 1 to 4 are not true, the learner's understanding is estimated to be standard.

4 Experiments

4.1 Outline of Experiment

We held the "Matsudai Science Course" for the students in Matsudai High School in Niigata Prefecture and its neighboring high school and conducted experiments on the learning of the two programming languages, the C programming language (18 high school students) and the Scratch programming language (16 high school students). The experimental setup is presented in Fig. 5. All students were beginners in programming. Assuming the remote learning of blended learning and e-learning, the examinees were allowed to browse slides that explained the basics of the C and Scratch programming languages, during which we measured their brain waves. We used a part of the "Matsudai Science Course (9:00 AM to 15:50 PM)" to conduct experiments on the C and Scratch programming languages for 5 min each (10 min in total).

Fig. 5. Photograph of the examinees participating in the experiment

4.2 Browsing History Acquiring Method

In the experiments, we collected the learning history using the learning-log-collection system described in Sect. 2.1. This system was used to collect log information, such as learner ID, content number, page number, open and closed times, and number of seconds the page was viewed. It is connected to the Moodle system, and by authenticating the user of the Moodle system, various log information can be obtained together with the authenticated user name. The study content included 8 slides about the C programming language and 16 slides about the Scratch programming language.

4.3 Brain Wave-Measuring Method

The simple EEG we employed in our experiments is called the MindWave Mobile headset (NeuroSky, Inc.). This headset can detect potential differences (voltage) between the forehead (F_{P1} position of the international 10–20 system for EEG) and the ear (A_1 position), as presented in [20]. The signals are passed through low-pass and high-pass filters to retain signals in the range of 1–50 Hz. Aliasing correction, 128 Hz sampling, noise artifact detection and correction, and frequency component transform (fast Fourier transform (FFT)) were performed on the headset.

As presented in Fig. 6, after converting the brain wave data, the headset sends the data to the ThinkGear connector via Bluetooth. The log-collection system collects the brain wave data from the ThinkGear connector via the transmission control protocol/Internet protocol. The ThinkGear connector is a middleware driver provided by NeuroSky Inc., which is only used to transfer the converted EEG data within the headset to the user application.

The brain waves that can be obtained by the MindWave Mobile headset are presented in Table 1. The data that can be obtained is a 4-byte (unitless) floating-point value [21]. This headset can also collect attention and meditation values called eSense. These values are between 1 and 100 and are described as follows [22]: values between 40 and 60 are considered as neutral, those between 80 and 100 are considered as high, and those between 1 and 20 are considered as very low. Three types of data were used in the proposed method: α_l, β_l, and attention.

4.4 Experimental Results

The browsing history logs of which pages the examinees viewed for how many seconds was collected. Moreover, the α and β waves and attention and meditation values were measured at 1-s intervals using a simple EEG. Since (low β wave)/(low α wave) represents the difficulty level of the task [16], we refer to that value of (low β wave)/(low α wave) as "contemplation degree."

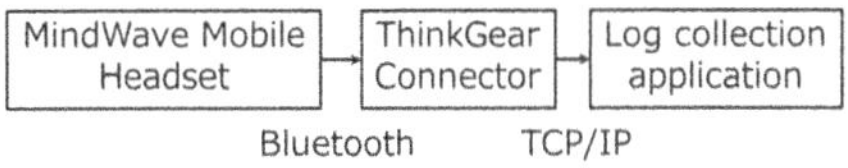

Fig. 6. Outline of the brain wave measurement

Table 1. Acquired brain waves

Type	Frequency (Hz)
δ wave	0.5–2.75
θ wave	3.5–6.75
Low α (α_l) wave	7.5–9.25
High α (α_h) wave	10–11.75
Low β (β_l) wave	13–16.75
High β (β_h) wave	18–29.75
Low γ wave	31–39.75
Mid γ wave	41–49.75

5 Analysis of Experimental Results

Table 2. Estimated results obtained from studying the C programming language (based on Table 2 of [17])

ID	TM_i	T_i	$\overline{AT_i}$	$\overline{BW_i}$	B_i	$B_i + T_i$	P_i	Estimated results*				
ma001	154	−39.50	66.60	1.70	34.69	−4.81	3					ST
ma002	247	53.50	67.29	1.14	−21.50	32.00	11				PU	
ma003	225	31.50	43.19	1.45	9.90	41.40	4	NC		(TD)		
ma004	241	47.50	50.43	1.86	50.73	98.23	5			TD		
ma005	177	−16.50	57.21	0.94	−41.71	−58.21	4		TE			
ma006	231	37.50	44.06	1.37	1.95	39.45	7	NC			(PU)	
ma007	199	5.50	50.12	1.32	−3.55	1.95	0					ST
ma009	134	−59.50	50.78	1.88	52.62	−6.88	0					ST
ma011	98	−95.50	54.59	1.02	−33.49	−128.99	0		TE			
ma013	147	−46.50	66.97	1.16	−19.73	−66.23	0		TE			
ma014	168	−25.50	59.25	1.28	−7.27	−32.77	0					ST
ma015	243	49.50	65.75	1.34	−1.53	47.97	0			TD		
ma016	219	25.50	79.24	1.36	0.86	26.36	8				PU	
ma021	211	17.50	59.81	1.47	11.93	29.43	0					ST
ma022	283	89.50	30.25	1.26	−9.33	80.17	0	NC		(TD)		
ma023	158	−35.50	42.93	0.89	−46.34	−81.84	1	NC	(TE)			
ma024	133	−60.50	65.82	1.67	31.27	−29.23	7				PU	
ma026	215	21.50	46.52	1.26	−9.51	11.99	6	NC			(PU)	
Average	193.5	0.00	55.60	1.35	0.00	0.00	3.1					

* NC: non-concentration, TE: too easy, TD: too difficult,
PU: partial understanding, ST: standard understanding.
Symbols without () are the final estimated results.

5.1 Analysis Results

Using the logs obtained as a result of the experiment, the learning state of the learners was estimated using our proposed method. The following formulas were used for the four conditions of the proposed algorithm:

$$\overline{AT_i} < 50 \qquad \text{(Condition 1)}$$
$$B_i + T_i < -40 \qquad \text{(Condition 2)}$$
$$B_i + T_i > 40 \qquad \text{(Condition 3)}$$
$$P_i > 6, \qquad \text{(Condition 4)}$$

Table 3. Estimated results obtained from studying the Scratch programming language

ID	TM_i	T_i	$\overline{AT_i}$	$\overline{BW_i}$	B_i	$B_i + T_i$	P_i	Estimated results*			
ma001	482	86.0	56.20	1.62	16.19	102.19	3			TD	
ma002	474	79.0	47.84	1.18	−27.48	51.52	1	NC		(TD)	
ma003	547	151.0	69.13	1.40	−5.73	145.27	5			TD	
ma004	575	179.0	45.24	1.10	−35.69	143.31	8	NC		(TD)	(PU)
ma005	159	−237.0	49.19	1.54	8.27	−228.73	2	NC	(TE)		
ma006	351	−44.0	47.13	1.28	−17.71	−61.71	6	NC	(TE)		(PU)
ma007	149	−247.0	36.55	1.24	−21.75	−268.75	1	NC	(TE)		
ma008	379	−16.0	64.82	2.24	78.59	62.59	2			TD	
ma009	512	117.0	46.49	2.01	55.35	172.35	1	NC		(TD)	
ma010	563	168.0	54.73	1.20	−26.32	141.68	4			TD	
ma011	438	42.0	58.83	1.39	−7.31	34.69	10				PU
ma012	548	152.0	50.20	1.34	−12.03	139.97	8			TD	(PU)
ma013	242	−154.0	63.44	1.63	16.67	−137.33	1		TE		
ma014	382	−14.0	55.43	1.15	−30.60	−44.60	5		TE		
ma015	318	−78.0	60.59	1.03	−43.35	−121.35	2		TE		
ma016	211	−184.0	58.60	1.99	52.88	−131.12	3		TE		
Average	396.0	0.0	54.03	1.46	0.00	0.00	3.9				

* NC: non-concentration, TE: too easy, TD: too difficult,
PU: partial understanding, ST: standard understanding.
Symbols without () are the final estimated results.

where

$$\overline{AT_i} = \Sigma_j AT_{ij}/n_i \qquad (1)$$
$$B_i = 100 \times (\overline{BW_i} - \overline{BW}) \qquad (2)$$
$$T_i = TM_i - \overline{TM} \qquad (3)$$
$$\overline{BW_i} = \Sigma_j BW_{ij}/n_i \qquad (4)$$
$$\overline{BW} = \Sigma_i \overline{BW_i}/m \qquad (5)$$
$$\overline{TM} = \Sigma_i \overline{TM_i}/m, \qquad (6)$$

where AT_{ij} denotes the attention of examinee i at time j; BW_{ij}, the β_l/α_l of examinee i at time j; TM_i, the reading time of examinee i; n_i, the number of measurement datasets from examinee i; P_i, the number of page-return times of examinee i; and m, the number of examinees.

Condition 1 is an expression determining whether the participants in the experiment were able to concentrate. The average value of the concentration of the participants was utilized for the judgment. Condition 2 is an expression determining whether the participants felt that the learning materials were too easy. We used the ratio of the α-waves and β-waves, which is said to indicate the degree of difficulty from previous studies, and the time to learn (read) the page. If the electroencephalogram value is low and the time is short, the learning materials are judged to be too easy. Condition 3 is an expression determining whether the participants felt that the learning materials were too difficult; the types of numerical values used are the same as in Condition 2. Condition 4 is an expression determining whether or not the learning materials are partially understood. The high number of participants returning to the previous page during the learning indicates that their understanding is partial. Therefore, we used the number of page returns as the conditional expression.

Tables 2 and 3 present the estimated results of the learning state obtained using the above formulas. Table 2 presents the results obtained from studying the C programming language, whereas Table 3 presents those obtained from studying the Scratch programming language. In the Estimated results column, the symbol without () indicates the final result. Conversely, the symbols with () indicate the possible estimated results other than the final result. The possible estimated results indicate the results that can be determined by the algorithm in Fig. 4, assuming that the above conditions are not satisfied.

5.2 Consideration on the Validity of the Experimental Results

In this section, we statistically compare and analyze the results obtained from the questionnaires administered after the experiment with the learning state of the learners estimated using the proposed algorithm. The questionnaire items were as follows:

Q_1: Did you think the learning materials were easy to understand?
Q_2: Did you think the learning materials were difficult to understand?
Q_3: Did you concentrate during your studies?

The possible answers to each question item were as follows:

A_1: I agree.
A_2: I agree a little.
D_2: I disagree a little.
D_1: I disagree.

Questionnaire Results Obtained from Studying the C Programming Language. The questionnaire results obtained from studying the C programming language are presented in Table 4. Two examinees who were classified as

TE (ma011 and ma013) completely understood (Q_1 was A_1) the learning materials and did not think that they were difficult to understand (Q_2 was D_1). Those classified as PU (ma002, ma016, and ma024) answered "Disagree" or "Disagree a little" in response to the item asking if the learning materials were difficult to understand (Q_2 was D_1 or D_2). This can be interpreted as having difficulty in understanding due to going back to the page and trying to understand because there were difficult parts. "Partial understanding" may also be interpreted as "there were parts that could not be understood at first, and understanding was deepened by page return." The examinees who were classified as TD (ma004 and ma015) responded that the learning materials were difficult to understand (Q_2 was A_1 or A_2).

Table 4. Questionnaire results obtained from studying the C programming language

ID	Estimated results					Questionnaire results		
						Q_1	Q_2	Q_3
ma001					ST	A_2	A_2	A_2
ma002				PU		A_2	D_2	A_2
ma003	NC		(TD)			D_2	A_2	A_2
ma004			TD			A_1	A_2	A_1
ma005		TE				A_2	A_1	A_2
ma006	NC			(PU)		A_1	D_1	A_1
ma007					ST	D_2	A_2	D_2
ma009					ST	A_2	A_2	A_1
ma011		TE				A_1	D_1	A_1
ma013		TE				A_1	D_1	A_1
ma014					ST	A_1	A_1	A_1
ma015			TD			A_1	A_1	A_1
ma016				PU		A_1	D_2	A_1
ma021					ST	D_2	A_2	A_2
ma022	NC		(TD)			A_2	A_2	A_2
ma023	NC	(TE)				D_2	A_2	A_1
ma024				PU		A_1	D_1	A_1
ma026	NC			(PU)		–	–	–

Questionnaire Results Obtained from Studying the Scratch Programming Language. The questionnaire results obtained from studying the Scratch programming language are presented in Table 5. Four examinees who were classified as TE (ma013, ma014, ma015, and ma016) completely understood the learning materials (Q_1 was A_1). All of them did not think the learning materials were difficult to understand (Q_2 was D_1), except for ma014. Two examinees who were classified as TE and NC (ma006 and ma007) completely understood the learning materials (Q_1 was A_1 or A_2) and did not think that they were difficult to understand (Q_2 was D_1 or D_2). Four examinees who were classified as TD (ma003, ma008, ma010, and ma012) responded that the learning materials were difficult to understand (Q_2 was A_2). There was only one examinee that was purely classified as PU (ma011), so it was difficult to analyze this result. The proposed method was effective for the estimated results of the TE, TD, and NC, as well as in the experiment involving the studying of the C programming language.

Statistical Analysis. In this section, we statistically analyze the results presented in Tables 4 and 5. In Tables 6, 7, and 8, the cross tabulation of the estimated results of our proposed method and the questionnaire results is presented. The numbers shown in the cross tabulations are the sum of the C programming language (Table 4) and the Scratch programming language (Table 5). Note that in Table 4, ma026 is not subject to statistical analysis due to the lack of questionnaire results.

Table 5. Questionnaire results obtained from studying the Scratch programming language

ID	Estimated results				Questionnaire results		
					Q_1	Q_2	Q_3
ma001			TD		A_1	D_1	A_1
ma002	NC		(TD)		A_1	D_2	A_1
ma003			TD		A_2	A_2	A_1
ma004	NC		(TD)	(PU)	A_2	A_2	A_2
ma005	NC	(TE)			D_2	A_1	D_2
ma006	NC	(TE)		(PU)	A_1	D_1	A_1
ma007	NC	(TE)			A_2	D_2	A_2
ma008			TD		A_2	A_2	A_2
ma009	NC		(TD)		A_2	A_2	A_1
ma010			TD		A_2	A_2	A_2
ma011				PU	A_1	D_1	A_1
ma012			TD	(PU)	A_2	A_2	A_2
ma013		TE			A_1	D_1	A_1
ma014		TE			A_1	A_1	A_1
ma015		TE			A_1	D_1	A_1
ma016		TE			A_1	D_1	A_1

Table 6. Crosstabulation of Q_1 results

	A_1	A_2	D_2	D_1
NC	3	4	3	0
TE	6	1	0	0
TD	3	4	0	0
PU	3	1	0	0
ST	1	2	2	0

Table 7. Crosstabulation of Q_2 results

	A_1	A_2	D_2	D_1
NC	1	5	2	2
TE	2	0	0	5
TD	1	5	0	1
PU	0	0	2	2
ST	1	4	0	0

Table 8. Crosstabulation of Q_3 results

	A_1	A_2	D_2	D_1
NC	1	5	2	2
TE	2	0	0	5
TD	1	5	0	1
PU	0	0	2	2
ST	1	4	0	0

We conducted a χ^2 test on the results presented in Table 9 and found significant differences in the Q_2 result.

In response to this result, we then conducted a residual analysis on the Q_2 result. With regard to reference, we also conducted a residual analysis on Q_1 and Q_3. The values of the adjusted standardized residual are presented in Tables 10, 11, and 12. The items in bold with "*" or "**" indicate significant differences (i.e., "*" indicates that the score is greater than 1.96 or lesser than −1.96, and "**" indicates that the score is greater than 2.58 or lesser than −2.58).

First, we consider Q_2 (Table 11), which was significantly different from the χ^2 test. The number of students classified as TE (too easy) who answered "A_2: I agree a little that the learning materials were difficult to understand in some places" is significantly low, whereas the number of those who answered "D_1: I do not agree that the learning materials were difficult to understand in some places" is significantly high. Although it was not a statistically significant difference, the number of students classified as TD (too difficult) exhibits an opposite trend from the number of students classified as TE. The number of students classified as PU (partial understanding) who answered "D_2: I do not agree a little that the learning materials were difficult to understand in some places" is significantly high. As presented in Sect. 5.2, this result is statistically supported by the fact that "partial understanding" should be interpreted as "there were parts that could not be understood at first, and understanding was deepened by page return."

Next, the χ^2 test did not exhibit any significant difference, but as can be seen from Table 10, the number of students classified as TE (too easy) who answered "A_1: I think that the learning materials were overall easy to understand" is significantly high.

Similarly, the χ^2 test did not exhibit any significant difference, but as can be seen from Table 12, the number of students classified as NC (non-concentration) who answered "A_1: I concentrate during my studies" is low.

Table 9. χ^2 test results

Question	p-value	Result
Q_1	0.1361 (>0.05)	
Q_2	0.0205 (<0.05)	Significant difference
Q_3	0.6919 (>0.05)	

Table 10. Residual analysis of Q_1

	A_1	A_2	D_2	D_1
NC	−1.40	0.29	1.57	–
TE	**2.22***	−1.37	−1.26	–
TD	−0.34	1.29	−1.26	–
PU	1.13	−0.50	−0.90	–
ST	−1.38	0.18	1.68	–

* : $p < 0.05$ C ** : $p < 0.01$

Table 11. Residual analysis of Q_2

	A_1	A_2	D_2	D_1
NC	−0.54	0.58	0.91	−0.85
TE	1.12	**−2.56***	−1.11	**2.67****
TD	−0.07	**1.75**	−1.11	**−1.04**
PU	−0.90	−1.83	**2.48***	0.91
ST	0.33	1.85	−0.90	−1.60

* : $p < 0.05$ C ** : $p < 0.01$

Table 12. Residual analysis of Q_3

	A_1	A_2	D_2	D_1
NC	**−0.82**	0.54	0.63	–
TE	1.53	−1.20	−0.76	–
TD	−0.21	0.60	−0.76	–
PU	0.63	−0.38	−0.54	–
ST	−1.02	0.34	1.42	–

* : $p < 0.05$ C ** : $p < 0.01$

6 Conclusion

In this study, we proposed a system to estimate the learning state of the learners through an integral analysis of the learning history and brain wave. We evaluated the learning state of high school students learning the C and Scratch programming languages using our proposed. Moreover, by comparing the estimated results with those obtained from a questionnaire administered after the experiments, we evaluated the effectiveness of our proposed method.

We have estimated the learning state of the learners for the entire learning time. However, we believe that by further estimating the learning state (e.g., for each page of the learning material), guidelines for the creation of learning materials can be provided. In our future work, we will establish a policy for setting the thresholds and coefficients of the four conditions in the proposed algorithm. Moreover, when estimating the learning state during learning, which involves editing texts, such as English and programming, rather than just browsing the teaching materials, this proposed method should be integrated with the editing history system. When the proposed method is employed in actual classes, we need to consider the validity of the learning contents, the learning conditions, and the educational curriculum, as well as the alternative devices to EEG, such as facial expression identification using a webcam. Furthermore, it is extremely important to compare and analyze the learning processes of text languages, such as the C programming language, and visual languages, such as the Scratch programming language. We believe that this analysis will be useful for beginners in programming languages to achieve a smooth transition from learning visual languages to text languages.

Acknowledgments. Part of this work was supported by JSPS KAKENHI Grant Numbers JP20K03082 and JP19H01721.

Research Ethics. The Research Ethics Committee of Shonan Institute of Technology has approved these experiments. We also have received consent to participate in this experiment from participants and their parents.

References

1. Sugimura, A., Ozaki, M., Takeoka, S., Adachi, Y.: The effective use of the Web teaching materials in class. In: The Institute of Electronics, Information and Communication Engineers (IEICE) Technical report, ET, vol. 108 (470), pp. 7–12 (2009)
2. Suzuki, Y.: The effects of seamless combining digital textbooks and e-learning. In: Japan Universities Association for Computer Education, Journal of Educational Application of Information and Communication Technologies, vol. 14, no. 1, pp. 31–35 (2011)
3. Umezawa, K., Ishida, T., Kobayashi, M., Hirasawa, S.: Effectiveness evaluation of practical use of the electronic teaching materials for university education. In: National Conference of JASMIN 2013 Autumn, Japan Society for Management Information, pp. 45–48 (2013)
4. Aramoto, M., Koizumi, D., Suko, T., Hirasawa, S.: The e-learning materials production supporting system based on the existing PDF file. In: 76th National Convention of Information Processing Society of Japan, vol. 4, pp. 359–360 (2014)
5. Aramoto, M., Kobayashi, M., Nakazawa, M., Nakano, M., Goto, M., Hirasawa, S.: Learning analytics via visualization system of edit record - system configuration and implementation. In: 78th National Convention of Information Processing Society of Japan, vol. 4, pp. 527–528 (2016)
6. Nakano, M., Aramoto, M., Yoshida, S., Koutou, K.: Learning analytics via visualization system of edit record - application to English writing task: error gravity and error correction time. In: 78th National Convention of Information Processing Society of Japan, vol. 4, pp. 531–532 (2016)
7. Goto, M., Mikawa, K., Kumoi, G., Kobayashi, M., Aramoto, M., Hirasawa, S.: Learning analytics via visualization system of edit record - analytics model based on edit record and evaluation score data for C-programming courses. In: 78th National Convention of Information Processing Society of Japan, vol. 4, pp. 533–534 (2016)
8. Ardimento, P., Cimitile, M., Bernardi, M.L., Maggi, F.M.: Evaluating coding behavior in software development processes: a process mining approach. In: 2019 IEEE/ACM International Conference on Software and System Processes (ICSSP), pp. 84–93 (2019)
9. Ardimento, P., Bernardi, M.L., Cimitile, M., Ruvo, G.D.: Mining developer's behavior from web-based IDE logs. In: 2019 IEEE 28th International Conference on Enabling Technologies: Infrastructure for Collaborative Enterprises (WETICE), pp. 277–282 (2019)
10. Giannitrapani, D.: The role of 13-HZ activity in mentation. In: The EEG of Mental Activities, pp. 149–152 (1988)
11. Uwano, H., et al.: Evaluation of software usability using electroencephalogram - comparison of frequency component between different software versions. J. Hum. Interface Soc. **10**(2), 233–242 (2008)

12. Yoshida, K., Sakamoto, Y., Miyaji, I., Yamada, K.: Analysis comparison of brain waves at the learning status by simple electroencephalography. In: Proceedings, Knowledge-Based Intelligent Information and Engineering Systems (KES 2012), pp. 1817–1826 (2012)
13. Hirai, F., Yoshida, K., Miyaji, I.: Comparison analysis of the thought and the memory at the learning time by the simple electroencephalograph. In: Multimedia, Distributed, Cooperative, and Mobile Symposium (DICOMO 2013), pp. 1441–1446 (2013)
14. Hirai, F., Yoshida, K., Miyaji, I.: Trial of the EEG state feed-back learning system at the time of the memory work by the simple electro-encephalograph. In: Multimedia, Distributed, Cooperative, and Mobile Symposium (DICOMO 2014), pp. 633–638 (2014)
15. Umezawa, K., Ishida, T., Saito, T., Nakazawa, M., Hirasawa, S.: Collection and analysis of the browsing history, editing history, and biological information for high school students. In: National Conference of JASMIN 2016 Autumn, Japan Society for Management Information, D_2-1, pp. 1–6 (2016)
16. Umezawa, K., Ishida, T., Saito, T., Nakazawa, M., Hirasawa, S.: A judgment method of difficulty of task for a learner using simple electroencephalograph. In: Information Processing Society of Japan (IPSJ) SIG Technical Report, pp. 1–6 (2016)
17. Umezawa, K., Saito, T., Ishida, T., Nakazawa, M., Hirasawa, S.: Learning state estimation method by browsing history and brain waves during programming language learning. In: Proceeding of the 6th World Conference on Information Systems and Technologies (World CIST 2018), pp. 1307–1316 (2018)
18. Crk, I., Kluthe, T., Stefik, A.: Understanding programming expertise: an empirical study of phasic brain wave changes. ACM Trans. Comput.-Hum. Interact. **23**, 1–29 (2015)
19. Lee, S., et al.: Comparing programming language comprehension between novice and expert programmers using EEG analysis. In: IEEE 16th International Conference on Bioinformatics and Bioengineering (BIBE), pp. 350–355 (2016)
20. ThinkGear measurements (MindSet Pro/TGEM). http://support.neurosky.com/kb/science/thinkgear-measurements-mindset-protgem. Accessed 12 Nov 2020
21. ThinkGear Serial Stream Guide. http://developer.neurosky.com/docs/doku.php?id=thinkgear_communications_protocol. Accessed 12 Nov 2020
22. MindWave Mobile: User Guide 5 August 2015

Making Use of Virtual Reality for Artificial Intelligence Education

Sølve Robert Bø Hunvik(✉) and Frank Lindseth

Department of Computer Science, Norwegian University of Science and Technology, Trondheim, Norway
srb.hunvik@gmail.com

Abstract. This project explored how virtual reality (VR) can be used in artificial intelligence (AI) education. A prototype VR application was developed to give students an introduction to deep learning using the Oculus Quest. The application applied escape room elements as an attempt to let students learn the curriculum in an engaging way by doing 3D-puzzles, calculations, and quizzes based on the course-material. The topics were split into separate rooms to let students progress through the curriculum intuitively. 15 people tested the application and responded to a questionnaire. 26 people evaluated the application's concepts after watching a video. Based on the evaluation, we believe that using such a VR application in AI education can be a good supplementary tool to introduce students to new topics in an engaging way. The main advantage of using VR in this context is to use interactive 3D-visualizations and hands-on activities that are challenging to experience by other means. The questionnaire's respondents were very positive to the concept, and it could potentially be beneficial in other types of STEM-education as well.

Keywords: Virtual reality · Immersive learning · Mobile learning · Artificial intelligence · Deep learning · Educational escape room · Learning technologies

1 Introduction

Universities are applying technological tools for teaching, such as video lectures, interactive projects, and other supportive tools. However, universities mainly apply traditional teaching methods, and new alternative methods are rarely introduced. Furthermore, the difficult times of the global pandemic in 2020 have shown that having good technological tools in education is more important than ever.

Electronic supplementary material The online version of this chapter (https://doi.org/10.1007/978-3-030-67435-9_5) contains supplementary material, which is available to authorized users.

L. S. Agrati et al. (Eds.): HELMeTO 2020, CCIS 1344, pp. 56–70, 2021.
https://doi.org/10.1007/978-3-030-67435-9_5

The need for competence in artificial intelligence (AI) has increased at a high rate around the world in recent years. That is due to the discoveries of new successful applications of AI and advancements in hardware and cloud solutions. In January 2020, Norway released a national strategy to be at the forefront of AI education, research, and innovation [17]. With the large need for AI competence, universities worldwide need to focus on educating students on the topic. Companies also need to put their employees through lifelong learning programs. AI is currently taught through traditional methods like lectures, assignments, and hands-on projects. Students can also learn about AI through interactive projects like Google's Machine Learning crash course [7].

Since the release of the consumer virtual reality (VR) headsets in 2016, VR has shown potential in multiple sectors, including education. According to Gartner, VR was considered an emerging technology until 2017. In 2018, Gartner stated that the technology had reached a mature stage, due to the variety of successful use-cases [5]. Even though successful ways of using VR have been discovered, VR has not yet had a mainstream breakthrough. Newer technological advancements make the technology more promising than ever. In May 2019, the Oculus Quest was released. The device proved that a room-scale and fully standalone VR headset could provide a highly immersive experience, without the need of an expensive PC and a cumbersome setup with cables and tracking sensors. The device shows potential in education since it can be brought anywhere and is easily set up for multiple students.

Studies have shown that the feeling of presence in VR can increase the users' ability to recall information, compared to using a monitor [11]. With the emergence of educational escape rooms, and its successful use in programming education [14], this concept was thought to have potential in VR as well. The goal of this project has been to investigate how VR can be used as a tool for learning in AI education. As a topic within AI, we have tried to discover if VR can be used to give an engaging introduction to deep learning and to see what students think about using such an application.

2 Background and Related Work

Through the literature study, we did not find any VR applications used in AI education and little research about using VR in computer science education. To understand how an application could best be applied in an AI course, we studied VR applications used in STEM-courses to understand what makes these applications beneficial for learning. A study from 2016, defined some main aspects of what makes VR beneficial in education [15]. Their key points were that VR enhances the learning experience through studying 3D models, which further increases their motivation and engagement. In VR, they can interact, manipulate, and get immediate feedback, which can improve the learning outcome and experience. The new level of presence caused by being fully immersed in a virtual world that tracks the user's movement and gives physical feedback through haptics shows the potential of creating experiences that would otherwise be impossible.

Game-based learning and gamification of education have also shown positive results for increasing engagement, motivation, performance, and learning outcome [8,10,21]. Effective educational games take advantage of the user's ability to interact with the game to solve problems and reach goals. They also let the student control the learning experience, make the learning experience challenging and rewarding, and stimulates the user through the audiovisual works [20].

Few projects have explored the use of VR in computer science topics. Some of the previous projects at the Norwegian University of Science and Technology explored the use of VR in algorithms and data structures [13]. The project results showed positive indications that students were interested in solving tasks in a "learning-by-doing" setting to get a hands-on experience, where they were immediately scored based on performance. The thesis concluded that one of the main advantages of the application was to provide experiences that are otherwise hard to recreate. The tool showed the potential of being used as a supplementary tool. Since few projects have explored the use of VR in computer science topics, it is unknown how applying VR in this context affects learning outcome and performance. However, other projects where VR has been applied in STEM-courses has had a positive impact on learning. Examples of applications are the LabsterVR application [12], where students can learn topics from various subjects within biology, ecology, and physiology. In the application, they can do experiments that could otherwise be expensive or dangerous to conduct. VR is also currently being applied in various courses as a supplementary experience of the current subject being taught. By using ClassVR [2], teachers hand out teaching plans, and students use immersive experiences within a simple VR headset as part of the lesson.

Educational escape rooms are currently an emerging field. Students solve puzzles, riddles, and other activities to progress through one or more rooms. The activities often facilitate collaboration through class-room activities, but single-player escape room games have become widely popular among VR enthusiasts [3]. An educational escape room was applied in a web programming course successfully [14]. The learning activity has also been applied successfully in other fields, like pharmacy [4]. No studies were found where the educational escape room concept was exclusively applied within VR. However, the concept was thought to have much potential in VR by combining it with the elements that make other educational VR games useful. In the programming course study [14], they stated that the physical puzzles had a very positive impact on the experience, but that they could not be recreated for the digital tools. However, VR shows the potential for recreating almost anything from the real world, which we thought could prove beneficial in this context.

3 Methods and Implementation

3.1 Research Methodology

The project followed the Design and Creation strategy [18, chap. 8] to implement the VR application for giving an introduction to deep learning. The research

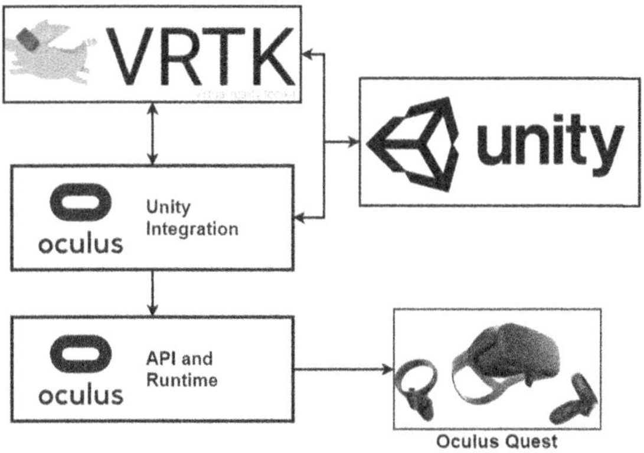

Fig. 1. This figure is a simple representation of the chosen architecture.

strategy was considered suitable since there was no existing literature about using VR in AI education. The application was developed, following the steps of defining requirements, design, implementation, and testing from the waterfall development methodology [6]. Git was used for version control, with a simple workflow, to make sure that the project could be rolled back to a stable version in case something went wrong. The project is available in a public repository on Github [22].

3.2 Technology

Figure 1 shows a simple representation of how the chosen technologies described below were related.

It was decided to develop the VR application for the Oculus Quest for two reasons; to be able to conduct user tests on multiple students simultaneously and to create a more accessible tool for students, compared to other VR headsets. The Oculus Quest is the first fully standalone room-scale device to reach the consumer market. It requires little effort to set up since there is no need for a powerful PC, cables, and external sensors. However, the device's hardware is similar to 2017–2018 smartphones. Because of this, applications developed for the device requires higher optimization efforts, compared to other VR headsets to maintain good performance in not too complex environments.

Unity [24] was used as a game engine since it is easier to learn and use for independent developers and smaller teams, compared to alternatives such as Unreal Engine. The Oculus Integration SDK [25] was used for hardware integration, and the Virtual Reality Toolkit (VRTK) [28] was used for setting up interactions and locomotion. The fundamentals of the application were set up with inspiration from the Unity Learn course by Oculus [26]. It was decided only to use free assets found on the internet, to focus on developing a functional prototype. Prefabs were implemented for various objects, to effortlessly reuse them for activities, learning material, and other events triggered through the application. One thing that had a significant impact on the development efficiency was the use of Unity Snaps [27]. Unity Snaps consists of a variety of resources for efficiently creating real-size room structures.

3.3 Concept

Before developing the application, another VR application had been developed for the project. It was user-tested, and we revealed that the project had potential. However, many of the activities and the presentation of learning material did not justify the use of VR. Also, the learning material lacked structure. A new concept was defined based on the evaluation results and the literature study.

The new concept was to introduce educational escape room elements, like puzzles, calculations, and quizzes based on the course material. The different topics within deep learning were split into separate rooms to give the user intuitive progress through the curriculum. The sequence and topics of the different rooms were designed with inspiration from Nielsen's book on deep learning [16] and the deep learning curriculum from a course called Visual Computing Fundamentals at our university. The idea was to split the curriculum into the topics; neurons, cost functions, gradient descent, and backpropagation, and further split the more complex topics into multiple rooms. The rooms were meant to have a close link to the sequence of the student's learning goals. The idea of splitting topics into rooms was inspired by the learning technique, virtual memory palace, which has been used since the ancient Greek/Roman times. Throughout the application, users progress through rooms by solving puzzles or other activities. The puzzles should apply 3D-objects and interactive 3D-visualizations to immerse the student in the curriculum. The intended target audience was students in introductory AI and deep learning courses, but a final application could also be made accessible to anyone interested in the topic. A thorough tutorial for teaching every type of interaction was needed since most people in the target audience were assumed to be new to VR.

3.4 Evaluation

Two alternative ways of evaluating the application were planned and conducted due to the Covid-19 situation. The application was evaluated quantitatively through questionnaires that measured opinions related to various statements on a 1–5 scale. The questionnaires were designed to measure engagement, opinions about the concept and to see what students thought about using the application for learning. Also, the questionnaire used for the participants that tested the application attempted to measure usability and discomfort. The results of the questionnaires were analyzed by studying the average score on each statement and describing possible reasons for negative and positive results. The results of the two questionnaires were compared where it was possible. The application was also evaluated qualitatively through written feedback. All data collected was anonymous, and could not be used to identify a respondent. The goal was to get as many participants as possible in the period from the beginning of April until the middle of June 2020, despite the challenging situation with Covid-19.

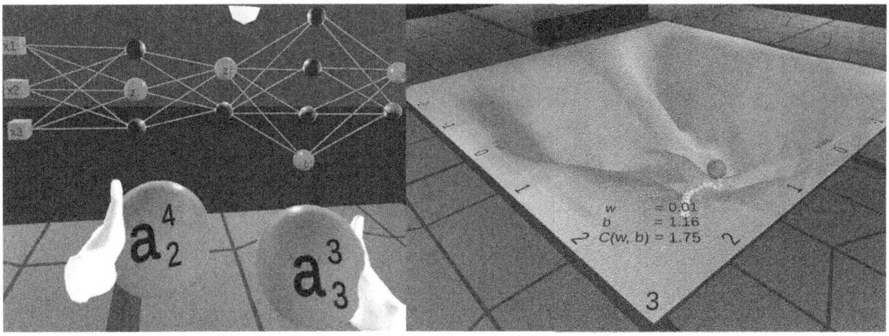

Fig. 2. Image to the left shows a task where users learn neural network notation by correctly placing neurons. Image to the right shows a visualization of gradient descent. Unity's terrain builder tool was used to mimic a cost function surface with two-dimensional inputs. The ball simulates gradient descent's process of taking small steps in the direction of the negative gradient, to reach a minimum.

Online User Tests. The application was distributed online in the IMTEL network [9] and the Reddit VR communities r/OculusQuest and r/oculus. People with VR headsets participated from home. They were given a guide for installing the application on any Oculus device and enough context to participate. Upon completion of the application, they submitted feedback through a questionnaire. Some of the first author's classmates also participated. The online user test evaluation started in the beginning of April 2020.

Video Evaluation. A 5-min YouTube video explaining the application's core concepts [23] was created and distributed online, along with a questionnaire. Most of the participants from the online user tests were highly experienced with VR. Therefore, it was attempted to reach out to AI research groups, AI students, and the Reddit AI communities r/artificial and r/ArtificialIntelligence and the groups involved in the online user tests. People were requested to respond to the questionnaire as well as they could, after watching the video. They were also given a chance to watch a full play-through for more insight. The questionnaire was designed knowing that the participants would not have the same insight as the people in the other group. Also, since the video evaluation started in the middle of May 2020, the questionnaire was improved and extended compared to the other questionnaire.

4 Results

4.1 Prototype Application

The resulting VR application is described in a 5-min YouTube video [23]. In the associated video description, there is also a link to a full play-through of the application and the tutorial. More work is needed before applying the application in a course. Therefore, it is considered a prototype.

Fig. 3. This figure illustrates the application's quiz system area, where users can bring cartridges loaded with quizzes. The unfinished red cartridge has been inserted in the cartridge player on the right side of the image. The quizzes appear on the big screen, and the user can respond to it using the physical buttons in front of it. When every cartridge in the application is won, the user can collect them to complete the application.

Learning Material. Since the application was developed by a single person only, the main focus was on creating engaging activities and some 3D-visualizations. 3D-visualizations were developed for neural networks and gradient descent, as shown in Fig. 2. The application ended up having many text panels, which we knew were not optimal for VR. The plan was to apply more immersive types of learning material, such as audio, 3D-visualizations, and videos. However, an extensive amount of work was put into creating the contents of the text panels, so they show potential for being conveyed in more immersive ways. The curriculum's topics were split into separate rooms, and within each room, the learning material was presented in a logical order. The learning material content was made with inspiration from Michael Nielsen's book about deep learning and neural networks [16] and the 3Blue1Brown series on YouTube [1].

Activities. The application has three main types of activities. The first one is the puzzles, where the user needs to place 3D-cubes, and spheres for learning notation and building neural networks. An example is shown in Fig. 2. The second type of activity is calculations, where the user needs to calculate a neuron's output. This is partly done using mental arithmetic, but since one part of the calculation is too complex for mental arithmetic, the student can use a calculator. The final type of activities is quizzes. The user finds cartridges loaded with quizzes after learning each topic. They are then brought to the quiz system, shown in Fig. 3. The user completes the application by winning each of the quizzes and placing the cartridges in a bookshelf.

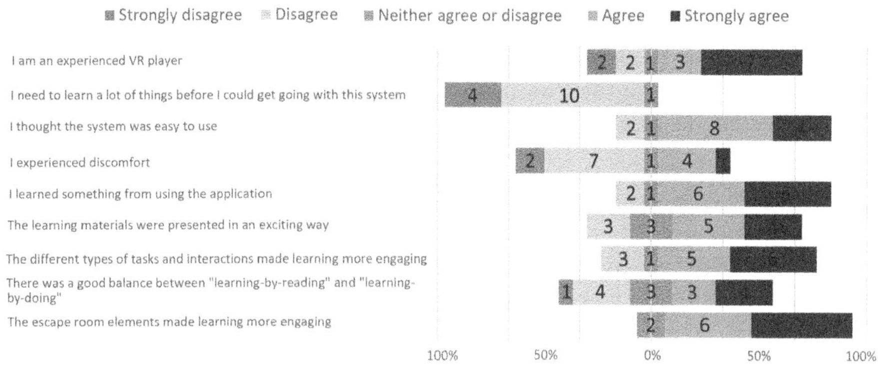

Fig. 4. Responses to the online user test questionnaire.

4.2 Evaluation

The application was distributed in the places mentioned in Sect. 3.4. 15 people responded to the online user test questionnaire. The respondents were either current or previous computer science students. Their experience in terms of AI was varying. Most of them were highly experienced with VR. 9 of the users were from the groups reached out to online, and 6 were classmates with the first author.

26 people responded to the video evaluation questionnaire. 88% were previous or current computer science students. 62% of them were current students, and we can assume that most of them were students in their third to fifth year of computer science, taking the Computer Vision and Deep Learning course at the Norwegian University of Science and Technology. We can assume this considering the time of the response, compared to when the questionnaire was shared. The rest of the previous or current computer science students were researchers, lecturers, or employed, and we can assume that most of them were members of AI research groups considering the time of the response. The participants' experience with VR was ranging evenly from low to high. Their experience with AI and deep learning was also somewhat varying, but most of them had a higher experience.

Questionnaires. The most interesting results from the questionnaires have been visualized as Diverging Stacked Bar charts [19]. Figure 4 shows the responses to the online user test questionnaire. Figure 5 shows the responses to the video evaluation questionnaire. The vertical axis shows the various statements, while the horizontal axis represents the total amount of responses on both the agree and disagree side of the scale. The numbers on a bar represent the number of people with that response. A positive or negative response can be on either side of the scale, depending on the statement.

Written Feedback. 12 respondents to the online user test questionnaire submitted written feedback. 8 submitted written feedback to the video evaluation questionnaire. Through their feedback, there were some key elements addressed. Most of the feedback covered below was submitted by the people who tested the application.

- **Concept.** Multiple respondents had positive feedback considering the application's concept. Some stated that dedicated rooms for each topic helped progress, and the room layouts looked good but should be more easily distinguishable. Also, the users enjoyed escape room elements like doing puzzles to progress.
- **3D-visualizations.** The respondents stated that they thought visualizations of gradient descent and neural networks were helpful. Some also stated that this was the best utilization of the technology. The users were interested in seeing more interactive 3D-visualizations.
- **Too much text.** Most respondents stated that the amount of text used for learning material was too high. They suggested replacing the text panels with more immersive types of learning material, such as audio, 3D-visualizations, and possibly videos.
- **Activities.** Multiple users stated that they thought the activities would be useful for learning. However, for backpropagation, some users were confused and ended up solving tasks by trial-and-failure since the learning material was somewhat lacking or confusing. Multiple users also enjoyed the quiz system solution and stated that collecting cartridges made the experience more engaging and rewarding. One user stated that collecting cartridges felt unnecessary. One user compared the activity for learning neural network notation to a lecture and felt that the hands-on experience made learning easier.
- **Applying the application in a course.** One of the respondents of the video evaluation questionnaire compared the method of learning with traditional methods. His key point was that the application's strengths were through the use of practical tasks and calculations for learning the curriculum. However, compared to traditional methods, he considered the application inefficient for entirely understanding a topic since this would require mass-training.

5 Discussion and Limitations

5.1 Research Outcome

The present study explored what students, researchers, employees, and others related to AI and VR thought about the application. The questionnaires mainly measured engagement, opinions about the concept, usability, how students would like to use the application, and attempted to get an indication of whether the participants felt that they learned something or not. The results show that the respondents of both questionnaires were generally highly interested in the application's concept. The Background and Related Work section mentioned the successful usage of classroom escape rooms in a variety of contexts, but no previous

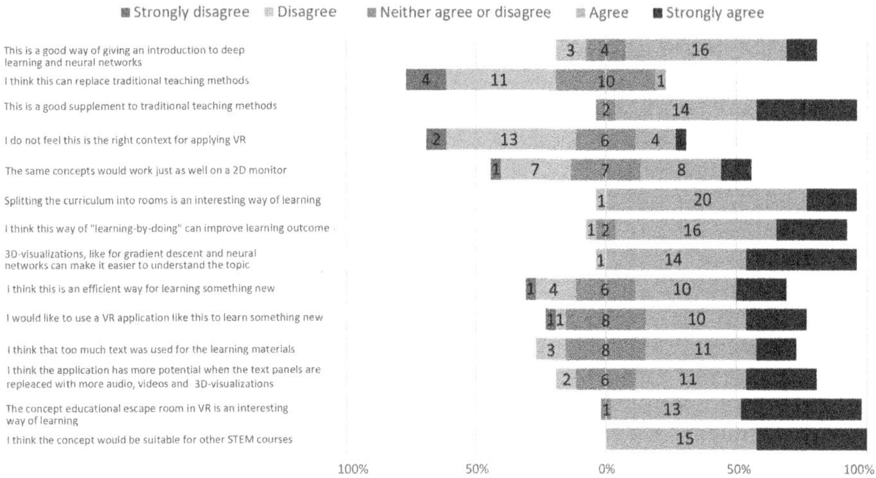

Fig. 5. Responses to the video evaluation questionnaire.

studies had explored the exclusive use of educational escape rooms in VR. This project shows that physical puzzles can indeed be ported to VR experiences, and be received with interest from users. The current escape room games for VR have reached high popularity, and with the participants' interest in the concept, it can potentially prove beneficial in education in general. One of the main advantages of applying VR in this context is through the use of interactive 3D-visualizations, that are otherwise hard to replicate. The participants showed great interest in the visualization of gradient descent and requested more 3D-visualizations of the curriculum. Therefore, separating complex topics into different rooms can potentially prove to be beneficial in other courses that require a visual understanding, such as STEM-courses.

The activities used throughout the application was also met with interest. The application developed for the project showed an improvement of the activities compared to the first application we evaluated since the activities were mapped to 3D-objects in the virtual world. The users seemed to enjoy the task of getting the right output on a neuron, doing calculations, and quizzes. The notation activities seemed to be useful for some users. However, since others ended up solving these tasks through trial-and-failure, either the activity type or the learning material needs to be improved or redesigned.

Considering how the application can be applied in a course, we see from the results that the users were positive about using it as a supplementary tool, but not using it as a replacement of traditional learning methods. The interactive 3D-visualizations and hands-on tasks were met with engagement and interest from the users. However, the large use of text panels for learning material did not justify the use of VR. Multiple users stated that they felt the amount of text was too high and suggested replacing it with more immersive types of learning material, such as audio, 3D-visualizations, and videos. This feedback was expected since there was not enough time to create such learning material, considering the project's scope. The results do not imply that text panels should be fully replaced, but that they should be designed for comfort, and the number of panels and amount of text should be kept to a minimum. Some parts of the curriculum, such as formulas, are better conveyed through text and smaller pieces of information. However, their contents can be conveyed through a combination of text and other types of learning material. The reading experience was somewhat worsened throughout the application since the performance was not optimal in parts where large amounts of content were being drawn. More efforts need to be put into optimization to fulfill the performance requirements laid out by Oculus. Furthermore, the results indicate that using such an application in this context could work well if the students can use it to get an introduction to new topics, and then proceed with traditional learning methods. Therefore, the application might be a suitable replacement for some lectures but mainly a supplementary tool for the rest of the teaching methods. However, it is important to keep in mind that VR can not replace the mass-training required to get the deeper understanding of the curriculum.

5.2 Limitations

This study did neither compare the learning method to other learning methods nor attempt to measure learning outcomes. For future work, this would be required to determine if using VR in this context is useful compared to other learning methods. The study shows some positive indications of what can make the tool useful, but developing for VR is more resource-intensive than developing for-instance an interactive website. Even though VR opens for new possibilities for conveying the curriculum, the method should be compared with traditional methods and other digital tools. However, the study shows that VR applications for learning can be developed efficiently with the right set of tools, assets, reusable contents, and good design and architecture.

The VR application was designed and developed by a single person with a software-engineering background. It would have been beneficial to develop the application using a dedicated team of designers, software developers, and more pedagogical content-creators.

The questionnaires were somewhat biased towards positive feedback and could have focused more on getting feedback from a more pedagogical point of view since this is an important aspect of the project. The questionnaire used for the online user tests was designed at an earlier stage than the one for video evaluation. During the period of online user testing, we discovered limitations with the questionnaire. Therefore, the questionnaire was revised and drastically improved for the video evaluation as an attempt to bias participants more towards negative feedback and attempt to discover more specific elements of engagement. One disadvantage of doing this was that it made the results more difficult to compare. For future work, there should be a more consistent and well-designed questionnaire for all evaluation. Future questionnaires need to be better designed to better cover the application from a more pedagogical and technical point of view. Also, there needs to be a better balance between gathering positive and negative feedback.

Due to the difficult times of the global pandemic of 2020, the application could not be tested on the intended target audience. The initial plan was to evaluate the application using students from an introductory deep learning course in a laboratory. This would be done in groups using six Oculus Quests. When we evaluated the other application developed for the project, we used this method and conducted interviews and observations. Conducting interviews were highly valuable to get more insightful feedback. Since this was not possible when Covid-19 broke out, we chose to alternatively evaluate the application using what we thought was the best alternative. However, the people that tested the application during the online user tests were generally highly experienced with VR, with some participants that had a lower experience. Therefore, the participants could have been more positive about using VR than the average person in the target audience. The respondents of the video evaluation reflected the target audience better. However, they did not have the same insight since there was no guarantee that they watched more than the 5-min concept video. Trying the VR application would be a highly different experience. The participants of the video evaluation could not interact and feel a presence in the virtual world like the groups from the other evaluation did. However, the questionnaire used for the video evaluation was designed with this in mind, so that the participants would not have to respond to statements that would require testing the application. Therefore, even though the participants responded somewhat based on assumptions, the evaluation method led to some valuable feedback, which would not otherwise be possible to gather during the global pandemic. For future work, the application should be user-tested by people that better reflect the target audience using the initially planned methods.

6 Conclusions and Future Work

Based on the feedback gained, we believe that the application's concept of splitting the curriculum's topics into separate rooms and encouraging students to solve hands-on puzzles to progress is an engaging and rewarding way of learning. The concept of an "educational escape room in VR" could potentially be beneficial in other types of STEM-education as well. There are two main advantages of using VR in the context of AI. The first one is to apply interactive 3D-visualizations based on the curriculum's concepts that are otherwise difficult or impossible to convey. The second advantage is through "learning-by-doing" activities that the students need to solve to progress. Compared to other teaching methods, the VR solution gives students a new level of immersion in the curriculum and a more hands-on experience. From the results, we saw that the participants felt that they learned something. However, the VR solution needs to be compared with other methods to measure the effectiveness of learning in this setting. Still, we believe that we have uncovered a teaching methodology that can be beneficial in courses that require a visual understanding of the curriculum.

We believe that a VR application like this could work well in the context of AI if the tool is used for learning something new. The focus should be on teaching what is challenging to convey through other means. One possible use case for the final application is for students to get an introduction in VR and then let them proceed with traditional learning methods to understand a topic entirely. The application shows what is possible to develop by a single person with little experience with VR development prior to the project. However, the application suffered from some unresolved performance issues. Therefore, we believe that standalone VR headsets such as the Oculus Quest could be a great and more accessible tool for students when more resources are put into optimization and development. A tethered VR headset would require dedicated rooms for using a VR application, while multiple standalone VR headsets can be brought anywhere by the course staff. Companies who are putting their employees through lifelong learning programs can also apply VR applications with ease. Since some courses require prior knowledge in deep learning, the final application can also get students who lack this knowledge up to pace with the other students.

For future work, more efforts need to be put into improving the current application and designing new activities, learning material, and interactions. Before applying the final application in a course, greater efforts would be needed for replacing text panels, adding more interactive 3D-visualizations, improving and adding more activities, optimizing the application, and improving learning material contents. Furthermore, the application should be user-tested on a group that better reflects the intended target audience. Also, the VR application should be compared to alternative technological and traditional learning methods to measure the learning outcome and effectiveness of using VR. An interesting approach to this could be to apply the final version of the VR application in a course, comparing the effectiveness with a control group that exclusively uses the current methods for learning the curriculum.

Seeing how positive users were to the concept of an educational escape room in VR, some interesting future work would be to see how the VR application's concept can be applied in other STEM-courses, such as physics or chemistry.

Acknowledgments. We would like to thank the staff of the VR labs at the Norwegian University of Science and Technology for providing us the right tools and tips for conducting the project. Also, we would like to thank the staff and participants of HELMeTO 2020 for letting us participate in the conference and giving feedback. Furthermore, we would like to thank the reviewers of the paper for giving us valuable feedback for improving the paper and future work. Finally, a special thanks to everyone that participated in the evaluation, who made it possible to conduct the project during such difficult times.

References

1. 3blue1brown, deep learning. https://youtu.be/aircAruvnKk. Accessed 13 July 2020
2. Class VR. https://www.classvr.com/. Accessed 12 July 2020
3. Escape room VR games. https://youtu.be/E6N4SmUgNgc. Accessed 12 July 2020

4. Eukel, H.N., Frenzel, J.E., Cernusca, D.: Educational gaming for pharmacy students-design and evaluation of a diabetes-themed escape room. Am. J. Pharm. Educ. **81**(7) (2017)
5. Virtual reality is reaching a mature state according to gartner. https://skarredghost.com/2018/08/27/virtual-reality-is-reaching-a-mature-state-according-to-gartner/. Accessed 12 July 2020
6. Classical waterfall model. https://www.geeksforgeeks.org/software-engineering-classical-waterfall-model/. Accessed 12 July 2020
7. Google machine learning crash course. https://developers.google.com/machine-learning/crash-course. Accessed 12 July 2020
8. Hwang, G.J., Sung, H.Y., Hung, C.M., Huang, I., Tsai, C.C.: Development of a personalized educational computer game based on students' learning styles. Educ. Tech. Res. Dev. **60**(4), 623–638 (2012)
9. Imtel. https://www.ntnu.edu/ipl/imtel. Accessed 12 July 2020
10. Jong, B.S., Lai, C.H., Hsia, Y.T., Lin, T.W., Lu, C.Y.: Using game-based cooperative learning to improve learning motivation: a study of online game use in an operating systems course. IEEE Trans. Educ. **56**(2), 183–190 (2012)
11. Krokos, E., Plaisant, C., Varshney, A.: Virtual memory palaces: immersion aids recall. Virtual Real. **23**(1), 1–15 (2018). https://doi.org/10.1007/s10055-018-0346-3
12. Labster VR. https://www.labster.com/vr/. Accessed 12 July 2020
13. Lindseth, F., Windsrygg, S.: Learning algorithms in virtual reality as part of a virtual university. Master's thesis, Norwegian University of Science and Technology (2019)
14. López-Pernas, S., Gordillo, A., Barra, E., Quemada, J.: Examining the use of an educational escape room for teaching programming in a higher education setting. IEEE Access **7**, 31723–31737 (2019)
15. Martín-Gutiérrez, J., Mora, C.E., Añorbe-Díaz, B., González-Marrero, A.: Virtual technologies trends in education. EURASIA J. Math. Sci. Technol. Educ. **13**(2), 469–486 (2017)
16. Nielsen, M.A.: Neural Networks and Deep Learning, vol. 2018. Determination Press, San Francisco (2015)
17. The national strategy for artificial intelligence. https://www.regjeringen.no/en/dokumenter/nasjonal-strategi-for-kunstig-intelligens/id2685594/. Accessed 12 July 2020
18. Oates, B.J.: Researching Information Systems and Computing. Sage, Thousand Oaks (2005)
19. Diverging stacked bar charts, peltier tech blog. https://peltiertech.com/diverging-stacked-bar-charts/. Accessed 12 July 2020
20. Shute, V.J., Ke, F.: Games, learning, and assessment. In: Ifenthaler, D., Eseryel, D., Ge, X. (eds.) Assessment in Game-Based Learning, pp. 43–58. Springer, New York (2012). https://doi.org/10.1007/978-1-4614-3546-4_4
21. Sung, H.Y., Hwang, G.J.: A collaborative game-based learning approach to improving students' learning performance in science courses. Comput. Educ. **63**, 43–51 (2013)
22. Deep learning introduction in VR github project. https://github.com/SolveH/deep-learning-intro-in-VR. Accessed 12 July 2020
23. Deep learning introduction VR application. https://youtu.be/TvlN-dxAn4M. Accessed 12 July 2020
24. Unity game engine. https://unity.com/. Accessed 12 July 2020

25. Oculus integration for unity. https://developer.oculus.com/downloads/package/unity-integration/. Accessed 12 July 2020
26. Design, develop, and deploy for VR. https://learn.unity.com/course/oculus-vr. Accessed 12 July 2020
27. Unity snaps. https://unity.com/products/snaps. Accessed 12 July 2020
28. Virtual Reality Toolkit (VRTK). https://www.vrtk.io/. Accessed 12 July 2020

Online Learning Pedagogical Frameworks: Models, Perspectives and Application

Professional Development with Digital Practices and Collective Intelligence

Muriel Frisch[1(✉)], Jean-Marc Paragot[2(✉)], Simon-Joseph Ndi[1(✉)], and Victoria Pfeffer-Meyer[1(✉)]

[1] Cérep, Reims, France
muriel.frisch@univ-reims.fr, {simon-joseph.ndi-mena, victoria.meyer}@etudiant.univ-reims.fr
[2] AM2IDEKI, Nancy, France
jean-marc.paragot@univ-lorraine.fr

Abstract. We propose a four-voice reflection on forms of collective intelligence based on the work carried out within the IDEKI network and various research projects. This work links research to the dimensions of real professional activity by crossing the orientations in didactics and the fields of professionalization, construction of professionalism, accompaniment and professional development. We will focus on two different professional communities and the analysis of their practices and the impact on the professional development of the actors. First, school nurses who work with digital professional tools and the question of disembodied labor, secondly, librarian-teachers who develop digital writing practices in blogs and the question of the intersubjective relationship.

Keywords: Collective intelligence · Professional development · Digital writing · Pedagogical framework studies · Distance education

1 Introduction

The concept of "counter-transposition" in didactics allows to analyze the "doing" of the actors in situation [1]. Associated with the concept of "collective intelligence", they constitute an entry point to reflect and questioning the relationship to knowledge and to the construction of professionals' knowledge. Develop the link between theory and practice is a fundamental issue for training in higher education. The goal is to bring professionals to understand and transform their practice, to make it intelligible.

We propose to reflect with four voices on forms of collective intelligence based on the work carried out within the IDEKI network and various research projects. This work links research to the dimensions of real professional activity by crossing the orientations in didactics and the fields of professionalization, construction of professionalism, accompaniment and professional development. This work falls within the framework of the Cérep[1] laboratory. We link, among other things, the field of professionalization and the construction of professionalism with the different forms of didactics.

[1] Centre d'Etudes et de Recherches sur les Emplois et les professionnalisations (Center for Studies and Research on Jobs and Professionalizations).

L. S. Agrati et al. (Eds.): HELMeTO 2020, CCIS 1344, pp. 73–85, 2021.
https://doi.org/10.1007/978-3-030-67435-9_6

We will focus on two different professional communities, the analysis of their practices and the impact on the professional development of the actors. Firstly, school nurses, who are involved in devices for analyzing practices in training to support transformations through processes of conceptualization of their activity with digital professional tools. Secondly, librarian-teachers and the way in which they implement digital writing practices in blogs. We questioned the impact that digital writing can have on knowledge and the construction of knowledge for information-documentation related to professional development. These didactics works feed university program of professional development. The elements showed in this study will enable the construction of training scenarios adapted to the demands of disembodied work or from mediated exchange work such as blogs. These proposals are repeated in certain sequences of training clinic or university pedagogy. The work of resuming studies and training during development or employment are today part of the missions of the university.

2 Method

From a point of view of what we can call a general methodology, the work carried out mobilizes a reflection on collective intelligence and analyzes carried out in counter-transposition. This means that in the didactic process, knowledge can be transposed but also counter-transposed [1], that we analyze the reality of the activity with learners and professionals. We carry out forms of extraction of knowledge from action related to the activity, the practice and the doing. We are going to expose examples of work that involve collective intelligence, counter-transposition with digital in and for human professions. First, we would like to come back to the concept of collective intelligence. By making a focus on IDEKI Network which develops the importance to enable all actors involved in educational action to develop practices; the importance of transforming research object into training objects and vice versa; by exposing different significations developed by authors witch bring a conceptual clarification of collective intelligence and by asking the question of the implementation of these forms of collective intelligence in the different didactics. Second, we would like to come back to the concept of collective intelligence. In a collective approach and in didactic "counter-transposition" [1] it will be a question of reflecting on and understanding the conditions under which collective work today would be a producer of knowledge and a generator of skills. With the group of school nurses, we mobilize "effective thinking" indicators [1] to study the "reflexive reality" engaged during the disembodied practice in analysis workshops.

We analyze the knowledge and skills developed using distance training tools in a university device, the master's degree in engineering for the training of trainers.

Concerning the professional group of librarian-teachers, we have built up a corpus of 56 blogs by carrying out a search via generalist engines and, on a directory of professional blogs entitled "Prodocopshere". We use three process to study related describe experience of the actors. First, we establish a documentary ranking to organize the posts. Then we use method of discourse and digital content analysis to bring out professional activities, reflexion and didactic situations. Finally, we focus the analysis on learning's situations. We use a model derived from didactics to bring out the characteristics of the specific learning situation to the teaching of information documentation. This work can then be invested in university training, initial or continuing training.

3 The Collective Intelligence in Didactic Approach

3.1 Conceptual Approach to Collective Intelligence in the IDEKI Network

Navarro [2] emphasizes the importance of "sharing knowledge, representations and common references in order to collaborate in action". Frisch and Paragot, in founding the IDEKI network, also aim, through processes of sharing, creation and exchange, to enhance the value of human professions and enable all actors involved in educational action to develop practices by transforming research objects into training objects and vice versa, from training objects into research objects.

In these different objects where knowledge and skills intersect, the interdisciplinary dimension occupies a very important place, as Frisch [3] points out. According to the author, it is on the basis of the "construction of interconnections" between the educational sciences and the information and communication sciences that "school disciplines" didactise knowledge, while vocational education and training didactises skills to a greater extent. This analytical grid demonstrates the positive impact of the concept of co-construction operated by the IDEKI network, which constitutes a springboard for the dissemination of knowledge between all the actors of the education system regardless of the context and their area of activity.

3.2 Collective Intelligence Yes, But in What Forms?

The evocation of forms of collective intelligence aims first of all at characterizing the concept itself. According to Levy [4], collective intelligence is an "intelligence that is distributed everywhere, constantly valued, coordinated in real time, and which leads to an efficient mobilization of skills". In his book entitled "Collective intelligence, the invisible revolution", Noubel [5] insists on the importance for our society of learners and even of governments not to limit themselves to "pyramidal collective intelligence. Muriel Frisch and her team use this viewpoint in action research and collective research projects, for example with the EvalNuts[2] project. The particularity of this project is that collective intelligence manifests itself in different forms, and that Arnaud and Caruso Cahn [6] (p.15) designate on the one hand by the concept of cooperative intelligence, i.e. a collective organization of work in which the goals are common but the tasks are distributed" and on the other hand, the concept of "co-elaborative intelligence" which they characterized as the fruit of innovation carried out collectively and which also leads to the emergence of collective intelligence. In a socioconstructivist approach and by its exploratory, multisectoral and interactive nature, these different forms of intelligence that we have just mentioned converge and contribute to creating a dynamic of interaction that involves professionals, trainers, field actors and the populations subject to the project. It should also be noted that a real knowledge of the actions to be carried out, a global vision of the fields of study, a general adhesion of all the actors concerned, and a sociological analysis of the target populations at the origin of the project are required. Emphasis must also be placed on better harmonization of exchanges between field professionals and trainers.

[2] Nutrition and Sensorially, a research-action and collaborative project agreed in January 2020 between the URCA and the "Maison de la nutrition" (nutrition house).

3.3 The Orientations in Didactics of Collective Intelligence

The new didactic approach, resulting from the work of certain researchers, has made it possible to develop and better understand the impact of didactics in the field of education, training but also in the human and relational space in general [7]. Frisch follows on the work of Jean-Pierre Astolfi (constructivist epistemology) and in a socio-constructivist approach. She has harmonized his thinking on "three strong poles": didactics, human professions and collective intelligence. These three poles integrate all the "subject-situation" interactions that occur and base on the one hand on the process of conceptualization, modelling and elaboration and on the other hand on research and professional practices.

3.4 Collective Intelligence for All Didactics?

Frisch's analysis [8] (p. 91), teach us through his writings that knowing how to build a didactic approach also means having the capacity to adapt one's practices to the contexts and situations in which the activity is carried out. This adaptation responds to the need for all didacticians to put collective and collaborative work methods at the forefront in the practice of their discipline, whether in the didactics of disciplines such as mathematics, language didactics, science didactics, French didactics, information and documentation didactics, and many others. The central matrix of all didactics is forged on the interaction between the actors involved; one can then imagine that the manifestation of collective intelligence cannot occur without these interactions.

4 Didactics, Human Professions and Collective Intelligence with Digital Technology

4.1 Confinement and Analysis of the Distance Reflexive Practices of the Nurses of the National Education System

The covid-19 global health episode (13 March–11 May 2020) has forced us to deal with the extant availability to collectively assume forms of continuity in development, training [9] education and learning. The work undertaken in direct, human and sensitive intersubjectivity has been adapted in order to allow the monitoring of professional collaboration and the co-construction of reflexive skills at a distance. Various support tools were used (Via, zoom, teams, WhatsApp…). The annual supervisions for the IENES, trainers for the professional practice analysis workshops have been maintained. A listening cell for professionals working in the "front line" (Macron, 25 March in Mulhouse) was set up to support IENES[3] who found themselves, whether voluntary or requisitioned, in an unusual professional context.

Work Sessions

Four sessions of three hours each were offered in June 2020 in order to guarantee the continuity of the supervisory work carried out over the past seven years. For each of them we gathered a group of ten people for a working session. This configuration in

[3] IENES in French: Infirmières de l'Education Nationale.

"clinical" groups, with a mixture of the origins of the geographical locations of exercise was unprecedented. Each time, it will have been necessary to create the group, the individual recognitions and the dynamics of the exchanges (respect, confidentiality and not judgment).

The planned scenario was followed each time. It consists of four periods always in the same chronology. We (the Technical Advisor to the Rector and the facilitator/researcher) first presented the meeting and the specific operating conditions linked to covid-19 and then the framework of this research-action (Helmeto). The following time allowed for individual presentations of the participants who do not all know each other, and we launch the "What's New" Talk Tour [10]. Then came an update on the local operation of each workshop and/or listening cell. Finally, we note the training requests in connection with the development of reflective workshops.

The exchanges were recorded and then returned to the participants in order to benefit from their reactions "après coup". The feedback was classified into three groups: Questions renewed due to the historical situation (ten years of experience and covid-19), avenues for developing the device to make it sustainable and adapt it to renewed contexts and finally, the proposals concrete in the short term. We take them up below and confront them with the realities of distance supervision work.

Renewed Questions

The framework of the AAPP is alive, the history of this action in the academy of Nancy and Metz is crossing a new course: after the era of the pioneers and we must question our self-reliance, our implicit. This is what started during these four dates, in the form of distance exchanges. If the aims of professional "holding" [11] have remained, in this period of communication, we propose to consider how the actors involved were able or knew how to develop existing systems and divert digital tools to carry out the project maintenance of social and professional ties. We will focus on how they contribute to expanding the phorique function in human occupations.

First of all, it is a question of reinforcing the separation of the moments of the day of meetings: hospitality, exchanges of tips and news then development of reflexivity. The mosaic of images should allow the facilitator to address each and every one. Discussion in the space dedicated to written messages promotes delayed reactions. Facilitators have video work rights which allow them to announce the aims as well as the stages of each form of work and to guarantee the time allotted by the sessions. While inviting participants to co-own the time frame (to avoid spilling over into speeches) and allow the facilitators not to be aiming at the image of the wrong instance. Guarantee a time of "self-recovery" through writing or silence before speaking for the "what's new" as for the expression of the fragment. The "my virtual cl@sse Via" space allows you to produce a text or a drawing during discussions.We take up the idea of a "hayloft" or a "space of flavors and knowledge" in order to make available the theoretical elements that will support the emerging blocks in real time by displaying book references and searchable sites. The traces produced are saved and thus available at the end of the session. Thus, it may be easier to involve the participants in this work in the intermediate time between two workshops.

The work of welcoming and announcing after the "what's new" will allow to maintain the announced framework and will thus support the work and the existence of the group [12].

During these four supervision sessions, several avenues for developing work with professional practice analysis workshops were considered. We offer a few.

Development Tracks

Very quickly involve colleagues in the work of documentation which promotes and participates in reflexivity (indicators M. Frisch and JM Paragot) [1].

The workshops are also to be offered as workspaces that can produce personal welcome and professional inclusion of contract workers or new colleagues who are members of the development project by the AAPP.

Following the effects of confinement, it will be wise to offer IENES interventions in AAPP for other education personnel in order to build a common space of work, speech and reflexivity in the service of the school's missions. (Benevolence, support, social resilience).

Short-Term Proposals

- Organize inter-academic days aimed at comparing practices and benefiting from the findings made by others ("but how are others doing?"). These days would be planned for AAPP facilitators. Today that would represent around 70 people in activity for four academies (Besancon, Dijon, Nancy-Metz and Reims).
- Open a training course for trainers in Lorraine in 2020/2021.
- Participate in days, conferences, and press interviews to continue to publicize the realities of the profession.
- Participation of IENES in the IDEKI International conference (December 2020).

Some Questions

What intersubjectivity with distance Learning Tools?

Intersubjectivity is the essence of so-called impossible professions, human professions (care, educate, train, support, supervise). How does she resist these forms of relationship? How do distance learning tools force us to rethink the connection that would then become more important than otherness? That is to say that in these work situations the protagonists would seek to establish, preserve, and strengthen the link in a form of essential dyad. The infra-linguistic elements or collusion in situational interlocutions would in fact become more secondary. A posture of "palliative" reciprocity which signifies to the Other, through our presence, the humanity that brings us together, would become essential to the continuity of the link.

A disembodied relationship more than a long-distance relationship?

The use of the phrase "at a distance" does not capture the reality that is constructed from a "clinical" point of view. Moreover, the "face-to-face" designation refers to another field of understanding this reality. We propose to consider the effects of the absence of the body, of total incarnation by naming this work situation: disembodied. We would avoid the pitfall of the illusion of taking for reality a representation that becomes a quasi "avatar" of the personal and professional self of each interlocutor. By accepting this question, it seems possible to us to revisit the engineering departments that use digital tools. The proliferation of names (hybrid, synchronous, asynchronous, etc.) which qualify the forms of learning and training situations in no way resolves this question of the body, of presence, of sensory and thinking complexity, which then disappear from concern for guarantors of training systems.

Understand professional activity in its context, a current requirement?

To avoid generalizing work situations which are in essence unique, it is incumbent on us to work on analyzing them in context. The singularity thus perceived, understood, and expressed may find itself confronted with other singularities which gradually become common sense or collective intelligence. The professional writings involved are then so many clinical fragments. We can work them with researchers and professionals. Research finds their new links, bottom-up confirmations, and training transforms knowledge from practice into knowledge. Conceptual support is carried out by working together professionals and researchers. The opposition between theory and practice is thus often erased in favor of a real co-construction of knowledge.

Momentary Conclusions

The work of the "listening cells" is the subject of a questionnaire cross-referenced with "clinical" writings of the IENES engaged in hospital care contexts. While digital and remote communication media will have enabled us to respect the "barrier gestures" linked to confinement without replacing human relations, they will also have obliged us to develop forms of research with temporalities adapted to singular, social or professional demands. We will also question the limits of these scattered initiatives and try to show how the networking of all these innovations relayed by conceptualizations should make it possible to make the invisible of these totally emerging practices visible.

It is up to us to instruct several questions relating to this transformation of workshop work from an incarnate and influential presence to a virtual and partial (disembodied) form of long-distance relationship, for example:

The impact of remote working conditions on these supervisions.

Support Speeches.

Time running out and time objectified in the face of the temporalities of professional development.

The professionalization of school nurses gradually leans on scholarly knowledge by a game of didactic back and forth.

4.2 Analysis of Writing Practices on the Blogs of Librarian-Teachers of the French National Education System

Context and Objectives of the Study

The aim of our research work, which started in 2018, is to understand and develop forms of analysis of activity in "counter-transposition" [1]. We are particularly interested by processes of writing and publishing blogs in secondary school librarian-teachers in France. On the job, for this professional, using digital tools is a habit. They employed them for the management of the resource center but also to train students. The originality is that some professionals use digital social media to share their own experience to the professional community. This digital practice exists for the librarian's teachers since the end of the 2000's. These activities take place outside workspace, which give them a new direction. We have noticed that writing with blogs have two interest for the professionals. First, they can share experiences and resources to the community. Secondly, through the virtual community a discussion can appear because readers can comment posts. Digital writing becomes a kind of "mediator" to share the experience, to look back on what happened and to mutualize the didactic productions.

So, we are wondering about impact that this form of writing can have on knowledge and on the construction of knowledge for information - documentation at school. But we are also interested in the emergence of knowledge and skills, linked to professional development, with aim of enriching training practices of librarian-teachers, whether in pre-service or in-service training.

Our questioning brings together several fields that we wish to interconnect in our reflection. First, the field of didactics of information - documentation, which makes it possible to reflect on the knowledge, skills and practices generated by librarian-teachers to develop information - documentation at school. Then, the digital work, with blog tool, which, studied with a didactic orientation, makes it possible to reflect on new forms of knowledge construction and the relationship to knowledge. And last, professional development, which refers to the conditions of professionalization.

Theoretical Framework

The concept of "Didactic counter-transposition" serves as a frame of reference to construct our purpose. It initially comes from association of two concepts that are put in tension each other, entitled "double movement of transposition and didactic counter-transposition" [1]. It is developed in the field of research on the didactics of information and documentation.

The "counter-transposition" movement illustrates a perception of construction of knowledge from "bottom up". We focus on this movement because it studying "Doing", "Saying" and Writing based on professional practice of the actors in order to "identify elements of knowledge" [1], and then to give elements of conceptualization and knowledge.

We think that blogs are originals workspace to develop skills and knowledge, according to following process. First, the professional lives an experience at work from which he elaborates a subject. After, he explains it on blog. Publication's tool allows to edit day to day articles, ante-chronologically. Multimedia elements can be integrated on it (video - photos - hyperlinks). We consider that it is in this multimedia writing process that we can identify forms of elaboration of professional knowledge. Consequently, we believe that write about the practice in blogs can be generator of professional development. This process of didactic counter transposition it shows below Fig. 1.

In this way, this original digital writing opens two direction for our reflection. First, the place given to the intimate, to the expression of introspection. It is a first-person writing, which can be compared to the form of a logbook or a personal diary. The first intention is to talk about oneself, called "the writing of oneself" [13]. The second is the "public" dimension which is marked by the numerical condition: "one writes also for

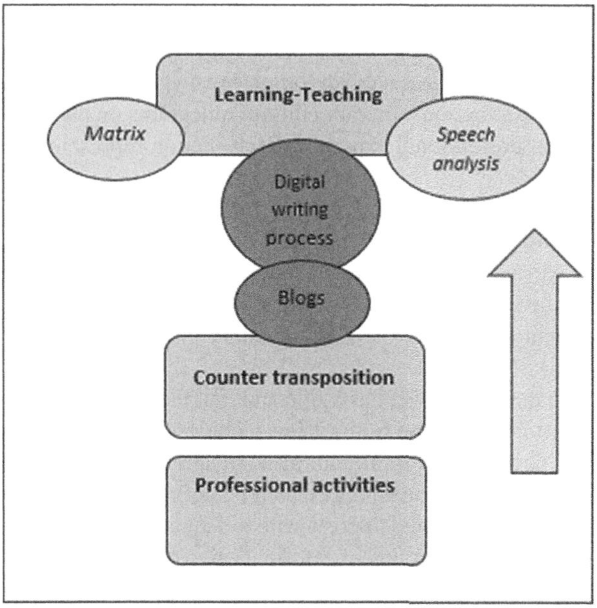

Fig. 1. "Didactic counter transposition" model with blogs writing about professional activities (Author: Pfeffer-Meyer V.)

others, to be read". [14], since the publications are freely accessible on the Internet and listed by search engines, everyone can visit them. According to Dominique Cardon and Hélène Delaunay-Téterel, blogs take on both a process of "intimate enunciation" and of "experience sharing". They represent a "tool for interpersonal communication" because they integrate a collective's dimension thanks to the communication generated by the comments [15].

Arguments and discussion created on posts give actors the feeling to belong to the same community, get together around a same practice. In addressing professional development, we see blogs as a means of create a kind of "professional archive" in a process of knowledge building. It based on a "resumption afterwards" work carried out through a writing practice [16]. Therefore, publications would be a means of bringing one's practice to light and confronting it with one's peers. In this way, it would become a manner of storing and pooling resources, but also of exposing one's work to the opinions and ideas of professional community. Posts allow to formalize the practice with words and leading to forms of reflexivity.

Consequently, one may ask under what condition this "voluntary" digital writing can become a reflexive practice and give to actors means to build professional skills?

Data Collection

To collect data and build our *corpus*, we have implemented three strategies. We crossed results of several search engines. Next, we used many "friend links" found in blogs in the form of hypertext links. And finally, we used a specialist directory "profdocosphere" developed by a professional and independent site "Docspourdocs". Our current *corpus* is composed of 56 Blogs. We have conducted an in-depth reading of the publications over two or more years. We have carried out a thematic classification of posts on each blog. We have identified concordances to establish topics. We focused on following items: daily life at library; learning situations; literary culture; reflections on profession; information watch; exchanges on professional expertise. Each section represents the content of the main publications.

Data Processing and Preliminary Analysis

Data analysis is carried out from three angles. We conduct a complete analysis of blog, to understand its organization. We have identified in some blogs common points between arrangement of the posts and documentary processing that can be carried out in a database.

First, we notice that every post has a title and that the text is formatted according to different characteristics who come from current technics of documentation. For example, each post also includes keywords in natural language. Or yet, all posts are classified according to different types of headings created by authors.

The second analysis is devoted to posts who tell about learnings situations. Through on model developed in the didactics of information - documentation, we seek to identify knowledge *in, and, for* information - documentation at schools. And we associate contexts and actors involved in the situation. Our approach is global, systemic. With the "*Matrice curriculaire et Développement*" [17], we seek to re-construct the learning situation to show its didactic construction. Writings are narratives of a learning sequence that will be carried out or that has already taken place. The enunciation by the actor himself allows him to understand intention of his action. This reality, which takes the form of "fragments", is represented by text, but also by video, photo of the class or the pupils' work. We observe the "representation" of reality from the point of view of the actor himself, which we confront with our eye as a researcher. Consequently, it's the "narrated experience" in different digital forms (writing - video - photo) we focus on for our reflection.

The third working angle invites us to observe and analyze the elements of digital discourse [18]. We identify typical characteristics of blogs, but also documentary and digital practices imported from librarian - teachers. These professionals of documentation use all possibilities of tool and sometimes go so far even as to introduce other digital tools to give the most accurate possible trace of their actions. Librarian - teachers are producers of didactic and pedagogical content. We noticed that they produce their own tutorials and training materials to publish them to their peers. These documents, which are accessible online, could be studied and analyzed with students in training situations on university.

Impact from Digital Writing Process with Blog

Based on the observation of 56 blogs, we have highlighted several major elements that we organize around tree points illustrated on Fig. 2. The first point is what is happened for the community sphere social media: first, for the actors-authors and next for the readers. Thirdly is what we can do with narrated experience in training situations.

For the actors-authors, the theme addressed on the blogs represent different areas of intervention of professionals. We can say that they "counter transpose" their practice on the blog. In about the act of writing which adopts a reflexive attitude by going back on his action and constructing a rewriting of what he has lived through, like a new form of professional writing. To explain it we noticed that actors take time to write a complete post. Every article has a title who show a professional object which is discussed on the post. Several signs of reflexivity are found in the discourse: "effective thinking", astonishment", "awareness" [1], "pride", and "questioning".

For the readers, the subject addressed by the article is often accepted and shared by the professional community. Readers comment posts with their own experiences or some questions.

Last one is training situation. Some posts can be used as a working document to begin an analysis of professional practice with students. The interaction between subjects, situation and experiences create a new learning situation in which develop forms of collective intelligence.

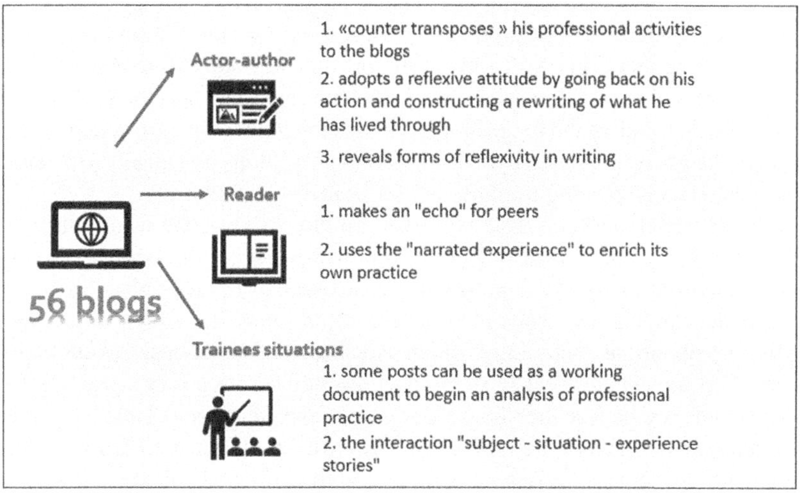

Fig. 2. Three possible impacts from digital writing process with the blogs (Author: Pfeffer-Meyer V.)

Discussion and Conclusion

As a researcher, the compilation of "stories – testimonies" leads us to access "fragments" of reality of practice who are usually inaccessible and reserved for the professional space. We have spotted on the blogs elements of actors' practice that we have identified as didactic engineering. Published "testimonies" represent postpone traces of action. In the discourse, authors carry out a kind of "return on action".

Preliminary analysis of the data shows that with blogs, authors are appropriating the codes of digital writing and proposing a new form of professional writing that integrates the "writing of oneself", of a professional self. It also becomes a space of construction where actors confront their actions to the virtual community that follows them. However, it should be noticed that although signs of reflexivity are found in the discourse, but for the moment, it's difficult to estimate in what conditions these realizations can become real knowledge leading to a transformation in professional practice. Nevertheless, we can establish that blogs constitute a rich and essential archive through which we can open up two workspaces. The first is focused on professional support, the blog allows him to keep track of the actions carried out. So, it gives him the opportunity to write and give a reflexive dimension to current or past action. The approach of "writing to be read" engages the author in a long-term writing process. He or she develops periodic, daily, or weekly writing to maintain the relationship with his or her readers. He or she shares his or her reflections and introspections, which can then be the subject of professional exchanges. We believe that a professional culture develops through this virtual community, which regularly meets on web to read and share about the profession. Teachers have, with a blog, the possibility to build expert knowledge, individually and collectively, with an actor who shares his story thanks to exchanges and sharing with the community.

The second area we are developing in our work concerns training. To make trainee students think about professional practices, we can use "stories – testimonies" on blogs to examine them collectively with aim of bringing out knowledge. Interaction "subjects - situation - stories of experience" gives inexperienced actors an opportunity to understand issues at stake in training and to develop questions inherent to the profession. Following example of the analysis of activity, use of learning situations associated with a didactic analysis can be an interesting training tool for trainee students.

Therefore, observation of posts published on blogs shows that as a writing tool, it allows one to carry out a work of putting into words one's professional activity. The analysis of writing processes shows that a reflexivity form takes place in writing. It leads to understanding and tends to make the actors' practice evolve. But it also has repercussions on virtual community, which uses "narrated experience" to enrich its own practices. This movement create an echo phenomenon between peer's practices.

To conclude, we believe that there are two training situations with the blog. It is both a personnel space to "Tell-Write" one's activity, and it can also be used as a work medium to investigate and observe learning situations and to developed collective intelligence's forms.

5 Conclusion

We analyzed elements of "real" activity, based on examples of professional collaboration and co-construction of distance reflective skills with nurses from the French National Education system. We also analyzed blog posts related to the professional activities of teachers-librarians. Blogs offer a multiplicity of possibilities for digital writing. The work in collective intelligence at several levels is a producer of knowledge and a generator of research skills and professional development. For this to happen, there must be a real commitment on the part of the actors, a progressive construction of common references, a conceptualization work as well as a "thought adaptation" to tools and situations, with a new temporality without giving up the aims in a perspective of transformation of devices and professional development.

This ambition implies an important work of didactic act. From these reference practices, analyzes carried out in connection with the fields of education and training, we can continue the didactic work within the framework of a pedagogy and university didactics integrating the use of digital technology, remote devices in a human perspective, that is to say that respects a principle of co-construction taking into account the experience and practice of everyone.

References

1. Frisch, M.: Émergences en didactiques pour les métiers de l'humain. L'Harmattan, Paris (2016)
2. Navarro, C.: Une analyse cognitive de l'interaction dans les activités de travail. Le Travail Humain **54**(2), 114–128 (1990)
3. Frisch, M.: Constructions de savoirs et de dispositifs. L'Harmattan, Paris (2018)
4. Lévy, P.: L'intelligence collective: Pour une anthropologie du cyberespace. La découverte, Paris (1997)
5. Noubel, J.-F.: L'intelligence collective, la révolution invisible. Guide pratique de l'intelligence collective (2004)
6. Arnaud, B., Caruso Cahn, S.: La Boîte à outils de l'intelligence collective. Dunod, Paris (2019)
7. Moral, M., Lamy, F.: Les outils de l'intelligence collective-La favoriser, la comprendre, la stimuler. Etude (broché), p. 40. InterEditions (2013)
8. Frisch, M.: La didactique de l'Information-Documentation en France comme ressources pour l'enseignement: Une histoire et une épistémologie plurielle. Didactica Historica **4**, 87–91 (2018)
9. Paragot, J.-M.: Parcours d'un responsable de formation: Du métier vers la profession. L'Harmattan, Paris (2014)
10. Lafitte, P.-J.: Coopération, éducation, formation. La pédagogie Freinet face aux défis du XXI° siècle. L'Harmattan et.AFIRSE. Paris, pp. 155–170 (2018)
11. Delion, P.: Fonction phorique, holding et institution. ERES, Toulouse (2018)
12. Anzieu, D., Martin, J.-Y.: The dynamics of restricted groups (1968). PUF, Paris (2012)
13. Deseilligny, O.: Le blog intime au croisement des genres de l'écriture de soi. Itinéraires, 2010-2, 73–82 (2010)
14. Miele, P.: L'écriture de soi et les nouveaux outils de communication. https://memoire.pm-pm.pm. Accessed 19 Aug 2020
15. Cardon, D., Delaunay-Téterel, H.: La production de soi comme technique relationnelle: un essai de typologie des blogs par leurs publics. Réseaux **138**(4), 15–71 (2006)
16. Pfeffer-Meyer, V.: L'écriture réflexive dans la relation tutorale avec des professeurs-documentalistes. Éducation et socialisation 52 (2019)
17. Frisch, M.: Des modèles et des concepts en question pour une didactique de l'Information-Documentation et proposition d'une matrice curriculaire dynamique. Tréma **45**, 43–57 (2016)
18. Paveau, A.-M.: L'analyse du discours numérique, dictionnaire des formes et des pratiques. Hermann Editeurs, Paris (2017)

Improvement of Art Creative Skills by the Means of Signature Pedagogy in Online Musical Education

Svetlana V. Karkina[1](✉), Juan J. Mena Marcos[2], and Roza A. Valeeva[1]

[1] Kazan Federal University, Kazan, Russia
s.karkina@mail.ru
[2] University of Salamanca, Salamanca, Spain

Abstract. The paper introduces the possibilities of online musical education based on signature pedagogy as a main trend of research work. Facing COVID19 Emergency in Higher Education stated the challenge that required to design new methods in teaching and learning specially in musical education include the process of training performance skills. The methodological basis of the research was the signature pedagogy as a reflection of the way of thinking as a professional for establishing the most progressive methods of learning for future music teachers. The data were collected from the online resource in Kazan Federal University such as students' essays, musical instrumental performance for quantitative data and feedback of students for qualitative data. Based on the results of research work were concluded that the implementation of signature pedagogy approach in musical education by the means of methods of critique and activation of creative potential through the online format allows to improve the piano class educational process and in particularly the development of students' performance skills.

Keywords: Online learning · Technologies · Education · Distance education · Signature pedagogy · Musical education

1 Introduction

In the modern world leading universities offer a wide range of online resources. On the Coursera platform there are lot of music learning courses including such as 'Introduction to Classical music' (Yale, USA), 'How Music Can Change Your Life' (Melburn, Australia), 'The Place of Music in 21st Century' (Sydney, Australia), 'Write Like Mozart – An Introduction to Classical Music Composition' (Singapur), 'The world of the string quartet' (Philadelphia, USA), 'Jazz improvisation' (Berklee, USA), 'Developing your musicianship' (Berklee, USA). Besides teachers of such courses as 'Introduction to Public Speaking' (Washington, USA) state a question of the possibility to improve performance skills through online format. Teachers who gave positive response for this question were based on two main points: performance skills can be improved through online learning through unlimited access to the information and stimulation of productive student's practice [1].

L. S. Agrati et al. (Eds.): HELMeTO 2020, CCIS 1344, pp. 86–99, 2021.
https://doi.org/10.1007/978-3-030-67435-9_7

The e-learning theory was researched very actively [2]. The e-learning strategies for delivering knowledge in digital age develop rapidly [3]. In higher education it is additionally demanded that both teachers and students use online learning resources to support knowledge acquired from the formal face-to-face context [4]. The use of Massive Open Online Courses (MOOCs) are an example of new model of distance education [5] which allows to realize modern pedagogical approaches [6]. The majority of distance learning research were conducted of the use of Moodle [7] and focused on the problem of virtual education environment quality [8]. According to researches the most important benefits of these studies are accessibility, flexibility and interactivity of the learning process [9]. The online environment allows to realize the learning without any barriers such as socio-economic status and geographical location [10].

Research of perspective of distance learning realization opens new possibilities of interaction between students from different countries including comparative aspects of opportunities [11]. Current researches indicate in the field of musical education insufficient demand for student's artistic and creative improvement in art [12], including all trends such as instrumental and vocal teacher education [13]. The experience of synchronous online piano teaching realization demonstrated the benefits for students who do not have access to learn piano directly through the free activization of art creative skills and showed new ways and methods in the musical study process organization [14].

The using of online resources offers possibilities to implement some characteristics of special professional environment in educational process such as unlimited access to wide range of professional knowledge include professional web-resources and libraries, changing forms of teacher-students interaction include individual work, flexible correction of course content based on recent changes in professional reality, opportunity to contact with a lot of numbers of respondents and monitoring the real professional process through the way of hidden surveillance technologies. All these benefits allow to implement the key idea of Shulman's concept of signature pedagogy of teaching through the educational process to think like a real professional [15].

Despite the fact that Shulman studied the signature pedagogies in the fields of medicine, law and the clergy only other researchers have found this method as useful to observe closely the pedagogy of the professionals in action. Wattiaux [16] researches the signature pedagogy in agriculture, Bauer-Dantoin [17] studied this problem in the biological sciences, Christie [18] have taken research experiences in computer science, Ernie [19] and others studied signature pedagogies in mathematics, Komoto [20] published paper in the area of geography and Lattery [21] researches physics in the aspect of main characteristics of teaching and learning process.

Some researchers are studying signature pedagogies in arts, such as Meacham [22] whose paper offer the research of vision and re-vision in creative writing pedagogy; Don [23] studied theory and practice of signature pedagogies in music theory and performance.

In the art pedagogy majority of authors understood signature pedagogy as a "critique". According to Shulman this method is a prime setting for developing "habits of mind" [15]. Kornetsky [24] offers to use arts critique as a method of signature pedagogy in the learning process of the performer in theatre arts. Motley [25] researches the role of critique in the graphic design classroom.

Facing with an emergency COVID19 in higher education has become like a challenge that required to design new methods in teaching and learning specially in musical education include the process of performance skills training offers the using of online technologies not only as a necessary tool, but priority and sometimes the only mean.

Based on the literature review, the objectives of research were follows:

1. Which methods could use anybody for musical teaching education practice in professional preparation process through the online format in the field of music?
2. What are the benefits for student in musical training educational process through an online learning format?
3. What are the limits for a teacher in using of online technologies in the musical education process?

2 Methods

This research presents the study process for music teacher education at Kazan Federal University include bachelor, master and teacher training program. In an emergency situation of rapid changing from face-to-face to the online way only in a pandemic all forms of work with students were turned among them lectures, practices, seminars, exams, as well as practices of training music performance skills.

The methodological basis of the research was the signature pedagogy of musical education. According to Shulman's works the signature pedagogy approach means "the characteristic forms of teaching and learning" that allows to teach students during the educational process to think like a real professional [15]. This approach is necessary in the process of professional education for preparation a person for accomplished and responsible practice in the service to others. The base statement of this approach is recognizing the gap between an academic discipline and real professional practice. The essence of this approach is attempts to create new methods for the process of professional preparation include values and hopes of real persons in professional area. The realization of this approach based on the methods of critique and activization of creative potential.

In the process of research study 50 students of Kazan Federal University took part in the experimental work. Based on the signature pedagogy approach in musical education the methods of critique and activation of creative potential were implemented. The experiment was organized in online way for students who enrolled piano class. The data were collected from the online resource such as results of student's passing the exams of piano training course include the marks obtained on the exam as a quantitative data and feedback of students and teachers as qualitative data. Student's piano performance works and critical essay were evaluated on a tenth point scale according to their creativeness.

We understand creativeness in this paper as the capacity of "production of relevant and effective novelty" based on knowledge, special skills and techniques [26]. The level of creativeness was evaluated through the quality of originality of students' responses in essay and piano performance. The most creative works demonstrated the most innovative and unique art solutions received 10 marks, when works without creative results copy any well-known art solutions could receive 0 mark.

The form of feedback consisted of four questions that allowed to clarify the level of satisfaction of students and teachers with learning process through the online way only and their readiness to continue this form in the future.

The process of data analysis was based on the method of expert evaluation and statistical methods the median and standard deviation. During the experiment several teachers evaluated students' results in essay and piano performance as experts. The using of median method allowed to count an average values without limitation such as kind or asymmetric of distribution. The method of standard deviation was used for counting the level of differences between the students' test results.

3 Data Analysis

In the process of analysis of essay results ten questions as criteria of essay were used. The using of the method of median demonstrated the average level of students' responses while equal number of answers were less and more than any result in the Table 1. For each criterion ten points scale was used. The lowest level of results was received in the first criteria that demonstrated two musical pieces used in essay. This is normal result because some students analyzed in their essays one or two musical pieces only. Also that was a reason why many of students used not more than two real facts from musical history (criteria 3). All other results were more than six points that is an evidence of very high level of critical essays quality. The highest level of results equal nine points was in two criteria: "the creativity in answering the questions" and "the correct form of written statement". The quality of results was measured by the method of standard deviation. All the obtained results were in the interval from 0,7 to 1,8 points that is too close to 1 point and means the lowest level of deviation between all the expert evaluations for students' responses of each of them. The statistical analysis of the results of students' essays demonstrated the high level of their critical thinking skills and ability to creativity in the musical meaning and content interpretation.

In the process of analysis of piano performance results five questions as criteria of performance were used. For each criterion ten points scale was used. The using of the method of median demonstrated the average level of students' piano performance while equal mark of playing piano were less and more than any result in the Table 2. All the results were high enough while the median of the results of three criteria reached eight point and of two criteria were nine point. The highest results were received on criteria of "technical level of performance" and "creativity in achievement artistic goals". The quality of results was measured by the method of standard deviation. All the obtained results were in the interval from 0,7 to 1,1 points that is too close to 1 point and means the lowest level of deviation between all the results of expert evaluations for each student in all the criteria of students' performance. The statistical analysis of the results of students' piano playing demonstrated the high level of their creative skills in the musical performance.

In the process of analysis of piano class students' feedback results four questions in survey were used. In answering the first question "How many attempts did you for home recording?" students were able to give any response without a limit. The test of median of their responses demonstrated the 20 as the average level of students' home attempts

Table 1. Analysis of essay results.

Question	Number of students	Median	Standard deviation
1. The number of musical pieces	50	2	1,327265
2. The level of the analysis of a musical meaning		6	1,821078
3. The using of the real facts from musical history		2	1,488048
4. The deep knowledge of the music theory		7	1,425139
5. The using of the appropriate arguments		8	1,244744
6. The knowledge of the lectures of the course		8	0,880631
7. The creativity in answering the questions		9	0,718275
8. The clarity and conciseness of thought		8	0,973946
9. The logic in the construction of arguments		8	1,111168
10. The correct form of written statement		9	1,005292

Table 2. Analysis of students' performance.

Question	Number of students	Median	Standard deviation
1. Overall quality of performance	50	8	0,880630572
2. Technical level of performance		9	0,718275
3. Artistic expression		8	0,973946
4. Creative art solutions		8	1,111168
5. Creativity in achievement artistic goals		9	1,005292

for doing the musical record (Table 3). This result shows that equal number of students' attempts were below and high than this mark. According to students' responses each of them used several attempts doing the home record. Majority of them did much more than 20–25 attempts that demonstrated their strong desire to create the best performance. This process had been very necessary also for activization the students' self-reflection as an extremely useful part of their self-preparation.

The lowest result of students' feedback by the means of method of median was received in answering the question "Had you any difficulties with technical equipment?". The obtained result was only two point in ten points scale that demonstrated too low level of technical equipment problems in creating musical records at home where students had such problems as possibility to use only synth instead of wooden piano, and to have available piano in a good tuning quality.

For the last two questions equal results as 8 point in ten points scale were received that means high level. These questions were the next: "Did you understand the teacher's instructions?", "Have you satisfied with the final result?". The high level of results were received during the feedback means that the way of getting instruction by teacher was understandable for students while all the teachers' advice were in a printed text only, but available for rereading by students as much time as they needed. The high level of students' satisfaction of the performance results also very necessary in the process that had been managed in the new way for this group of students. The quality of results was measured by the method of standard deviation. All the obtained results that were used ten points scale were in the interval from 1,2 to 1,6 points that is too close to 1 point and means the low enough level of deviation between all the results of students' feedback of each person. The standard deviation for the first question "How many attempts did you for home recording?" was equal to 8,07 point that could be interpreted as not so low and demonstrates the difference in art creative process self-management where each student needs an own way for doing home exercise and to create a musical record.

The statistical analysis of the results of students' feedback in total demonstrated the high level of their ability to improve their musical performance way in online way and to feel a satisfaction from this process and an art result.

Table 3. Analysis of piano class students' feedback.

Question	Number of students	Median	Number of point scale	Standard deviation
How many attempts did you for home recording?	50	20	50	8,074273
Did you understand the teacher's instructions?		8	10	1,468583
Had you any difficulties with technical equipment?		2	10	1,610679
Have you satisfied with the final result?		8	10	1,244744

4 Results

The results of the experimental work demonstrated the high level of students' critical thinking skills, ability to be creative in musical performance include a musical interpretation and activity in self-improvement of piano playing. Based on data analysis were found that implementation of signature pedagogy in musical education using such methods as critique and activation of creative potential could be effective and allow to manage the process of students' studying in musical performance class through an online format.

5 Discussion

The necessary to bridge the gap between academic knowledge and real professional practice stated by Shulman [15] in his works where he pointed the distinctive qualities of professional preparation in the fields of medicine, law and the clergy. Also the researcher highlighted three fundamental dimensions of any profession: thinking, performance and acting with integrity. These dimensions included into the approach named as signature pedagogy were divided by him on three levels: surface structure (educational process that includes all forms of classroom interaction between teacher and students); deep structure (the knowledge about effective methods in the subject area) and implicit structure (values and dispositions of professional experience).

The signature pedagogy approach could be implemented in musical education by the means of online resources. The online way allows to implement all three dimensions were pointed by Shulman.

The surface structure including different forms of classroom interaction between teacher and students can be implemented through online way using such resources as forum, chat, webinar, that allows to recreate the traditional classroom in online environment. The benefit of online way is an opportunity to individual interaction with each student for special purposes include work with students with special needs, consultation and closing knowledge gaps, control of students' home work.

The deep structure including improvement knowledge about effective methods in the subject area can be implemented in online way by the unlimited correction the course content for adding recent information in professional reality include effective methods, resources, experience. The online way allows to add any information according to changes in real professional field to improve educational resources. The benefit of deep structure online implementation is opportunity to capture the professional field knowledge from the best resources.

The implicit structure including values and dispositions of professional experience can be implemented through online resources in several ways. Firstly, this way opens unlimited access to wide range of professional knowledge include professional web-resources and libraries. These resources contain sets of books, art and musical collections, art illustrations and records. All these materials can be very useful for different professional tasks. The gathering rich professional collections in one place can keep student's time instead for looking for them during the educational process. Besides that special professional sites can provide access to the professional community for sharing experience, ideas and news, discussion problems.

Secondly through this way students can get an opportunity to learn more about values and dispositions of a person had reached great level in the professional field. Historically well-known the fact from composers' biographies when they learnt other famous persons professional experience in distance way. J.S. Bach during his childhood rewriting the musical text wrote by great organists for learning their music and analysis the principles of composition. This way was such as school education for him because any other opportunities for listening the music or learning directly by that composers were unavailable. The life of W.A. Mozart was beginning in the small town Salzburg was rich by excellent musical traditions of brilliant chamber art of such composers as G. Biber lived and died much earlier than Mozart was born. The learning of these traditions in the childhood gave to Mozart opportunity to reach the highest level of art compositions in the musical history. Hungarian composer F. Liszt became one of the best pianist in the world trying to follow and repeat the success of Italian violinist N. Paganini whom personality was the leading for the pianist in the process of self-improvement. After the invention and rapidly improvement technical equipment for the professional recording and home listening to music majority of people received an opportunity to choose musical piece and artist for whom they prefer to listen include professional purposes while such records can become as an ideal for self-improvement. Trying to follow the best art example of a great person students learn more about his life and biography, his values system and professional dispositions. Also they can find an opportunity to meet to contact with real people who is working in the professional field for getting an advice from them or even a consultation. All these attempts allow them to reach deepest level in education that Shulman named as an implicit structure for learning the core of the professional skills such as values and dispositions of professional experience.

All these dimensions implemented through online way allowed to realize the key idea of Shulman's concept of signature pedagogy of teaching through the educational process to think and act like a real professional. According to the Shulmans' words that any profession is much more than an academic discipline and needs to find new methods for the preparation of students for future professional activity the set of effective methods for musical education was chosen. Firstly, based on the works of majority researchers who studied art [24, 25] the method of critique had been chosen as a way for filtering, structuring and understanding information from unlimited internet sources include musical pieces. In addition, this method is necessary for understanding the artistic content and meaning of any musical work is a key skill for any musician, as well as for a music teacher. Secondly the method of activization of creative potential was chosen for a set that demonstrates a main trend in professional activity of musician. Both methods of critique and activization of creative potential were used in a set for implementation of signature pedagogy approach in the musical education process in Kazan Federal University.

The using of method of critique in the educational process was implemented in the students' work with essay. That was the task for them to write the essay with musical analysis. According to the instruction they could choose one way for their work from the next options:

1. To compare the records of several musical pieces.
2. To describe the art content of musical piece.
3. To explain of an art idea of musical performance.
4. To compare the musical content with the origin literature piece.
5. To compare the key characteristics of west and east music.

Also students received detailed explanation of their task as the necessity to base on real musical facts such as history and theory of music, to generalize and explain the main art idea of the musical piece and proof it by musical and expressive means. Their choice of music for analysis was free and students were able to choose any musical pieces according their personal taste and preferences.

Before the writing of essay students were instructed about the criteria of valuation their works include the number of musical pieces chosen for analysis, the quality of the text. Beside the demonstration of knowledge of musical history and theory that was important as evidences of an idea the critical way of analysis was based on the ability to use appropriate arguments that were in strict logical construction. The main idea in essay was to be proof by arguments correctly as well as the form of written essay without errors. The importance of this work based on the presumption that not for all students the task of explanation the meaning of music is common enough and they able to do it properly. Despite this point the analysis of results demonstrated the high level of improvement of students' critical skills through the work with essay based on the method of critique.

The same method of critique also was used by students in their self-preparation work at home where they created records of piano performance. This work is the regular part of training performance skills in any musical class learning process. The organization of this work in online way required direct teacher's instructions by texting in the chat personally for each student. Trying to prepare the record before sending to teacher after home exercises students did several attempts for improvement the quality of performance. This process was very useful when was based on critical self-assessment and activated students' self-reflection of their piano performance. The final analysis of all records let us to state the great difference between the first and the last musical record of each student that reflected much efforts of them in trying to improve their performance based on teacher advice.

For the evaluation of students' piano works five criteria were chosen for expert judgment. In the beginning of assessment the "overall quality of performance" was expertise include the general view on the musical image as well as a compliance of the performance to the composer's idea without errors. The second criterion was the "technical level of performance" that allow to establish an appropriate level of playing the piano according to the musical text remarks. For the assessment of this criterion were evaluated special playing piano skills such as ability to play in appropriate tempo according to the text, to change dynamic and correctly distribute the elements of a musical text in their integral structure. These two criteria reflected the total level of piano playing skills and they are common for any musician as an obligatory requirement.

The level of creativeness of students' works was reflected by last three criteria. The artistic expression demonstrated the brightness and memorability of a musical image, as well as ability of a student to perform any musical details in the best way according to the musical meaning. During the process of preparation of the art plan of musical performance each musician can add some creative details for reaching more expression and for implementation of the personal preferences. This skill of student based on the understanding of musical content and ability to recognize and create the personal plan of musical piece interpretation. The criterion of "creativity in achievement artistic goals" is the most important in the evaluation of musical performance skills. The ability of student to diversify the timbre, dynamics, strokes, as well as to achieve a more flexible intonation reflects a high level of artistic creativity, the achievement of which reflects the quality of the student's performance training.

All these criteria reflect the great meaning of creativeness in musical educational process in particularly the training performance skills as a process for self-realization of artistic capacity of any person. The management of this process by implementation of signature pedagogy approach allowed to find a way for improvement of students' piano performance skills by the means of online educational process.

The using of online resources during the quarantine because of COVID19 was uncommon for majority of students in particularly for training musical performance skills. The most part of students never had have an experience to learn teacher's instructions through the Internet only. Taking into account the need to analyze the implementation of unique way of musical education process through online the using of students' feedback as a method was justified and necessary.

By the means of feedback four questions were asked to students to clarify the details of their home self-preparation work, technical conditions and problems, the ability to understand teacher's instructions through the online way and the level of satisfaction of the result.

The relevance of the issue about the number of students attempts for creating the home musical record is based on the well-known problem of any artist that effect as a "fear of camera". For majority of people the creating of any record is the most difficult task requiring many attempts before a satisfactory result will be achieved. The same task for students can be useful for activization their reflection the musical performance, when the ambition to improve the record can stimulate personal development of wide range of musical skills. The students' responses on the question "how many attempts did you for home recording" proof the point of view that any record needs in strong efforts while the majority of students wrote down in the feedback the number of their home attempts much more than 15. This fact is confirmed by the quality of students' piano playing records validated by teacher as higher than in regular face-to-face work because they sent for assessment only the best result.

The understanding of teacher advice in musical class work is one of the most important condition based on the good relations between student and teacher as well as on ability of teacher to give appropriate instructions for fruitful work of any student according to his/her personality and art capacity. The possibility to explain an instructor point of view in face-to-face work not the same as in online format. When in traditional class a teacher able to point any art detail for working in online way he must to reduce and specify the instruction in more general way but pointing the core of the problem or lack in performance. At the same time the online way allows to keep instruction as a text that available for rereading by student as many times as he needs.

The question about the home technical equipment is not common for relations between teacher and student in higher education tradition, but necessary as evidence of home cultural environment of student while allows to get some new personal information about a student. The result of feedback demonstrated that not all the students have home good quality piano. Some of them do not have any instrument at home at all while nobody of them have any problems with technical equipment such as gadgets allow to create a record. The knowledge about home cultural environment where each of student lives allow for teacher to correct the requirements of the study program in trying to choose the most appropriate way of personal development for musical performance skills improvement.

The last question about the personal satisfaction of the performance result demonstrated the success of online work in total and allowed to state the possibility to implement this way in the future. The positive responses of the majority of students proof the preferences of students to be more independent in their art work and to get more freedom in creation decisions. During the receiving less control from teacher than in face-to-face way of interaction students get an opportunity to express their artistic personality in more individual way that allow them finally to achieve more satisfaction.

Based on the result of students' feedback analysis as well as on the results of the quality of their essays and piano performances it is possible to highlight the main benefit of using online technologies for learning purposes such as opportunity to offer flexible approach for each student according to his art capacity, individual preferences and professional purposes. The using of online access to education is relevance in rapidly changing world while each person gets an opportunity for self-improvement and the management become an able to bridge the gap between education and professional reality for their close interaction.

6 Conclusions

Based on the results of research work becomes possible to conclude that the implementation of signature pedagogy approach in musical education by the means of methods of critique and activation of creative potential through the online format allows to improve the piano class educational process and in particularly the development of students' performance skills.

According to the research the evidences were found by methods of expert evaluation and the set of statistical methods include the median and standard deviation proof that the using of online format in musical training educational process allows students to achieve such benefits as:

- Unlimited access to the content of knowledge and teachers' advice and recommends for improvement of musical performance skills;
- Possibility to eliminate different restrictions of traditional education such as time-limit, locations, social-cultural distinctions, level of development of piano performance skills, professional experience in the field of music;
- To use digital resources such as illustrative visual aids, audio and video learning tools and open online sources in the most appropriate way;
- Active exchange of musical experience between wide range of participants, discussion of them, critical analysis of actual problems;
- Activization of students' self-reflection during the process of records of their own piano performance and selection the best one from all attempts for sending to teacher;

- Offering a comfortable way for self-improvement of students' art creative skills through the productive training practice without direct teachers' instructions and strict requirement to follow the limited way of performance.

Besides was stated that the management of musical education process through the online way needs special tools while a teacher must keep in mind some limits such as:

- During the online teaching necessary to remember about musical development of student in general and to pay attention for improvement of art creative skills as well as to improve the knowledge about history and theory of music and musical performance and increase the motivation to creativeness.
- The online format by using the records for teaching musical performance skills not appropriate way for students who do not passed the first level of playing instruments for receiving the bases skills;
- For fruitful work with student teacher's instruction must be very direct and touch the core of difficulty or problem in student performance;
- The instructions consist of a lot of details that touch the way of self-expression of student could be useless for understanding and will lock personal imagination that is necessary for creative performance.

Development of the online learning content very necessary in modern world where distance learning technologies becomes an important mean of delivery of knowledge in the environment of unlimited education for young generation. Besides main benefits for students such as accessibility, flexibility and interactivity the online format could demonstrate new trends in development of methods in musical education offering from another point of view ways for improvement of students' art creative skills within the frameworks of performance training process.

7 Limitations

The paper has a limitation such as diagnostics only two criteria include critical thinking and art creative skills that had been chosen according to the methods of research work the critique and activation of creative potential. The diagnostics of another criteria such as motivation and art knowledge will be used in our future research works when the systematic approach in paper will embrace all components of personal development based on the proof of their changes under the action of methods the critique and activation of creative potential in the frameworks of signature pedagogy approach.

Acknowledgments. The work is performed according to the Russian Government Program of Competitive Growth of Kazan Federal University.

References

1. Coursera Structure Sample Speech. Introduction to Public Speaking. https://www.coursera.org/learn/public-speaking-deprecated/lecture/AU0OL/structure-sample-speech. Accessed 15 Apr 20195

2. Aparicio, M., Bacao, F., Oliveira, T.: An e-learning theoretical framework. J. Educ. Technol. Soc. **19**(1), 292–307 (2016)
3. Perla, L., Agrati, L.S., Vinci, V.: The 'sophisticated' knowledge of e-teacher. Re-shape Digital Resources for Online Courses. In: Burgos, D. (ed.) Higher Education Learning Methodologies and Technologies Online. HELMeto 2019. Communications in Computer and Information Science, vol. 1091, pp. 3–17. Springer, Heidelberg (2019). https://doi.org/10.1007/978-3-030-31284-8_1
4. Ni, A.Y.: Comparing the effectiveness of classroom and online learning: teaching research methods. J. Public Affairs Educ. **19**(2), 199–215 (2013)
5. Bozarth, J., Chapman, D.D., LaMonica, L.: Preparing for distance learning: designing an online student orientation course. J. Educ. Technol. Soc. **7**(1), 87–106 (2004)
6. Blackmon, S.J.: MOOC makers: professors' experiences with developing and delivering MOOCs. Int. Rev. Res. Open Dist. Learn. **19**(4), 76–91 (2018)
7. Ziebarth, S., Hoppe, H.U.: Moodle4SPOC: a resource-intensive blended learning course. In: Rensing, C., de Freitas, S., Ley, T., Muñoz-Merino, P.J. (eds.) Open Learning and Teaching in Educational Communities. EC-TEL 2014. LNCS, vol. 8719, pp. 359–372. Springer, Cham (2014). https://doi.org/10.1007/978-3-319-11200-8_27
8. Caverly, D.C., MacDonald, L.: Designing online developmental education courses. J. Dev. Educ. **23**(1), 36–37 (1999)
9. Olmos, S., Mena, J., Torrecilla, E., Iglesias, A.: Improving graduate students' learning through the use of moodle. Educ. Res. Rev. **10**(5), 604–614 (2015)
10. Ramirez-Montoya, M.-S., Mena, J., Rodriguez-Arroyo, J.A.: In-service teachers' self-perceptions of digital competence and OER use as determined by a xMOOC training course. Comput. Hum. Behav. **77**, 356–364 (2017)
11. Widoretno, S., Dwiastuti, S.: Improving Students' thinking skill based on class Interaction In discovery Instructional: a case of lesson study. J. Pendidikan IPA Indonesia Sci. Educ. Study Program FMIPA UNNES Semarang **8**, 347–352 (2019)
12. Abankwa, J., Mikkila-Erdmann, M.: Piano teacher education in Finland and Germany: Targeted competencies and respective learning environments of two cases. Int. J. Music Educ. **36**(4), 616–629 (2018)
13. Lennon, M., Reed, G.: Instrumental and vocal teacher education: competences, roles and curricula. Music Educ. Res. **14**(3), 285–308 (2012)
14. Pike, P.D.: Improving music teaching and learning through online service: a case study of a synchronous online teaching internship. Int. J. Music Educ. **35**(1), 107–117 (2017)
15. Shulman, L.S.: Signature pedagogies in the professions. Daedalus **134**, 52–59 (2005)
16. Wattiaux, M.A.: Signature pedagogy in agriculture. In: Gurung, R.A.R., Chick, N.L., Haynie, A. (eds.) Exploring signature pedagogies: Approaches to Teaching Disciplinary Habits of Mind, pp. 207–223. Stylus Publishing, Sterling (2009)
17. Bauer-Dantoin, A.: The evolution of scientific teaching within the biological sciences. In: Gurung, R.A.R., Chick, N.L., Haynie, A. (eds.) Exploring Signature Pedagogies: Approaches to Teaching Disciplinary Habits of Mind, pp. 224–243. Stylus Publishing, Sterling (2009)
18. Christie, D.: Signature pedagogies and SOTL practices in computer science. In: Gurung, R.A.R., Chick, N.L., Haynie, A. (eds.) Exploring signature pedagogies: Approaches to Teaching Disciplinary Habits of Mind, pp. 244–259. Stylus Publishing, Sterling (2009)
19. Ernie, K., LeDocq, R., Serros, S., Tong, S.: Mathematical reasoning. In: Gurung, R.A.R., Chick, N.L., Haynie, A. (eds.) Exploring Signature Pedagogies: Approaches to Teaching Disciplinary Habits of Mind, pp. 260–279. Stylus Publishing, Sterling (2009)
20. Komoto, C.: Moving toward a signature pedagogy in geography. A close reading of the Landscape. In: Gurung, R.A.R., Chick, N.L., Haynie, A. (eds.) Exploring Signature Pedagogies: Approaches to Teaching Disciplinary Habits of Mind, pp. 121–138. Stylus Publishing, Sterling (2009)

21. Lattery, M.J.: Signature pedagogies in introductory physics. In: Gurung, R.A.R., Chick, N.L., Haynie, A. (eds.) Exploring Signature Pedagogies: Approaches to Teaching Disciplinary Habits of Mind, pp. 280–294. Stylus Publishing, Sterling (2009)
22. Meacham, R.: Vision and re-vision in creative writing pedagogy. In: Gurung, R.A.R., Chick, N.L., Haynie, A. (eds.) Exploring Signature Pedagogies: Approaches to Teaching Disciplinary Habits of Mind, pp. 59–80. Stylus Publishing, Sterling (2009)
23. Don, G.G.C., Sadeghpour, M.: Theory and practice. Signature pedagogies in music theory and performance. In: Gurung, R.A.R., Chick, N.L., Haynie, A. (eds.) Exploring Signature Pedagogies: Approaches to Teaching Disciplinary Habits of Mind, pp. 81–98. Stylus Publishing, Sterling (2009)
24. Kornetsky, L.: Signature pedagogy in theatre arts. Arts Hum. High. Educ. **16**(3), 241–251 (2017)
25. Motley, P.: Critique and process: signature pedagogies in the graphic design classroom. Arts Hum. High. Educ. **16**(3), 229–240 (2017)
26. Cropley, A.J.: Definitions of creativity. In: Runco, M.A., Pritzker, S.R. (eds.) Encyclopedia of Creativity, pp. 511–524. Academic Press, San Diego, CA (2011)

A Multiple Case Study on Blended and Online Educational Strategies

Chiara Panciroli(✉), Laura Corazza, Anita Macauda, and Simona Nicolini

Department of Education Studies "Giovanni Maria Bertin", University of Bologna, Bologna, Italy
Chiara.panciroli@unibo.it

Abstract. This paper aims to investigate how three specific didactic strategies, arts-based learning, flipped learning and role-playing, adopted within the scope of blended and online teaching support the involvement and the interactions between student and student and between students and teacher, as well as the elaboration of new forms of knowledge, promoting active learning. Sectoral studies indeed show how the inter-relation between didactic strategies, disciplinary contents and technological applications, have an impact on the transformative nature of learning and teaching processes. The use and the sharing of different stimulus materials, along with the work developed in collaboration using digital environments and instruments, have turned out to be particularly significant. In this regard, the students' observations and comments show how the adoption of the three strategies, also developed within digital environments have provided opportunities to improve the cognitive processes with positive implications for motivation, participation, the re-elaboration of knowledge. This paper presents and discusses a multiple case study based on three different interventions made within the scope of university teaching (University of Bologna, academic year 2019–2020).

Keywords: Arts-based learning · Flipped learning · Role-playing

1 Theoretical Framework

A large scientific literature shows [1–5] how in the didactic field, the interrelationship between didactic strategies, disciplinary contents and technological applications, impacts on the transformative nature of the learning and teaching processes. In regard to these studies, the didactic strategies should move towards a systemic approach. The "systemic method" indeed leads us to consider education as an "open" and "autopoietic" structure [6] characterized by an interdependency between organization and environment. Within a holistic approach that underscores the relations between subject and context, a priority role is acquired by the technologies. It is indeed shown how the boundary between physical and digital space is by now no longer so identifiable, in an entanglement between

This contribution, developed and shared jointly by the four authors, was drawn up as follows: Sect. 1, 2 and Conclusion by Chiara Panciroli; Subsect. 3.1 and 4.1 by Anita Macauda; Subsect. 3.2 and 4.2 by Laura Corazza; Subsect. 3.3 and 4.3 by Simona Nicolini.

L. S. Agrati et al. (Eds.): HELMeTO 2020, CCIS 1344, pp. 100–114, 2021.
https://doi.org/10.1007/978-3-030-67435-9_8

heterogenous media and environments [7, 8], with the positive consequence that also technologies contribute to a particularly significant model of integrated didactics [9]. Inside this model a priority role is played by the didactic strategies understood as "a set of intentional. coherent and coordinated actions, addressed to the achievement of an educational objective" [2, p. 11]. The experimentation conducted in this specific field have shown how the use of didactic strategies that stimulate discussions and reflections in the classroom and drive students to a greater participation through collaborative workgroups have a more meaningful impact on the development of active learning [4].

In that regard, with reference to didactic pathways realized in digital environments, Banna, Lin, Stewart and Fialkowski [10] underline how involvement plays a central role in stimulating learning. Lear, Ansorge and Steckelberg [11] state that the interactions with the contents, the interactions between student and student and between student and teacher lead to a more meaningful learning process and to more effective results. Interaction and involvement are indeed closely correlated: students' involvement is developed through interaction. Recalling the seven principles for good practices in university didactics of Chickering and Gamson [12], it transpires that the students are more involved when the didactic strategy: 1. increases the relationship between student and teacher; 2. offers the students opportunities to work in collaboration-cooperation; 3. encourages the students to use active learning strategies; 4 provides timely feedback as to academic progress; 5. calls for the students to dedicate quality time to their academic assignments; 6. establishes high standards for an acceptable academic work; 7. responds to the students' different demands in the learning process. In regard to these aspects, Martin and Bolliger [13] have shown the importance of involvement strategies finalized to increasing the students' motivation to learn, reducing the sense of isolation and improving their attainment. The use and sharing of different stimulus materials, together with the work developed in collaboration using instruments of digital communication, have been defined as the most advantageous involvement strategies, along with project work and the proposal of case studies have been particularly significant for relating different concepts to one another and applying them in real situations.

Within the scope of integrated didactics, the use of several media within a multimodal perspective [14] valorizes the different methods of achieving knowledge. Indeed, recourse to challenging materials stimulates the elaboration of new ideas [3]. In this sense, there is a growing convergence between linguistic mediators (visual, audio, gestural) that, connected to the spaces (physical and digital) enable the students to construct important conceptual-logical bridges [15–17]. Indeed, learning becomes more meaningful when the ideas, the words and the abstract concepts are associated to images, sounds and to corporeity [18, 19]. In this regard, sectoral studies show how students achieve the best results when they are provided with contents through, for example, the use of visual languages such as images, videos, diagrams, graphs [20, 21]. Furthermore, the images can contribute to activating pre-knowledge, to developing problematization skills, to creating connections, besides stimulating emotional and motivational intelligence [22–24].

2 Method

A multiple-cases approach was adopted [25] to compare three different study cases that are situated within the scope of university teaching[1] focusing attention on the declination of specific didactic strategies with reference to categories such as presence-distance and synchronous-asynchronous modality. The sample involved 370 students altogether.

1) The first study case was conducted within the scope of course in Museum Didactics of the three-year degree Social and Cultural Educator and course in Iconography and Iconology of the single Cycle Degree in Primary Teacher Education of the University of Bologna. The reference is to an experience of arts-based learning developed remotely on a specific technological platform; the languages used are mainly visual (paintings, photographs, performances…).
2) The second case was performed within the laboratory of Didactic Technologies and was addressed to fourth year students of the degree in Primary Education Science of the University of Bologna. The students were involved between attendance and distance learning and according to a flipped learning approach, exploiting the opportunities offered by Moodle, by online software of multimedia presentations (Prezi and Powtoon) and by YouTube as a social environment of archiving and sharing.
3) The third case study was performed within the laboratory of professional specialization of the postgraduate degree in Education of the University of Bologna. The reference is to the role-playing strategy tested remotely, on a technological platform (Teams).

The data were collected both by means of final questionnaires and observation made *in itinere* by teacher of course/laboratories on the trends of the intermediate feedback provided by the students, in relation to the assigned tasks. For the collection and return of these comments, a chart freely inspired by the SWOT matrix was shared, applied to each strategy in order to identify their strengths and weaknesses, their opportunities and risks.

Each case will be described hereunder, carefully examining its working and its activities. Indeed, as Stake [25] underline: "Qualitative understanding of cases requires experiencing the activity of the case as it occurs in its contexts and in its particular situation".

3 Results and Discussion

3.1 Arts Based Learning

The first study case led to the testing of an experience focused on Art-Based Learning (ABL) finalized to promoting art-based learning through different expressive forms in view of learning styles [26, 27]. The reference is to the application of "teaching strategies where there is significant learner involvement with art forms" [28]. Reference is made specifically to the intentional use of artistic skills, processes and experiences as

[1] "For multicase research, the cases need to be similar in some ways" [25].

Table 1. Arts-based learning

Work phases
Presentation of the activity to clarify the aims, illustrate the activities, reflect in groups (Teams – synchronous modality)
Autonomous use of visual contents drawn from the art world shared on a technological platform (Moodle – asynchronous modality)
Identification by each of student of an artistic work with which to relate activating the sensorial channels evoked by the image itself (Teams – synchronous modality)
Initial feedback: sharing in a large group by means of brainstorming key words/thoughts/emotions evoked by the image (Teams – synchronous modality)
Reinterpretation and design of a new aesthetic production in small groups through different languages (narrative, musical, performative and photographic, audiovisual). (Teams – synchronous modality – Moodle – asynchronous modality).
Feedback *in itinere*: sharing the works/work in progress on the platform (Teams)
Creation of a digital environment for the presentation/communication of the new aesthetic productions (MOdE-synchronous and asynchronous modality)
Final feedback in the large group (Teams – synchronous modality).

Activities
Autonomous use of the images of some artworks made available on the platform
Sensorial/emotive reading of the visual material
Brainstorming in large groups
Work in small groups
Reinterpretation of a work through performance and graphic-pictorial re-elaborations
Creation of digital environments for the presentation/communication of new aesthetic productions
Presentation to large groups

Materials, tools and digital environments
Teams platform for the video-lectures in synchronous modality
Moodle platform for the use and study of the materials
Visual stimulus materials (reproductions of stimulating works of art)
App for the graphic production/re-elaboration of visual and video contents
MOdE-Museo Officina dell'Educazione for the creation of the artifacts

Working time organization
The asynchronous and individual work is alternated with the synchronous one in small groups and in large groups
The hours of work in synchronous modality are for encounter/restitution and co-construction; the hours of work in asynchronous modality are for individual viewing/reading/analysis of the proposed materials.

Teacher's Role
The teacher chooses the materials and organizes the activities.
The teacher conducts the brainstorming and supports the discussion and the analysis
The teacher guides and supports the students' choices
He/she supervises the works and monitors the intermediate results *in itinere*
He/she conducts the final communication phase

educational instruments to foster learning in non-artistic disciplines and sectors[2]. The aim is to involve the students on the cognitive, socio-relational and aesthetic-affective levels, using the arts (visual, musical, performative…) as means through which the imagination, creativity and innovation find expression, giving rise to processes of transformative learning [29]. The students can take part by creating their own artistic product or by interacting with the works of other artists. Two of the most used approaches are the project thinking process and the visual thinking strategies. Both forms can: lead to involving experiences on the emotional level and transformative on the cognitive level; promote creative thinking and the problem-solving capacities; increase the observation and collaboration capacities while working inside groups; enhance emotional intelligence competencies [30, 31]. Further, art-based learning can help students to develop confidence and self-esteem and to construct effective communication and socio-relational competencies.

Art-based learning can take place in a physical (classroom, laboratory, museum space, workshop) or digital space. In this specific case, art-based learning was conducted online via the use of digital platforms, Teams, Moodle, MOdE-Museo Officina dell'Educazione on which the students worked in synchronous and asynchronous modalities. The realization of the ABL experience developed according to four macro-phases: 1. the autonomous use of visual contents drawn from the art world; 2. the choice by each student of a work with which to come into a sensorial relationship; 3. the realization of a new aesthetic production; 4. the creation of a digital environment. The experience consisted of the continuous production of intermediate feedback by the students stimulated by the lecturer, provided by comments expressed by the spoken word (microphone) or in written form (chat). From the analysis of the answers in the chat revealing elements emerged both in terms of the valorization of the participative dimension and of "reciprocal listening", and in terms of valorization of the sensorial, aesthetic-affective dimension, and in terms of construction of new semantic connections (Table 1).

[2] The Art of Science Learning examined the interrelationship between art-based learning and innovation and creativity in STEM (science, technology, engineering and mathematics) students and professionals (https://www.artofsciencelearning.org/). Furthermore, art-based learning can be effectively incorporated in the medical training for future doctors to develop critical thinking and collaborative capacities and to increase their confidence levels [32].

3.2 Flipped Learning

The second case is an experience of laboratory activities structured according to the rationale of the flipped learning, freely adapted to respond to the characteristics of the specific training activity, with moments of access to materials for distance learning and students in attendance. The work also envisaged, according to the rationale of flipped learning, tasks to be performed individually or in pairs or in small groups, moments of shared reflection, problem-solving and public presentations [4, 33, 34]. The laboratory, thought of for future teachers and addressed to students in their fourth year of Primary Education Science, seeks to arouse a reflexive/critical attitude in respect to the use of the digital image and the multimedia/audio-visual language in the contexts of teaching/learning. It also has the objective of testing environments/instruments for the presentation of concepts in the form of multimedia map or animated product. For this the students tested the use of Prezi for the production of animated concept maps, and Powtoon, for multimedia presentations with small animations. The reflection on such instruments came in the light of the concepts of multimediality/multimodality and with particular attention to the relationship between digital artifacts, didactic mediation [21, 35–37] and visual thinking [19, 38, 39].

For the sharing of the products made YouTube was chosen, a clear example of how a digital environment for diffusion and sharing can influence one's personal productive capacities by becoming a de facto social network. At the basis of a laboratory set-up of this kind there is indeed the belief that the environment in which one operates to distribute, archive and share the products made, also conditions the didactic relationship and the learning process. In the case of YouTube, the students/teachers must learn to move in a strongly multimedia environment and one having a great impact for distance relations, being a matter of an instrument with all the characteristics of a social network [40].

From the analysis of the observation provided by the students during the pathway, three elements were highlighted: 1. the situation created was defined as "shared learning", in which there was not the concern of giving the right or the wrong answers but the need to share the thoughts of each one so as to reach conclusion enriched by the remarks of the many; 2. the type of commitment required was defined by some as "research", highlighting how the people were driven to put themselves into play to find solutions autonomously to problems that progressively arose; 3. the situation in attendance was experienced as stimulating and the remote commitment as necessary (Table 2).

3.3 Role-Playing

The third case – Inside a laboratory of professional specialization addressed to educationists held on a distance-learning platform two experiences of role-playing were carried out in Teams. The role-playing technique, which sinks its roots in the Morenian psychodrama as therapeutic technique, lends itself to an articulated and different use depending on the context, the objectives and the addressees [41]. In the case of the Laboratory of specialization it was deemed important to support the students in their pathway of learning, which specifically concerned the laboratory of project competence, but above all put play the learning of competencies and functions of the educationist within the

Table 2. Flipped learning

Work phases
In-class attendance (4 hours) to clarify the objectives, illustrate the activities, reflect in group by means of brainstorming.
At home: use of video documentations (provided by the teacher on the platform) of activities in *flipped learning* with the use of maps and multimedia presentations. Questions and thoughts are to be noted at the same time.
In-class attendance (4 hours): in-class discussion and analysis of the *flipped learning* strategy and on the use of multimedia presentations.
At home: use of multimedia presentations (provided by the teacher on the platform) with the task of choosing one as an example for his/her own creation in pairs in class.
In-class attendance (4 hours): in pairs or in small groups tests with the use of Prezi and Pow-toon and design of a multimedia presentation.
In-class attendance (4 hours): creation of a short multimedia presentation.
At home: use of YouTube channels by teachers ad design of one's own channel.
In-class attendance (4 hours): pair activities or in small groups with YouTube.
In-class attendance (4 hours): presentation of one's own work.

Activities
Individual viewing at home of audiovisual and multimedia materials.
Individual exercises.
Pair work.
Group discussion in attendance.
Production of multimedia materials.
Presentation of one's own product to the class.

Materials, tools and digital environments
Network systems for the sharing of materials and management of distance communication flows.
Multimedia and audiovisual materials.
Software for the production of conceptual maps and multimedia presentations.
LIM in class.
YouTube for the publication and the sharing.

Work time organization
Individual work at home is alternated with that in classroom attendance
The hours of presence are Laboratory hours, the hours at home are counted as individual study.

Teacher's role
The teacher becomes a tutor, a facilitator, a guide for the laboratory, group or individual experiences.
He/she choose the materials, organizes the activities, prepares personalized pathways.
He/she conducts brainstorming sessions and debates for the in-class checking of exercises and for a shared reflection on the topics dealt with in the videos.

pathway of the social planning. The learning of the role requires putting into play one's own reflexive competencies in contact with acting, that is Reflection-in-action [42]. From this need arises the decision to draw on the role-playing instrument, a ductile instrument, that can act as a go-between in the construction of experiences for the students. The two role-playing experiences realized in particular were of the structured role-playing type [43, 44]. Aim of the exercise was to let the students experience some competences relating to the project; in particular, the first role playing was mostly focused on the phase of detection and analysis of the problem and on the direct involvement of the actors on the field; the second role playing was mostly addressed to the management of the conflict within the project group and to the definition of the objectives.

The pathway was articulated in this way: 1. Initial presentation of the main contents of the project; 2. Realization of the role playing; 3. Elaboration in the Teams classroom of impressions, consideration, learning on the role playing. These three moment were repeated (synchronously via Teams) for each one of the role-playing experiences. 4. Elaboration of the group's training balance: synchronous encounter via Teams was dedicated to the group's training balance. 5. Drafting of an individual report on the experience: at the end of the whole pathway, each one of the students sent in his/her own report vis-à-vis the pathway, indicating the main learnings, the resources and the difficulties encountered. Specifically concerning the role-playing experience, the customary canvass was followed, with some differences: the figure of the observer was not defined (everyone observes in real-time), the preparation of the role-playing came about in subgroups divided by role to be studied, via Teams; the viewing of the game was then strongly focused on the players' view (the "thumbnails" that opened on the Teams screen).

From the analysis of the responses and the observations, we can infer that: 1. Before and during the role-play many interventions by the participants were recorded; many students report that they had been able to better overcome their shyness. 2. The role-playing methodology was much appreciated as a way to deal with the critical aspect of a real project group context. 3. There were difficulties, reported by the students themselves, in working in the online subgroups in preparation for the role-playing. In a general sense, the group of students have positive evaluations bearing in mind the exceptional circumstances of the, but they also reported the peculiarity of the situation (the whole pathway was undertaken remotely), which did not allow people to "know each other in person".

The Teams medium, that is the distance modality, besides fostering the intervention of many people, also allowed the participants' responses to be recorded in timely fashion, with a further analysis of the outcomes around the figure of the pedagogist, observed from different angles (Table 3).

Table 3. Role-playing

Work phases
Initial presentation of the work contents and of the Role-Playing methodology
Realization of the role-playing: preparation, enactment, action, conclusion.
Live group discussion via Teams synchronously and collection of impressions via chat
Individual elaboration at home of the experience by means of a document sent to the teacher

Activities
Initial presentation of the text, first collection of impressions
Student's self-candidature for a role
Work in subgroups divided by role; choice of the player and the contents to bring
Realization of the role-playing: enactment, action, conclusion
Initial collection of spontaneous impressions
Group debate and elaboration of the method and contents.

Materials, tools and digital environments
Before and during: written text on which to perform the role-playing
Siteography and reference bibliography for home

Work time organization
All of the laboratory pathway is performed via Teams
At the end, the student drafts an essay on the experience.

Teacher's role
The teacher leads the pathway. In the specific case of role-playing he7she acts to construct a methodological setting, with materials, schedules, activities for the preparation and leading of the game. In the end, he/she provides a critical elaboration of what has taken place.
During the role-playing, the teacher acts to detect, observe, record what is happening.
He/she conducts a brainstorming session, a conclusive debate, fosters the critical elaboration of what has happened; he/she uses reading competencies of the group dynamics and elaboration and reflection on the professional practices.

4 Results and Discussion

4.1 Arts-Based Learning

The art-based learning module provided for a didactic structure developed remotely, via activities performed in synchronous (Teams) and asynchronous (Moodle, MOdE) modality, by means of an individual work (use of materials), in small groups (design and construction of artifacts, creation of digital environments) and large groups (brainstorming, moments of shared analysis, presentation/communication of the artifacts).

The following table (Table 4) collects a summary of the main elements emerging from the observations left by the students in the Teams chat and/or final questionnaire of teaching satisfaction.

Table 4. Arts-based learning. SWOT analysis

Strengths	Weaknesses
- I was able to come to terms freely with visual contents without prejudice - The activities proposed allowed me to connect theory with practice - I had the chance to work in groups - I was able to communicate via different languages and expressive forms	- Often spaces of creative construction shared with the other companions were lacking - The corporeal relationship was missing both with the works proposed and with the companions - I found it rather hard to participate in the activities of creative re-elaboration proposed owing to the fact that I am not very skilled in using the instruments and programs needed for the creations
Opportunities	Threats
- Development of the fanta-cognitive/creative dimension - Motivating feedback (not only for the teacher, but also the groups sustain each other reciprocally via intermediate feedback) - Development of the collaborative and cooperative dimension within the group/groups	- The students are concerned with the creative capacities - Fear of not being able owing to a lack of art knowledge - Impossibility to participate owing to technical difficulties

Reflecting on the risks and elements of weakness emerging from the students' reflections, we tried to highlight some recommendations to improve the ABL experiences (Table 5).

Table 5. Recommendations drawn from the analysis of the experience

Recommendations to limit the risks and exploit the opportunities
- Not focusing one's attention on the artistic perfection but on the creative expression and on the process of learning. - Providing few images to start up the reflection. - Giving more space inside the groups to moments of discussion/reflection. - Providing the students with the time needed to elaborate the whole experience and the emotions evoked by the images. - Suggesting spaces/environments in which to share and re-elaborate the material. - Suggesting instruments/applications for the graphic-pictorial re-elaboration. - Proving the assistance or guidance necessary to the students during the whole experience.

4.2 Flipped Learning

The 24-h laboratory was designed, as we have seen, according to the flipped learning rationale, including in the didactic structure the hours that are usually dedicated to the activity of free study at home. The use of the materials and the activities of production of multimedia artifacts are developed between remote and in attendance. the work also provided for assignments to be done individually, in pairs or in small groups, moments of shared analysis, problem-solving and public presentations.

The following Table (Table 6) collects a synthesis of the main elements emerging from the analyses developed with the students during the laboratory

Table 6. Flipped learning. SWOT analysis

Strengths	Weaknesses
- The phase of ideation and search for solutions is easier, as there is time dedicated to such an activity (such as individual distance work) - The discussion in class on what was done at home gives confidence and is stimulating - To work in pairs it is necessary to find useful mediations for learning new things	- The degree course requires many hours in the classroom and it is hard to find the time to carry out the required tasks - Working in pairs requires a harmony that is not always straightforward to find when we don't know each other - Even at home at times it is necessary to find the way to discuss things with others
Opportunities	Threats
- The type of activity required at home consists in reflecting on contents without the anxiety of having to be judged - In the classroom I am stimulated to pay attention - You can also make a mistake because the work is a research one - Working with others one can overcome one's own fears with regard to the use of instruments one doesn't know	- Not finding the time needed at home. - Letting yourself be demoralized looking at the proposed videos thinking you aren't good enough - Getting stuck owing to the technical difficulties

Reflecting on the risks and elements of weakness emerging from the students' observations we have tried to highlight some recommendations to improve the application of the method (Table 7).

4.3 Role-Playing

The laboratory was set up wholly by means of the Teams platform in synchronous modality. The duration was 24 h and involved students on the master's degree course in Education. During the pathway, the students left comments in the chat in relation to the experience performed, and at the end of the pathway they sent off an individual report; from those materials we have gathered some of the following considerations (Table 8).

Table 7. Recommendations drawn from the analysis of the experience

Recommendations to limit the risks and exploit the opportunities
The material to be used at home autonomously must not be too complex. If it is video these should be short (10 minutes at most); very short clips are useful as well.
It is necessary to have a shared environment (e.g. Moodle) where the teacher can suggest the selected products, listing them in a structured way to facilitate their comprehension and with introductory or explicatory notes.
The observation of the videos must be accompanied by an activity of annotation of doubts and queries by the student, to be addressed to the teacher and to the class preferably in attendance.
The pair-work should be constantly followed by the teacher who must play the role of facilitator.
It is very important to share the products created and the use of social networks that enable the creation of an environment of exchange and viewing of the work of others, with the possibility to put everything into connection fostering the realization of a community of practices.

Table 8. Role-playing. SWOT analysis

Strengths	Weaknesses
Very intense work: it was an unexpected way of learning We have been able to intervene more, overcoming any shyness I have been able to optimize the study time, using an experience that otherwise I could not have done In the role-playing you can see the actors' expressions very well	In-class attendance would have allowed us to know each other better as a group Some students, more accustomed to traditional methods, struggled to adapt to the work in subgroups (prior to the play) The actors' proxemics and gestures were lacking It was not possible (owing to the synchronous presence of the whole group) to use the figure of the observer, who has a particular role in the role-playing The leader was not able to intervene in the role-playing by means of some possible modalities (the technique of the "double," and the technique of the "aside")
Opportunities	Threats
The remote role-playing is less daunting, it is easier to intervene and make observations via the chat The working time is more concentrated. The observation of the role-playing is more focused in the action	Scarce analysis in the preparation of the game (the so-called "enactment" cannot be developed") It is harder to keep the boundaries, in the action, between those who play the role and those who instead must only observe (everyone is present in the Teams screen view) The actors can have greater difficulty to "separate" from the context: they have no way to "turn their backs" to the audience

In conclusion, we present some recommendations to performing a role-playing online (Table 9).

Table 9. Recommendations drawn from the analysis of the experience

Recommendations to limit the risks and exploit the opportunities
• Defining carefully the timing of the game, also envisaging a greater "dispersion" in the preparation prior to the action. • Reinforcing the dimensions of the setting that allow for the definition of the players' roles and vice-versa that of the observers, for example asking the observer to turn off the cameras and not to use the chat during the action. • Asking for immediate feedback by means of the chat following the role-playing. • Conducting the role-playing with minimal ad hoc interventions.

5 Conclusions

The comparative analysis of the three cases shows how the didactic strategies have become an attendance-distance integrated didactics, to improve the level of involvement but also to foster the development of the situated knowledge. In these situations, the technologies do not merely have the instrumental role of allowing the students to participate in the lesson but become environments in which to participate in the development of the learning process, in which different experiential, emotive and cognitive worlds contribute.

Within the scope of a model of integrated didactics, these three cases have shown how the digital environment is configured not as a treasure trove of didactic resources to be studied at home, not as a web conference space for the video-lectures, but as an environment capable of supporting the three didactic strategies tested. Specifically, the students are enabled to use the strategies to construct new meanings, to intervene and make observations via the chat; to reflect on the contents without the fear of being judged; to overcome their own anxieties in respect to the use of instruments/applications that they did not know before; to express themselves/communicate through the use of different languages and expressive forms.

References

1. Kanchanachaya, N.: Development of a blended learning model based on creative problem solving principles using lateral thinking to enhance creative problem solving abilities for instructional media production of pre-service teachers. Chulalongkorn University, Bangkok (2012)
2. Bonaiuti, G.: Le strategie didattiche. Carocci, Roma (2014)
3. Seechaliao, T.: Instructional strategies to support creativity and innovation in education. J. Educ. Learn. **6**(4), 201–208 (2017)

4. Panciroli, C., Corazza, L., Vignola, P., Marcato, E., Leone, D.: Didattica innovativa. Soluzioni efficaci per contesti complessi. FORM@RE **18**(2), 116–129 (2018)
5. Panciroli, C.: Per una didattica integrata: il modello CLAS. In: Panciroli, C. (ed.) Animazione digitale per la didattica, pp. 19–33. FrancoAngeli, Milano (2020)
6. Maturana, H.R., Varela, F.: Autopoiesi e Cognizione. Marsilio, Venezia (1980)
7. Rivoltella, P.C.: La previsione. Neuroscienze, apprendimento, didattica. Editrice La Scuola, Brescia (2014)
8. Panciroli, C.: Innovare le architetture della didattica universitaria. Educ. Sci. Soc. **9**, 39–57 (2018)
9. Rossi, P.G., Giaconi, C. (eds.): Micro-progettazione: pratiche a confronto. PROPIT, EAS, Flipped Classroom. FrancoAngeli, Milano (2016)
10. Banna, J., Lin, M.-F.G., Stewart, M., Fialkowski, M.K.: Interaction matters: strategies to promote engaged learning in an online introductory nutrition course. J. Online Learn. Teach. **11**(2), 249–261 (2015)
11. Lear, J.L., Ansorge, C., Steckelberg, A.: Interactivity/community process model for the online education environment. J. Online Learn. Teach. **6**(1), 71–77 (2010)
12. Chickering, A.W., Gamson, Z.F.: Seven principles for good practice in undergraduate education. AAHE Bull. **39**(7), 3–7 (1987)
13. Martin, F., Bolliger, D.U.: Engagement matters: student perceptions on the importance of engagement strategies in the online learning environment. Online Learn. **22**(1), 205–222 (2018)
14. Kress, G.: Multimodality: a Social Semiotic Approach to Contemporary Communication. Routledge, London (2010)
15. Lacelle N., Boutin J.-F., Lebrun M.: La littératie médiatique multimodale appliquée LMM@. Presses de l'Université du Québec, Québec (2017)
16. Ragone, G., Ilardi, E., Tarzia, F.: Verso la blended education Riflettendo su immaginari, media e apprendimento. Mediasc. J. **5** (2015)
17. Panciroli, C., Macauda, A.: Feedback images in university teaching. FORM@RE **19**, 234–246 (2019)
18. Calvani, A.: Principi di comunicazione visiva e multimediale. Fare didattica con le immagini, Carocci, Roma (2011)
19. Cicalò, E.: Intelligenza Grafica. Aracne, Roma (2016)
20. Benedek, A.: The imagistic turn in education: opportunities and constraints. In: Proceedings of International and Interdisciplinary Conference IMMAGINI? Image and Imagination between Representation, Communication, Education and Psychology, vol. 1, p. 855 (2017)
21. Panciroli, C., Corazza, L., Macauda, A.: Visual-graphic learning. In: Cicalò, E. (ed.) IMG 2019. AISC, vol. 1140, pp. 49–62. Springer, Cham (2020). https://doi.org/10.1007/978-3-030-41018-6_6
22. Goleman D.: Intelligenza emotiva. Adelphi, Milano (1995)
23. Tuffanelli, L. (ed.): Intelligenze, emozioni e apprendimenti. Le diversità nell'interazione formativa, Erikson, Trento (1999)
24. Balboni, E.P.: Il ruolo delle emozioni di studente e insegnante nel processo di apprendimento e insegnamento linguistico. EL.LE **2**(1), 7–30 (2013)
25. Stake, R.E.: Multiple Case Study Analysis. London, The Guildford Press, New York (2006)
26. Bradley, J., Moore, E., Simpson, J., Atkinson, L.: Translanguaging space and creative activity: theorising collaborative arts-based learning. Lang. Intercult. Commun. **18**(1), 54–73 (2018)
27. Zakaria, Z., Setyosari, P., Sulton, S., Kuswand, D.: The effect of art-based learning to improve teaching effectiveness in pre-service teachers. J. Educ. Gifted Young Sci. **7**(3), 531–545 (2019)
28. Rieger, K.L., Chernomas, W.M.: Arts-based learning: analysis of the concept for nursing education. Int. J. Nurs. Educ. Scholarsh. **10**(1), 53–62 (2013)

29. Brenner, M.Y.: Art based learning and leadership development: a case studi. Columbia (2010). https://pqdtopen.proquest.com/doc/816838065.html?FMT=AI
30. Goldman, K., Yalowitz, S.,Wilcox, E.: The impact of arts-based innovation training on the creative thinking skills, collaborative behaviors and innovation outcomes of adolescents and adults. National Research Foundation. Audience Viewpoints Consulting, Herndorn (2016)
31. Seifter, H.: Proof of impact: arts-based learning leads to improvements in creative thinking skills, collaborative behaviors and innovative outcomes. The Art of Science Learning (2016)
32. De la Croix, A., Rose, C., Wildig, E., Willson, S.: Arts-based learning in medical education: the students' perspective. Med. Educ. **45**, 1090–1100 (2011)
33. Maglioni, M.: Capovolgiamo la scuola. Le cinque leve Flipnet per un nuovo sistema educativo. Erickson, Trento (2018)
34. Maglioni, M., Biscaro, F.: Innovare la didattica con la flipped class-room. Trento, Erickson (2014)
35. Rossi, P.G.: Gli artefatti digitali e i processi di mediazione didattica. Pedagogia Oggi **2**, 11–26 (2016)
36. Rivoltella, P.C., Rossi, P.G. (eds): L'agire didattico. Manuale per l'insegnante. La Scuola, Brescia (2017)
37. Panciroli, C.: Ecosistemi digitali. In: Corazza, L. Apprendere con i video digitali. Per una formazione online aperta a tutti, pp. 13–32, FrancoAngeli, Milano (2017)
38. Arnheim, R.: Il pensiero visivo. Einaudi, Torino (1974)
39. Floridi, L.: La logica e il pensiero visivo. Iride **24**(2), 343–358 (1998)
40. Corazza, L.: Apprendere con i video digitali. Per una formazione online aperta a tutti. Milano, FrancoAngeli (2017)
41. Schutzenberger, A.: Moreno Jacob Levi. In: Barus-Michel, J., Enriquez, E., Lévy, A. (eds.) Dizionario di psicosociologia, pp. 228–236. Raffaello Cortina, Milano (2005)
42. Schön, D.A.: Il Professionista riflessivo: per una nuova epistemologia della pratica professionale. Dedalo, Bari (1993)
43. Capranico, S.: Role Playing. Manuale a uso di formatori e insegnanti. Raffaello Cortina, Milano (1997)
44. Masci, S.: Giochi e role playing per la formazione e la conduzione dei gruppi. FrancoAngeli, Milano (2017)

New Perspectives for Using the Model of the Use and Acceptance of Technology in Smart Teaching

Giusi Antonia Toto(✉) and Pierpaolo Limone

University of Foggia, Foggia, Italy
giusy.toto@unifg.it

Abstract. This article intends to investigate the theme of mental representations, perceptions and visions of teachers with respect to the use of digital technologies in the classroom. The UTAUT questionnaire was administered to a sample of 350 teachers during a training course in ICT in the period between September 2019 and January 2020. Descriptive and inferential statistical analyses were conducted through the use of the t-test, correlation and ANOVA. The results that emerged describe a strong relationship between resistance to the use of technology and years of service or gender of respondents. The purpose of this article is to provide an innovative look at the research into the use of digital technologies in the school context.

Keywords: UTAUT · Smart teacher · ICT · Acceptance technology · E-learning

1 Introduction

The Unified Theory of Acceptance and Use of Technology (UTAUT) emerges and presents itself as an extension of the primitive TAM model (Fig. 1) developed by Davis and enriched with two further constructs, namely *social influence* and *facilitating conditions.*

Both in the first TAM model and in its second revision of 1989, social factors remained excluded, still considered external variables not relevant for the assessment of the acceptance of technological innovations. In this way, not only social factors acquire considerable importance, but the UTAUT model aims to explain the end user's intentions to use technology and to foresee the real decisions and behaviours in relation to the use/non-use of the physical and virtual equipment. To determine behaviour following the adoption of technological innovations, this model considers four fundamental dimensions which determine the intentions of use. These dimensions are performance expectancy, effort expectancy, social influence and facilitating conditions. Furthermore, it should be noted that variables related to gender, age, experience, and voluntariness mediate the impact of the four fundamental dimensions on the intention of use and behaviour.

L. S. Agrati et al. (Eds.): HELMeTO 2020, CCIS 1344, pp. 115–125, 2021.
https://doi.org/10.1007/978-3-030-67435-9_9

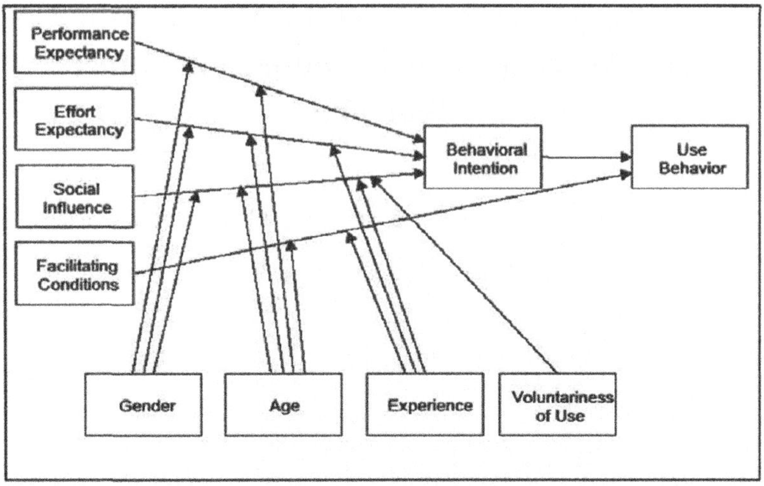

Fig. 1. UTAUT – source: Venkatesh, (2003, p. 194).

The models proposed so far (Table 1) make it clear how in a twenty-year period (1990–2010) the technology acceptance theory was created starting with instances sometimes in stark contrast and incorporating increasingly complex dimensions and aspects. The confluence of different knowledge and sciences has enriched the epistemological background of the theory, still in the process of definition. An unpublished version of the UTAUT questionnaire, translated and adapted to the Italian school context, is now proposed. As a matter of fact, there have been several experiments of the model in Italian organisational contexts [1, 2] but a validated version had not yet been produced in the educational context. The effective use of technologies in educational contexts depends on its acceptance, which represents a prerequisite and at the same time a critical factor for the improvement of the learning process [3]. Birch and Irvine [4] explored the factors that influence teachers' acceptance of the integration between information and communication technologies (ICT) and classroom teaching. In line with the foregoing, the Unified Theory of Acceptance and Use of Technology (UTAUT), developed by Venkatesh et al. [5], shows a greater construct validity compared to the previously presented models and has reasonably predicted the teachers' intention of use. The key roles of performance expectancy, effort expectancy, social influence and facilitating conditions in the dynamics of technology acceptance by teachers clearly emerges from the authors' reflections. Schools attempt to integrate ICT into teaching processes, in increasingly complex patterns, to improve the teaching strategies adopted. The didactic innovation makes the teacher once again the main responsible during the management and monitoring phases of the students' learning to achieve educational success. The conclusions of a recent experiment conducted by Radovan and Kristl [6] confirmed that the introduction of digital technologies in current teaching models is subject to the acceptance and willingness of teachers to use these innovative tools. Finally, in addition to the instrumental value of technology, a fundamental element is also represented by the presence of virtual learning

Table 1. Overview theories about technology acceptance

Theory	Construct	Reference model
Technology Acceptance Model of Davis (1989) TAM Technology Acceptance Model	Perceived Usefulness Perceived Ease of Use	Evolution of the Reasoned Action Theory BET and Motivational Model MM
Combination Theory of planned bahaviour (TPB) e Tam (Taylor e Todd)	Attitude Toward Behavior Subjective Norm Perceived Behavioral Control Perceived Usefulness	Combination with the Reasoned Action Theory TRA and Tachnology Acceptance Model TAM
PC use model (MPCU)	Job Fit Complexity Social factor Long-term Consequences Affect towards Use Facilitating Conditions	Human Behavior Theory of Triandis
Innovation diffusion Theory (IDT)	Relative Advantage Ease of Use Image Visibility Compatibility Results Demonstrability Voluntariness of Use	Innovation diffusion Theory of Rogers
Social Cognitive Theory of computer utilization	Outcome Expectations – Performance Outcome Expectations – Personal Self-efficacy Affect Anxiety	Social cognitive Theory of Bandura
Unified Theory of Acceptance and Use of Technology (UTAUT)	Performance Expectancy Effort Expectancy Social Influence Facilitating conditions	TRA, TAM, TPB, MM (motivational model), Model of Pc utilization (MPCU), IDT e SCT (social-cognitive Theory)

environments, hybridised to school practice that structurally reform this ongoing process. The necessary transition to a dialoguing condition of technology holding together numerous instances, including formal and informal, teaching and learning, has already been outlined by post-constructivism [7], which represents the natural outcome of this complex process that occurred in the time span of thirty years.

2 Method

The UTAUT questionnaire in the original version of Venkatesh, Morris, Davis, and Davis [3] is composed of 31 items and investigates 8 constructs, based on the Unified Theory of Acceptance and Use of Technology (UTAUT) presented in this paragraph. Specifically, the dimensions (Table 2) concern: performance expectancy (PE), effort expectancy (EE), attitude toward using technology (ATUT), social influence (SI), facilitating conditions (FC), self-efficacy (SE).

Tabel 2. UTAUT questionnaire – fonte: Venkatesh, Morris, Davis, e Davis (2003).

	Dimension	Under-size	Numero item
1	Performance Expectation (PE)	PU - Ease of Use (Davis, 1989)	1
		RA - Relative Advantage (Rogers, 2003)	2
		OE - The expectation of results (Compeau and Higgings, 1995)	1
2	Difficulty expectation (EE)	PEU - Perception of Ease of Use (Davis, 1989)	3
		EU - Ease of use (Moore and Bembasat, 1991)	1
3	Attitude to the use of technologies (ATUT)	AtB - Aptitude to Experience Behavior (Fishbein, and Ajzen, 1975)	1
		AtU - Attitude towards use (Thompson et al., 1991)	2
		A - Preference (Compeau and Higgings, 1995)	1
4	Social influence (SI)	SN - Subjective Norms (Ajzen, 1991)	2
		SF - Social factors (Thompson et al., 1991)	2
5	Facilitating Conditions (FC)	PBC - Perceived Behavior Control (Ajzen, 1991)	3
		FC - Facilitating conditions (Thompson et al., 1991)	1
6	Self-efficacy (SE)	SE - self-efficacy (Compeau and Higgings, 1995)	4
7	Anxiety (AN)	AN - Anxiety (Compeau and Higgings, 1995)	4
8	Behavioral Intention to Use a System (B)	B - Behavioral intention (Davis et al., 1989)	3

In this test, subjects are required to answer each question on a Likert-type scale (from completely disagree to completely agree with a range of choices from 1–5).

The sample of this research was recruited 368 teachers (MAge = 38.69, SD = 4.30; F = 315 M = 53) enrolled in a training course for the support of the University of Foggia from different school levels (infancy, primary, secondary I and II grade) who attended a training course in ICT in the period between September 2019 and January 2020. The data collection period spanned a week before the beginning of the training course. The teachers participated voluntary and responded to the battery of questionnaires anonymously. The completion of the battery took approximately 20 min. The questionnaire was translated from English into Italian separately by the Italian authors of this study. The resulting Italian version was then back-translated into English by a native speaker to establish the comparability and to resolve any discrepancies [8].The methodological approach involved descriptive and causal analyses. As for the descriptive analyses, minimum, maximum, means and standard deviations of each score were calculated. The sample was divided into four groups on the basis of the grade of school, i.e., the first group teacher of infancy school (n = 85), the second of primary school (n = 85), the third Secondary of I grade (n = 102) and Secondary of II Grade (n = 96). Mean differences between the two groups were calculated by using independent samples t-test. Bivariate correlations were applied to analyse the associations between the variables of interest. As for the causal analyses, a stepwise linear regression analysis. Data analyses were conducted using SPSS 20.0.

3 Results and Discussion

In the translated and adapted questionnaire, Cronbach's alpha statistical indicator, which measures reproducibility over time and homogeneity of the questions, was used to evaluate the internal consistency or the coherence between items. It refers to the degree of correlation between the analysed variables; in general, if values higher than 0.70 are obtained, a questionnaire has good internal consistency. The same procedure was used in the present study. This value in relation to the 31 items processed shows a very high reliability of 0.834.

Reliability statistics

Cronbach's Alpha	N. of element
,834	31

In the independent-samples t-test, using gender as a grouping variable, differences emerge in relation to items 7, 9 and 12, i.e. in relation to the perception of the use of technology, ease of use and the pleasure of using technology at work, respectively. This demonstrates a difference in the perception and use of technology in the two genders (men and women). Given the small number of male teachers in the sample investigated (due to the specificity of school work), and the considerable sample of women (n = 315), it is evident that even today female teachers have some resistance to digital technology. Conducting the same type of analysis (the general linear model and multivariate tests are used for this comparison) with respect to the variable years of service or substitute, the sample is divided into three macro categories: those who have not had any experience (n = 142), those who have 1 to 8 years of experience, and those who have 10 to 27 years of experience. The greatest differences emerge between the first and third groups and are inversely proportional to the acceptance of technology at school. To demonstrate the strong link between years of experience and resistance to change, this is specifically expressed in the use of technologies at school. The correlations then bring out a strong relationship between age and question 6 'Would it be easy for me to become competent in the use of technology?' and question 8 'Learning to use a new technology is easy for me.' Confidence in the use of technology decreases with increasing age. This is a somewhat different consideration from the reality where digital technology has entered all social contexts and everyday life. The age of the candidates also correlates with question 14, which is linked to the influence of the family context in the use of ICT in the workplace, and with questions 18 and 20, aimed at the acquisition of new technical skills and the effective use of technology [9]. Finally, age correlates strongly with items 25, 27 and 29, in relation to prevention, fear and anxiety about the use of technology in the professional field, as well as from an emotional point of view. This dimension that appeared strong in the first studies on UTAUT is also confirmed in our research on digital technology in the school environment [10]. Furthermore, the relationship between items 1, 2, 3 and 4 with all 31 items in the questionnaire emerges from the analysis of the correlation (Pearson's correlation) between the items (Table 3).

Table 3. Relationship of items 1, 2, 3, 4 with the other test items

	ITEM 1	ITEM 2	ITEM 3	ITEM 4
Significance at the two-tailed 0.01 level	2, 3, 4, 5, 6, 7, 8, 9, 10, 11, 12, 13, 14, 15, 16, 17, 18, 20, 21, 23, 28, 29, 30, 31	1, 3, 4, 6, 8, 9, 10, 11, 12, 14, 15, 16, 17, 18, 20, 21, 23, 29, 30, 31	124 6 8 9 10 11 12 14 15 16 17 18 20 21 28 29 30 e 31	12357 8 9 10 12 13 14 15 16 19 21 22 24 29 30 e 31
Significance at the two-tailed 0.05 level	27	5, 7, 19	23, 26, 27	18, 20, 23

The first four items of the questionnaire relate to the dimension of performance expectation (Table 2). Question 1 follows the 'ease of use' sub-dimension theorised by Davis [11], questions 2 and 3 relate to the 'relative advantage' sub-dimension studied by Rogers [12], and question 4 defines 'expectation of results' elaborated by Compeau and Higgings [13]. Therefore, it seems clear that the main intuition of the creators of the questionnaire is confirmed by this series of data, i.e. the expectation of performance forms the basis of the model of acceptance of the use of technology. Specifically, ease of use represents how difficult the use of a technological innovation is considered to be; the relative advantage is understood as the perception of an innovation that can produce an improvement compared to the previous innovation AND the expectations of results are understood as a consequence of one's own internal behaviours of professional results

Table 4. Anova with gender variable

Model	Sum of squares	Gl	Quadratic mean	F	Sign.
Regression	8,313	33	,252	2,574	,000b
Residue	32,684	334	,098		
Total	40,997	367			

a. Dependent Variable: gender

b. Predictors: (constant), item 31, 19, 5, 24, 20, 9, 15, 11, 13 26, 2, 4, 1, 21, 17, 6, 7, 23 ,28, 22, 3, 16, 10, 25,29, 18, 8, 30, 14, 27, 12.

Coefficients[a]

Model	Not Standardized coefficients B	Not Standardized coefficients Standard error	Standardized coefficients Beta	t	Sign.
1(Costant)	1,888	,198		9,515	,000
Age	,000	,003	-,003	-,051	,959
Years of service or substitute	,007	,004	,100	1,832	,068
1	-,071	,026	-,171	-2,779	,006
2.	,030	,026	,077	1,174	,241
3.	,012	,026	,030	,448	,655
4.	-,011	,019	-,033	-,559	,576
5	,010	,028	,019	,339	,735
6	,059	,027	,157	2,161	,031
7.	,068	,024	,182	2,856	,005
8	-,003	,028	-,009	-,110	,912
9	-,049	,017	-,163	-2,930	,004
10	-,017	,026	-,048	-,671	,503
11	,055	,031	,143	1,758	,080
12	-,086	,032	-,242	-2,685	,008
13	,014	,021	,053	,703	,483
14	,002	,022	,009	,112	,911
15.	-6,320E-5	,017	,000	-,004	,997
16	-,022	,020	-,076	-1,116	,265
17	,012	,024	,033	,493	,622
18	-,049	,028	-,129	-1,735	,084
19	-,035	,016	-,118	-2,170	,031
20	,064	,019	,200	3,427	,001
21	,012	,022	,037	,559	,576
22	,015	,018	,054	,801	,423
23	,012	,018	,041	,643	,521
24	-,043	,019	-,152	-2,288	,023
25	-,011	,018	-,042	-,601	,549
26	,006	,016	,026	,377	,706
27	,025	,026	,086	,989	,323
28	-,016	,027	-,049	-,583	,561
29	,010	,031	,024	,323	,747
30	,024	,028	,067	,854	,394
31	-,043	,028	-,123	-1,555	,121

a. Dependent Variable: Gender

Table 5. Anova with variable years of service

ANOVA[a]

Model		Sum of squares	Gl	Quadratic mean	F	Sign.
1	Regression	1018,117	31	32,842	1,389	,086[b]
	Residue	7945,535	336	23,647		
	Total	8963,652	367			

a. Dependent variable: Years of service or substitute

b. Predictors: (costant), items 31, 19, 5, 24, 15, 10, 13, 20, 9, 28, 2, 17, 4., 6, 1, 26, 21, 7, 23, 22, 3, 16, 11, 25, 29, 18, 8, 30, 14, 27, 12.

Coefficients[a]

Model		Not Standardized coefficients		Standardized coefficients		
		B	Standard errors	Beta	t	Sign.
1	(Costants)	-9,069	3,267		-2,776	,006
	Age	,219	,037	,312	5,832	,000
	1	,626	,383	,102	1,638	,102
	2.	,098	,381	,017	,257	,797
	3.	-,296	,381	-,053	-,777	,438
	4.	,324	,280	,068	1,158	,248
	5	,059	,418	,008	,142	,887
	6	,509	,406	,091	1,254	,211
	7	-,591	,352	-,108	-1,677	,094
	8	-,658	,417	-,121	-1,578	,116
	9	,308	,251	,069	1,227	,221
	10	,513	,379	,097	1,355	,176
	11.	,654	,461	,115	1,417	,157
	12.	-,714	,476	-,136	-1,499	,135
	13	-,033	,304	-,008	-,107	,915
	14	-,077	,325	-,019	-,238	,812
	15	,383	,244	,093	1,572	,117
	16	-,111	,290	-,026	-,384	,701
	17	-1,172	,344	-,227	-3,410	,001
	18	,483	,414	,087	1,166	,244
	19	-,066	,237	-,015	-,279	,780
	20	-,033	,282	-,007	-,118	,906
	21	-,091	,327	-,018	-,277	,782
	22	-,241	,271	-,060	-,888	,375
	23 .	,167	,264	,041	,633	,527
	24	-,167	,282	-,039	-,592	,555
	25	-,260	,268	-,068	-,972	,332
	26	,207	,240	,059	,860	,390
	27	,057	,378	,013	,150	,881
	28	,346	,394	,074	,878	,381
	29	-,213	,459	-,035	-,464	,643
	30	,184	,419	,034	,438	,662
	31	,276	,413	,053	,667	,505
	Sesso	1,474	,804	,100	1,832	,068

a. Dependent variable: Years of service or substitute

and personal achievement. All these components have effects on all the other dimensions investigated, i.e. aptitude for the use of technology, social influence, facilitating conditions, self-efficacy, broad, and behavioural intention to use the system. In the regression analysis, on the other hand, an ANOVA was conducted using the years of service and temporary post as a dependent variable. From the analysis of the results, it emerged that there is a strong correlation between length of service and item 1 'I would like to find a useful technology for my work'. The same significant relationship also forms with the ease of use of technologies and again with items 7 and 8, i.e. the willingness to learn how to use a new technology. In teaching practice, a very strong element that emerged from this analysis is the latent awareness described in item 17, i.e., that of possessing all the cognitive resources necessary to use technology, which therefore only need application and study for the working context. This relationship has the highest significance in the statistical elaborations carried out (Tables 4 and 5).

4 Conclusion

The delicate issue of teachers' mental representations with respect to the use of digital technologies in the classroom has aroused strong interest in the international scientific community which traces further evolution in the studies of recent years. The specialisation of a professional teacher is characterised by constitutive elements: the training and theoretical background (1) specific to the discipline that must teach techniques for the transfer of knowledge, and (2) the application of the knowledge learned. Theory and practice must be in a close and constant empirical relationship to obtain satisfactory and effective professional and individual results [14]. The success of the teaching/learning process occurs through overcoming the gap between theory and practice, since the success of every human action consists of solving real problems through creative solutions. To achieve this goal, a preventive and standardised didactic action is essential, aimed at dialoguing with the contexts to which the subjects belong and proposing unprecedented responses to real educational emergencies. The affirmation of constructivism that started in the 1980s (as a natural continuation of cognitivism) reinforced the idea that every change and knowledge starts from something already acquired. Consistently building and reconstructing personal mental representations becomes, according to this school of thought, vital to the very existence of the learning process [15]. The transition from resistance to technologies in the didactic field to their professional use by teachers is going through a complex process of professional redefinition. Technology, in general, has produced more incisive transformations in playful, relational and social contexts to the point of accentuating the strong pre-existing divergence between intra- and extracurricular reality. The debate initiated by Postman (1979) [16] on the conservativeness of teaching still appeared relevant when teaching technology emancipated itself as an autonomous science, underlining the limen between teaching without technology and technology-centred teaching. Contemporary research still tries to mediate between these two extreme positions: on the one hand, it is argued that technology has no effect on learning, but only represents a modification of the object substrate of the tools for learning [17]. Therefore, there is no difference between a book or a tablet except the format of content presentation. On the other hand, it is the intrinsic characteristics of digital media that produce cognitive modifications and build operational skills compared to traditional teaching, and they are more in step with youths' cultural background. Studies also show that the greatest resistance complained of by teachers regards the actual lack of technological resources, ease of access, and adaptation of the school context to multimedia learning environments [18]. Perceptions also play a role in reinforcing the resistances described; in fact, they are influenced by the personal characteristics of teachers and their motivation, affecting their sense of effectiveness and the real use of ICT in teaching practice. Many scholars have been fascinated by the theme of accepting the use of technologies in a professional context, and numerous theories and interpretative models have emerged from this fruitful debate [19, 20]. Fred Davis, in his pioneering contribution Perceived Usefulness, Perceived Ease of Use, and User Acceptance of Information Technology from 1989, started from reflections of social psychology and adapted the Theory of Reasoned Action (TRA) to the emerging paradigm of Technology Acceptance [13]. In fact, Davis showed how the two constructs – Perceived Usefulness, understood as the ability to advantageously use a particular technology to improve one's work performance, and Perceived Ease of Use, the degree of ease of use of a particular tool that limits it to the maximum effort – were competitors in the acceptance of the use of technology in work contexts.

References

1. Mariani, M.G., Curcuruto, M., Gaetani, I.: Training opportunities, technology acceptance and job satisfaction: a study of Italian organizations. J. Workplace Learn. **25**(7), 455–475 (2013)
2. Limone, P., Toto, G.A.: Peer learning and peer assessment to enhance participation in online courses: a brief theoretical overview of research findings and strategies. In: Examining the Roles of Teachers and Students in Mastering New Technologies, pp. 1–26. IGI Global (2020)
3. El-Gayar, O., Moran, M., Hawkes, M.: Students' acceptance of tablet PCs and implications for educational institutions. Educ. Technol. Soc. **14**, 58–70 (2011)
4. Birch, A., Irvine, V.: Preservice teachers' acceptance of ICT integration in the classroom: applying the UTAUT model. Educ. Media Int. **46**(4), 295–315 (2009)
5. Venkatesh, V., Morris, M.G., Davis, G.B., Davis, F.D.: User acceptance of information technology: toward a unified view. MIS Q. **27**(3), 425–478 (2003)
6. Radovan, M., Kristl, N.: Acceptance of technology and its impact on teachers' activities in virtual classroom: integrating UTAUT and CoI into a combined model. Turk. Online J. Educ. Technol.-TOJET **16**(3), 11–22 (2017)
7. Rossi, P.G.: Tecnologia e costruzione di mondi: post-costruttivismo, linguaggi e ambienti di apprendimento. Armando Editore, Roma (2010)
8. Presser, S., et al.: Methods for testing and evaluating survey questions. Public Opin. Q. **68**(1), 109–130 (2004)
9. Hu, S., Laxman, K., Lee, K.: Exploring factors affecting academics' adoption of emerging mobile technologies-an extended UTAUT perspective. Educ. Inf. Technol. **25**(5), 4615–4635 (2020). https://doi.org/10.1007/s10639-020-10171-x
10. Ifenthaler, D., Schweinbenz, V.: The acceptance of tablet-PCs in classroom instruction: the teachers' perspectives. Comput. Hum. Behav. **29**(3), 525–534 (2013)
11. Davis, F.D.: Perceived usefulness, perceived ease of use, and user acceptance of information technology. MIS Q. 319–340 (1989)
12. Rogers, E.: Diffusion of Innovations, 5th edn. Free Press, New York (2003)

13. Compeau, D.R., Higgins, C.A.: Computer self-efficacy: development of a measure and initial test. MIS Q. 189–211 (1995)
14. Makovec, D.: The teacher's role and professional development. Int. J. Cogn. Res. Sci. Eng. Edu. **6**(2), 33 (2018)
15. Garavaglia, A., Petti, L.: Strategie di uso dello smartphone degli studenti della scuola secondaria di secondo grado = Secondary school students' strategies for using the smartphone. In: Le Società per la società. Ricerca, scenari, emergenze, vol. 3, pp. 40–50. Pensa Multimedia (2020)
16. Postman, N.: Teaching as a conserving activity. Instructor **89**(4), 38–42 (1979)
17. Giancola, O., Grimaldi, E., Romito, M.: La digitalizzazione della scuola. Temi, teorie e metodi di ricerca. Scuola Democratica **10**(3), 461–479 (2019)
18. Carenzio, A., Triacca, S., Rivoltella, P.C.: Education technologies and teacher's professional development. The project Motus (Monitoring Tablet Utilization in School) run by Cremit. REM–Res. Educ. Media **6**(1), 25–38 (2014)
19. Cortiana, P., Barzanò, G.: Docenti e nuove tecnologie: l'esperienza del Teamblogging. Form@re **17**(2), 266–279 (2017)
20. Toto, G.A.: Expertise docente. Teorie, modelli didattici e strumenti innovativi. FrancoAngeli (2019)
21. Toto, G.A., Limone, P.: Hybrid digital learning environments for college student education. In: CEUR Workshop Proceedings (2020)

Learning Between Real and Virtual. Narrative and Cognitive Elaborations of University Teaching

Marco Piccinno(✉)

Università del Salento, Lecce, Puglia, Italy
marco.piccinno@unisalento.it

Abstract. Cognitive styles express the preferential way of engaging personal resources in learning processes and represent one of the most important predictors of success in academic paths. The mental representations of university students related distance and presence learning are in some way related to these styles, which orient personal dispositions towards one or another mode of teaching organization. The present research work explores these representations and identifies the variables that students take as a reference point to establish the personal meaning attributed to the experiences of learning in presence and at at distance.

Keywords: Cognitive style · Meaning · Context

1 Introduction

The didactic action, today more than ever, is called to deal with the transformations that affect the learning project.

The recent events due to the pandemic have prompted the spread of distance learning in university contexts and require a reflection on the formative value of this learning method, as well as that of its comparison with face-to-face teaching systems.

The questions that arise in the didactic field refer both to the choice of content and to the activation of the mental and operational procedures that oversee learning in the two different contexts.

In more specific terms, the questions posed to the research refer to issues concerning the focus of resources, forms of intelligence and the typology of cognitive styles stimulated by the dynamisms acting in such scenarios.

Face-to-face teaching and distance teaching cannot be considered as simple containers of processes that take place independently of the characteristics of the two areas. Presence and distance are not simple "containers" of procedures. They should rather be considered as "frames" [1–4], that is, as a set of presuppositions and conditions from which the meaning of the actions that take place within them is defined.

The fact of engaging paradigmatic or narrative thinking [5–11] one or the other of the multiple forms of intelligence [12–16] or understanding [17], or the dynamisms of a particular cognitive style [18–20] in the learning processes, appears as a consequence

L. S. Agrati et al. (Eds.): HELMeTO 2020, CCIS 1344, pp. 126–138, 2021.
https://doi.org/10.1007/978-3-030-67435-9_10

of the interaction that is established in the two scenarios between personal orientations and configuration of the frames.

The outcome of this interaction is largely affected by the specificity of the situations in which they take place; however, the configurations in which it leads can be placed within a polarized structure on two extremes, one focused on the learning of the elemental elements of the objects of knowledge and the other focused on the representation of the meaning that this object assumes for the subjectivity of the student [21, 22].

The first polarity (focusing on the constituent elements of the object of knowledge) is expressed through epistemic acts incardinated on paths of predicative type [23–25]. The mental operations it promotes are expressed through attributive paths, which consist in the construction of internal representations that connect a set of attributes to a specific object. The logical and linguistic scheme that exemplifies the meaning of such an operation can be identified in the fundamental declarative structure, attributable to the statement "A is B", in which the quality B (the predicate) is assigned to the object A. The dynamism that governs the process is ascribable to paradigmatic thinking [3], which is expressed within cognitive acts oriented towards the thematicization of the "object itself". It encodes the content of knowledge as an entity essentially free from the subjectivity of the knower.

The second polarity (focus on the meaning that the object assumes for subjectivity), is aimed at representing objects of knowledge based on the value they assume for the one who knows them. It takes consistency within epistemic acts that thematicize a content from the meaning that it assumes "for the Self" [21, 22, 26]. The mental operations placed on this polarity are intended to connect knowledge to subjectivity. They introduce into learning the "scenario of consciousness", and, for these reasons, promote content processing not in terms of structure, but in terms of "meaning". The mental resource that governs such elaborations is narrative thinking, which represents the subjective disposition that promotes the genesis of the meanings related to objects of knowledge [3].

The frames that characterize real and virtual learning contexts, as well as the orientation of learning paths towards one or the other polarity, can be identified starting from the linguistic-narrative elaborations that emerge from the testimonies of the students of the university courses. The present survey has explored these dimensions through an instrument divided into two sections.

In fact, these reconstructions make it possible to extrapolate the context configuration, as represented by the subjects acting within them. In this regard, the distinction between paradigmatic thought and narrative thought, already highlighted previously, is particularly fruitful. It allows to structure a set of inducers able to bring out the paradigmatic and narrative representations from which the subjects codify the learning experiences in presence and distance.

The answers provided by students to these questions contain, in fact, a set of elements suitable to identify the perception of the frames and the type of mental operations that they activate when they act in the two contexts. More precisely, the data obtained from the students' reports allow to identify the traits that they recognize as constitutive of both contexts, as well as the orientation of the learning paths on structural elements or dimensions of meaning.

2 Research Methodology

a) Research object

The research focuses on the mental representations of "in presence" and "at distance" learning, detected in a group of 121 undergraduate and master's degree students.

Mental representations can be considered as the result of the attitudes with which students orient themselves towards the product and process variables that structure the didactic action [13, 14]. The characterization of these attitudes is defined with respect to the degree of autonomy that the students seek in the organization of learning paths. While on the one hand there are students who feel comfortable in contexts focused on the teacher's initiative, on the other hand there are students who express the need to learn in contexts that allow the autonomous management of contents and paths.

The degree of preference accorded to one or the other organizational form also appears to be influenced by the configuration of each student's specific cognitive style. The cognitive style indicates the preferential way of engaging personal resources in the performance of teaching tasks, and, according to R. Stenberg [18, 19], allows for the identification of three different categories of subjects:

a) those who like to commit their resources to tasks in which they must move within a set of instructions constructed by others (executive style);
b) those who like to commit their resources to tasks in which they have to produce personal comments and evaluations on products built by others (judicial style);
c) those who like to commit their resources to tasks in which they are called to create something "out of nothing".

The representations of presence and distance learning are presented as the outcome of the interaction between these subjective dispositions (degree of autonomy in the management of processes and products and specific cognitive style of the subjects).

For these reasons, their joint exploration allows for the development of an interpretative model suitable for identifying both the needs and the resources that the subjects are able to activate in comparison with the contexts in which learning takes place.

b) Method of analysis

The survey involved 273 students of the bachelor's and master's degrees. The research tool was administered through the google forms application, and was filled in by 121 students.

The results of the questionnaire were analyzed using the following statistical indices:

a) Correlation between the intensity of each cognitive style and the levels of satisfaction declared by the subjects with respect to learning in presence and at a distance;
b) Identification of the recurring headwords in the narrative processing of learning experiences in presence and at a distance;

c) Identification of the lexical categories relating to the lexical characteristics to which the headwords expressing the perception of students with respect to learning in presence and at a distance refer;
d) description of variables

This survey explored the dimensions described in the previous paragraph, through the administration of a detection tool focused on the following variables:

a) Perception of in-presence learning: it is the dimension that refers to the characteristics that students identify as constitutive of the teaching in presence. It refers to past or ongoing educational experiences.
b) Perception of distance learning: it is the dimension that refers to the characteristics that students identify as constitutive of distance learning. It refers to the educational experience of the previous academic year.
c) background of didactics in presence: it is the dimension that refers to the subjective experience that students experience in learning activities in presence.
d) bakground of distance learning: it is the dimension that refers to the subjective experience that students experience in distance learning activities. It refers to these activities carried out in the previous academic year

The survey also found the "level of liking" declared by students in relation to the two teaching modes (in presence and at distance), as well as the type of their cognitive style.

Cognitive style "non è una abilità, ma piuttosto un modo preferito di usare una abilità. La distinzione tra stile e abilità è cruciale. Una abilità si riferisce al grado di bravura con cui una persona sa fare qualcosa. Uno stile si riferisce al modo in cui a una persona piace fare qualcosa"[1]. Style, therefore, does not refer to the person's resources, but to his preferential way of using those resources.

The research explored the following cognitive styles [19]:

a) Executive style: it is the style of those who prefer to engage personal skills in tasks in which they have people who prefer to act in a system of established rules and conditions;
b) Judicial style: it is the style of those who prefer to engage personal skills in tasks in which they have to make judgments and assessments of tasks and performance performed by others;
c) Legislative style: it is the style of those who prefer to engage personal skills in tasks in which they have to build something "out of nothing", that is, regardless of the rules or what has already been produced by others.

[1] [Cognitive Style] Cognitive style "is not a skill, but rather a preferred way of using a skill. The distinction between style and skill is crucial. A skill refers to the degree of skill with which a person can do something. A style refers to the way a person likes to do something" Sternberg, R. Teorie dell'intelligenza. Una teoria tripolare dell'intelligenza umana, Bompiani, Milano (1987), p. 24 [19] (Translated by Author).

d) These styles were detected in order to explore the correspondence between each of them and the preference declared by students for the two modes of learning (in presence and distance).
c) Metodology of research.

The research was carried out by administering a questionnaire divided into two sections.

The first section consists of the following 8 open-ended questions, of which the English translation is reported:

1. Think about your learning experience in presence and try to describe it briefly (maximum 5 staves). In the end, try to synthesize it all into one or two adjectives that, in your opinion, highlight its characteristics
2. Think about your distance learning experience in the previous academic year and try to describe it briefly (maximum 5 staves). In the end, try to synthesize it all into one or two adjectives that, in your opinion, emphasize its characteristics.
3. Indicate with 5 words those that, in your opinion, represent the strengths of the learning in presence and with 5 other words those of distance learning
4. Indicate with 5 words those that, in your opinion, represent the weaknesses of the teaching in presence and with 5 other words those of distance learning
5. Indicate, on a scale of 1 to 10 (1 minimum score, 10 maximum score) your level of liking of "in presence" learning;
6. Indicate, on a scale of 1 to 10 (1 minimum score, 10 maximum score) your level of liking of "in distance" learning;

The questions in the first section refer to the variables described above, namely:

- Item 1 refers to variable c);
- Item 2 refers to the variable d);
- Item 3 refers to the variable a);
- Item 4 refers to variable b);
- Item 5 refers to the level of liking of "in presence learning";
- Item 6 refers to the level of liking of "at distance learning";

The research procedures explored finally, the orientation of the students towards two fundamental dimensions of didactic action: the dimension of the contents and the dimension of the processes. These variables have been polarized according to the following modalities:

a) Preference for contents decided by the teacher Vs preference for contents decided autonomously by the student;
b) Preference for processes decided by the teacher Vs preference for processes decided autonomously by the students.

The exploration of the contents was proposed through the following item: *Consider the two methods of didactic organization indicated in the following question and indicate with an X the point that corresponds to your level of preference (−10 maximum preference for contents decided by the teacher; +10 maximum preference for learning contents decided independently by you; 0: intermediate preference between one and the other).* The text of the items described below is in English.

-10										0										+10

I prefer learning methods in which the teacher decides the subjects of study.

I prefer learning methods in which I decide the subjects of study.

The exploration of the processes was proposed through the following item: *Consider the two methods of didactic organization indicated in the following question and indicate with an X the point that corresponds to your level of preference (−10 maximum preference for contents decided by the teacher; +10: maximum preference for learning content decided independently by you; 0: intermediate preference between one and the other).* The text of the items described below is in English.

-10										0										+10

I prefer learning modes in which the teacher decides the teaching and learning procedures.

I prefer learning modes in which I dedide the teaching and learning procedures.

The results of this section of the survey were analyzed by arranging them in two dimensions on a system of Cartesian axes which shows the evaluations relating to the "content" variable on the abscissa, and the evaluations relating to the "process" variable on the ordinate (Fig. 1).

The intersection of the axes allows to define four different types of didactic intervention:

Area 1: Contents decided by the student/processes decided by the teacher.

Area 2: Contents decided by the pupil/Processes decided by the student.

Area 3: Contents decided by the teacher/Processes decided by the student.

Area 4: Contents decided by the teacher/Processes decided by the teacher.

The subjects participating in the survey were distributed in their respective quadrants and their answers were grouped into a single group, each relating to a quadrant.

The subsequent operation made it possible to explore the set of recurring characteristics of the subjects located in each section of the Cartesian plane.

The graph in question is focused on the levels of autonomy of the student, which can be identified through 4 different configurations:

a) Maximum autonomy: this is the situation outlined by quadrant 2, in which are placed students who prefer learning context that allow to decide independently both

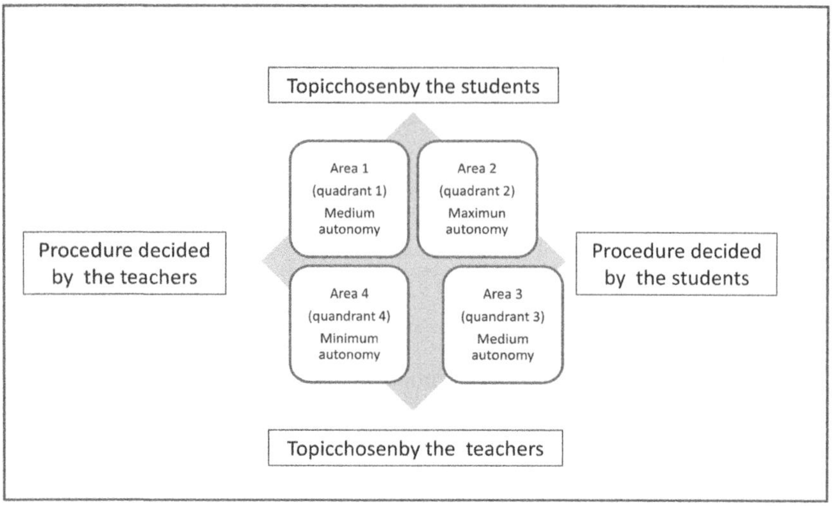

Fig. 1. Level of student's autonomy

the arguments and the learning paths. This sector includes students who, in both variables, have expressed levels of preference from 1 to 10.

b) Minimum autonomy: this is the situation outlined by quadrant 4, in which are placed the students who declare to prefer context in which the is teacher to decide both the topics and the procedures. This sector includes students who, in both variables, have expressed levels of preference from −10 −1.
c) Minimum autonomy (focus on process autonomy): this is the situation outlined by quadrant 3, in which are placed the students who declare that they feel at ease in situations where it is the teacher who decides the content, but it is they who decide the processes. This sector includes students who, in both the "content" variable have expressed preference levels from −10 to −1 and in the process variable, have expressed preference levels from +1 +10.
d) Minimum autonomy (focus on the autonomy of contents): this is the situation outlined by quadrant 4, in which are placed the students who declare they feel comfortable in situations in which the teacher decides the processes, but it is they who decide the contents.
e) This sector includes students who, in the "content" variable, expressed preference levels from 1 to 10 and in the process variable, they expressed preference levels from −10 to −1.

The analysis of the narratives and reports produced by the students interviewed made it possible to highlight, for each quadrant of the graph, some peculiar characteristics that are associated with the relative level of autonomy.

3 Results

The analysis of the headwords highlights the following results.

The headword that finds the greatest number of occurrences in narratives on learning in presence is "relationship", followed by "participation". This didactic model is identified as a form of intervention that allows you to "learn from the teacher's gaze and posture", to "know things through physical closeness with others", to "experience the emotions linked to the knowledge that is presented". It is also identified as a form that supports the community learning experience. Which favors "human contact not only with professors but also with fellow students" [27–30].

The lemma that finds the greatest number of occurrences in narratives on "at distance learning" is "aseptic", followed by "comfortable" and "efficient ". It is perceived as a form of learning without emotional feedback ("it does not make me perceive the emotions connected to topics), which occurs in an indefinite dimension ("they looked like words that came from an unidentified place"), which induces disorientation and a feeling of loss of control of the situation ("I have difficulty in identifying the right way to follow the lesson").

At the same time, however, distance learning is recognized as a form of learning that facilitates the understanding of concepts ("things were clear to me that I have always had difficulty understanding in class"), and which is characterized by make it easier to use the lessons ("it's convenient, because I can follow from home and not worry about bus timetables").

The survey also explored the average of the levels of satisfaction connected to each form of learning, the average of each cognitive style and the correlation between the intensity of cognitive styles and the level of satisfaction of presence and distance teaching declared by the participants.

The cognitive evaluation of the two forms of teaching was detected starting from the data provided by the answers to items 1 and 2, which were classified according to the semantic areas of belonging.

The average level of satisfaction of presence learning in presence is 8,2, while that relating to distance learning is 8.5. The Legislative cognitive style detects an average of 5,23 (maximum value: 8); the Executive style records an average of 4.78 (maximum value: 8); the judicial style records an average of 4.46 (maximum level 8).

The correlation indices between the cognitive styles and the level of satisfaction of the two forms of distance learning are shown in the following tables:

Table 1. Correlation between cognitive styles satisfaction to learning in presence.

Style	Chi sq.	Gdl	p.
Legislative	**143,56**	**120**	**0,07**
Executive	**146,56**	**120**	**0,05**
Judicial	**115,52**	**120**	**0,6**

The satisfaction learning in presence shows positive correlations with all cognitive styles explored by the survey, even if it detects a significant correlation ($p \leq 0.05$) only with the executive cognitive style (Table 1).

The appreciation of distance learning shows positive correlations with all cognitive styles, even if it detects a significant correlation ($p \leq 0.05$) only with the judicial style (Table 2).

Table 2. Correlation between cognitive styles satisfaction to distance learning

Style	Chi sq.	Gdl	p.
Legislative	**124,22**	**120**	**0,3**
Executive	**115,57**	**120**	**0,5**
Judicial	**149,23**	**120**	**0,03**

The positive and negative characteristics ascribed to face-to-face teaching are shown in the following table:

Positive lemmas	Negative lemmas
Engaging	Repetitive
Partecipatory	Boring
Community	Passive
Reassuring	Stiff

The positive and negative characteristics ascribed to distance learning are shown in the following table:

Positive lemmas	Negative lemmas
Convenient	Aseptic
Clarifier	Disorienting
Individualized	Dispersive
Stimulating	Abstract
Varies	Disordered

The data emerging from the correlation indices highlight the following trends:

a) "at Distance learning" is a form of learning particularly suitable for meeting the needs of those who prefer to commit their resources to tasks in which they have to move within pre-established coordinates (Executive Style).
b) "in presence learning" is a form of learning particularly suitable for meeting the needs of those who prefer to commit their resources to tasks in which they have to make personal assessments on learning contents proposed or constructed by others. (Judicial Style) [31, 32].

The quantitative and qualitative data detected by the illustrated procedures were subsequently analyzed on the basis of their distribution in the four quadrants represented by the Cartesian graph which crosses the preferences relating to the content variables with the preferences relating to the process variables (Graph 1).

The subjects who are placed in the first quadrant (moderate autonomy with focus on procedures of learning) are 13% of the total and show a predominantly judicial cognitive style. Above all, they manifest needs related to the mastery of the self-regulation procedures of learning, even if they prefer is the teacher to select the topics, since they consider their preparation inadequate to discern the scientific relevance of the contents. They note a marked preference for the learning in presence, since they consider it as a form of learning that facilitates the acquisition of the procedures necessary to learn knowledge [33–35]. The reason for this choice lies in the fact that they perceive the teacher as a model of scientific competence, whose direct observation allows to acquire the devices and strategies that preside over the understanding of the contents. In this sense, they show a certain preference for the tasks in which they are asked to express personal evaluations on what is proposed by the teacher (Judicial style), in which they recognize both an accreditation and validation agent both of their cognitive operations, and a model to be reproduced in their learning tasks. These subjects declare that they are not comfortable with distance learning, because they believe that this form of organization of learning neutralizes the modeling strategies that represent, instead, their fundamental need.

The Subjects who are placed in the second quadrant (high autonomy) are 40% of the total and are those who declare that they prefer learning situations in which they can decide on both topics and procedures. They express both the need to acquire a clear conceptual profile of knowledge and the need to identify the personal and social value of the same. They declare a marked preference for distance learning, as they consider it a form of learning that better meets their needs. Such students recognize the flexibility and the possibility of declining learning in according to the subjective orientations, as a peculiar characteristic of distance learning. At the same time, they believe that in-present learning is devoid of these caracteristics and declare that this context causes them difficulties difficulties and esperiences of distress. The cognitive style that detects the highest levels of intensity is the judicial one (prevalent in 60% of subjects), even if there is a conspicuous number of students (30%) which detects the highest scores in the legislative one. Decidedly smaller (10%) are the allieviche, in this quadrant, they have an Executive style.

The subjects who are placed in the third quadrant (moderate autonomy with focus on processes) are 30% of the total. They declare the need for a didactic intervention that supports the path of conceptual clarification, but also the need for a learning process that solicits personal elaboration and the shared construction of the meanings of knowledge. Their need for relationships finds its generative reason in the need for a systematic comparison with peers and with the teacher, that involves not so much the emotional dimension, but rather the definition of a clear and defined profile of the learning paths. They believe that these objectives are promoted by learning in presence, which is recognized as a context that facilitates face-to-face exchange and guarantees mutual support in the construction of learning. Almost all the students who are placed in this quadrant have the highest score in the judicial style (87% of subjects).

The subjects who are placed in the fourth quadrant (minimum autonomy, preference for contents and procedures decided by the teacher) are 17% of the total and are those who declare to be at ease in situations in which the teacher decides topics and procedures. The cognitive style that points out the highest scores is the executive one (detected in 80% of the students who are placed in this section), while the students who show higher levels in the other two styles are decidedly lower. They are students who detect a strong need for involvement and direct contact with the teacher and classmates and who show a marked preference for te learning in presence. The students who are placed in this area of the graph consider distance learning as aseptic and without emotional feedback and declare that they have difficulty following the lessons because they cannot see the teacher and cannot feel the proximity of their peers. These subjects also declare that they are unable to identify points of reference and indications in distance learning that can suggest how to organize the study activity, because they are considered lacking the possibility of activating such exchanges. For these reasons, they consider distance learning to be substantially demotivating.

The data point out by the survey, although partial and not yet subject to generalization, allow, however, to highlight some trends.

The distribution of the results in the four quadrants outlined by the intersection of the content and process variables allows some reflection, albeit provisional.

Distance learning is developed as a context suitable to involve the totality of personal dimensions (emotion, volition, cognition), only if students are motivated by needs for clarity and relationship. They identify in this form of organisation the context suitable to satisfy these instances, since they recognize that it allows both autonomy in the choice of content and personal initiative in identifying learning paths (quadrant 2). A confirmation of this conclusion can be found in the fact that those who show a prevalence of the judicial style, they are also the ones who value this form of teaching only if these requirements are safeguarded. On the contrary, when these requests are disregarded (as in the forms of organization identified by quadrant 3), the judicial style, although prevalent, does not allow for an enhancement of distance learning.

When students' requests focus on the acquisition of a study method (quadrant 1), or around the need for relational involvement (quadrant 3) or, again, around the need to acquire teaching contents in a purely replicative way (quadrant 4), the organization model that finds the preferences of these students (who represent 60% of those who answered the questionnaire) is the one in presence. These students, in fact, express a disorienting and dispersive experience of distance learning, since they do not find in it the solicitations or anchor points that can suggest to them the contents, procedures and strategies for obtaining knowledge.

The possibility of recognizing a value in distance learning is largely correlated with the ability of the students to perceive in themselves both the ability to self-regulate learning processes and to elaborate a personal meaning of the contents being studied.

In cases where the students' motivational system does not jointly meet these needs, it does not promote a positive vision of distance learning and, on the other hand, consolidates the positive experience of presence learning. The latter is identified, in these cases, as a context that guarantees a clear presentation of the concepts, an example (identified above all in the teacher) of self-regulation of cognitive paths, a community context of belonging that stems the sense of insecurity deriving from the feeling of not mastering the operations necessary to carry out academic tasks. In any case, it should be emphasized that the representations of distance learning obtained from this survey refer to experiences originated in emergency situations (the pandemic), which did not allow for a complete organization of the relative learning paths.

In any case, these results may represent, as already indicated above, some trend lines, which can provide the reference point for organizing search activities on a larger sample and within distance learning experiences organized in a more complete way.

References

1. Mente e natura, Adelphi, Milano (1979)
2. Bateson, G.: Verso un'ecologia della mente. Adelphi, Milano (1989)
3. Bateson, G.: Questo è un gioco, Cortina, Milano (1996)
4. Mead, G.: Mente, Sé e società. Giunti, Milano (2010)
5. Bruner, J.: Psicologia della conoscenza, Armando, Roma (1976)
6. Bruner, J.: Verso una teoria dell'istruzione, Armando, Roma (1978)
7. Bruner, J.: La mente a pià dimensioni, Laterza, Roma-Bari (1978)
8. Bruner, J.: La ricerca del significato. Per una psicologia culturale, Bollati Boringhieri, Torino (1990)
9. Bruner, J.: La cultura dell'educazione. Feltrinelli, Milano (1997)
10. Smorti, A.N.: Cultura, memorie, formazione del Sé, Giunti, Firenze (2007)
11. Groppo, M., Locatelli M.C.: Mente e cultura. Tecnologie della comunicazione e processi educativi, Raffaello Cortina, Milano (1996)
12. Gardner, H.: Formae mentis. Feltrinelli, Milano (1981)
13. Gardner, H.: La nuova scienza della mente. Storia della rivoluzione cognitiva, Feltrinelli, Milano (1988)
14. Gardner, H.: Sapere per comprendere. Discipline di studio e discipline della mente, Feltrinelli, Milano (2009)
15. McKenzie, W.: Intelligenze multiple e strategie per la didattica, Trento, Erickson (2006)
16. Fodor, J.A.: La mente modulare. Saggio di psicologia delle facoltà, Il Mulino, Bologna (1988)
17. Egan, K.: La comprensione multipla. Erikson, Trento (2012)
18. Sternberg, R.: Teorie dell'intelligenza. Una teoria tripolare dell'intelligenza umana, Bompiani Milano (1987)
19. Sternberg, R.: Stili di pensiero. Differenze individuali nell'apprendimento e nalla sluzione di problemi, Erickson, Trento (1987)

20. Sternberg, R., Grigorienko E.: Misurare il l potenziale di apprendimento. Iltesting dinamico, Armando, Toma (2017)
21. Piccinno, M.: Apprendere e comprendere. ETS, Pisa (2019)
22. Piccinno, M.: Imparare a conoscere per imparare a pensare. Pensa, Lecce (2016)
23. Kempson M.R.: La semantica, Il Mulino, Bologna (1981)
24. Levinson, S.: La pragmatica, Il Mulino, Bologna (1983)
25. Levi-Strauss, C.: Mith and Meaning. Toronto University Press, Toronto (1978)
26. Johnson-Laird, P.N.: Modelli mentali. Verso una scienza cognitiva del linguaggio, dell'inferenza e della coscienza, Il Mulino, Bologna (1990)
27. Lowen, A.: Il linguaggio del corpo, Feltrinelli, Milano (2015)
28. Argyle, M.: Il corpo e il suo linguaggio, Zanichelli, Bologna (2015)
29. Berthoz, A.: La vicarianza, Codice, Torino (2015)
30. Sibilio, M. (ed.): Vicarianza e didattica. Morcelliana, Brescia (2017)
31. Rossi, P.G., Rivoltella, P.C.: Il corpo e la macchina. Scholé, Brescia (2019)
32. Watzslawick, P.: Pragmatica della comunicazione umana. Astrolabio, Milano(1972)
33. Morrison, A., McIntyre, D.: Insegnanti e insegnamento. La Nuova Italia, Firenze (1977)
34. Nathorp, P., La pedagogia sociale. Teoria dell'educazione alla ragione nei suoi fondamenti sociali, Sanna, Bari (1977)
35. Neisser, U., Conoscenza e realtà., Il Mulino, Bologna (1981)

Facing COVID19 Emergency in Higher Education Teaching and Learning: Tools and Practices

Conducting a College Through COVID-19: The Evolving Leadership Challenge

Neil Mort(✉) and John Daniel

Acsenda School of Management, 200-666 Burrard Street, Vancouver, BC V6C 2X8, Canada
neil.mort@acsenda.com, odlsirjohn@gmail.com

Abstract. Prior to the COVID-19 pandemic erupted, Acsenda School of Management (ASM) in Vancouver, Canada was engaged in change management to integrate technology enhanced learning throughout its curriculum. But when the pandemic struck ASM, like many higher educational institutions (HEIs) worldwide, had to move all its programs and operations online, and vacate the campus in a short time, which called for crisis management. Based on surveys of students, faculty and staff carried out during and after the first term online, ASM responded successfully. ASM is now charting its future for the rest of 2020 and 2021, using the approach of change leadership. It is aimed at creating a resilient institution that will be able to thrive in the uncertain times that will follow COVID-19. Change leadership may also involve occasional recourse to crisis management, since new waves of infection could occur at any time and require operations to go back online at short notice.

Keywords: Change management · Crisis management · Change leadership · COVID-19

1 Introduction[1]

ASM is a privately-owned higher education business school in Vancouver, Canada with some 1,200 students from 40 countries (Acsenda 2020). This paper is inspired by the events of this unprecedented academic year as the institution responded to the COVID-19 pandemic. It draws from the experiences and challenges that leadership faced and applies what it has learned through the response to this crisis.

Like many higher education institutions (HEIs) around the world, ASM has been through three distinct phases during the 2020 calendar year. ASM began the year 'normally', that is to say teaching all its programmes on its downtown Vancouver campus. In mid-March, after the COVID-19 pandemic arrived in Vancouver, ASM decided to move all teaching and services online and vacated the campus by the end of that month. Since June, ASM has been planning for the autumn session against a background of considerable uncertainty and evolving guidance from public health officials.

[1] This paper is adapted from the keynote address by the authors at the HELMeTO 2020 Conference. The authors are, respectively, Neil Mort, President and Sir John Daniel, Chancellor of the Acsenda School of Management (ASM), Vancouver.

L. S. Agrati et al. (Eds.): HELMeTO 2020, CCIS 1344, pp. 141–150, 2021.
https://doi.org/10.1007/978-3-030-67435-9_11

The challenge of change in higher education is the theme of this paper. The literature of change distinguishes different approaches to preparing for and managing change, each appropriate to particular situations.

Before the COVID-19 pandemic erupted, ASM was engaged in change management through strategic planning. The change management process can be described as an intentional or planned alteration of organizational components of which the purpose is to improve the effectiveness of the institution (Cawsey et al. 2012; Kotter 2012). However, when the pandemic struck ASM, like most HEIs worldwide, had to take all its operations online and vacate the campus in a short time. HEIs faced a complex situation of significant magnitude that was continually changing and where a definitive answer or solution did not exist. This situation required a different type of approach and one which can be referred to as crisis management (Pauchant and Mitroff 1992). Based on feedback from surveys of students carried out during and after the first term online, ASM appeared to respond successfully in its response to the crisis. ASM is now charting its future for the rest of 2020 and 2021, using the approach of change leadership. It is aimed at creating a resilient institution that will be able to thrive in the uncertain times that will follow COVID-19. Change leadership may also involve occasional recourse to crisis management, since new waves of infection could occur at any time and require operations to go back online at short notice. Resilience is far more than a specific response, it is building the capacity of the institution to deal with future disruptions and involves a developing a capacity to learn from its experiences (Lane et al. 2013).

We begin by recalling the key features of COVID-19 and its impact on societies, noting its effects on education. This will lead us to address the practical issues of responding to the pandemic, using the experience of ASM and juxtaposing it with theories of change management. We conclude by asking how educational institutions and governments can build resilience to address future crises. We must not let this COVID-19 crisis go to waste. These are turbulent times, so future threats like political unrest and climate change will require education systems to adjust again. We must prepare to cope with disruptions.

2 The Impact of Coronavirus and COVID-19

The coronavirus behind the COVID-19 disease has attracted daily news coverage and commentary worldwide for months, so we make just two points.

First, COVID-19 is a very infectious and lethal disease, especially for older people and those with other illnesses. It is now present in all countries of the world and had infected over 20 million people and killed more than 750,000 by mid-August 2020. At that time the number of new cases per day was still rising quickly (WHO 2020; CDC 2020).

Second, in order to try to slow and limit the spread of the disease, most countries imposed restrictions on movement and economic activity. This caused widespread hardship, so governments are now trying to strike a balance between lifting these restrictions and containing the disease. COVID-19′s incubation period is up to 14 days, so the many large gatherings and protests held around the world in mid-2020, when there was often less physical distancing among people than medical advice recommended, are having a delayed impact on the global tally of new infections and additional deaths (WHO; CDC; BCCDC 2020).

COVID-19 has caused great difficulty for education systems. According to UNESCO (2020), 90% of students were out of schools and universities by the end of April 2020. This created huge uncertainty for students and parents about how education would continue and for teachers about how they would provide it. Students were torn suddenly from their friends and social groups, reminding us how important schools and colleges are as social units. Because the change was sudden, teachers had very little time to train and prepare for a new way of teaching.

COVID-19 will not be the last global or local upheaval to impact education. This major crisis provides an opportunity to build resilience into our education systems so that they can cope better with sudden change. During the pandemic HEIs 'crashed into online learning' and most did not do it very well (Bates 2020). Now is our chance to integrate elements of open, distance and online learning into whole education system so that we can perform better next time.

How did HEIs respond to the pandemic? We take ASM as an example. How did it cope with this challenge of change? Tracking the example of ASM allows us to see how proceeding through the processes of change management and crisis management has led us to the approach of change leadership.

3 Effecting Change: Theory and Reality

Higher education is made up of complex organizations. They have highly educated work forces, whose members usually know something of the concepts of organizational design, leadership and change. But despite their commitment to ideas, learning and innovation, HEIs are not always amenable to change. Their decision-making follows the collegial tradition of academia, which values discourse and dialogue. This does not usually sit easily with the bureaucratic approaches of traditional theories of change management.

3.1 Change Management – Theory

HEIs are influenced by many factors: political, economic, social, technical, and environmental. Organizational cultures embed values that affect how an institution functions and how it approaches change. Therefore, embarking on a change process normally requires a considered plan that integrates these factors and lays out an appropriate leadership approach to preparing the organization for change. Complex environments place high demands on information, so systems which collect and manage information are vital for the decision-making process (Smart and Verinsky 1984).

Lewin posits a three-step process of "unfreezing" the organization before it can change, and then re-freezing it after the change is made (Lewin 1947; Cawsey et al. 2012, p. 56–58). People often react negatively to change. Indeed, Kubler-Ross compares their reactions to change to the five-step process of grieving at the prospect of death, where individuals go through stages of denial, anger, bargaining and depression before they reach a point of acceptance (Kubler-Ross 2005).

People are resistant to change not because they fear change, but because they fear loss (Buller 2015 p. 30). Kotter proposed a change management process in eight steps. 1. Create Urgency; 2. Form a Powerful Coalition; 3. Create a Vision for Change; 4.

Communicate the Vision; 5. Remove Obstacles; 6. Create Short-Term Wins; 7. Build on the Change; and 8. Anchor the Changes in the Corporate Culture (Kotter 2012). Previously he had explained the difference between change management and change leadership and the uses of tools and structures to control the process to minimize the impacts of change (Kotter 2011).

The Beckhard and Harris approach to change management puts greater emphasis on why change is needed, and the 'people' factor in the change process, as does the change path model, which identifies four stages of change as awakening, mobilization, acceleration and institutionalization (Cawsey et al. 2012; Deszca et al. 2020). In the case of higher education, Kezar and Eckel emphasize the importance of helping people make sense of change (Kezar and Eckel 2002).

3.2 Change Management: The ASM Reality

Before the COVID-19 pandemic erupted, ASM was engaged in change management through strategic planning. One aim was to assess how best to incorporate online technologies into ASM's future teaching and learning activities. This planning work called for gradual change and a blend of teaching and learning methods. It was not intended to convert ASM into a largely online institution.

The general view was that Acsenda's key strength, and the characteristic most valued by students, was the personal contact among students, faculty and staff, implying that online teaching and learning might be helpful at the margins but was not a mainstream objective. Nevertheless, in 2017 the Strategic Planning Committee was asked to examine the potential use of online methods in more detail, to assess the pedagogical, organizational, and technological opportunities that they might afford, and to make recommendations. This led to the presentation of a Strategic Technology Plan in November 2019.

This plan aimed to achieve the following impacts between 2020 and 2022:

- To use technologies that enable ASM to achieve efficiencies in the deployment of institutional resources.
- To use technologies that enhance the quality of programme curricula, improve flexible access to courses, and enhance learning effectiveness.
- ASM graduates can demonstrate competencies related to using technologies that support continuing education activities throughout their lives.

Key outcomes of the plan are to:

- Use a 3-h block format for all courses.
- Render students and faculty competent in the use of common business technologies.
- Improve efficiencies of scheduling and facilities use.

3.3 Crisis Management - Theory

Most institutions aspire to be strategic in their planning. However, change can also occur as a result of a major event, such as COVID-19; which was both unexpected and very problematic, since it both threatened corporate goals and also required a rapid response. Herman (1972), calls such a situation a crisis.

Leonard (2020) explains that crises are qualitatively different from routine emergencies. In crises, the situation is unfamiliar and there is no playbook for responding. Organizations face a real-time decision-making situation which feels chaotic and unsettling. Crisis management requires "rapid innovations, under stress and embedded in fear". In a new and unprecedented situation, priorities conflict in odd ways. In the COVID-19 crisis, for example, HEIs were faced with decisions juxtaposing safety and business continuity. Leonard emphasizes that "crisis management does not need answers, it needs a process". Leadership in crisis requires rapidly setting up a critical incident team to help the organization learn its way through the response (Leonard 2020). Effective leaders must be honest about the realities of the situation, while at the same time offering hope, which is referred to as the Stockdale Paradox (Collins 2001).

Institutions can respond to crises in different ways. A crisis can provide an opportunity for entrepreneurial responses, that can lead institutions in new directions, or more adaptive responses, which tend to result in less change to the organization. Long term-entrepreneurial responses are seen as strategic approaches; short-term-entrepreneurial responses are considered as tactical. Whereas long-term adaptive responses are referred to as a planning approach, short-term adaptive responses are often called 'fire-fighting' (Smart and Vertinsky 1984). An effective crisis management strategy, however, is not a response but a planning approach.

For Pauchant and Mitroff (1988), crisis management is not about the specific response, but more about the organization's process for anticipating and preparing for potential crises, thus allowing it to respond effectively, mitigate possible damage and let the business recover and learn from the experience. Crises bring opportunities for change. Attitudes evolve and systems then become permeable. Nevertheless, if the change is to be deep, long-lasting and strategic, it must win acceptance within the underlying organizational culture.

The hard challenge for institutional leaders is to keep the organization ready for change at all times. Safi Bahcall, in his book Loonshots, applies concepts from physics to organizational change, concluding that a leader's role is maintain a state of agitation so that things can easily be reconfigured (Bahcall 2019). Whereas Lewin suggests that organizations must unfreeze, change and refreeze, Bahcall might say that they should remain in a constant state of slush.

3.4 Crisis Management: The ASM Reality

When COVID-19 struck, ASM's two-year plan for change became a two-day plan. We had to transform completely our methods of instruction as well as our administrative, student and support services. Change management became crisis management. A collaborative, distributed approach promoted engagement in the process and ensured that processes and changes occurred quickly. Acsenda responded effectively and minimized the financial and organizational impact of what could have been a disaster for this small private-for-profit degree granting institution.

Information gathering had an important role in the response to the crisis and provided data to evaluate the effectiveness of the organization's response and illuminate its future choices. ASM introduced an evaluation component early in the process and collected data on different aspects of its response to COVID-19. This included feedback from various stakeholders: returning students, new students, faculty and staff, information which is helping to guide decisions and provide a basis for future change. It allowed ASM to identify what it has done well, which is an important guide both in the short term, with the prospect of another term of online learning, and in the longer term with a return to on-campus delivery of courses and services. One of the authors prepared a narrative account of the experience (Daniel 2020).

How did ASM rise to the challenge of crisis management successfully? Key elements were:

- Good leadership at all levels of the organisation, with a senior team that met daily and made decisions quickly, benefiting from some previous planning for going online.
- Effective communication across the organisation.
- A collegial, caring and collaborative work environment with a strong focus on individual support and care for students.
- A competent and well-networked professional staff.
- An owner, EduCo International Group, that gave consistent support and encouragement.

3.5 Change Leadership: Theory

Today, as it looks to the future, ASM's focus is on both change leadership and the management of future crises. Unlike a process change, which can be done with a management approach, change leadership means modifying the organization's underlying principles. This transformation can be profound and involve fundamental changes to the organization, to its culture, to its beliefs, and in the basics of what it does and how it does it. The distinction between leading change and managing change is that leading is about the 'how' of change more than about the 'what'.

Kotter considers change leadership as more suited to larger scale, 'big vision' changes which require a broader organizational effort (Kotter 2011). Change leadership places greater focus on the process and the skill of influencing people to engage in change and helping them to transition from the current state to a future state. In contrast to a management approach, "change leaders have to see themselves as part of the system being changed, not as controlling it from on high". Leading change means understanding the organization and its people, nurturing the institutional culture to accept change, building a 'coalition' for it and support around it, and helping people make sense of what they are experiencing so they can develop meaning from it (Buller 2015; Hawkes 2015; Kezar 2018).

3.6 Change Leadership: ASM's Aspirations

As it adopts the approach of change leadership, ASM will also continue to employ a crisis management strategy, including ongoing environmental scanning, the development of signal detectors and scenario planning to prepare responses to potential future crises, whether from further waves of COVID-19 or other causes.

Six months into the COVID-19 pandemic, ASM has responded to the crisis well. Teaching and learning have continued. Enrolment has remained strong, although new student enrolment has declined. We have ensured the continuity of ASM's services. People have settled into a new routine. ASM has not had to lay off any employees. However, a new challenge looms: when and how do we return back to the delivery of classes on campus?

The province of British Columbia, Canada has made good progress in containing the virus. It has moved into Phase 3 of its plan and aims to have elementary and secondary schools open in September. Higher education has been somewhat more cautious but some HEIs along with ASM are planning to resume some classes on campus. On-campus delivery is important for a number of reasons. First, while we have adapted to online delivery of classes and are doing it quite well, according to feedback from students, we are not equipped to compete with larger, more established online programs. Second, ASM caters to international students who want to come to Canada. If international students are unable to come to study in Canada, they may choose to defer or change their educational plans. Canada's Immigration and Border Services are also restricting travel to Canada unless it is 'non-discretionary'. If students could study online with ASM in their own countries, their travel to Canada would be considered discretionary and therefore, they would not be admissible at this time. Students must also demonstrate that they are prepared for their travel and, in particular, have a detailed arrival plan in place for a 14-day quarantine period. Institutions must provide the necessary support and monitoring of students during this time, as well as evidence that appropriate safety measures are in place on campus.

ASM will introduce a hybrid instructional approach for the term beginning in October 2020. A limited number of classes will be offered on campus and students in those classes will rotate; with two groups of students coming to class in person in alternate weeks. Students not on campus will participate simultaneously through a video conferencing system. We recognize that, in a crisis, an institution must be readily adaptable to constantly changing conditions. Therefore, ASM's planning process has anticipated multiple scenarios and the ability to adjust quickly in the event of an outbreak of COVID-19 recurring. Faculty, staff, and students are aware that they may need to revert to fully online delivery at a moment's notice. Planning must also take into account the possible reluctance of some students, faculty and staff to come on campus. We have given priority for campus attendance to first year students and to courses on English language development, mathematics, and accounting. We have made it voluntary for faculty to teach on campus. Likewise, student participation on campus will be optional.

We see this partial return to campus as both an interim solution and also as a broader part of a return to campus strategy. This process will guide the gradual re-introduction of faculty and staff to the workplace. While we have been successful in making the change from on campus to online learning for the last six months, we realize that people have adapted and adjusted to new work environments and methods. We now sense resistance in some quarters to returning to the workplace. The leadership challenge is both to maintain a crisis management process, while also preparing people for this transition. We have learned much so far and have discovered better ways to deliver our services and our academic programs, which will change much of what we do in the future. We recognize that there will be a 'new normal', but its shape is still evolving. We are, however, clear that we need to continue with the effective process used throughout the COVID-19 pandemic, which has emphasized a team approach to planning, effective communication and a culture of learning and innovation.

3.7 The Evolving Leadership Challenge

The case of ASM shows us that change can occur in organizations as a result of planned process, and it can also be influenced or accelerated by a crisis. In either scenario there needs to be a driving force, which Kotter defines as the action or event that creates a sense of urgency (Kotter 2012). Regardless of the reason for change, organizations must understand that change is inevitable, and the key roles of leadership are creating a culture that is ready for change, and one that is adaptive, flexible and resilient. We see that even in the case of crisis management, theories suggest that the process is not as much responsive as it is anticipatory. Effective leadership of change also takes into account the culture of the organization (Paul 2015), its employees, students and other stakeholders, in order to help them make sense of and understand what they are experiencing and why it is happening. This is the key role for change leaders .

4 Conclusion: Building Resilience

What does ASM's experience in 2020 tell us about the future? It provides a telling case study about how an HEI prepares for change and responds to it. What began as a gradual change management process quickly changed to crisis management and is now an opportunity for change leadership as the institution moves forward. Its aim must be to make ASM more resilient to shocks of all kinds. Analogous to the cybernetic Principle of Requisite Variety, this means having systems ready with responses for the crises most likely to confront them (Naughton 2017).

There were several factors which contributed to ASM's ability to respond effectively and adapt to the COVID crisis. First, through an inclusive planning process, the organization was thinking about change and envisioning the future. Kezar notes that "when institutions embark on change, they often do so in a reactionary way that is unpredictable and prompted by a sudden crisis" (Welton et al. 2018, p 7). This often does not allow for appropriate measures to garner support or buy in to a long-term solution, sustainable solution. However, in the case of ASM, all sectors of the organization were engaged in the process and this contributed to a state of readiness to adapt. Second, a crisis management approach helped ASM prepare for different scenarios, which allowed the organization to remain flexible and adjust to constantly changing conditions. It has also reinforced the importance of ongoing crisis management practices where the organization is now anticipating future events that could occur in order to mitigate future disruptions. Third, this experience has reinforced the importance of providing the necessary support for those affected to adjust to change. In the case of ASM, this included providing training sessions in the use of the new online tools, a responsive system for receiving feedback and regular discussion forums to provide the opportunity to share experiences and ideas. Fourth, during a change process, communication is important.

ASM provided regular updates to all stakeholders on developments, the challenges that the institution was facing and our response. The ASM senior leadership group met daily throughout the first four months and continues to meet weekly. Regular updates were provided to students through email and social media. The communication strategy also included other stakeholders such as the parent company, Academic Council, educational agents, peer institutions and the Ministry of Advanced Education. Finally, it was very beneficial to develop an evaluation plan early in the process so that we could collect data. This was important to monitor and measure the effectiveness of our responses as well as reinforcing a culture of learning and continual improvement.

So far ASM has responded effectively and minimized the financial and organizational impact of a crisis that could have been a disaster for a small private-for-profit HEI highly dependent on international students. An important aspect of its success in managing this crisis was that, as well as taking teaching online, ASM gave strong and consistent attention to providing student services at a distance and animating social life through virtual connections among students confined to their homes. As it moves into the future ASM must hold fast to the holistic view that its relationships with students are not only academic and pedagogical but also, just as importantly, social, technological and psychological.

References

Acsenda School of Management: www.acsenda.com (2020)

Bahcall, S.: Loonshots: How to nurture the crazy ideas that win wars, cure diseases, and transform industries. St. Martin's Publishing Group (2019)

Bates, T.: Crashing into online learning: A report from five continents and some conclusions. Online Learning and Distance Education Resources (2020). https://www.tonybates.ca/2020/04/26/crashing-into-online-learning-a-report-from-five-continents-and-some-conclusions/

BCCDC-British Columbia Centre for Disease Control: COVID 19 (2020). https://www.bccdc.ca/health-info/diseases-conditions/covid-19/data

Buller, J. L.: Change Leadership in Higher Education: A Practical Guide to Academic Transformation. Jossey-Bass (2015)

Cawsey, T.F., Deszca, G., Ingols, C.: Organizational Change: An Action-Oriented Toolkit, 2nd edn. Sage Publication, Thousand Oaks (2012)

CDC-Centers for Disease Control and Prevention (2020) https://www.cdc.gov/coronavirus/2019-nCoV/index.html

Collins, J.C.: Good to great: Why some companies make the leap ... and others don't. HarperBusiness (2001)

Daniel, J.S.: COVID-19: A two-week transition from campus to online at the Acsenda school of management. Canada. J. Learn. Dev. **7**(3), 264–278 (2020)

Deszca, G., Ingols, C., Cawsey, T.F.: Organizational Change: An Action-Oriented Toolkit, 4th edn. Sage Publication, Thousand Oaks (2020)

Hawkes, R.: How do you lead change? It's all in the definition. Linked In Learning (2015). https://www.linkedin.com/pulse/how-do-you-lead-change-its-all-definition-richard-hawkes/

Hermann, C.F.: Some issues in the study of international crisis. In: Hermann, C.F. (ed.) International crises: Insights from behavioral research, pp. 3–17. Free Press (1972)

Kezar, A.: How Colleges Change: Understanding, Leading and Enacting Change, 2nd edn. Routledge, Abingdon (2018)

Kezar, A., Eckel, P.: Examining the institutional transformation process: the importance of sensemaking, interrelated strategies, and balance. Res. High. Educ. **43**(3), 295–328 (2002)
Kotter, J.P.: Change management vs. change leadership: What's the difference? Forbes (2011). https://www.forbes.com/sites/johnkotter/2011/07/12/change-management-vs-change-leadership-whats-the-difference/#710f71db4cc6
Kotter, J.P.: Leading Change. Harvard Business Review Press (2012)
Kübler-Ross, E.: On Grief and Grieving: Finding the Meaning of Grief Through the Five Stages of Loss. Simon & Schuster, New York (2005)
Lane, K.E., McCormack, T., Richardson, M.D.: Resilient leaders: essential for organizational innovation. Int. J. Organ. Innov. **6**(2), 7–25 (2013)
Leonard, D.: Managing through crisis: What is crisis management? (2020) [Webinar]. Harvard Business School. https://www.youtube.com/watch?v=1evSfmArTRQ
Lewin, K.: Field Theory in Social Science. Harper & Row, New York (1947)
Mitroff, I.: Managing Crises Before they Happen: What Every Executive and Manager Needs to Know about Crisis Management. Amacom Editions (2001)
Naughton, J.: Ashby's law of requisite variety. Edge (2017). https://www.edge.org/response-detail/27150
Pauchant, T.C., Mitroff, I.: Crisis prone versus crisis avoiding organizations: Is your company's culture its own worst enemy in creating crises? Ind. Crisis Q. **2**(1) (1988)
Pauchant, T.C., Mitroff, I.: Transforming the Crisis-Prone Organization: Preventing Individual. Organizational and Environmental Tragedies. Jossey-Bass, San Francisco (1992)
Smart, C., Vertinsky, I.: Strategy and the environment: a study of corporate responses to crises. Strateg. Manage. J. (1984). https://doi.org/10.1002/smj.4250050302
Therrien, M.C., Valiquette-L'Heureux, A.: Crisis management. Encyclopedic Dictionary of Public Administration (n.d.). https://www.dictionnaire.enap.ca/dictionnaire/docs/definitions/definitions_anglais/crisis_management.pdf
UNESCO: 1.37 billion students now home as COVID-19 closures expand (2020). https://en.unesco.org/news/137-billion-students-now-home-covid-19-school-closures-expand-ministers-scale-multimedia
Welton, A.D., Owens, D.R., Zamani-Gallaher, E.M.: Anti-racist change: a conceptual framework for educational institutions to take systemic action. Teach. College Rec. **120**(14) (2018)
WHO-World Health Organization: Coronavirus disease (COVID-19) pandemic (2020). https://www.who.int/emergencies/diseases/novel-coronavirus-2019. Accessed 15 Aug 2020

The Educational Relationship Between Teachers and Young Tennis Players Continued During the Covid-19 Outbreak: Is the Online Teaching a New Start also for the University?

Valerio Bonavolontà, Stefania Cataldi(✉), Davide Maci, and Francesco Fischetti

Department of Basic Medical Sciences, Neuroscience and Sense Organs, University of Bari «Aldo Moro», Bari, Italy
stefania.cataldi@uniba.it

Abstract. During the lockdown children, teenagers and young adult university students discovered a new type of distance learning through online platforms and conferencing tools. Extra-school sports activities were also suddenly stopped with a sharp interruption of all the social and pedagogical processes involved. Aim of the present work was to evaluate if the educational relationship between pupils and teachers continued during the lockdown; secondly, to monitor the levels of physical activity and the level of enjoyment and motivation in children and adolescents in the emergency context. 140 among children and adolescents filled in three questionnaires: one to investigate their sports and physical activity habits, the second was the Physical Activity Questionnaire to monitor the physical activity status and the third one was the Physical Activity Enjoyment Scale (PACES) . About 90% of pupils attended online school classes and about the same percentage received indications from Tennis School about home-exercises and other forms of distance learning. More than 40% of the sample did not follow physical education classes and 45% declared to be inactive during free time. PACES questionnaire revealed that pupils mostly enjoyed doing physical activity staying at home and did not consider it as a frustrating or annoying practice. Also, for higher education, it would be advisable to potentiate the traditional didactics with some of the best digital practices experienced during the lockdown.

Keywords: Distance learning · Physical and sport activities · Enjoyment

1 Introduction

During the period going approximately from March the 12th until May the 4th, in Italy, as in most of the European and worldwide countries, a severe lockdown was held to protect the population from the spreading of SARS-CoV-2 virus (also known as COVID-19) which had initially originated in China. Closures and strict restrictions as well as bans on travel, cultural and sporting events, and social gatherings were introduced by national

L. S. Agrati et al. (Eds.): HELMeTO 2020, CCIS 1344, pp. 151–157, 2021.
https://doi.org/10.1007/978-3-030-67435-9_12

authorities [1]. To contain the spreading of COVID-19 epidemic, Italy has been the first European country to adopt unprecedented measures to restrict individual mobility, and to promote social distancing, with the aim of interrupting transmission of the SARS-CoV-2 virus. Following the detection of the first cluster of COVID-19 cases in Lombardy, on 21 February 2020, the government adopted an increasing number of strict orders, ranging from school and university closures, limitations placed on social gatherings, closure of bar and restaurants with the exception of essential business and services, and a national stay-at-home order [2].

Therefore, one of the main issues connected to the lockdown is the nationwide closure of all level's education system: over 100 countries have imposed the closure of all educational facilities [3]. UNESCO estimates that at least 138 countries and as close as 900 million learners have been affected by the closure of educational institutions and have been removed from the educational context [4]. Recently, it was also claimed that school closure could be only marginally effective on the fight for pandemic diffusion: in fact, some experts suggest that the potential advantages of school closure, if present, have to be balanced against the secondary adverse effects such as social and economic consequences [5]. In addition, in a recent systematic review, Viner et al. [6] showed that there are no data on the relative contribution of school closures to SARS-CoV-2 transmission control.

Anyway, as a matter of fact, in a very short time children, teenagers and young adult university students were forced to discover a new type of distance learning filtered by the screen of their home personal computers. In particular, the higher education system has overturned, in a few days, the traditional teaching methods as well as the conduct of the examinations and even the discussions of the dissertations. Online platforms and conferencing tools like Microsoft Teams, Google Meet and Zoom have been promptly set by local Universities to host meeting between teachers and students, to carry out online curricular lessons, to conduct exams either *vis a vis* and/or in written form, and even the discussion of the final thesis that were presented from the students' houses in such an extraordinary context.

Children and teenagers have been confronted with online distance learning with their own devices, until now mainly used for leisure time, chatting on social networks and online gaming. In a way, mandatory distance learning has finally given these tools their educational potential, which has long been overwhelmed. From the other side, not all the students have the same digital facilities and condition, as these depends on the heterogeneity of the national connection network: indeed, Italian Agency AGCOM estimated that about 12.7% of the students could not regularly attend lessons and were then unable to keep on going with their education process. Moreover, 10% of the students did not have a proper device and about 25% of students, although in possession of a digital device could not account on a 30 mbps internet connection, necessary to join these educational meeting [7].

The World Health Organization (WHO), as well as the Italian Medical Sports Federation and other sources of scientific information, have provided indications to promote a correct lifestyle for the whole population who could not practice sport, encouraging, in particular, regular physical activity for all age groups. As a result of school closure, many children are unlikely to reach the 60 min of physical activity suggested by WHO and will suffer from the lack of social assistance provided by the school environment [8]. Hammami et al. [9] proposed that implementing an adapted physical training program at home during the period of the pandemic would decrease the negative physiological and psychological impact of sedentary behaviors. The same authors claimed that many people followed duly the official advice to self-isolate and stay at home, and that these actions will negatively affect people's physical activity behaviors, with more time spent sitting watching screens and a subsequent impact on physical health, well- being, sleeping patterns and quality of life. There are also reasons for concern about the physical and mental health of children, due to the prolonged closure of the school and confinement at home. Evidence suggests that when children do not go to school (e.g. on weekends and summer holidays), they are physically less active, have irregular sleep patterns and less favorable diets, resulting in weight gain and weakened cardiovascular fitness [10, 11]. Regarding mental health, Golberstein [12] recently reported that the COVID-19 pandemic may have worsened existing mental health problems and lead to more cases among children and adolescents because of the unique combination of the public health crisis, social isolation, and economic recession. Economic crises are also associated with increased mental health issues for youth that may be affected by adult unemployment, adult mental health, and other social scenarios connected to the pandemic emergency.

In addition to this complex and difficult formal education context, extra-school sports activities were suddenly stopped and pupils were not allowed to go playing their usual physical and sports activities with the unavoidable consequence of a sharp interruption of all the social and pedagogical processes and relationships involved in that.

Although the practice of physically active lifestyles is recommended to counteract health and mental consequences of the COVID-19 pandemic [13], individual and team sport activities were totally shutdown either for amateurs as well as for professional. Some sport clubs or sport teams provided, anyway, to give to their athletes and pupils online assistance, either live or not, to keep them active and to reduce the isolation.

To our knowledge, no studies were conducted to investigate the role of distance learning in physical and sports activities in adolescences and young adults during the Covid-19 emergency.

Therefore, aim of the present work was to evaluate if the educational relationship between pupils and their teachers continued during the Covid-19 lockdown and in which form; secondly, to monitor the levels of physical activity and the level of enjoyment and motivation in children and adolescents in the emergency context.

2 Method

140 among children and adolescents (60 aged 6–11 and 80 aged 12–15, 66% males and 34% females; 25 attending primary school, 57 and 58 attending middle and high school, respectively) recruited from 23 different Tennis Clubs of the six provinces of Apulian region voluntarily participated in this study; participants filled in three questionnaires via Google Forms at the end of April: the first one was created *ad hoc* to investigate on their sports habits and physical activity behaviors during the Covid-19 lockdown period and it was based on some indications given by the Italian Tennis Association inthat period; the second questionnaire administered was the Physical Activity Questionnaire for Older

children (PAQ-C) [14, 15] or for Adolescents (PAQ-A) [16], depending on the age range, to monitor their physical activity status during the previous 7 days: both PAQ-C and PAC-A are scored with a scale ranging from 1 to 5 and are adapted versions of the International Physical Activity Questionnaire (IPAQ) which was initially developed to measure health-related physical activity in populations. The third questionnaire proposed was the Italian version of the Physical Activity Enjoyment Scale (PACES-It) [17] that evaluates the level of enjoyment during physical and sports activities; PACES questionnaire is based on 16 items scored with a scale from 1 to 5 and the final score obtained by the sum of positive and reversed negative items ranges from 16 (no enjoyment) to 80 (total enjoyment). The beginning stem of PACES was modified to better fit with the pandemic scenario by asking subjects "During the lockdown, when I am physically active…". Data were analyzed by comparing percentages and means of the result obtained from the above-mentioned questionnaires.

3 Results

Data from the first questionnaire indicated that 90.8% of pupils were following online school classes and 82.9% had also received indications from their Tennis School under a home-based form of distance learning such as online video-streaming with teachers (29.3%), recorded videos (17.9%) or a list of exercises to do at home (35.7%).

PAQ questionnaires mean value was 2.69 ± 0.76 on a scale ranging from 1 to 5. Not surprisingly, more than 43% of the sample did not follow physical education (PE) classes in the previous 7 days and 44.4% declared to be inactive during free time; by the contrary, 40.8% and 36% of pupils maintained a frequency of physical activity of > 5 times/week and of 2 to 3 times/week respectively, suggesting that PE lessons had a small contribution to the total amount of activity for most of them.

PACES questionnaire showed that subjects liked the home physical activities with a mean value of 65.2 ± 11.8 (female: 64.7; male: 65.45) with higher values from those who received online support and guidance from their regular instructors respect to their peers who did not (66.45 vs 59.17); moreover, higher values from PACES were obtained by middle school children respect to primary school children and high school adolescents (67.89, 63.92 and 63.42 respectively).

4 Discussion

The worldwide lockdown and Covid-19 outbreak have created a new unpredictable and unseen scenario that deeply affected the whole socio-economic context and forced the educational system to deeply modify its procedures and social interactions.

Aim of our study was to assess the sports habits, the amount of physical activity and the level of enjoyment during physical and sport activities of children and young adolescents of the Apulian region in the emergency context.

Data from the first questionnaire revealed that about 90% of the sample has followed online didactics, in line with the UNESCO report [4] confirming that low income families and areas with limited internet coverage need to be supported by the national authorities. Instead, it seems positive that more than 80% of the pupils received indications and support by their sports teams and clubs, suggesting a good pedagogical praxis that could be maintained over time in order to strengthen the relationship between educators and youngsters.

PAC-C and PAC-A results revealed an amount of physical activity in line with a regular period as it was shown by Crocker and colleagues that reported a mean value ranging from 2.56 to 3.16/5 [14]: it is a remarkable data that suggest that children and adolescents do not stop moving and playing actively during the quarantine confinement at home, despite the smaller space available in most of cases. It is not unexpected, instead, that curricular PE lesson did not significatively contribute to the total amount of physical activity as many school teacher experienced several issues carrying out their habitual class virtually and rather have preferred to show to their students videos and theoretical aspects of the subject, also for security reason.

Interestingly, from a pedagogical point of view, PACES results revealed that pupils mostly enjoyed doing physical activity staying at home during the lockdown and did not consider it as a frustrating or annoying practice (Table 1). Table 1 shows that home-based physical activity had a high impact on enjoyment and motivation and that items representing negative feelings had low agreement by pupils. It is interesting to remark that subjects reported positive feedback on the home distance education modality even if, actually, they were not allowed to go to the usual location to play their favorite sport.

Thus, the relationship between young tennis players and their instructors was maintained during the lockdown in line with the mandatory education process between school teachers and their pupils. In addition, most of active time was attributable to extra-school physical activities.

Therefore, in order to strengthen the educational relationship between teachers and their pupils, it would be advisable to potentiate the onsite traditional didactics with some of the best digital practices that were experienced and appreciated during the lockdown [18]. Thus, an integrated approach between school settings and informal contexts could be more beneficial for the education of children and adolescents.

Moreover, as Tennis is also present in the Physical Education and Sport Sciences university curriculum, the present findings may be extended to higher education system, fostering and implementing the traditional live didactics, which remains essential for an effective learning process.

As recently reported by Giovannella, [19] although university students seem to miss live settings and face to face activities, the sudden switch from physical to fully virtual setting has been positively absorbed and suggests that the new generation of students are mostly ready to receive a blended education that integrates activities in presence with those online.

Additionally, if online didactics will be preferentially used at the beginning of the forthcoming academic year, the distance methodology will allow also those practical activities, such as for Didactics of Tennis, suspended during the lockdown, to be carried out, even if adapted and with some limitations, in the university courses. The blended modality could benefit either traditional curricular subjects and practical ones and there are rising studies indicating that students show positivity towards e-learning [20] and that 26% of students would like to study fully online, while majority of students, (49%) are in favor of studying through blended learning system [21]. Moreover, as previously proposed by Picerno et al. [22] exergames and e-tivities could facilitate the interaction between students and teachers about selected physical activities thus favoring the learning process.

In the very last days, in Italy, schools of all levels have reopened and will be facing probably the most difficult challenge ever. Educational system, to avoid a dramatic new school closure has studied alternative strategies to contain transmission, such as reducing class size, physical distancing, and hygiene promotion: when social distancing is not possible, due to space availability and structural limitations, blended didactics or a shorter schedule is the only solution provided by the schools.

Higher education system could implement its offer with the blended e-learning modality, but it will probably need the support of the Ministry of the Education and University as well as an attitude change and technological literacy by the students [23] and teachers . In conclusion, distance learning and online teaching, even in an unprecedented scenario like the Covid-19 outbreak, can be effective modalities to carry on educational relationship between students and teachers , also in the higher education system, that could continue some of the best practices experienced also in normal conditions.

Table 1. PACES Questionnaire report. Pupils were asked "During the lockdown, when I am physically active…".

Item	Disagree a lot	Disagree	I Am not sure	Agree	Agree a lot
I enjoy it	1	18	19	49	53
I feel bored	75	43	12	10	0
I dislike it	95	23	16	6	0
I find it pleasureable	4	18	18	50	50
It's no fun at all	91	29	11	8	1
It gives me energy	7	12	20	42	59
It makes me sad	113	12	11	4	0
It's very pleasant	6	22	15	55	42
My body feels good	3	16	15	47	59
I get something out of it	10	18	22	43	47
It's very exciting	16	20	31	44	29
It frustrates me	99	26	11	4	0
It's not at all interesting	104	17	14	4	1
It gives a strong feelings of success	16	23	31	34	36
It feels good	3	17	18	36	66
I feel as though I would rather be doing something else	75	33	15	9	8

References

1. Parnell, D., Widdop, P., Bond, A., Wilson, R.: COVID-19, networks and sport. Managing Sport Leisure (2020)
2. Pepe, E., et al.: COVID-19 outbreak response, a dataset to assess mobility changes in Italy following national lockdown. Sci. Data **7**(1), 1–7 (2020)
3. Nicola, M., et al.: The socio-economic implications of the coronavirus pandemic (COVID-19): a review. Int. J. Surg. **78**, 185 (2020)
4. Educational Disruption and Response, UNESCO. https://en.unesco.org/themes/education-emergencies/coronavirus-school-closures. Accessed 20 Mar 2020

5. Esposito, S., Principi, N.: School closure during the coronavirus disease 2019 (COVID-19) pandemic: an effective intervention at the global level? JAMA Pediatr. (2020)
6. Viner, R.M., et al.: School closure and management practices during coronavirus outbreaks including COVID-19: a rapid systematic review. Lancet Child Adolescent Health **4**, 397–404 (2020)
7. AGCOM: L'impatto del Coronavirus nei settori regolati. Allegato alla relazione annuale (2020)
8. Van Lancker, W., Parolin, Z.: COVID-19, school closures, and child poverty: A social crisis in the making. Lancet Public Health **5**(5), e243–e244 (2020)
9. Hammami, A., Harrabi, B., Mohr, M., Krustrup, P.: Physical activity and coronavirus disease 2019 (COVID-19): specific recommendations for home-based physical training. Managing Sport Leisure, 1–6 (2020)
10. Brazendale, K., et al.: Understanding differences between summer vs. school obesogenic behaviors of children: the structured days hypothesis. International J. Behav. Nutr. Phys. Activity **14**(1), 100 (2017)
11. Wang, G., Zhang, Y., Zhao, J., Zhang, J., Jiang, F.: Mitigate the effects of home confinement on children during the COVID-19 outbreak. Lancet **395**(10228), 945–947 (2020)
12. Golberstein, E., Wen, H., Miller, B.F.: Coronavirus disease 2019 (COVID-19) and mental health for children and adolescents. JAMA Pediatr. (2020).
13. Lim, M.A., Pranata, R.: Sports activities during any pandemic lockdown. Irish J. Med. Sci. (1971-), 1–5 (2020)
14. Crocker, P.R.E., Bailey, D.A., Faulkner, R.A., Kowalski, K.C., McGrath, R.: Measuring general levels of physical activity: preliminary evidence for the physical activity questionnaire for older children. Med. Sci. Sports Exerc. **29**, 1344–1349 (1997)
15. Gobbi, E., Elliot, C., Varnier, M., Carraro, A.: Psychometric properties of the physical activity questionnaire for older children in Italy: testing the validity among a general and clinical pediatric population. PLoS ONE **11**(5), e0156354 (2016)
16. Kowalski, K.C., Crocker, P.R.E., Donen, R.M.: The Physical Activity Questionnaire for Older Children (PAQ-C) and Adolescents (PAQ-A) Manual. College of Kinesiology University of Saskatchewan, Saskatoon, Canada (2004)
17. Carraro, A., Young, M.C., Robazza, C.: A contribution to the validation of the physical activity enjoyment scale in an Italian sample. Soc. Behav. Pers.: Int. J. **36**(7), 911–918 (2008)
18. Fiorentino, G., Salvatori, E.: La didattica a distanza, dall'emergenza alle buone pratiche. Umanistica Digitale, vol. 8 (2020)
19. Giovannella, C.: Effect induced by the Covid-19 pandemic on students' perception about technologies and distance learning SLERD Conference, Bucharest (2020)
20. Radha, R., Mahalakshmi, K., Kumar, V.S., Saravanakumar, A.R.: E-learning during lockdown of Covid-19 pandemic: a global perspective. Int. J. Control Autom. **13**(4), 1088–1099 (2020)
21. Almuraqab, N.A.S.: Shall universities at the UAE Continue distance learning after the COVID-19 pandemic? Revealing students' perspective. Int. J. Adv. Res. Eng. Technol. (IJARET) **11**(5), 226–233 (2020)
22. Picerno, P., Pecori, R., Raviolo, P., Ducange, P.: Smartphones and exergame controllers as BYOD solutions for the e-tivities of an online sport and exercise sciences university program. In: Burgos, D., et al. (ed.) HELMeTO 2019. CCIS, vol. 1091, pp. 217–227. Springer, Cham (2019). https://doi.org/10.1007/978-3-030-31284-8_17
23. Krishnapatria, K.: From 'Lockdown' to letdown: Students' perception of e-learning amid the COVID-19 outbreak. ELT Focus **3**(1), 1–8 (2020)

University Students' Online Social Presence and Digital Competencies in the COVID-19 Virus Situation

Edit Kővári[1(✉)] and Gerda Bak[2]

[1] Faculty of Business and Economics, University of Pannonia, Veszprém, Hungary
kovari.edit@gtk.uni-pannon.hu
[2] Doctoral School in Management Sciences and Business Administration, University of Pannonia, Veszprém, Hungary

Abstract. 2020 is the year of change and adaptability. The COVID19 pandemic immensely influences our everyday routines. Education is no exception as schools have to transform their classroom teaching to distance online tutoring. It is not easy on either side as educators and students encountered gaps in digital capabilities. Moreover they suddenly happen to be an online medium where different social behavior pattern immerged. We were very much interested how young adults endure and overcome this situation. In the present study the first result of our ongoing research that aimed to explore the digital competence and social presence among the students of the University of Pannonia are presented. The main objective was to see how students perceive their social situation online with their digital abilities, knowledge and level of competences. The results indicated that although on average perceived online social presence is not affected by individuals' digital competences, significant relationships were found between some factors.

Keywords: Digital competence · Social presence · COVID19

1 Introduction

As technology develops, so do the tools in the education scheme, with the traditional schoolroom often being changed by a virtual learning environment. Social presence is a relevant factor in distance learning [1–4]. Enrolment in distance education has steadily increased in recent years, with the proportion of university students registered in minimum one distance learning course in the United States from 25.9% increased to 31.6% between 2012 and 2016 [5]. This rise of online learning has further increased rapidly in recent months due to the coronavirus (COVID-19). Online education replaced traditional education at all levels and reduced physical contact [6, 7]. The sudden transition to online learning posed several challenges for faculty and students similarly. A recent survey by Barnes & Noble College Insights asked 432 students in the United States what their expectations and concerns might be about the shift from traditional classroom education to online courses in the wake of the COVID-19 pandemic. The majority of respondents expressed various concerns about the transition. 64% of respondents believed that

L. S. Agrati et al. (Eds.): HELMeTO 2020, CCIS 1344, pp. 158–169, 2021.
https://doi.org/10.1007/978-3-030-67435-9_13

online education would not affect their learning processes, and 55% expressed concern that they would be depressingly affected by the lack of social interaction in the online learning environment [8]. Accordingly, it has become more critical than ever to evaluate and understand how to optimize and improve online learning and learning experience effectively.

According to the social presence theory, the mediating medium influences the communication between actors and their listeners [9, 10]. It, in turn, boosts the user's feelings of taking part in social interactions [11–13]. The critical role of social presence in social interactions is unquestionable [14].

Our present life is characterized by rapid development: computers and the Internet have become available to almost everyone in developed countries [15, 16], and almost everyone has a smartphone [17]. These tools and technologies have become important and determining factors of our lives [18]. Digitalization has led to many professions changes, and several jobs have been lost, and new ones have been created [19]. As a result, people have to master their tasks and operate many unprecedented new tools. These newly almost indispensable skills, abilities, and knowledge become part of necessary skills at an ever-increasing rate with technological innovation [20]. The literature calls these skills, abilities, and knowledge of digital competence (DQ). The European Parliament and the Council have highlighted the Eight Key Competences for Lifelong Learning and developed a digital framework to acquire these competencies [21]. The first digital competence framework was established in 2016 and revised a year later in 2017 [22, 23]. The framework was needed because digital technology affects many aspects of our lives, be it work, fun [18], or even a weekend shopping [24].

2 Social Presence

Until now, the literature on online learning agrees that the ability to perceive social presence or others in an indirect environment [25] is of paramount importance for fostering online classroom relationships. Richardson et al. [25] found that when students perceive a more significant social presence in the online classroom, they experience higher satisfaction ($p = 0.56$) and higher levels of learning ($p = 0.51$). Other research has shown that social presence promotes a willingness to participate in future online courses [26], perseverance [27], and motivation to participate [28, 29], and student performance [30]. These results are of great importance in large-scale online learning environments, where educators are looking for tangible ways to maximize and enhance their online learning experience.

Social media networks are socio-virtual environments in which individuals and groups communicate to share their thoughts and tap-tables. The theory of social presence (SPT) evolved from the use of telecommunication devices. It shows how individuals participate in social media use; how it is perceived as a means of communication, how it influences their behaviour, which predicts individuals' extent and form of intelligence and social acceptance [31]. Social presence, which was originally used to assess how the social context influences media choice, was defined as "the degree of salience of the other person in the interaction and the consequent salience of the interpersonal relationships' [32 p. 65]. It suggests that social presence bridges perceived distance and assumes a degree of closeness between participants, which also depends on the media's wealth of information [10].

Although the theory of social presence embodies social interactions, it is not intended to present social cognition in the traditional sense but to highlight how technology can influence, distort, and improve certain aspects of social cognition [33]. Starting from this assumption, Short et al. [32] highlighted two concepts related to social presence: the concept of 'intimacy'; and the concept of 'immediacy'. While'intimacy is a function of the subject of eye contact, closeness, conversation, immediacy means the psychological distance between the communicator and the recipient' that is "verbally and non-verbally generated' [31 p. 28]. It suggests that social presence contributes to increasing intimacy in terms of the outcome of social interactions, allowing people to communicate instantly or immediately both non-verbally (physical proximity, images, and facial expressions) and verbally [34].

Social presence can be defined as the perception of another individual and the interpersonal relationship [1–4]. Biocca [35] defined social presence as a more complex phenomenon: a minimal level of social presence when a user's sense of the presence of another intelligence is triggered by a form, behaviour, or sensual impression. The characteristics of the medium and the perception of the user determine the degree of social presence. By degree of social presence means the effect that a given user is affected by another's intelligence, intentions, and sensual impressions. According to Reeves and Nass [36], the other's perception is an emotionally coloured and inner state of the individual in which the individual feels as if he or she is there with another individual. During face-to-face contact, several factors contribute to social presence: facial expression, vocal cues, posture, dress, verbal, and non-verbal. Social presence was initially seen as a property of the medium [2]. Many research [34, 37, 38] have concluded that perception of social presence varies among users. Because social presence is a dynamic variable, individuals can distinguish between different types of social presence on each media interface [31].

3 Digital Competence

Research in digital technology and digital literacy has developed rapidly over the past decade. Scientists are increasingly concerned about the conditions and implications of working with digital technologies and the digital skills associated with this. However, this requires theoretically sound, more reliable, and validated tools to measure the individuals' skill levels and their development [39].

In the current situation caused by the COVID-19 pandemic, students need to participate effectively in digital media even more inevitably while still expressing themselves in the virtual classroom. Previous literature has shown that students need to acquire the skills and competencies essential for digital learning, such as the ability to view digital texts and problem-solving ideas in digital media and the ability to understand and motivate each other to communicate effectively with others [40–44]. It is a challenge at all levels of education to ensure that students can effectively develop their digital literacy [44].

Digital literacy can also be defined as the ability to understand and use information in different formats. This approach focuses on critical thinking rather than skills and abilities related to information and communication technologies [45]. We spend more and more time in front of smart devices, with continuous communication taking place indirectly anywhere on the screen [40]. For this reason, Gee [46] believes that people need skills to interpret and decode different texts, symbols, and figures. Lankshear and Knobel [47] highlighted that due to technological advances and the use of new digital tools and the many social sites [48], people need to equip themselves with a new kind of knowledge. Digital literacy and media literacy and information literacy, play an essential role at any level of education [49]. This idea is also supported and followed by the Partnership for 21st Century Learning [50], which aims to create an education that provides students with 21st-century knowledge and skills. Many large companies and educational institutions also participate in cooperation. The collaboration has identified and gathered the skills and competencies needed in the 21st century and their definitions and meanings, with particular reference to educational needs [51].

Digital literacy involves the use of software or the operation of digital devices and a variety of complex cognitive, sociological, and emotional skills that users need to be able to move effectively and perform tasks in a digitally controlled environment [52]. Digital literacy should also include an individual's awareness, attitude, and ability to collectively communicate, express themselves, and establish social interactions in specific life situations using digital tools [53].

The authors identify several forms of digital literacy (digital competence) in the literature that include information and communication technologies (ICT), media literacy and visual literacy, and Internet skills. Behind the broad approach, there are researchers and ideas from different disciplines [54]. These academics [54–61] with the UNESCO [62] and other digital literacy literature contributors agree that digital literacy is a multidisciplinary concept. However, the authors differentiate between the specialized disciplines that make up digital literacy. Our study identifies five disciplines: information literacy, computer literacy, media literacy, communication, and technology literacy, predominantly referred to heterogeneous skills [54].

4 The Present Study

The relationship between digital competence and technology is apparent, but the content and formulation are less. It can be traced back, among other things, to the fact that researchers of the topic examine the phenomenon from many different aspects and find numerous variances in terms of its content [63]. In connection with digital competence, it is worth mentioning digital literacy, computer literacy, or media literacy, which covers the same phenomenon [64], but according to others, the mentioned terms are different aspects of digital competence [59].

In the present research, we examined the dimensions of digital competence in parts of the DQ models based on the previous literature. The existence and assessment of digital competencies have also been justified by the current COVID-19 virus situation, with many schools closing their doors and teaching taking place online. This new circumstance creates an unusual and challenging situation for the majority.

The changes brought about by the COVID-19 virus justify the online social presence, the other pillar of our research, which is related explicitly to so-called computer-mediated communication (CMC) [65]. In our case, we measure learning in an online environment with a social presence.

Online education is viral due to its flexibility and personalization [66] and the spread of the Internet [67]. However, in addition to the popularity of e-learning systems, it should be borne in mind that the implementation of online learning systems is challenging. The development of e-learning systems is costly, time-consuming, and more efficient than other systems [68]. Social presence is related to the extent to which individuals value online communication as 'real' [69]. The degree of social presence of participants in online courses varies, depending on the extent to which they are active in online training and how far one reveals him/herself [70].

Social presence is an essential factor in online learning experiences [71, 72], as it allows an individual to be a member of a community socially and emotionally [73]. However, online learning satisfaction is greatly influenced by how online learners perceive their online presence [74, 75] and how continuous communication is within the given group and course [76].

4.1 Method

The aim of the survey conducted with the involvement of the students of the University of Pannonia was to get to know the their digital competencies, feelings and experiences during online learning in the COVID-19 virus situation.

The study was conducted using a questionnaire, which was distributed online between 6 and 25 May 2020. It consisted 3 parts: demographic questions, he Internet Skill Scale (ISS) [39] and the Online Social Presence Questionnaire (OSPQ) [77]. To measure ISS and OSPQ, a 5 + 1 Likert scale was applied, on which 1 = strongly disagree, 5 = strongly agree, and respondents had the opportunity not to answer for each statement if they could not decide whether the answer was relevant.

We applied the Internet Skill Scale (ISS) tool developed by Van Deursen et al. [39] to measure digital knowledge. The instrument Internet Skills Scale is specifically designed to capture a full range of Internet skills from basic to advanced levels. The ISS contains 35 questions that can be classified into five factors. The five factors are *operational, information navigation, social, creative*, and *mobile*. The tool measures general and digital knowledge, avoiding device-specific activities and elements. An exception to this is the skills associated with mobile phones, which almost everyone has. Both of the Cronbach alpha's were calculated on our data, and for both questionnaires, a higher score means a higher level of digital knowledge or online social presence. The reliability coefficient of the Internet Skill Scale (ISS) obtained by Cronbach's alpha was 0.706.

To measure the social presence, we used the Online Social Presence Questionnaire (OSPQ) [77]. The OSPQ contains 19 items, which also fall into five factors. These five diemsions are *social respect, social sharing, open mind, social identity*, and *intimacy*. The reliability coefficient of the Online Social Presence Questionnaire (OSPQ) obtained by Cronbach's alpha was 0.932.

5 Results

The participants were recruited using a snowball sampling procedure. They were invited to participate in the online survey and were asked to share the questionnaires' link with their friends. The questionnaire was completed by 105 students (27 men and 78 women), mainly between 20 and 30 years (mean = 26.87, SD = 8.385). Most of the respondents were Ba/Bsc students, and a large proportion of the respondents were further education certificate (FEC) course students. Table 1 summarizes the descriptive data of the respondents.

Table 1. Demographic information of the respondents (N = 105).

Demographics		*Frequency*	*Percentage*
Gender	Male	27	25.7
	Female	78	74.3
Age	Under 20	2	1.9
	20–30	96	91.4
	Above 30	7	6.7
Education	FEC	31	29.5
	BA/Bsc	67	63.8
	MA/Msc	5	4.8
	5-year (BA + MA)	1	1.0
	Dual	1	1.0

At the beginning of our research, we made four assumptions, which are presented below.

H1: We assumed a relationship between Internet Skills and Online Social Presence. The results (Table 2) indicate no significant correlation between the two factors ($r = 0.081$, $p = 0.412$).

Table 2. Correlation between IS and OSP.

		Szum OSP
Szum IS	Pearson correlation	.081
	Sig. (2-tailed)	.412
	N	105

Note: * $p < 0.05$, ** $p < 0.001$

H2: We hypothesized that Internet skills are also related to social presence at the level of factors. At the bottom of the results presented in Table 3, it can be said that there is a week relationship between some of the factors of internet skills and social presence.

The results show that there is a significant relationship between the internet skill creative factor and the online social presence, social respect, and social identity factors ($p < 0.05$). The internet skill social factor is also significantly related to the online social presence social identity factor ($p < 0.05$), and the internet skill social and creative factors are related to the online social presence social sharing factor ($p < 0.001$). Furthermore, we found a significant relationship between the internet skill social factor and the online social presence intimacy factor ($p < 0.001$).

Table 3. Correlation between factors of IS and OSP.

	Social respect	Social sharing	Open mind	Social identity	Intimacy
Operational	.025	.025	−.043	.138	.126
Information navigation	−.064	−.081	−.028	−.100	−.087
Social	.144	.304**	.170	.250*	.347**
Creative	.229*	.342**	.190	.242*	.162
Mobile	.012	.020	-.039	.009	.159

Note: * $p < 0.05$, **$p < 0.001$

H3: We assumed that there is a negative correlation between age and the internet skill scale. The respondents' mean age was 26.87 years (SD = 8.385), and the mean score of the ISS was 137.067 (SD = 9.945). As shown in Table 4, there is no significant relationship between the two variables ($r = -0.167$; $p = 0.089$).

Table 4. Correlation between IS and Age.

		Age
Szum IS	Pearson correlation	−.167
	Sig. (2-tailed)	.089
	N	105

Note: * $p < 0.05$, **$p < 0.001$

H4: We assumed that men and women have the same OSP and ISS scores. Table 5 shows that ISS's mean score for men is 141.5158; while for women, it is 135.5256. A similar trend difference in OSP mean scores can be observed between the two groups. The average for men is 75.3333; while women scored an average of 75.1282 points on the OSP scale.

Based on the results, we can say that there is a significant difference between the group of men and women in terms of ISS ($p = 0.006$; $t = 2.785$), but there is no significant difference in terms of OSP ($p = 0.955$; $t = 0.056$), so we reject the hypothesis in part.

Table 5 shows the descriptive statistics of internet skills and online social presence.

Table 5. Descriptive statistics of IS and OSP scores.

	N	Min	Max	Mean	SD	Variance
Total ISS score	105	112.00	175.00	137.0667	9.94530	98.909
Male	27			141.5185	10.33430	
Female	78			135.5256	9.39014	
Total OSP score	105	28.00	95.00	75.181	16.2147	262.919
Male	27			75.3333	19.13917	
Female	78			75.1282	15.21223	

6 Conclusion

As online learning's popularity continues to grow, there is a need to understand how the learning experience can be further enhanced and facilitated for learners in online and video-centric environments. The rapid development of digital devices and the related digital intelligence and the limitations caused by the current pandemic make it difficult to understand all this. Online education and learning is in itself a completely different situation than the usual, personal form. In our current situation, several factors make the adaptation process challenging. Many people have been forced to change their plans, either in terms of their studies or work. Although the phenomenon of online education, as well as online social presence is not new, we did not find any research examining OSP as a function of digital knowledge.

Our present research was exploratory, intending to assess students' digital competence and their presence during online learning and the existence of a relationship between the two factors. This research aimed to pilot the applicability of the measuring tools in Hungary Overall, the Hungarian language versions of both questionnaires can be said to be excellent for other research purposes.

Based on our results, it can be said that the participants in the sample have a moderately-strong level of digital competence. This level was influenced by several factors, such as the amount of time spent using the Internet. Although we did not find a correlation between age and the level of digital knowledge based on the sample examined.

Further studies are needed to test the proposed hypotheses. A similar situation exists concerning gender differences. We found only a significant difference between the two genders, but this may be due, among other things, to the fact that it was a small and unequally distributed sample.

Regarding the online social presence, the respondents achieved a reasonably high level, which can probably be attributed to their age specificity and flexibility, but proving this requires further research. Although the results did not indicate a significant relationship between Internet skills and social presence, some factors have a positive correlation.

Our future aim is to extend the scales to a larger sample and conduct correlation studies between digital knowledge and online social presence. In this way, we would be able to identify each age group's characteristics, and we think it is worth repeating the research even after the COVID-19 pandemic.

In the present exposition, we have also encountered two limitations, which we intend to further develop in another paper. It is the first time that the present study focuses on students at the University of Pannonia. Our aim is to repeat the research in other universities and populations. Another such limitation is that our present research took place during COVID-19, as a result of which the sudden shift from offline education to online learning may have influenced the results. In the future, it will also be valuable to compare it with the results of students who have been studying online for a long time and not as a result of a forced change. The third limitation of the study is that in future research, it is necessary to examine to what extent the online social presence perceived by students contributes to their study results.

References

1. Rice, R.E.: Media appropriateness: using social presence theory to compare traditional and new organization media. Hum. Commun. Res. **19**(4), 451–484 (1993)
2. Short, J.A., Williams, E., Christie, B.: The Social Psychology of Telecommunications, vol. 3. John Wiley, London (1976)
3. Walther, J.B.: Interpersonal effects in computer-mediated interaction: a relational perspective. Commun. Res. **19**(1), 52–90 (1992)
4. Walther, J.B., Burgoon, J.K.: Relational communication in computer-mediated interaction. Hum. Commun. Res. **19**, 50–88 (1992)
5. Seaman, J.E., Allen, I.E., Seaman, J.: Grade Increase: Tracking Distance Education in the United States. Babson Survey Research Group (2018)
6. Burke, L.: Colleges Move Online Amid Virus Fears (2020). https://www.insidehighered.com/news/2020/03/09/colleges-move-classes-online-coronavirus-infects-more
7. Goldstein, D.: Coronavirus is shutting schools. Is America ready for virtual learning? (2020). https://www.nytimes.com/2020/03/13/us/virtual-learning-challenges.html
8. Brown Barnes, C.J.: Noble Education survey reveals college student preparedness split: technically ready for online learning, but emotionally unsure (2020). https://www.businesswire.com/news/home/20200408005156/en/
9. Chang, C.M., Hsu, M.H.: Understanding the determinants of users' subjective well-being in social networking sites: an integration of social capital theory and social presence theory. Behav. Inf. Technol. **35**(9), 720–729 (2016)
10. Cui, G., Lockee, B., Meng, C.: Building modern online social presence: a review of social presence theory and its instructional design implications for future trends. Educ. Inf. Technol. **18**(4), 661–685 (2013)
11. Dunlap, J.C., Lowenthal, P.R.: Tweeting the night away: using twitter to enhance social presence. J. Inf. Syst. Educ. **20**(2), 129–136 (2009)
12. McLean, G., Wilson, A.: Evolving the online customer experience… is there a role for online customer support? Comput. Hum. Behav. **60**, 602–610 (2016)

13. McLean, G., Osei-Frimpong, K.: Examining satisfaction with the experience during a live chat service encounter-implications for website providers. Comput. Hum. Behav. **76**, 494–508 (2017)
14. Shen, K.N., Yu, A.Y., Khalifa, M.: Knowledge contribution in virtual communities: accounting for multiple dimensions of social presence through social identity. Behav. Inf. Technol. **29**(4), 337–348 (2010)
15. Statista, Share of households with a computer at home in developed countries from 2005 to 2019. https://www.statista.com/statistics/748557/developed-countries-households-with-computer/. Accessed 21 may 2020
16. Statista, Global digital population as of April 2020. https://www.statista.com/statistics/617136/digital-population-worldwide/. Accessed 21 May 2020
17. Statista, Forecast number of mobile users worldwide from 2019 to 2023. https://www.statista.com/statistics/218984/number-of-global-mobile-users-since-2010/. Accessed 21 May 2020
18. Janssen, J., Stoyanov, S., Ferrari, A., Punie, Y., Pannekeet, K., Sloep, P.: Experts' views on digital competence: commonalities and differences. Comput. Educ. **68**, 473–481 (2013)
19. World Bank: ICTs are creating new jobs and making labor markets more innovative, inclusive, and global – World Bank study. https://www.worldbank.org/en/news/press-re-lease/2013/09/10/icts-are-creating-new-jobs-and-making-labor-markets-more-innovative-inclusive-and-global-world-bank-study. Accessed 01 Feb 2018
20. Ilomäki, L., Paavola, S., Lakkala, M., Kantosalo, A.: Digital competence–an emergent boundary concept for policy and educational research. Educ. Inf. Technol. **21**(3), 655–679 (2016)
21. European Community: Key competences for lifelong learning - A European framework. Publication Office for Official Publications of the European Communities, Luxembourg (2007)
22. Vuorikari, R., Punie, Y., Carretero Gomez S., Van den Brande, G.: DigComp 2.0: The Digital Competence Framework for Citizens. Update Phase 1: The Conceptual Reference Model. Luxembourg Publication Office of the European Union, Luxembourg (2016)
23. Carretero, S., Vuorikari, R., Punie, Y.: DigComp 2.1: The Digital Competence Framework for Citizens with eight proficiency levels and examples of use. Publications Office of the European Union, Luxembourg (2017)
24. Brečko, B., Ferrari, A.: The Digital Competence Framework for Consumers. Publications Office of the European Union, Luxembourg (2016)
25. Richardson, J.C., Maeda, Y., Lv, J., Caskurlu, S.: Social presence in relation to students' satisfaction and learning in the online environment: a meta-analysis. Comput. Hum. Behav. **71**, 402–417 (2017)
26. Reio, T.G., Jr., Crim, S.J.: Social presence and student satisfaction as predictors of online enrollment intent. Am. J. Distance Educ. **27**(2), 122–133 (2013)
27. Berger, J.B., Milem, J.F.: The role of student involvement and perceptions of integration in a causal model of student persistence. Res. High. Educ. **40**(6), 641–664 (1999)
28. Swan, K., Shih, L.F.: On the nature and development of social presence in online course discussions. J. Asynchronous Learn. Netw. **9**(3), 115–136 (2005)
29. Mazzolini, M., Maddison, S.: When to jump in: the role of the instructor in online discussion forums. Comput. Educ. **49**(2), 193–213 (2007)
30. Hughes, J.N., Luo, W., Kwok, O.M., Loyd, L.K.: Teacher-student support, effortful engagement, and achievement: a 3-year longitudinal study. J. Educ. Psychol. **100**(1), 1–14 (2008)
31. Tu, C.H.: Online learning migration: from social learning theory to social presence theory in CMC environment. J. Netw. Comput. Appl. **23**(1), 27–37 (2000)
32. Short, J., Williams, E., Christie, B.: The Social Psychology of Telecommunications. John Wiley, Hoboken (1976)

33. Biocca, F., Harms, C.: Defining and measuring social presence: contribution to the networked minds theory and measure. Proceedings of Presence **2002**, 1–36 (2002)
34. Gunawardena, C.N.: Social presence theory and implications for interaction and collaborative learning in computer conferences. Int. J. Educ. Telecommun. **1**(2), 147–166 (1995)
35. Biocca, F.: The cyborg's dilemma: progressive embodiment in virtual environments. J. Comput.-Mediated Commun. **3**(2), JCMC324 (1997)
36. Reeves, B., Nass, C.I.: The Media Equation: How People Treat Computers, Television, and New Media like Real People and Places. Cambridge University Press, Cambridge (1996)
37. Gunawardena, C.N., Zittle, F.J.: Social presence as a predictor of satisfaction within a computer-mediated conferencing environment. Am. J. Distance Educ. **11**(3), 8–26 (1997)
38. Perse, E.I., Burton, P., Kovner, E., Lears, M.E., Sen, R.J.: Predicting computer-mediated communication in a college class. Commun. Res. Rep. **9**(2), 161–170 (1992)
39. Van Deursen, A.J., Helsper, E.J., Eynon, R.: Development and validation of the internet skills scale (ISS). Inf. Commun. Soc. **19**(6), 804–823 (2016)
40. Kress, G.R.: Literacy in the New Media Age. Routledge, London (2003)
41. Kress, G.R., Van Leeuwen, T.: Reading Images: The Grammar of Visual Design, 2nd edn. Routledge, Florence (2006)
42. Jolls, T.: Literacy for the 21st Century: An Overview & Orientation Guide to Media Literacy Education: Center for Media Literacy (2008)
43. Ohler, J.: Digital Storytelling in the Classroom. Learning, and Creativity. Corwin Press, Thousand Oaks, New Media Pathways to Literacy (2008)
44. Frazel, M.: Digital Storytelling Guide for Educators. International Society for Technology in Education, USA (2010)
45. Gilster, P.: Digital Literacy. John Wiley, New York (1997)
46. Gee, J.P.: What Video Games Have to Teach as About Learning and Literacy?, 1st edn. Palgrave Macmillan, New York (2003)
47. Lankshear, C., Knobel, M.: New Literacies: Changing Knowledge and Classroom Learning. Open University Press, Buckingham England (2003)
48. Ibrahim, N., Shariman, T.N.T., Woods, P.: The Concept of Digital Literacy from the Perspective of the Creative Multimedia Industry 2013 International Conference, pp. 259–264. IEEE (2013)
49. Koltay, T.: The media and the literacies: media literacy, information literacy, digital literacy. Med. Cult. Soc. **33**(2), 211–221 (2011)
50. Partnership for 21st Century Learning. Framework for 21st Century Learning (2015), 12 October 2016. https://www.p21.org
51. Voogt, J., Roblin, N.P.: A comparative analysis of international frameworks for 21st century competences: implications for national curriculum policies. J. Curriculum Stud. **44**(3), 299–321 (2012)
52. Eshet-Alkalai, Y.: Digital literacy: a conceptual framework for survival skills in the digital era. J. Educ. Multimed. Hypermed. **13**(1), 93–106 (2004)
53. Goodfellow, R.: Literacy, literacies and the digital in higher education. Teach. High. Educ. **16**(1), 131–144 (2011)
54. Bak, G.: Digitális kompetencia: új trend vagy szükséges tudás? In: Conference Proceedings of VI. Winter Conference of Economics Ph.D. Students and Researchers, pp. 6–13. Doktoranduszok Országos Szövetsége, Gödöllő (2020)
55. SCONUL Working Group on Information Literacy. The SCONUL Seven Pillars of Information Literacy (2011). https://www.sconul.ac.uk/sites/default/files/documents/coremodel.pdf
56. Lankshear, C., Knobel, M.: Digital Literacies: Concepts. Policies and Practices. Peter Lang, New York (2008)

57. Greene, J.A., Yu, S.B., Copeland, D.Z.: Measuring critical components of digital literacy and their relationships with learning. Comput. Educ. **76**, 55–69 (2014)
58. SIEMENS. African Digitalization Maturity Report (2017). https://www.siemens.co.za/pool/about_us/CG_17-015_African_Digitalization_Maturity_Report.pdf
59. Covello, S., Lei, J.: A Review of Digital Literacy Assessment Instruments. Syracuse University, pp. 1–31 (2010)
60. McKinsey and Company: Offline and Falling behind: Barriers to Internet Adoption, September 2014. https://www.mckinsey.com/industries/high-tech/our-insights/offline-andfalling-behind-barriers-to-internet-adoption
61. Ridsdale, C., et al.: Strategies and Best Practices for Data Literacy Education: Knowledge (2015)
62. UNESCO Institute for Information Technologies in Education. Digital Literacy in Education. Policy Brief, May 2011 (2011). https://unesdoc.unesco.org/images/0021/002144/214485e.pdf
63. Gallardo-Echenique, E.E., de Oliveira, J.M., Marqués-Molias, L., Esteve-Mon, F., Wang, Y., Baker, R.: Digital competence in the knowledge society. MERLOT J. Online Learn. Teach. **11**(1), 1–16 (2015)
64. Calvani, A., Cartelli, A., Fini, A., Ranieri, M.: Models and instruments for assessing digital competence at school. J. E-learn. Knowl. Soc. **4**(3), 183–193 (2008)
65. Kang, M., Choi, H., Park, S.: Construction and validation of a social presence scale for measuring online learners' involvement. In: EdMedia+ Innovate Learning, pp. 1829–1833. Association for the Advancement of Computing in Education (AACE), Waynesville (2007)
66. Allen, I.E., Seaman, J.: Online Report Card: Tracking Online Education in the United States. Babson Survey Research Group, Massachusetts (2016)
67. Horzum, M.B.: Interaction, structure, social presence, and satisfaction in online learning. Eurasia J. Math. Sci. Technol. Educ. **11**(3), 505–512 (2017)
68. Bloom, M.: E-learning in Canada: findings from 2003 e-survey: top line findings from a survey of the Conference Board of Canada's customers on current e-learning practices: a special report. Conference Board of Canada, Ontario (2003)
69. de Bruyn, L.L.: Monitoring online communication: can the development of convergence and social presence indicate an interactive learning environment? Distance Educ. **25**, 67–81 (2004)
70. Christopherson, K.M.: The positive and negative implications of anonymity in internet social interactions: "On the internet, nobody knows you're a dog." Comput. Hum. Behav. **23**, 3038–3056 (2007)
71. Cobb, S.C.: Social presence and online learning: a current view from a research perspective. J. Interact. Online Learn. **8**(3), 241–254 (2009)
72. Shin, N.: Transactional presence as a critical predictor of success in distance learning. Distance Educ. **24**(1), 69–86 (2003)
73. Garrison, D.R., Anderson, T., Archer, W.: Critical inquiry in a text-based environment: computer conferencing in higher education. Internet High. Educ. **2**(2/3), 87–105 (1999)
74. Richardson, J.C., Swan, K.: Examining social presence in online courses in relation to students' perceived learning and satisfaction. J. Asynchronous Learn. Netw. **7**(1), 68–88 (2003)
75. Gunawardena, C., Lowe, C.A., Anderson, T.: Analysis of a global online debate and the development of an interaction analysis model for examining social construction of knowledge in computer conference. J. Educ. Comput. Res. **17**(4), 397–431 (1997)
76. Poquet, O., Kovanović, V., de Vries, P., Hennis, T., Joksimović, S., Gašević, D., Dawson, S.: Social presence in massive open online courses. Int. Rev. Res. Open Distrib. Learn. **19**(3), 43–68 (2018)
77. Sung, E., Mayer, R.E.: Five facets of social presence in online distance education. Comput. Hum. Behav. **28**(5), 1738–1747 (2012)

Virtual Internship as Mediatized Experience. The Educator's Training During COVID19 Emergency

Laura Sara Agrati[1(✉)] and Viviana Vinci[2]

[1] 'Giustino Fortunato' University, Benevento, Italy
ls.agrati@unifortunato.eu
[2] Mediterranea University of Reggio Calabria, Reggio Calabria, Italy
viviana.vinci@unirc.it

Abstract. The work presents the multimodal study on the didactic solutions adopted for virtual internship of the Degree Course 'Educational Sciences' at the Giustino Fortunato University in response to the COVID19 emergency. It focuses on how the internship - assumed as an 'active mediation device' – has been reshaped in virtual form – i.e., it has been 'mediatized' - and set objectives of investigation as: the effect of specific LMS sources, the interactive web seminars taken within the e-tivities structures, on educational skill, such as the professional thinking that is explicit in the design of interventions; the use of iconic means in the simulations of cases and problems. The synthesis of two different types of analysis and documents - verbal interaction-exchanges on webinar transcriptions and iconic mediators used to illustrate the simulated case – shows that: a. if virtual internship provides targeted e-tivities on specific skills, it would be useful for building of professional thinking and skills; b. specifically, web seminars - interactive between mentor and mentee and supported by explanatory means, such as images - can have an effect in the simulation of problematic cases and, in this way, exercise the design skill of intervention.

Keywords: Virtual internship · Mediatization · COVID-19 pandemic emergency

1 Introduction – *Internship Training and Effect of COVID-19 Pandemic Emergency*

Internships within higher education has nowadays spread in many country: it is increasingly assumed as a training 'device' that favors a 'filtered' entry into the concrete practice of jobs, a support to develop professional knowledge. As theorized by education researchers and learning scientists [1, 2], practical experiences in authentic and real contexts are taken as an effective complement to academic programs and classroom teaching. After an initial period of uncertainty due to often 'anecdotal' investigation methods [3, 4], the 'high-impact' of internship training practice has been demonstrated during the years by research: specifically, a causal relationship with the improving of student engagement and academic outcomes [5], more likely to be contacted for a job

L. S. Agrati et al. (Eds.): HELMeTO 2020, CCIS 1344, pp. 170–183, 2021.
https://doi.org/10.1007/978-3-030-67435-9_14

interview immediately after graduation [6]. Many degree courses in the educational and social sector provided increasingly intra-curricular internship practices for reasons related to the profession, not only the impact [7, 8]: the development of a specific practical knowledge, non-exhaustive sum of personal elements and procedures acquired [9, 10], alongside other 'reflective' training devices, such as laboratories or professional writing [11]. Numerous internship programs have been carried out over the years, different according to the duration, objectives and type of tutorship [12]. Thanks to the sophisticated information technologies - that make available simulations and virtual reality - and to the development of related e-learning models - such as 'integrated' [13, 14] -, in recent years the type of online or remote internships has gained importance [6] within the training of future professionals [15].

The COVID-19 pandemic in 2020 is impacting higher education and internships in a way that cannot yet be described [16].

As stated by the National Association of Colleges and Employers [17], about 80% of employers (400 companies) in the US have changed their internship programs by reducing the duration and distance relationship; the remainder took more extreme measures, canceling the programs. Cartus [18], an US job relocation service company, investigated on 50 companies: 30% of internship program have been switched to the virtual, 27% canceled, 16% have not been changed, 11% have been reduced in time. The aim of these first surveys is, however, to foreshadow the effects on the quality of vocational training and the impact in the case of complete cancellation.

As pointed out by Hora et al. [12], the choice of online internships as useful mode of "work-based learning for students around the world" has broader reasons including the growing job insecurity – linked to the so-called 'gig' economy - and the possibilities of remote access [6]. For this reason, the analysis on the impact of online internships would have to be conducted in a way functional to the emergency from COVID19 and to describe the so-called 'coronateaching'[1] [16, p. 25] but also to grasp the effective adaptation of the curriculum and of the teaching methodologies involved.

2 Objectives of the Study – *Virtual Internship in the Mediation Perspective*

National Association of Colleagues and Employers (NACE) generally defined internship as a "legitimate learning experience benefitting the student and not simply an operational work experience" [17, p. 78]. Internship is often associated, and sometime confused, with experiences of co-operation, student teaching, field experience, clinical placement, having each one unique formats, regulations, and educational goals [19].

There is a meaningful difference among online internships, in refers to the host organization, duration, compliance with standards. As noted by authors:

[1] "Transforming the presential classes to a virtual mode, without changing the curriculum or the methodology (…) abrupt entry into a complex teaching modality, with multiple technological and pedagogical options, and with a steep learning curve (that might imply) frustration and overwhelm due to adaptation to an educational modality never before experienced without the corresponding training" [16, p. 25].

"there is no single format or structure for an internship: in contrast to work-based learning programs such as students-teaching in K12 pre-service teacher training programs, where the experience is structured in accordance with the requirements state and/or professional certification requirements (…) college internships come in all shapes and sizes" [12, p. 4].

Hora et al. [12] propose to define 'online internship' as training programs and work-based learning experiences at post-secondary institutions, employers or third-party suppliers, which do not meet high quality criteria and to assume as 'virtual internship' the more elaborate and qualitatively valid experiences, such as the 'legitimate internships' proposed by NACE or CCWT (Center for Research on College-Workforce Transition) organizations (Table 1).

Table 1. Criteria for 'legitimate internship' (Adatt. [17]).

Extension	Activities must be an extension of the training course and provide for the application of the knowledge acquired, not only be functional to the employer process or linked to the duties that a regular employee would habitually carry out
Transferability	Acquired skills or knowledge must be able to be transferred to other working contexts, not be tied exclusively to the experiential context[a]
Temporal and formative description	Defined beginning and end of the experience and explanation of the activities in terms of learning objectives and professional profile within the course of study
Supervision	An experienced professional offers professional and educational guidance in the field of experience; another expert offers feedback as a process supervisor
Provided means	"Resource" and "equipment" are provided by the employer based on the learning objectives

[a]Hora et al. [12] are keen to clarify that the skills related to the face-to-face or online internship experience should not be of the 'soft' type or, also called, '21st century' - considered too ambiguous and generic (e.g. teamwork, communication skills, critical thinking and problem solving, etc.) - rather they should be linked to the specific professional profile instead.

Although the empirical research on the impacts of online internships on student outcomes is relatively little, nevertheless sufficient technology, pre-internship orientations, effective supervision and self-regulated learning seems to be important for successful experiences [12, p. 2]. Moore et al. [20] proposed for the virtual internship the same distinctive criterion used by scholars regards e-learning, distance learning and online learning. Specific surveys have investigated the characteristics of online/virtual internships, exploring specific aspects of teaching and learning in online setting: student-teacher and peer relation - from the cultural differences [21] and social network analysis [22] – and engagement with content knowledge [23]. Over the years, such didactic assumptions and the technological refinement allow to clarify the internship experiences through technological means and to distinguish characteristics as *virtual*, *computer-mediated*, *simulated* and *remote internship*.

Table 2. Typology of online internship. Adatt. [12]

Construct used	Definition	Description
Virtual internship [24]	Access to an environment supported by ICT, in which students interact with each other, regardless of space-time constraints. The aim is to carry out meaningful 'work-based' activities in line with the student's compulsory educational curriculum	Key elements, planning and evaluation of the virtual internship in Pakistan
Computer-mediated internship (e-internship/simulated internship) [25]	*E-internship* = real-world workstation where the trainee's interaction is mainly computer-mediated. *Simulated internship* = students are placed in a very structured learning experiences (as immersive virtual environment) "that replicates the real-world internship setting"	Conceptual literature review comparing hypothetical learning objectives (*traditional, e-internship, simulated internship*)
E-internship (virtual internship) [26]	Internships partially or entirely computer-mediated, provided by the employer or an institution	Empirical study on impact of mentoring on the e-trainee' satisfaction and on the development of skills
Remote internship [27]	Field tasks led by stakeholder entrusted to a student who performs them off-site and in flexible hours through generic or specific ICT tools	Dutch pilot study on communication tools and design prototypes for the use of students in a remote internship program
Virtual internship (Professional practice simulator) [28]	It simulates authentic problems and provides students with the opportunity to practice within a realistic professional environment	Complement to the introduction to the university course. Engineering students are involved in computer lab and work as a team on a virtual 'fictional' project under the control of design consultants
Micro-internship [29]	Real-world paid and monitored work experience	Description of a platform that connects numerous trainees to numerous mentors

Some types of online/virtual internships referred to the study by Hora et al. [6] are presented below (Table 2)[2].

Based on the specific literature related to the characteristics of the teaching-learning setting of the virtual internship (Moore et al. 2011) [20] and focusing on the tutoring support in the elaboration of the trainee's practical knowledge [23], an exploratory study was carried out on the first virtual internship adaptation, realized during the COVID-19 pandemic emergency at the 'Science of Education' graduation course of Telematic University 'Giustino Fortuntano'.

[2] Hora et al. [6] carried out a literature review with an integrative approach - review, critique and synthesis of a *corpus* of literature with the aim of providing a comprehensive understanding, regarding how online internships have been conceptualized. For more information on the inclusion/exclusion criteria, see p. 8.

Table 3. Characteristics of virtual internship as *analogical* mediator.

Type of analogy	Function	Criterion of validity	Examples
Representation	Re-present reality as it is	*Adequacy* (unconscious pretense)	Dream, illusion, hallucinogenic experiences (without de-briefing)
Simulation	Building another reality	*Verisimilitude* (conscious pretense)	Game, internship, virtual community (forum, chat) (with de-briefing)

Refers to the didactic theory of mediation [30, 31], virtual internship has been framed in the 'simulation of professional practice' model [28] and assumed as *analogical* mediator that creates an alternative reality to that of real experience - not as 'representation' (*adequacy* criterion) but 'simulation' (*verisimilitude* criterion) and 'attention' - and supports processing of knowledge and beliefs [32].

In contrast to previous studies on the perception of trainees [23], the support for the mediation of knowledge carried out by tutors in the online environment has been investigated, in particular the *verbal*, *analogical* and *symbolic* means that reproduced the professional reality of which to experience. The study therefore focused on how the internship - assumed as an 'active mediation device' [31] - is rendered in virtual form – i.e., it has been 'mediatized' [32] - and set the following objectives of investigation: in general, on the effect of specific LMS sources [13], the interactive web seminars taken within the e-tivities structures [33], on educational skill, such as the professional thinking that is explicit in the design of interventions; specifically, on the use of iconic means [34–36] in the simulations of cases and problems.

3 Method – *A Case-Study on 'Professional Thinking'*

Given the variety of organizational forms and the specificity of non-transferable academic virtual internship experiences [3, 37], a univocal method of analysis of the online teaching-learning setting is not yet available but it is possible to refer to some previous studies. For the training of future engineers, Chesler et al. [28] demonstrated that virtual internship, based on individualized mentoring and simulated authentic problems, supports students in solving real problems and trainers in evaluating 'engineering thinking' [38]. The simulation of concrete experience, supported by different mediators and mentors, allows the evaluation of learning processes and outcomes in different ways: analysis of the students' final projects, comparison between knowledge/attitudes pre-post experience:

> a "system automatically records students' (a) reports and other work products, (b) conversations with colleagues and mentors (…), (c) (…) notebook entries, and (d) final proposals or presentations (it) allows the analysis of student learning (…) and measure of the development of professional (…) thinking" [28, p. 3].

Through the epistemic discourse coding, the study by Chesler et al. [28] referred to the quantification and visualization of the learning epistemic structures theory [39] - keyword coding and coding scheme through Cohen's kappa -; it compared the emerged coding scheme and a standardized one. Referring to the studies on development of professional thinking [28, 40] the empirical analysis of the exploratory study was carried out on individualized *interactive-exchange* with mentors - realized through the web seminars and supported by iconic means - functional to the illustration of the problem [13] to be solved and to provide feedback to the elaboration of the project work.

3.1 Context and Case-Study Description

In the virtual internship of the 'Science of education' undergraduate courses at the UniFortunato, students have been involved in the simulation of educational intervention activities within a childhood service, where they design the adaptation of the space-section to be used by children with special educational needs (see Table 4 – structures of e-tivity) [33]. The simulated activity presents the characteristics of a 'case-study'[3].

Table 4. E-tivity structure of case-study Adatt: [33].

Salmon's item	Examples of transcriptions	LMS sources
Clarification/description	The space in the childhood nest	Lesson
Summary of activities	Educator has an area of 5 × 8 m available, 4 movable low-tables, 3 poufs, 3 hypoallergenic carpets	Task Case report
Spark	What should be excluded/included, considering the type of activity and the number of children?	Forum
Individual contribution	*I would eliminate the poufs because they are not functional for manual work. I'd rather arrange the tables...*	Webinar 1 forum
Dialogue	*'If you consider this specific aspect, it will seem easier then to choose the direction'* *'The direction is given by the direction in which the path can be traveled'*	Webinar 2
Moderator interventions		Forum

Each student starts the virtual internship by viewing a video lesson on the specific subject (*video lesson*), sustaining an initial online talk with mentor (*webinar 1*) and producing an early online report on the case (*case report*). During the 12 weeks of virtual internship (frequency: 13 h per week), the student works alone or collaborating with other trainees and mentors to complete the specific task related to the design of the

[3] 'Similar to problem-based learning, but presents a factually based complex problem in which there is not necessarily a right or wrong answer. The case is usually read individually and discussed as part of a larger group (class/team)', [13, p. 138].

educational intervention. Trainees can learn more about the case through literature made available by experts or through personal research, shared online. The trainee proposes a first project (*project work 1*), that is submitted to the internal staff of the virtual childcare service. One or more referents comment on whether the project presented meets known standards - respect for safety, reliability, feasibility [41]. Based on the feedback, reported via forum and second thematic webinar (*forum, webinar 1*), the trainee edits the final version of the project work in presentation version (*project work 2*), which is filed as official document (see Fig. 1, e-learning activities and Moodle's icons).

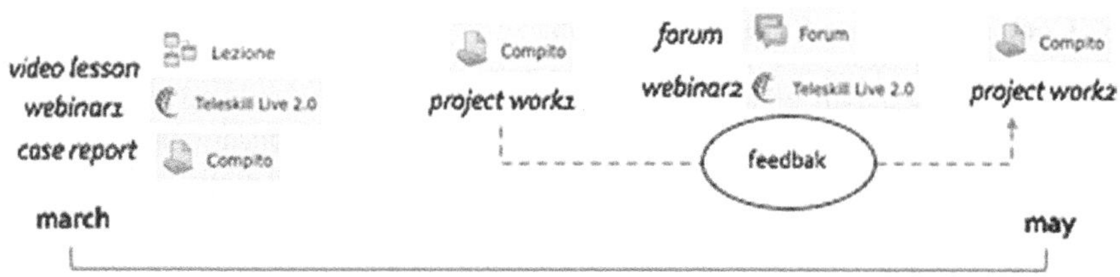

Fig. 1. Virtual internship e-learning activities – case-study

3.2 Data, Coding and Analysis

Based on the Kirkatrick model, adapted to the e-learning environment - which replaces four (reaction, learning, behavior, results) with three (interaction, learning, results) tips - [42], attention was focused on level 2 of learnings with reference to a case-study completed virtual internship (March–May 2020). The triangulation of methods in adult distance learning [43] has been the methodological basis of the study. Quali/quantitative data were collected in a Moodle environment via interface. The synthesis of two different types of analysis and documents has been done:

- analysis of verbal interaction-exchanges on webinar transcriptions, direct interactive exchange between trainee and mentor – see *webinar 1* and *webinar 2*;
- analysis of the iconic mediators used to illustrate the simulated case - see *lesson, task, webinar 1* and *webinar 2*.

Question n. 1 - How was the effect of interactive web seminars on the educational professional thinking during the design of interventions?

We started by asking which of the LMS resources used in the virtual internship path had had more weight in the elaboration of the final work (*project work2*) and in order to operationalize the issue we counted the number of accesses of the single student to the single resources and, for each them, the number of interactions and the permanence time - see Table 4 and Fig. 1. In reference to the interactive web seminars transcriptions, the method of a recent study on pedagogical mentoring in virtual exchange [44] has been used, refers to the Ware's [45] Linguistic and Interactional Features. In terms of operationalization, the transcripts of interactive exchanges are analyzed on the basis of established analytical categories (see Table 5).

Table 5. Linguistic and Interactional Features of Ware [45]. Adapt.: [44] p. 156.

Analytic category	Examples from transcriptions
"Emotive words and phrases (total sentences containing words or phrases that reflected the emotional state of the speaker)"	I'm not sure this is the correct way
"Personal forms of address" (number of times the interactive partner's name/appellation was used)	Dear, prof., please …
Topic development (sentences related the on topics in questions introduced by interactive partner)	Yes, other times I have resorted to…
"Question posing (total questions posed including declarative statements followed by a ?)"	Can we then assume it is right for us?
"Personal information" (sentences containing personal information that do not interest to the interactive partner)	I have already tried to change the layout of the desks with my pupils and I believe that I will continue to use this mode at other times
"Display of alignment" (phrases of support, agreement or praise)	So, well, it's very clear. In addition I add that…

Question n. 2 - How useful was the iconic means in the simulations of cases and problems?

Regarding the analysis of the iconic means, we focused on the images used during two e-tivity item - 'clarification/description' and 'summery of activities' of *lesson, task* and *case-report* (Table 4, Fig. 1, Fig. 2).

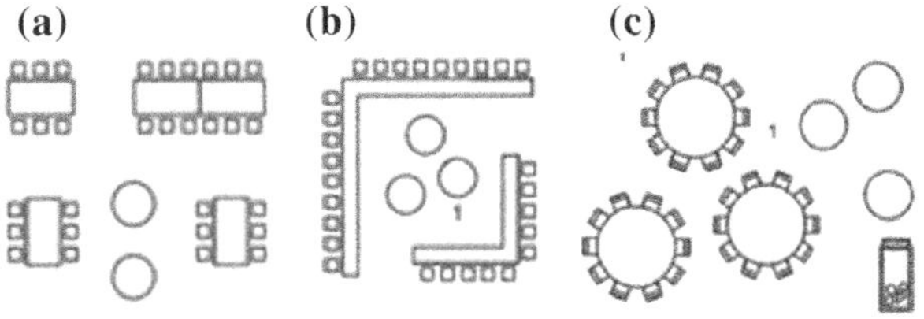

Fig. 2. a, b, c – Iconic mediators used during the simulation – Adapt.: [41] p. 78–83.

In order to observe how was useful the explanatory images in the description of the problematic case to be solved, the number of references to these means - a, b, c - during the verbal interactions (*web seminars1* and *2*) and the references to it in *project-work 1* were counted.

4 Results

Table 6 reports the total of expressions related to Ware's 6 linguistic and interaction categories as well as rate per 1.000 words, for what concern the interactive web seminars transcriptions.

Table 6. Use of linguistic and interaction features Adapt.: [45].

Linguistic and Interactional Features	Webinar1 (1h) (illustration of the case) 6896 words	Webinar2 (1h) (feedback on project work1) 7578 words	14474 words
Emotive words/phrases			
Total	84	53	137
% per 1000	12.2	7.0	9.5 (-5.2)
Personal forms of address			
Total	42	22	64
% per 1000	6.1	2.9	4.4 (-3.2)
Topic development			
Total	285	328	613
% per 1000	41.3	43.3	42.4 (+2.0)
Question posing			
Total	60	130	190
% per 1000	8.7	17.2	13.1 (+8.5)
Personal information			
Total	66	62	128
% per 1000	9.5	8.2	8.8 (-1.3)
Agreement			
Total	80	55	135
% per 1000	11.5	7.3	9.3 (-4.2)
Other			
Total	6279	6928	13207
% per 1000	910.5	914.2	912.5

In general, it should be noted that from the first to the second webinar the number of words per unit of time increases (n. 6896 and n. 7578) and that the expressions related to 'topic development' are the most numerous (n. 613), while lower are those on 'personal form of address' (n. 64). However, there is a noticeable shift in distribution between the first and second webinars: references from all categories decrease except for 'topic development' (+2.0) and 'question posing' (+8.5) - as shown in the third column of the Table 6 and in the graph of Fig. 3. The greatest decrease concerns the 'emotional words and phrases' (−5.2) and 'display of alignment' (−4.2) categories.

Table 7 reports the number of references to the iconic means used during the description of the problematic case - *lesson, task* and *case-report* - which it was possible to detect during the verbal interactions via web seminar 1 and 2 and within the first draft of project work.

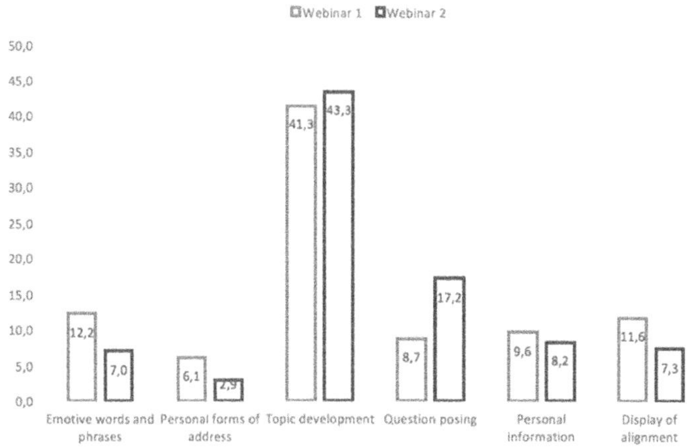

Fig. 3. Trend of linguistic and interactive categories between *webinars 1* and *2*.

Table 7. References to the iconic means in web seminars and project work.

Iconic means	Webseminar 1	Webseminar 2	Project work 1
a. – Space for kindergarten	3	4	8
b. – Space in the nursery	2	3	1
c. – Space in the playroom	4	5	7
Tot.	9	12	16

If the project work is assumed as the first personal elaboration, by the student involved in the virtual internship, to solve the simulated case, then from Table 7 it can be deduced that: the student's references to iconic means of expression increase in the transition from web seminars to project work - from 9 to 12 to 16; two out of three iconic mediators had a sort of effect - a. illustrating a situation in the kindergarten (n. 8) and c. describing a situation in the playroom (n. 7).

5 Discussion and Conclusions

The study highlights ultimately that the verbal interaction conducted during the web seminar of virtual internship between mentor and novice changes: it is less and less focused on themes of a personal nature and conducted with a formal style, instead it is more technical and focused on the description of professional aspects (Table 5). In order to clarify the problem to be faced by the novice, however, the iconic means were decidedly explanatory and useful, especially in the concrete representation of the situation (as evidenced by the use of them in the drafting of the project work - Table 7).

This investigation confirms the Moodle environment and related technological devices as useful to represented the internship activities in virtual form. This work argues, specifically, that if e-tivities are targeted on specific skills, virtual training would be useful for building professional skills, such as those of the educator [46]. It emphasizes the importance of well connecting, from the organizational system point of view, the activity, the LMS resource and the ability to support as claimed by the e-learning designer [13]. As regards the design competence, described within the broader construct of 'professional thinking' and defined by the interactive-linguistic categories, the study detected the increase of it. It also showed the possible direct connection of specific tools in increasing specific professional skills, such as web seminars on the ability to problematize in a personal way and project work on the ability to represent the problem to be solved. With reference to the design skill, also, task having characteristics of e-tivity - in particular, the iconic means used within the description/clarification of problem (see Table 6) - proved to be decidedly effective for the increase of the skill. For this reason, it also offers a contribution to the problematization of the e-learning training of the educator, specifically the building of 'professional thinking' [28, 40] which requires practical experience, is has always been considered a challenge for online vocational training - see universities and telematic degree courses [47] - and has become even more urgent in the current emergency situation due to COVID.

In conclusion, two considerations are highlighted: the criteria of 'legitimate internships' and the mediation function performed by internship.

As stated by Hora et al. [12] regarding 'legitimate internships' and clarified by NACE [17] with the proposal of the 5 criteria - *extension, transferability, time and training description, supervision, means provided* -, the providing of specific means should be further investigated. It has been defined as resources and equipment that facilities the employer's learnings based on the learning objectives. It is possible to note a relationship with the remarks by Vai & Sosuslki [13] on LMS sources and on 'virtual internship' - as defined by Chesler et al. [28] see Table 2). If the simulation effect is given by the use of sophisticated technological tools that ensure the simulation of experience and reality, then it becomes essential in the e-learning environment a correspondence between the didactic system and the technological support - so that the technology becomes itself mediator - as was seen in the study which resorted to the joint use of verbal interaction and the support of images. Finally, as stated within the framework of the theory of mediation [30, 31], the virtual internship can be compared to the model of the 'simulation of professional practice' [28] due to the mediation function analogical who owns. Referring to the characteristics of the virtual internship as analogical mediator - see Table 3 -, the study conducted shows that the analogical function of it consists in the ability to build another (*verisimilitude*) reality, not only to re-present (*adaptation*): the verbal descriptions of the mentor, combined with the enhancement of the iconic means used, are able to help the student to simulate the concrete problems of professional reality. Through a transdisciplinary analysis, which makes use of the verbal and iconic level of communication established between mentor and mentee and useful to underline the 'ternary' nature of mediation, some fundamental characteristics of the internship assumed as an analogical mediator - *replacing* and *amplifying* personal experience, guarantee of *concreteness* and *identification* - have been brought to light.

The results of this study will be than compared with three other complete traineeship path in order to derive possible trends, which will subsequently be extended through larger studies.

References

1. Dewey, J.: Experience and education. Touchstone, New York (1938)
2. Resnick, L.B.: The 1987 presidential address learning in school and out. Educ. Res. **16**(9), 13–54 (1987)
3. Bullock, K., et al.: Work placement experience: should I stay or should I go? High. Educ. Res. Dev. **28**(5), 481–494 (2009)
4. Mansfield, R.: The effect of placement experience upon final-year results for surveying degree programmes. Stud. High. Educ. **36**(8), 939–592 (2011)
5. Kuh, G.D.: High-Impact Educational Practices: What They Are, Who Has Access to Them, and why They Matter. Association of American Colleges and Universities, Washington (2008)
6. Hora, M.T., Wolfgram, M., Thompson, S.: What do we know about the impact of internship on student outcomes? Results from a preliminary review of the scholarly and practitioner literatures. Centre for Research on College-Workforce Transitions Research Brief 10, University of Wisconsin-Medison (2017)
7. Palmieri, C., Rossetti, S., Pozzoli, B., Tognetti, S., Alemani, C., Finzi, G., et al.: Pensare e fare tirocinio. Manuale di Tirocinio per l'educatore professionale. FrancoAngeli, Milano (2009)
8. Bastianoni, P., Spaggiari, E.: Apprendere a educare. Il tirocinio in Scienze dell'educazione. Carocci, Roma (2014)
9. Polanyi, M.: Personal Knowledge. University of Chicago Press, Chicago (1958)
10. Lynch, M.: At the Margins of Tacit Knowledge, Philosophia Scientiæ [En ligne], pp. 17–3 (2013)
11. Perla, L.: Scritture professionali. Metodi per la formazione. Progedit, Bari (2012)
12. Hora, M.T., Vivona, B., Chen, Z., Thompson, M., Brown, R.: What do we know about online internships? A review of the academic and practitioner literature. Centre for Research on College-Workforce Transition Research, Brief n. 10, University of Wisconsin-Medison (2020)
13. Vai, M., Sosulski, K.: Essentials Of Online Course Design, 2nd edn. Routledge, London (2015)
14. Limone, P.: Ambienti di apprendimento e progettazione didattica. Proposte per un sistema educativo transmediale. Carocci, Roma (2012)
15. Balamuralithara, B., Woods, P.: Virtual laboratories in engineering education: the simulation lab and remote lab. Comput. Appl. Eng. Educ. **17**(1), 108–118 (2009)
16. UNESCO-IESALC COVID-19 and higher education: today and tomorrow. http://www.iesalc.unesco.org/en/wp-content/uploads/2020/04/COVID-19-EN-090420–2.pdf. Accessed 13 Sept 2020
17. National Association of Colleges and Employers Position statement: U.S. Internships. National Association of Colleges and Employers. https://www.naceweb.org/about-us/advocacy/position-statements/position-statement-us-internships/. Accessed 13 Sept 2020
18. Cartus Corporation: COVID-19 impact on internships. https://www.cartus.com/files/4315/9172/6562/Cartus-Internship_Pulse-Survey-0520.pdf. Accessed 13 Sept 2020
19. National Survey of Student Engagement: Engagement insights: Survey findings on the quality of undergraduate education. NSSE, Bloomington (2018)
20. Moore, J.L., Dickson-Deane, C., Galyen, K.: e-Learning, online learning, and distance learning environments: are they the same? Internet High. Educ. **14**(2), 129–135 (2011)
21. Liu, X., Liu, S., Lee, S., Magjuka, R.J.: Cultural differences in online learning: international student perceptions. Educ. Technol. Soc. **13**(3), 177–188 (2010)
22. Ouyang, F., Scharber, C.: The influences of an experienced instructor's discussion design and facilitation on an online learning community development: a social network analysis study. Internet High. Educ. **35**, 34–47 (2017)

23. Mullen, G.E., Tallent-Runnels, M.K.: Student outcomes and perceptions of instructors' demands and support in online and traditional classrooms. Internet High. Educ. **9**(4), 257–266 (2006)
24. Ahsan, S.M., Hassan, A.: Increasing virtual education effectiveness by quantifying student leaning trajectories and virtual internships. Life Sci. J. **10**, 262–264 (2013)
25. Bayerlein, L., Jeske, D.: Student learning opportunities in traditional and computer-mediated internships. Educ. Train. **60**(1), 27–38 (2018)
26. Jeske, D., Linehan, C.: Mentoring and skill development in e-Internships. J. Work-Appl. Manag. **12**(2), 245–258 (2020)
27. Lansu, A., Löhr, A., van Dorp, C.: Professional development by e-learning: examples of effective remote internship models. In: M-2009 23rd ICDE World Conference on Open Learning and Distance Education. Maastricht. International Council of Distance Education (2009)
28. Chesler, N., Ruis, R., Collier, W., Swieck, Z.: A novel paradigm for engineering education: virtual internships with individualized mentoring and assessment of engineering thinking. J. Biomech. Eng. **137**(2), 1–8 (2015)
29. Suzuki, R., Salehi N., Lam M.S., Marroquin J.C.: Atelier: repurposing expert crowdsourcing tasks as micro-internships. In: CHI 2016: Proceedings of the 2016 CHI Conference on Human Factors in Computing Systems, pp. 2645–2656 (2016)
30. Perla, L.: La mediazione 'plurale' nel lavoro educativo. In: Perla, L., e Riva, M.G. (eds.) L'agire educativo. Manuale per educatori e operatori socio-assistenziali. La Scuola, Brescia (2016)
31. Damiano, E.: La mediazione didattica. Per una teoria dell'insegnamento. FrancoAngeli, Milano (2013)
32. Rézeau, J.: Médiation, médiatisation et instruments d'enseignement: du triangle au «carré pédagogique». ASp. la revue du GERAS (35-36), pp. 183–200 (2002)
33. Salmon, G.: E-tivities: A Key to Active Online Learning. Routledge, London (2002)
34. Paoletti, G.: Comprendere testi con figure. Immagini, diagrammi e grafici nel design per l'istruzione. FrancoAngeli, Milano (2011)
35. Clark, R.C., Lyons, C.: Graphics for Learning. Proven Guidelines for Planning, Designing, and Evaluating Visuals in Training Materials. Pfeiffer, San Francisco (2010)
36. Mayer, R.E. (ed.): The Cambridge Handbook of Multimedia Learning. Cambridge University Press, Cambridge (2005)
37. Crebert, G., Bates, M., Bell, B., Patrick, C.-J., Cragnolini, V.: Developing generic skills at university, during work placement and in employment: graduates' perceptions. High. Educ. Res. Dev. **23**(2), 147–165 (2004)
38. Morgan, B., Keshtkar, F., Greasser, A., Shaffer, D.W.: Automating the mentor in a serious game: a discourse analysis using finite state machines. In: Stephandis, C. (ed.) Human Computer Interaction International 2013, pp. 591–594. Springer, Berlin (2013). https://doi.org/10.1007/978-3-642-39476-8_119
39. Rupp, A.A., Gushta, M., Mislevy, R.J., Shaffer, D.W.: Evidence-centered design of epistemic games: measurement principles for complex learning environments. J. Technol. Learn. Assess. **8**(4), 4–42 (2010)
40. Arastoopour, G., et al.: Nephrotex: Measuring first year students' ways of professional thinking in a virtual internship. In: Proceedings of 119th ASEE Annual Conference and Exposition. American Society for Engineering Education (2012)
41. Presidenza del Consiglio dei Ministri – Dipartimento per le Politiche della Famiglia e l'Istituto degli Innocenti di Firenze 2015, Manuale dei servizi educativi per l'infanzia, http://famiglia.governo.it/media/1490/manuale-servizi-infanzia.pdf. Accessed 13 Sept 2020
42. Hamtini, T.M.: Evaluating E-learning programs: an adaptation of Kirkpatrick's model to accommodate E-learning environments. J. Comput. Sci. **4**(8), 693–698 (2008)

43. Hammond, M.: Learning through online discussion: a case of triangulation in research. Australas. J. Educ. Technol. **21**(3), 283–302 (2005)
44. O'Dowd, R., Sauro, S., Spector-Cohen, E.: The role of pedagoggical mentoring in virtual exchange. TESOL Q. **54**(1), 146–172 (2020)
45. Ware, P.: Teaching comments: intercultural communication skills in the digital age. Intercult. Educ. **24**, 315–326 (2013)
46. Pike, P.: Using a synchronous online teaching internship to develop pedagogical skills and explore teacher identity: a case study. J. Music Technol. Educ. **8**(3), 227–242 (2015)
47. Perla, L., Agrati, L., Vinci, V.: The 'sophisticated' knowledge of e-teacher. re-shape digital resources for online courses. In: Burgos, D. (eds.) Higher Education Learning Methodologies and Technologies Online. First International Workshop, HELMeTO 2019, Revised Selected Papers (2019)

Facing COVID19 Emergency in Higher Education Teaching and Learning: Frameworks and Overviews

Online Teaching in Higher Education with the Support of Start@Unito During Covid-19 Pandemic

Barbara Bruschi[1], Marina Marchisio[2], and Matteo Sacchet[2(✉)]

[1] Department of Philosophy and Education Sciences, University of Turin, Turin, Italy
barbara.bruschi@unito.it

[2] Department of Molecular Biotechnology and Health Sciences, University of Turin, Turin, Italy
{marina.marchisio,matteo.sacchet}@unito.it

Abstract. Online teaching, open online courses, and higher education form a close union of elements that orbit around the same objective: enhancing students' tertiary education quality. This entanglement has been emphasized by the new educational needs that arose during the recent Covid-19 crisis since many schools and universities worldwide shut down. Teaching paradigms usually undergo step-by-step changes, but sometimes, after a global event, the development is major and relevant. In this framework, the start@unito experience at the University of Turin appears as a useful model to shift didactics into an online setting. Start@unito is a Digital Learning Environment that promotes 50 Open Online Courses related to the main first-year disciplines. This paper analyzes the start@unito model from the teachers' perspective to understand how much teaching was facilitated through this experience. Data will be deeply investigated using quantitative and qualitative measures. Results also contain teachers' comments and remarks on their approach to students through start@unito.

Keywords: Digital learning environment · Open online courses · Start@unito

1 Introduction

Since its birth, online teaching in Higher Education has developed with three main paradigms: in-person, distance, and blended teaching. Research on this topic has been active [1]. The global pandemic period for Covid-19 gave an incredible boost to fully online teaching since schools and universities shut down worldwide, and students cannot be present and participate in classroom activities [2]. For many teachers, this modality change has been dramatic. However, it is highly probable that teachers who were already used to online teaching or with an open mind to Technology Enhanced Learning did not find it very hard to change their educational approach. These teachers may think of this challenge as a stimulus for adopting new methodologies and new tools and defining newly experimented pedagogies in a different learning environment. Moreover, colleagues benefited from their mutual emotional and professional support. Many countries tried to provide alternative initial teacher education programs during the Covid-19 outbreak,

L. S. Agrati et al. (Eds.): HELMeTO 2020, CCIS 1344, pp. 187–198, 2021.
https://doi.org/10.1007/978-3-030-67435-9_15

more open to candidates [3]. The prerequisite of the program described in [3] was an undergraduate degree in the relevant discipline. Candidates were required to undergo a special screening process to ensure their suitability for the program.

Fewer problems were experienced by those professors who had just prepared or were about to finish a full university module just before the pandemic. This is the case of start@unito [4, 5]. Start@unito (https://start.unito.it) is a Digital Learning Environment (DLE) that promotes 50 Open Online Courses (OOCs). One of its aims is to facilitate the transition from secondary school to university and from bachelor's to master's degrees because most OOCs are related to the main first-year disciplines. The OOCs are designed to help those who approach university studies for the first time, provide university guidance, and promote autonomous learning. The DLE is composed of a virtual learning environment integrated with different tools designed to help students in autonomous learning and improve engagement [6]. The DLE of start@unito uses an Automatic Formative Assessment (AFA) to give immediate and interactive feedback, an Advanced Computing Environment (ACE), to increase the interactivity, and other tools. The online platform development started in October 2017, with the first phase of 20 open online courses held from March 2018 and officially inserted in the university offer in the academic year 2018/2019. The number of OOCs increased to 50, with new courses implemented throughout 2019. Besides, many new courses are held entirely in English to enhance internationalization. All of them are available in the academic year 2019/20, which means just in time for the Covid-19 pandemic, which caused schools and universities' closure. Various actors participated in the learning process inside start@unito [7]. Teachers who developed the OOCs took advantage of the newly prepared contents, sharing this possibility with colleagues. University professors participating in start@unito were trained on topics related to online learning and teaching [8]. The Start@unito model was also evaluated before Covid-19 in comparison with in-person courses. The new emergency context changed the perception of its usefulness: in particular, the lockdown has prompted teachers and students to appreciate the flexibility of the modules and the units of start@unito. Forced distance teaching caused distress to many teachers, but those who had embarked on an online teaching experience such as start@unito found great benefits.

The paper discusses the model for OOCs developed through start@unito, also in the light of the Covid-19 pandemic and mainly from the teachers' perspective. Section 2 delineates the state of the art of Higher Education during and after the Covid-19 crisis. Section 3 defines the Research Questions, while Sect. 4 describes the adopted methodology to answer those questions. Section 5 shows the results obtained using quantitative and qualitative data, highlighting the benefits and positive support provided by the start@unito experience.

2 State of the Art

The shifting of courses into an online setting is a global common policy response from governments in response to the need to keep teachers, staff, students, and society as safe as possible and reduce interpersonal contact, minimizing virus transmission during the Covid-19 pandemic. However, this is not the first pandemic to impact education.

Some books were written about a quiescence period at various medieval universities after the fourteenth-century plague. More recently, the University of Oxford scholars and students retreated to their countryside estates during the Black Death [9]. Many institutions and organizations produced reports on the situation. As UNESCO reports, by the end of March 2020, over 166 countries implemented nationwide closures, impacting over 87% of the world's student population, around 1.52 billion students, and nearly 60.2 million teachers [10]. Online learning has become an essential tool for education. Technology can enable teachers and students to access materials in multiple formats and in ways that can bridge the forced distance. Due to the Covid-19 pandemic, many schools began conducting classes via videotelephony software. Online learning has its own requirements: as an example, students need a desk and silence, but 9% of 15-year-old students do not even have a quiet place to study in their homes [11]. Another obvious prerequisite to online learning is having access to a computer that students can use to study in their homes. The situation in this setting is quite different from country to country. Some of them have high percentages of students with a computer to use for working at home, but there tend to be huge gaps across socio-economic groups [11]. Even if these data concern secondary education, they represent some similar issues that arise in higher education.

There are three main primary responses to COVID-19: the first one is minimal or no response at all, the second one is the delayed beginning of study periods, postponing the entrance into classes and providing limited access to rooms, the third one is the rapid digitalization of curriculum [12].

Recommendations were also given to teachers. As an example, in Portuguese universities [13], the general guidelines concerned:

- Adjustment of teaching, learning, and assessment strategies according to the new learning environments in remote learning.
- Availability of educational resources for students to undertake learning activities in a diversity of timetables.
- Regular feedback to students about their learning progress.
- Recording of all activities, with lesson summaries and diaries, and taking notes about students' participation.

To answer the first of the guidelines, in [14], six more specific educational strategies are presented to enhance online teaching experiences for university instructors who are conducting online education during a pandemic:

1. Making emergency plans for unexpected problems, which may occur with more frequency when students are at home.
2. Dividing the teaching content into smaller units or segments to help students focus and learn step-by-step.
3. Emphasizing the use of "voice" in teaching because body language, facial expressions, and teachers' voices are all important communicative media.
4. Working with teaching assistants and gain online supports from them.
5. Strengthening students' active learning ability outside of class.

6. Combining online learning and offline self-learning effectively. Students should be required to read course-specific literature and submit assignments.

The study then states high-impact principles for online education, among which there is adequate support provided by faculty to students. Institutional policymakers should provide proper guidance to face new challenges.

3 Research Question

This research wants to analyze the start@unito model and understand how much teaching was facilitated through this experience. This model is different from MOOCs, Massive Open Online Courses, because students can access and start courses anytime, from anywhere, with a self-paced and adaptive approach. This kind of approach was taken into account while developing courses. Thus, this paper focuses on HE and education in the transition between secondary and tertiary education. In particular, we will focus on teachers' experience and the support provided by start@unito to online teaching. Thus, it is possible to summarize the aim of this work with the following Research Questions:

RQ1. How does the model of OOCs of start@unito help teachers improve their online teaching?
RQ2. To what extent did the start@unito OOCs facilitate teaching during Covid-19?

4 Methodology

To provide an answer to the RQ, we use both quantitative and qualitative data. The collection of data for this research relies on three modalities:

- Questionnaire: we asked every start@unito teacher to fill a non-anonymous online survey to understand each individual's perspective and relate the various criticalities to their subject of study. Numerical variables are presented with percentages, median, and IQR (Inter Quartile Range).
- Data collected from teachers' and students' interaction with the DLE of start@unito and their analytics.
- Teachers' open comments arising from the questionnaire, from focus group activities and other moments of discussion. Project coordinators set up different meetings, divided by thematic areas (economics, humanities, languages, law, science). During these gatherings, a person was in charge of taking notes of teachers' opinions. No recording was done. Thus, the comments reported are not literal but rephrased. Another motivation for this decision comes from the fact that the language during the meetings was Italian, and a translation in English would not have been effective. Open comments cover different aspects: expression of satisfaction, positive teacher, and/or student experiences, criticalities.

5 Results

The entire sample of teachers who are module leaders is composed of 69 teachers. Some of them are leaders of more than one OOCs.

5.1 Teacher Questionnaire

From the questionnaire, we collected answers from 47 teachers. 50% of the teachers who answered have been module leaders for 2 years. The OOCs of start@unito are completely open to everyone worldwide, but these modules have an analogous in-person module at the University of Turin. Students enrolled at the University of Turin can use the OOC to study the equivalent module or insert the OOC in their careers. In many cases, the online and in-person modules share the same teachers, generally the course developers, after proper training. In this way, teachers can then evaluate participation. With knowledge of the platform potentialities, they can experiment with using it in their online teaching, in person and remotely. We asked teachers how they used the online course with their students. Most of them (44.7%) said that they advise the OOC for revision, thus as a corollary of the usual module for theory (10.6%), exercises (34%), and automatic formative assessment (29.8%). Few teachers transformed their course into a blended one (12.8%) or required students to attend some online activities (8.5%). These percentages show that the situation of the various courses is quite different. In fact, some of the teachers were approaching online education for the first time (around 60%). In contrast, others already had some experience with technologies but had rarely experienced a fully online teaching approach (around 20%).

Table 1. Teachers evaluation of the opportunities provided by start@unito OOCs

Item	Median	IQR
O1: Expansion of the educational offer	4	2
O2: Anticipation of the students' career	4	2
O3: Support for the preparation of the exams	4	2
O4: Support for students not attending or with special needs	4	2
O5: Reusability of materials	4	2
O6: Continuous availability of materials	5	1
O7: Orientation in choosing the university path	4	1
O8: Creation of a bridge between university and secondary school degree	4	2
O9: Support for teachers of secondary schools who want to offer opportunities for further study and enhancement for their students	3	2
O10: Support for distance learning in the Covid-19 period	4	2

Teachers were asked about their opinion on the advantages of start@unito modules from the students' point of view over a 5-point Likert scale, in which 1 represents "not useful" and 5 represents "very useful". Results are summarized in Table 1, from which we can see that the model works, according to the teachers.

Detail of the results summarized in Table 1 is given in Fig. 1.

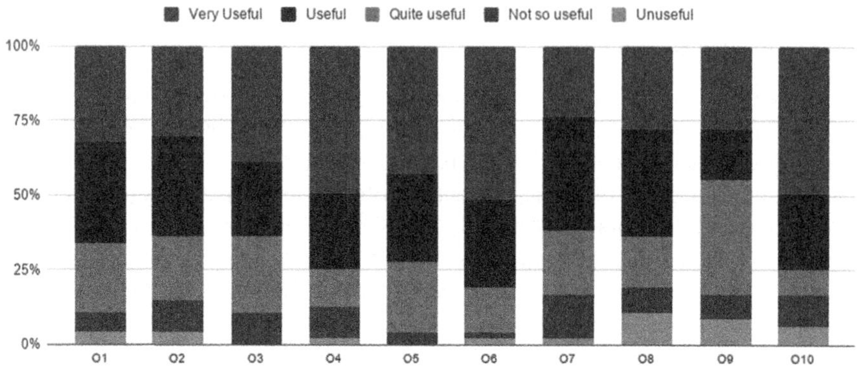

Fig. 1. Percentages of Likert scores about teachers' evaluation of the opportunities.

Most of the entries express high usefulness (4 is the average score), with a low rate of dispersion (IQR spanning from 1 to 2), meaning that most teachers agree on these advantages. Other opportunities highlighted by teachers concern students' chance to obtain ECTS with a self-paced study, which can be used to reach an application's requirements, for example, to a master's degree. We must stress that these are the opinions of teachers and that their interaction with students was generally rare, due to the self-paced nature of the courses, that students should attend in autonomy: many teachers never interact with their students before the exam (26.1%) or just interact once a month (34.8%). A similar percentage of teachers (30.4%) had contact with students almost once a week, and there was just one case of daily interactions.

Focusing on teachers' advantages, they emphasized their own development of online teaching skills (42.6%). Another advantage that teachers appreciated is the facility in the management of the exam (21.3%): in fact, for those who chose to adopt a computerized test, there was a person devoted to the assembly work, the assistance and the extraction of marks, while teachers were responsible for the questions and the verbalization. In fact, teachers were not left alone in the experience of online self-paced teaching: they were supported by staff, researchers, professors with strong experience in the field of Digital Education. Teachers were asked to evaluate the support they received over a 5-point Likert scale, in which 1 represents "bad support" and 5 represents "excellent support". The results are summarized in Table 2. Detail of the results summarized in Table 2 is given in Fig. 2.

It is worth mentioning that not all teachers provided an answer to all the entries. For example, the language support was dedicated to English-taught modules. Moreover, computerized exam support was dedicated to teachers who chose this modality, while teachers who adopted oral or written examinations received less support for exams. Most of the entries express high usefulness (the average score ranges between 4 and 5), with a low rate of dispersion (IQR spanning from 1 to 2), meaning that most teachers

Table 2. Teachers evaluation on the provided support by staff, researchers, professors

Item	Median	IQR
S1: Implementation of courses	5	1
S2: Language support (for English-taught modules)	5	1
S3: Course maintenance	4	1
S4: Computerized exam support: opening exams	4	1
S5: Computerized exam support: assignment assembly	5	1.5
S6: Computerized exam support: classroom assistance	4.5	2
S7: Computerized exam support: management of results	4.5	2
S8: Computerized exam support: viewing student tests	5	1.5

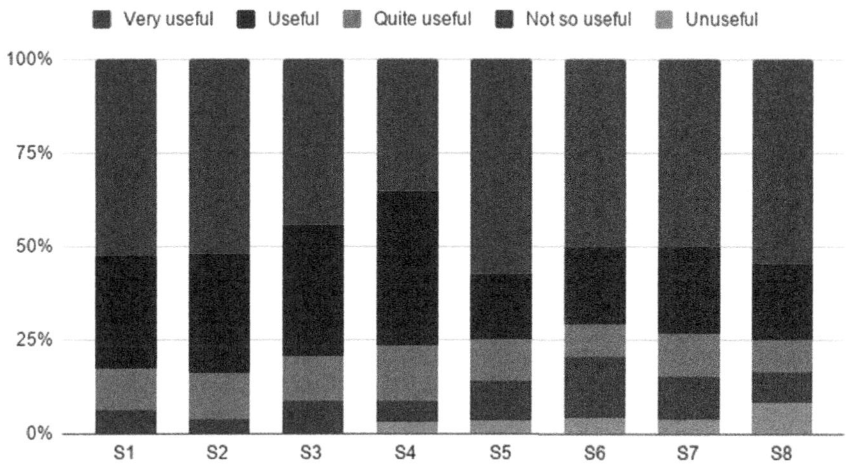

Fig. 2. Percentages of Likert scores about teachers' evaluation of the support.

received appropriate support. Even if the support was satisfactory, teachers highlighted their interest in hiring a tutor for their course (87.2%), which can add content support for students, but in any case, almost all teachers (97.9%) state that they will continue using the online course during the next academic year, emphasizing the positivity of the experience, expressed by a global satisfaction (Median 4, IQR 2 over a 5-point Likert scale).

We can state that the start@unito model is working since it can be used in different ways, and it brings advantages to both students and teachers, advantages which were highlighted during the Covid-19 global pandemic. Many start@unito teachers had the advantage of using already prepared online contents and appreciated it (Median 4, IQR 3 over a 5-point Likert scale). Its usage has increased, but not so prominently (Median 3, IQR 2 over a 5-point Likert scale). The reasons for this are shown in the open comments:

part of the modules belongs to the first semester, while the Covid-19 emergency occurred in the second semester.

5.2 Open Comments

In this section, we report a textual collection of what emerged from the meetings with teachers. Many of them stated that the experience of start@unito is good, very positive. The newly prepared courses were precious during the Covid-19 crisis, useful in the difficult moment, made available perfectly on time. For example, language modules adopted the same strategy: course attendance and online test submission were mandatory to take the final exam.

More generally, teachers highlighted other aspects: many subscribers (see Fig. 1), growing day by day, especially for new courses, but on the other side a low number of exams. There is a great difference between enrolled students and the number of exams. Some brand new courses had no exams, or just one person, about whom teachers were usually quite impressed, with an excellent examination in more than one case.

One teacher highlighted the positive effect on orientation: students from other regions attended the course during the summer and then came to attend lessons in presence during the semester; the online material was useful for non-attending students, especially those who had difficulties with Italian. For example, Polish students took exams in the framework of an agreement with foreign education institutions. Many teachers advised students to attend the online course, especially for those who had many absences, for those who had simultaneous courses, and in general for those who could not attend.

Some criticalities: some teachers with little experience in online education complained about difficulties in the extraction of test results and the grade book management. In fact, users can subscribe with multiple email addresses, and in these cases, data reports risk duplication. Generally, teachers require professional and technical support. Moreover, some courses, after two years of delivery, will need an update.

There is room for improvement and new ideas: reminder systems or modules outside degree courses for professional updates.

5.3 Data from the DLE

Even if many professors did not see the increased usage, this was detected by the online platform's activity. Let us start by splitting the academic year 2019/2020 into two parts, the pre-Covid period from September 1st, 2019 to February 29th, 2020 (6 months), and the Covid period from March 1st, 2020 to May 31st, 2020 (3 months). Globally, more than 25.000 new users registered on the platform, 47% of which during the shorter Covid period. Moreover, there were, on average, 72 new users every day, compared to an average of 41 in the pre-Covid period. Figure 3 shows the number of new users collected by months. The increased usage is not just connected to new users: even the distinct users' login number grew, from 266 daily distinct users' logins in the pre-Covid period to 504 during Covid (+90%). Figure 4 shows monthly distinct users' logins to the platform.

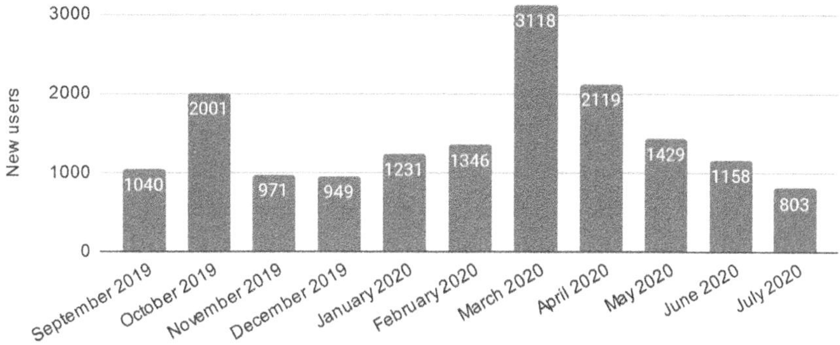

Fig. 3. Monthly new users in start@unito, September 2019–June 2020.

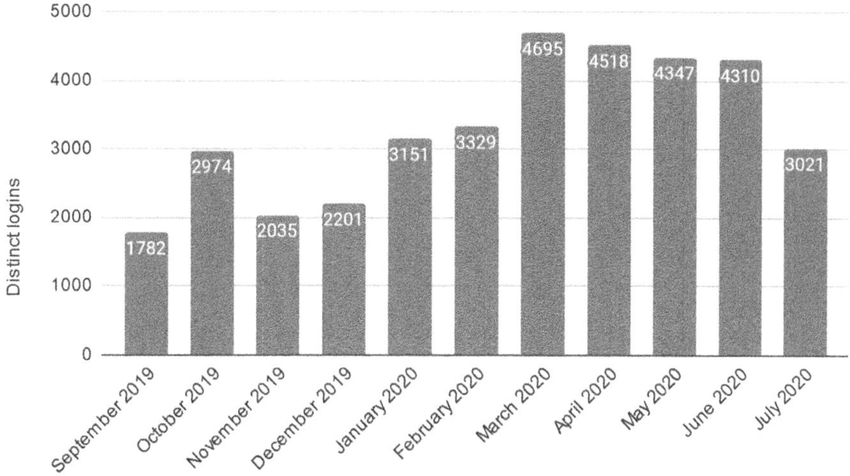

Fig. 4. Monthly distinct users' logins in start@unito, September 2019–July 2020.

Table 3 reports the data represented in Fig. 4 and 5. The last column of the table calculates the ratio between logins and distinct logins, giving a perspective of how many times a student logged in into the start@unito platform. The ratio is higher in the months closer to exam sessions, like September and January, while the ratio is lower during the Covid-19 period. This could mean that students were more interested in looking at the online courses, even though 20 logins for every student means that, if we think of one or two logins per day, that student was online attending courses for 10–20 days a month.

Table 3. Teachers evaluation on the provided support by staff, researchers, professors

Month	Logins	Distinct logins	Ratio
September 2019	90416	1782	50,74
October 2019	75147	2974	25,27
November 2019	54761	2035	26,91
December 2019	62051	2201	28,19
January 2020	123958	3151	39,34
February 2020	79718	3329	23,95
March 2020	117428	4695	25,01
April 2020	85882	4518	19,01
May 2020	93468	4347	21,50
June 2020	83812	4310	19,45
July 2020	62809	3021	20,79
August 2020	39877	1970	20,24

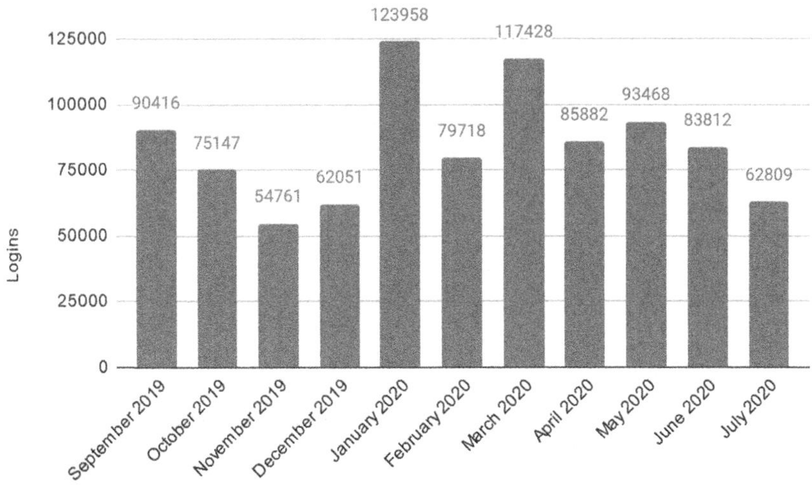

Fig. 5. Monthly users' logins in start@unito, September 2019–July 2020.

6 Conclusions

University professors are aware of the opportunities that OOCs can provide them and their students (RQ1) and felt very lucky to be a part of start@unito. The model must be enforced with new modules and didactic support, and it must be extended to other teachers. It is also true that the sample we analyzed is composed of teachers who agreed to develop an online course, but when start@unito began, we had some rejections, too. Even if this affected teachers differently, teachers' experience through the Covid-19 pandemic was facilitated by their previous experience in start@unito (RQ2). They appreciated what they learned during the training. This means that it is important to train every teacher on online didactics, especially after Covid-19.

The support would have been useless if it was not accompanied by quality measures, which play an important role. This topic is addressed by different stakeholders: higher education institutions, course providers, education companies, educational providers, national and international agencies. These actors are involved in preparing or attending common guidelines to enhance the quality of OOCs. Some indicators that can help analyze quality are provided by the learner's point of view, by pedagogy, instructional design, and outcome measures. These indicators were taken into account while dealing with the quality of start@unito OOCs [15].

Stat@unito was of great help in enhancing the internationalization process for two reasons: firstly, some OOCs are in English, and this allowed incoming Erasmus students to attend them, and secondly, outgoing Erasmus students can more easily take exams of non-attended courses. Moreover, during the Covid-19 pandemic, the Erasmus program was blocked, but the University of Turin agreed upon virtual mobility for international incoming students in the second semester.

Students' and teachers' online activity will be further investigated in future research to provide interventions and improvements in the experience of the various actors around education and develop new specific tools for educational purposes. Learning Analytics techniques will be adopted soon in the start@unito experience to understand and optimize learning and the context in which this happens [16].

The type of study and analysis has some natural limitations. First of all, in this investigation, it is tough to compare the point of view of start@unito teachers before and during the global pandemic because the health emergency has caught everyone by surprise in its seriousness, shifting attention to how to deal with it in the best possible way by enhancing quality present experiences. By the data of the experience and from the reflections that emerged from the teachers during the periodic meetings at the beginning and end of the semester, it is quite reasonable that start@unito was useful even before the Covid-19 crisis. A precise comparison could be made only for the modules already available on the start@unito platform in the second semester of the previous academic year. However, it is possible to imagine in the future, also given the ongoing emergency, a comparison between the impact of the start@unito model in the immediate future to respond to the emergency and in the medium term on the change of paradigms of teaching. This disruptive crisis will permanently transform higher education by requiring new solutions.

However, what was done is a good starting point. Some changes need to be made: 65.9% of teachers said their online course needs an update. This means that the support to teachers for online teaching must be continuous. We await them with a positive attitude since they want to repeat the experience: 93.2% said that they would take part in online teaching initiatives in the future.

References

1. Ghilay, Y.: Online Learning in Higher Education. Nova Science Publishers (2016)
2. Toquero, C.M.: Challenges and opportunities for higher education amid the COVID-19 pandemic: the philippine context. Pedagogical Res. **5**(4), em0063 (2020). https://doi.org/10.29333/pr/7947
3. Donitsa-Schmidt, S., Ramot, R.: Opportunities and challenges: teacher education in Israel in the Covid-19 pandemic. J. Educ. Teach. (2020). https://doi.org/10.1080/02607476.2020.1799708
4. Bruschi, B., et al.: Start@unito: a supporting model for high school students enrolling to university. In: Proceedings of the 15th International Conference on Cognition and Exploratory Learning in Digital Age (CELDA 2018), pp. 307–312, Budapest, Hungary (2018)
5. Marchisio, M., Operti, L., Rabellino, S., Sacchet, M.: Start@unito: open online courses for improving access and for enhancing success in higher education. In: Proceedings of the 11th International Conference on Computer Supported Education (CSEDU), vol. 1, pp. 639–646, Heraklion, Greece (2019). https://doi.org/10.5220/0007732006390646
6. Barana, A., Marchisio, M. Rabellino, S.: Empowering engagement through automatic formative assessment. In: 2019 IEEE 43rd Annual Computer Software and Applications Conference (COMPSAC), 2019, pp. 216–225, Milwaukee (2019). https://doi.org/10.1109/COMPSAC.2019.00040
7. Marchisio, M., Rabellino, S., Sacchet, M., Salusso, D.: Start@unito underground map for an e-learning trip. In: Conference Garr 2019 - Connecting the future - Selected papers (2019). https://doi.org/10.26314/GARR-Conf19-proceedings-22
8. Marchisio, M., Sacchet, M., Salusso, D.: Instructional design to train the trainers: the start@unito project at the University of Turin. In: Proceedings of the IADIS International Conference e-Learning 2019, pp. 195–202, Porto, Portugal (2019). https://doi.org/10.33965/el2019_201909F025
9. Courtenay, W.J.: The effect of the black death on English higher education. Speculum **55**(4), 696–714 (1980). https://doi.org/10.2307/2847661
10. UNESCO-IESALC: Coronavirus COVID-19 and Higher Education: Impact and Recommendations. https://www.iesalc.unesco.org/en/2020/03/09/coronavirus-covid-19-and-higher-education-impact-and-recommendations/. Accessed 15 Sept 2020
11. OECD, Learning remotely when schools close: How well are students and schools prepared? Insights from PISA. https://read.oecd-ilibrary.org/view/?ref=127_127063-iiwm328658. Accessed 15 Sept 2020
12. Crawford, J., Butler-Henderson, K.: COVID-19: 20 countries' higher education intra-period digital pedagogy responses. J. Appl. Learn. Teach. **3**(1), pp. 9–28 (2020). https://doi.org/10.37074/jalt.2020.3.1.7
13. Assunção Flores, M., Gago, M.: Teacher education in times of COVID-19 pandemic in Portugal: national, institutional and pedagogical responses. J. Educ. Teach. https://doi.org/10.1080/02607476.2020.1799709
14. Bao, W.: COVID-19 and online teaching in higher education: a case study of Peking University. Hum. Behav. Emerg. Technol. **2**(2), 113–115 (2020). https://doi.org/10.1002/hbe2.191
15. Marchisio, M., Sacchet, M.: Analysis items to assess the quality of open online courses for higher education. In: Proceedings of the IADIS International Conference e-Learning 2020, pp. 63–70 (2020)
16. Marchisio, M., Rabellino, S., Roman, F., Sacchet, M., Salusso, D.: Boosting up data collection and analysis to learning analytics in open online contexts: an assessment methodology. J. e-Learn. Knowl. Soc. **15**(3), 49–59. https://doi.org/10.20368/1971-8829/1135048

Agility of the Post COVID-19 Strategic Plan on Distance Learning at Cadi Ayyad University. An Opportunity Towards a Total Digital Transformation of the University

Hana Ait Si Ahmad, Khadija El Kharki, and Khalid Berrada(✉)

Transdisciplinary Research Group on Educational Innovation (Trans ERIE), Cadi Ayyad University, Prince Moulay Abdellah Avenue, PB:2390, Marrakech, Morocco
berrada@uca.ac.ma

Abstract. In early March 2020, Morocco, like most countries, decided to impose restrictive measures to limit the spread of the SARS-CoV-2 virus. Among these measures, all schools and universities, including Cadi Ayyad University (UCA), have been closed so far, forcing students to take distance learning courses.

Previously, students and professors were reluctant to use online platforms, but the new closure situation has forced everyone to experiment with these strategies. 14 UCA higher education institutions have joined forces to offer students e-learning as an alternative to overcome university closures and ensure that learning never stops. 15852 educational resources have been produced to date, covering all UCA programs, with about 70% of the resources produced since the beginning of the pandemic. For this first stage, the university has recovered the bulk of the educational needs.

The second phase of the non-disruptive learning process, consists of strengthening interactive online learning with learners to motivate them to prepare for their exams, which have been postponed to September 2020.

The last stage of the distance learning process is devoted to the redesign of post-COVID-19 education, taking into account the challenges and experiences gained in the first and second stages.

The objective of this paper is to analyze the measures taken to ensure non-disruptive learning in the context of COVID-19. This study will help higher education institutions and the Ministry of Higher Education to compare the different experiences in the country, as well as in other faculties around the world.

Keywords: E-learning · COVID-19 · Active learning · Disruptive learning · Distance learning · Crisis time

1 Introduction

Pandemic diseases or natural disasters have occurred worldwide, affecting not only human health but also several sectors such as the education sector. 2002 was disrupted by SARS, which affected several countries around the world. In order to contain the

L. S. Agrati et al. (Eds.): HELMeTO 2020, CCIS 1344, pp. 199–213, 2021.
https://doi.org/10.1007/978-3-030-67435-9_16

virus, classroom teaching was suspended in several regions of China. Similarly, in 2009, the H1N1 influenza epidemic affected many people around the world, resulting in the closure of schools in many countries and regions, such as Bulgaria, China, France, Italy, Japan, New Zealand, Serbia, South Africa, Thailand, the United Kingdom, and the United States [9].

Clearly, the global pandemic is not just a major public health emergency, but one of political, economic and social emergency as well. As per the beginning of the year 2020, news strokes the world about a new pandemic that is becoming a serious threat to all humanity. In the early march of the same year, most countries decided to impose restrictive measures to limit the spread of the SARS-CoV-2 virus, as the Coronavirus (COVID-19) spreads rapidly around the world, causing the infection of more than 26,000,000 people and the death of more than 810,000 others [36], affected countries have launched several strategies to contain the virus, including school closures.

According to results published by UNESCO, up to March 2020, the closure of schools has affected 165 countries, representing almost 1.5 billion children and young people, i.e. almost 87% of the world's student population [31, 37]. A prolonged suspension of courses will not only lead to learning losses in the short term but also in the long term will result in a further loss of human capital and reduced economic opportunities. In order to reduce learning losses, many countries are seeking to use distance education to manage and respond to this crisis [29].

Nevertheless, the question of how to continue learning without interruption has become a major challenge for the global education community, while this is an important transition for the global and Moroccan education systems, it is also an occasion to develop alternative educational opportunities. The question, then, is whether higher education is well prepared for the new generation of the digital age [17]?

Equity is, according to UNESCO, the top priority in this period of crisis as school closures have fatal effects on the one hand on the quality of education and the other hand on vulnerable and extremely disadvantaged learners, and alternative distance education strategies could even aggravate learning inequalities due to gaps in access to technology and the resources and capacities of schools and teachers [31].

As a result of the crisis caused by the coronavirus epidemic, decisions on digital innovations in universities and higher education that would normally have taken several years due to various regulations and constraints are now being rapidly introduced within days. This is mainly a consequence of the COVID-19 pandemic, which has triggered a digital transformation in universities and higher education.

In addition, infected countries have responded by using distance learning approaches and many have deployed e-learning solutions. However, a survey of school principals in 82 countries participating in the Program for International Student Assessment (PISA) revealed huge disparities among students attending schools with effective e-learning platforms, ranging from 35% to 70%. This is a testament to the ability of schools to support e-learning during school closures. The situation is much worse for low-resource environments in middle- and low-income countries, where Internet penetration rates are typically less than 50% and a large proportion of students do not have e-learning facilities at home. Countries are therefore turning to education programs on lower technology options such as television and radio to significantly increase access to distance learning [33].

Following the World Health Organization's declaration that COVID-19 is a pandemic, the Ministry of National Education, Vocational Training, Higher Education and Scientific Research in Morocco reports the closure of vocational training institutions, universities, private and public schools, language centers and foreign mission schools. In this context, disrupted classes from 16th of March 2020 affected most educational institutions in Morocco including Cadi Ayyad University (UCA) until now [22, 27]. Students and teachers were forced to stay at home, as they had to switch in record time to online, student-centered, interaction-based distance education, offering a learning environment from anywhere, at any time, with a variety of digital technology sources. It's a learning strategy that comes from active learning, a unique approach to keeping classes undisturbed.

In this context, Cadi Ayyad University and its administrative and educational teams were forced to be creative, critical, problem-solving, communicative, collaborative and flexible. Thus, demonstrating that there is another way of teaching that is more efficient and flexible.

Cadi Ayyad University has made a challenge to offer alternative modes of learning and education to students who are out of school, and to establish equivalency and transition programs, recognized and accredited by the State, to ensure flexible learning in emergency settings. We are conducting this article to answer the central research question: How does Cadi Ayyad University respond to the health crisis of COVID-19?

2 Method

In the field of education, we see that learning, media and technologies can and must contribute more directly to knowledge and practice during the COVID-19 pandemic, the shift to online and digital education formats and the development of distance education and learning forms due to the massive closures of universities. In this time of pandemic, when the means to manage and resolve the crisis are being tested at multiple levels, distance education has become a major concern for the authorities. Education has become a matter of urgency, and with it, educational technologies have been positioned as a front-line emergency service. In recent years, learning, media and technology has become a reference point for critics of education and technology [32]. In this time of crisis, the question is not how online teaching and learning methods can ensure quality education, but more about how academic institutions will be able to adopt e-learning on such a massive scale [12].

Usually, the pedagogical process at Cadi Ayyad University involves the students, teachers and all the administrative teams in the realization of a set of programmed actions, evolving in terms of knowledge acquisition and usually taking into account the physical presence of the student in the institution. Our pedagogical approach is mainly based on the physical presence of students and teachers in the classrooms and also on the administrative management and follow-up for the success of the educational process.

As in all educational institutions in the world, Cadi Ayyad University has established an emergency plan to limit the spread of the SARS-COV-2 virus and overcome the problem of school and faculty closures. According to the Organization for Economic Co-operation and Development [24], the emergency plan includes: information and training on the virus; training of teachers and school principals in distance learning; deployment of online classrooms at scale; and the establishment and training of working groups of counselors and teachers to support parents and students.

Previously, students and teachers were reluctant to use these tools, but the new lock-in situation has forced everyone to experiment with these strategies, reducing resistance and increasing adherence to innovative active learning methods. This type of learning environment can increase the learning potential of students. Students can learn anytime and anywhere, developing new skills as part of the process leading to lifelong learning. The Government also recognizes the growing importance of e-learning in this dynamic world [12]. Our goal is to list the various measures that the university has implemented that have enabled the transition to an all-digital mode to ensure the continuity of its activities. Therefore, teachers and higher education institutions must prepare quickly for this change with the necessary skills and tools. The lack of sophisticated technologies and experience in developing e-learning platforms is, however, the main challenge faced by players around the world [23]. In particular, we will take into consideration the contribution of the Trans ERIE research group, which aims to highlight the importance of the field of pedagogical innovation, action research and development of digital resources and distance learning platforms with an experienced team. In the meantime, the Trans ERIE research group has made available to the university a set of pedagogical materials, audio and video content and technological support teams and has enabled all parties involved to find common ground for effective e-learning.

In two and a half months, 14 UCA faculties and higher education institutions have joined forces to offer students e-learning as an alternative solution to overcome university closures and to ensure that learning never stops. The school is no longer there, but the class continues [35]. Both synchronous and asynchronous modes of learning have been taken into account; different formats of courses, assignments, interactive classes, seminars, round tables and others have been put in place. Most of these educational resources have been made available to learners through multiple dissemination channels.

2.1 LMS Platforms

Cadi Ayyad University's higher education institutions are widely accustomed to delivering online courses and have a rich bank of online materials, which facilitates the transition from face-to-face to online teaching to better follow courses without disruption in times of health crisis. The university's existing online distance learning platforms (UC@MOOC platforms: http://mooc.uca.ma; http://ucamooc.uca.ma) [7, 38] can offer courses and resources in various digital formats (PDF, video, video conferencing, etc.), usually with associated exercises. Generally, teachers can select courses and exercises that their students can watch and do, and coach them through social networks and synchronous classrooms. The university provides these students with a wide range of open educational resources that could be used.

2.2 Live Streaming Courses

Another form of distance learning, coaching and follow-up adopted by the university is the use of new online and synchronous learning platforms or so-called virtual classrooms. Students are invited to connect online and participate in the educational process using virtual classrooms, which simulate all the aspects of a digital educational environment. In addition, today more than ever, teachers are being asked to restructure their teaching practices and adapt to these changes, even if in record time [30]. Some "virtual classroom" services already exist online (e.g. ZOOM, Google Meet, Webex). Not forgetting the use of all appropriate electronic communication methods. In some places in Morocco where the infrastructure is obsolete, some older electronic methods (such as streaming television courses, radio channels) are more relevant.

2.3 UCA Digital CAMPUS

Cadi Ayyad University has released an intuitive and rich platform (UCA DIGITAL CAMPUS), consolidating the content of its fourteen institutions, allowing more than 95,000 students registered for the academic year 2019–2020 to successfully complete their distance learning. On the technical side, the platform is hosted on the site of the university presidency. For each of the 14 institutions, the student receives an identifier and an access code. A user's guide allowing him/her to consult the educational resources and activities by subject and study module. The teacher, for his part, has access to read, edit and create content, as well as technical support to help teachers if necessary. The e-Campus platform (https://www.uca.ma//fr/page/Cours_en_ligne) [39] offers these students and teachers a multifunctional digital environment with which the teachers can make knowledge tests to find out the students level of understanding of course program related topics, as well as video lectures, assignments and a calendar so that the teacher can inform his students about the dates of real-time lectures, assignments and tests.

Furthermore the Moroccan Ministry of Education in collaboration with the National Telecommunications Regulatory Agency (ANRT) [5] and the local mobile telecommunications network operators have managed to make outgoing and ingoing traffic to distance learning platforms free of charge, enabling students to access or download UCA's digital resources from the Internet, participate in the Discussion Forums and knowledge tests without impacting their data volume plans.

2.4 National TV Channel

The Ministry of Higher Education has hired some television and radio stations to broadcast courses in rural areas where mobile network coverage or capacity is lower. For example, the broadcasting courses of the TV channels Tamazight and Al Ayoun are aimed at primary and secondary school students, while the educational programs of the Arryadia TV channel are deliberately aimed at university students [13]. The Arryadia channel also broadcasts among its training programs, a part of a 6H per day whose content has been developed by the UCA and targets several disciplines.

2.5 Virtual Practical Work

According to Noam Ebner and Sharon Press [14], focusing totally on synchronous teaching methods may not be the best idea, from an educational or practical point of view. As teachers become more and more proficient with online technologies, they would do well to consider integrating other online teaching methods, including asynchronous simulations.

Laboratory experiments are an indispensable part of the scientific program. The objective of these experiments is to understand and describe the real world and to enable students to apply the knowledge acquired in a traditional course. In this respect, the EXPERES project in partnership with Cadi Ayyad University, aims to set up a platform for remote practical work within the training environment. These works will be envisaged as a pedagogical activity leading to a reinforcement of the efficiency and quality of the learners' knowledge [19]. For this reason, the UCA has integrated this virtual laboratory with a Moodle platform (LMS) as an activity to be linked with other learning activities (courses, tests, quizzes, etc.), the implementation of online simulated practical exercises allows students to repeat the experience as many times as they wish, at any time and in any place, so students also have the advantage of communicating interactively with the tutors to answer their questions and possible needs for formative evaluation [18]. This initiative allows learners to conduct virtual experiments that would be dangerous and forbidden to perform in a laboratory with the measure of university closure due to COVID-19.

2.6 OER (Open Education Resources)

In Morocco, Cadi Ayyad University and Ibn Zohr University were the two representatives of the OpenMed project which is a project co-financed by the Erasmus + higher education capacity building programs of the European Union, involving 14 partners from Europe and Southern Mediterranean countries (Morocco, Egypt, Palestine and Jordan). OpenMed is structured in three axes: review of good practices, broadening participation in OER, and training of trainers (openmedproject.eu). The objective of OpenMed is to adopt open educational resources in the four Southern Mediterranean countries, it promotes the role of universities as providers for their students, and for disadvantaged groups [34]. It is not just a matter of the selection of materials, as the true value of OER lies in the way they are integrated into the curriculum to feed into a pedagogy that is more closely linked to the needs of learners [26].

2.7 Social Networks

Different social networks (Facebook, Twitter, LinkedIn, WhatsApp, Youtube…) are used for certain teaching/learning tasks based on communication and sharing, teachers can use them to organize discussions, disseminate information, share videos, multimedia files and more. They can also create work groups through social networks such as WhatsApp for each class and share information, digital content and resources.

3 Results

Cadi Ayyad University was able to act quickly and decisively thanks to the solid infrastructure and rich digital educational resources put in place from the very beginning, i.e. existing resources were put in place years before the COVID-19 pandemic, paving the way for a new active learning strategy.

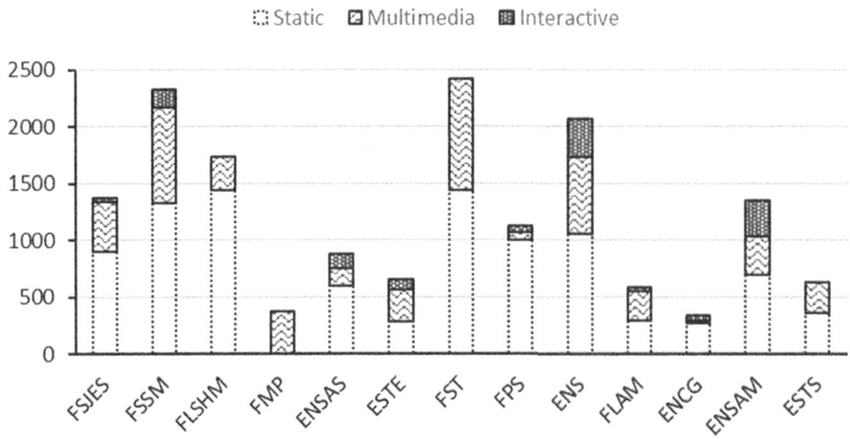

Fig. 1. Cumulative online resources count by category and by faculty

We can summarize the production of Cadi Ayyad University in terms of online digital educational resources, as shown in Fig. 1. We have seen that the production is classified into three main categories, static digital resources includes courses in PDF and PPT format, with a sum of 9662 materials, these course materials are the easiest to make by teachers and the most used by students because of their simplicity. The second category of digital educational resources are the multimedia supports including courses in Video, Audio format and capsules dedicated to broadcasting in the Arryadia TV channel, with a production of 5014 supports. The third category with 1176 supports, includes courses that are delivered through remote conferencing platforms or so-called virtual classrooms (ZOOM, Google Meet, Webex and Jitsi Meet are the platforms most used by Cadi Ayyad University), these platforms offer the possibility of interacting with students. In total, Cadi Ayyad University has produced 15852 online digital resources until June 2020 (Table 1).

Among the 14 faculties in the Cadi Ayyad University, as shown in the Fig. 2, the Semlalia Faculty of Sciences occupies a very important place in the process of producing video courses to integrate them into the Moodle (E-Campus) and EDX (UC@MOOC) platforms. It has managed to produce 786 video courses, i.e. 21%. In terms of live courses, the Fig. 3 shows that the Ecole Normal Supérieure (ENS), the National School of Applied Sciences of Marrakech (ENSAM), the Faculty of Sciences Semlalia (FSSM) and the National School of Applied Sciences of Safi (ENSAS) have ascended to the throne with a large number of productions of live courses, i.e. 79%.

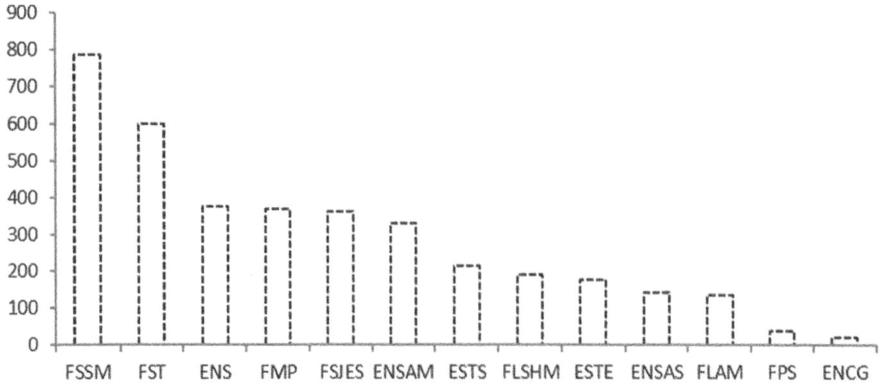

Fig. 2. Videos published by each faculty

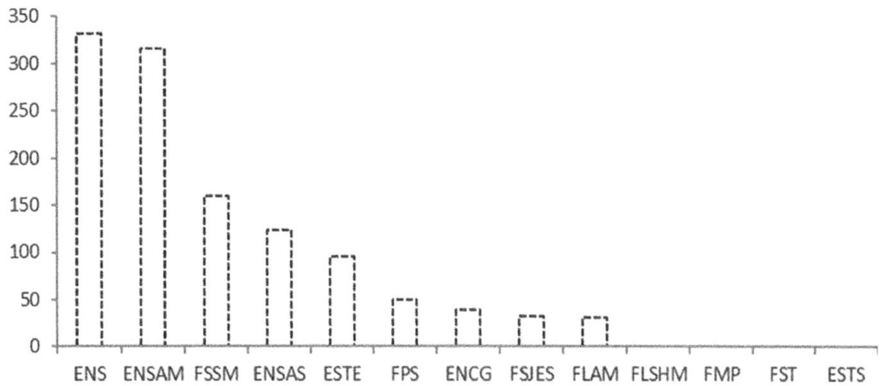

Fig. 3. Live courses delivered by each faculty

In addition, Experes' e-TP hands-on platform has had a very important impact, improving the quality of learning, with which the student can repeat the experience as many times as they want, anywhere, anytime. The platform has so far provided students with 12 labs and is used by 4 institutes belonging to UCA: FSSM, FST, Multidisciplinary Faculty and ENSA.

In term of infrastructure, the university has managed new studios for recording courses, reinforced its internet speed, offered teasers and tutorials to train staffs on the use of platforms and how to produce contents using low-cost solutions, etc. To succeed in the online teaching process, a large campaign of communication was organized overall faculties allowing over 100.000 students to be updated on time on what is going while the COVID-19 is progressing. Every student at UCA was delivered a personal email address to allow a free access to the LMS platform.

The transformation of teaching and learning models will necessarily have strengths and weaknesses. The new forms of teaching and learning will bring new challenges, as will the family situations, living conditions and consequences of the current situation of confinement are sources of disruptive stress that affect both the quality of teaching

Table 1. Table of online educational resources by faculty.

Faculties	Online educative resources						Total
	PDF	PPT	Videos	Audios	Live courses	TV/Radio	
FSJES	741	159	362	0	32	80	1374
FSSM	741	159	362	0	32	80	2324
FLSHM	1115	208	786	39	159	17	1731
FMP	1157	285	190	56	0	43	369
ENSAS	0	0	369	0	0	0	880
ESTE	509	89	144	13	123	2	654
FST	186	92	177	97	95	7	2420
FPS	1261	175	598	386	0	0	1124
ENS	884	121	39	30	50	0	2068
FLAM	827	229	376	300	332	4	587
ENCG	211	83	137	84	31	41	339
ENSAM	196	75	22	7	39	0	1350
ESTS	567	133	332	3	315	0	632
Total	7898	1764	3747	1073	1176	194	15852
%	49.82%	11.13%	23.64%	6.77%	7.42%	1.22%	100.00%

and the psychology of the learner. According to a study conducted at the University Ibn Tofail, which aims to examine the impact of distance education on the mental health of students. Research has shown that imposing distance education as a learning process on students produces a significant level of stress in 49% of the student population studied [25]. In such contexts, it becomes necessary to find ways to provide psychological support and meet the needs of the students. There is a need to identify the full range of student needs and to provide innovative ways to support students online. As part of its mobilization to deal with the COVID 19 health crisis, UCA is setting up a psychological support system for students during this period of confinement. This initiative is created by the Center for Inclusive Education and Social Responsibility of the UCA (CEIRS) and supervised by teacher-researchers in Psychology and volunteer external professionals. In this regard, the UCA has published on its website thematic capsules to raise awareness among students about the difficulties they may encounter during confinement (fear, anxiety, depression, lack of motivation, poor time management, or other …). For this purpose, interested students have the possibility to arrange a remote appointment with a professional [8].

4 Discussion

In conclusion, 15852 educational resources have been produced up to June 2020, covering all UCA curricula, with about 70% of resources produced since the beginning of the pandemic (see Table 1) thus offering students a wide range of educational resources adapted to their needs (see Fig. 1). For this first stage, the university has recovered the bulk of its educational needs.

After the first two months of online teaching and according to some online surveys distributed among students and other stakeholders on the perception of distance learning, taking into account the preliminary analytical results obtained throughout the LMS platforms (UC@MOOC and E-Campus) and the need to ensure quality assurance throughout this period, we have shown that:

- 20% of the students could not connect to their courses on the platforms, and 70% could not benefit from the interactive LIVE courses, due to the lack of computer tools and Internet connection, especially in rural areas because they do not have the necessary means.
- 60% of the resources produced were in PPT and PDF formats. The main advantage of this method is that the size of the files is reduced, which makes it possible to have courses with low-speed Internet access.
- The online evaluation was conducted through the LMS platforms, and the evaluation of online certification is not yet possible via LMS platforms. In this regard, the evaluation of learner certification is postponed to next September.
- Virtual practical work limited to 12 practical works have been proposed to students, according to the Experes platform, 1450 summer students are registered, of which 40 users are teachers. the platform is used by 5 faculties.

Cadi Ayyad University has responded to the closure of academic institutions by implementing an emergency strategy to engage and push these 14 institutes without exception to transform their courses from traditional mode to a purely online mode with a wide choice of online digital resources of a total of 15852 digital media. In comparison with other institutions worldwide, we can cite as an example the Australian higher education, which has responded to COVID-19 with varying degrees of effectiveness, some of its universities have temporarily stopped considering e-learning, some others have plans in place to continue face-to-face learning, while others have moved quickly to e-learning without suspending their courses [11]. In the case of higher education institutions in Pakistan [1], despite limited resources, some of the country's leading universities were even able to start their online courses immediately.

UCA's Moodle platform (E-Campus) and Edx platform (UC@MOOC) have managed to ensure a smooth running of teaching without disruption, these platforms offer a unique account for each student which allows access to the course resources and to post in the forums, participate in the chat, answer knowledge tests and send homework. They make available to students of the 14 faculties 3747 courses in video format in different streams and modules. In addition, the university has adopted the online course delivery tools (ZOOM, Google Meet, Webex and Jitsi Meet) to provide 1176 courses. Meanwhile, Teachers at the University of Massachusetts Amherst also used, as in the case of UCA, the learning management systems Moodle and Blackboard to communicate with students and share course content, such as lecture notes, PowerPoint slides, assignments and other course materials that can be downloaded, and to use Zoom to broadcast or record courses [15]. Peking University has launched live online programs of a total of

2,613 undergraduate courses and 1,824 graduate courses online to ensure normal teaching operations [3]. In addition, New York University in Shanghai and Duke Kunshan University have also been able to quickly adapt their teaching using the Zoom and Moodle video conferencing platform [2]. It is important to note that these universities already had experience with these technologies, which they were able to extend. However, the Moodle platform, used by the Faculty of Chemistry and Hydrocarbons (FHC) of the University of Boumerdes in Algeria, offers a wide range of communication tools with a simple interface, but the "Anonymous" option is an obstacle to interactivity. As it limits several functions of the platform, the universities of Boumerdes decided that students must be anonymous visitors to access their courses submitted by their professors on the university's Moodle platform. They can only access course resources and therefore cannot post in the forums, participate in the chat, answer tests, send assignments and add entries or comments to a glossary or database. The results of the adopted strategy revealed a negative perception of e-learning by students at the University of Boumerdes in Algeria during the COVID epidemic19 [6].

On the other hand, Georgia University of Commerce and Technology has based its teaching solely on Suite G for free tuition. 8 products were considered to be used in the new form of teaching: Gmail, Classroom, Forms, Calendar - for online conference planning, Drive - for storing recorded conferences, Jamboard and Drawings - for drawing and writing that can replace the whiteboard, Hangouts Meet - for live conference broadcasting with up to 100 participants and OBS - for streaming conference recordings [4].

Also, the e-TP practical work platform made available to students opens the door to autonomous teaching, it allows learners to conduct virtual experiments in simulation with JavaScript that it would be dangerous and forbidden to carry out in a laboratory with the university's closure measure because of COVID-19. In China, it has been proven that learning using video simulation of the dynamic mathematics software "Hawgent" has a positive impact on the learning attitude of students. With this software, students can easily understand the basic concept [28].

We are now starting the second phase of the undisruptive leaning process which consists of reinforcing interactive online learning with learners to motivate them to be prepared for their exams, which have been postponed at the national level to September 2020 as confirmed by the Moroccan Ministry of Higher Education. So far, many virtual classes will continue to be organized by teachers to interact with their students and recording sessions will be kept on platforms. We have also noticed that the Moroccan TV channel Arryadia which was previously in charge of the number of courses has moved their programs to deliver tutorials and interactive works helping learners in preparing the next step of face-to-face evaluation by September.

The last step of the Distance learning process is dedicated to the post COVID-19 reshape education taking into account challenges and experiences learned during the first and second steps. In fact, UCA is now working on its strategic plan of Distance learning from various angles as well as for many other public universities who are acting under the auspices of the Moroccan Ministry of Higher Education.

Before giving the picture of some pillars that UCA is now focusing on we need to mention the part of the scientific research developed locally in the era of Science education that was necessary to continue improving quality in teaching and giving guidance to some new adopted solutions at UCA. Among these solutions, we will highlight 8 pillars that seem to be the most relevant to build the university of tomorrow:

- Development of Internet networks, with wide coverage and acceptable quality and speed, and development of mobile applications.
- Enrich the university's data center with digital educational resources.
- Adapting teaching methods to the new generation of universities in the digital age, based on active learning strategies.
- Training staff and human resources in the adoption of ICT and distance education solutions.
- Content digitization, production and resource protection.
- Enhance policies and regulations regarding the adoption of distance education.
- Encourage and support research in pedagogical development (funding, surveys, teaching methods, interactive learning, evaluation, automatic learning, etc.).
- Support all stakeholders (students, teachers, administrative staff, technicians, civil society, curriculum designers, ...) in order to be in regular contact and create a link and synergy between faculties.

Solutions that are believed to be almost certain to work often contain flaws. As any adaptation requires modification to existing structures and resources to meet new requirements [21]. It is clear that the most important part of the process of resolving the problem of university closure is not only the implementation of a solution to transform face-to-face teaching into distance education, but rather the process of monitoring the results of applying the solution to the intended objectives. In times of crisis, UCA has often examined and monitored digital devices as they are implemented, and is considering ways to adapt them during their implementation.

Student satisfaction with the measures taken by the Ministry of National Education in Morocco against the closure of higher education institutions is measured through surveys that have been generalized to all higher education institutions throughout the kingdom. Most Moroccan students believe that, more or less, the measures taken by the Ministry of National Education in Morocco are sufficient to meet the needs of students to take their courses at a distance in the face of the covid-19 pandemic. Indeed, 33 percent of students consider these measures to be satisfactory, 43 percent consider them to be average, and 24 percent consider them to be poor [16]. At the international level, existing research shows that student performance in online learning is slightly better than in face-to-face courses [10, 20].

5 Conclusion

The COVID-19 pandemic is a learning experience for students by giving them the opportunity to better understand how they learn; they will tailor their learning to their needs. The lesson to be learned from this difficult situation is that the field of education in general needs greater interest from governments to improve the quality of education, and for the development of learning platforms that will be used in a blended learning model throughout the school year. Teachers need to be trained in ICTs, emphasizing that they can teach at a distance, and also create digital teaching devices and materials. The objective of this paper was to analyze the experience of Cadi Ayyad University to ensure non-disruptive learning in the context of COVID-19. This study will also help higher education institutions and the Ministry of Higher Education to compare the different experiences in the country, as well as in other faculties around the world in order to better prepare stakeholders to cope with the various requirements of the COVID-19 pandemic or any period of health crisis.

References

1. Adnan, M., Anwar, K.: Online learning amid the COVID-19 pandemic: students' perspectives. J. Pedagog. Sociol. Psychol. **2**, 2020 (2020). https://doi.org/10.33902/JPSP
2. Ali, W., Wahab, A.: Unraveling the inherent complexities of quality education: emerging implication for policy and practice view project online and remote learning in higher education institutes: a necessity in light of COVID-19 pandemic. High. Educ. Stud. **10** (2020). https://doi.org/10.5539/hes.v10n3p16
3. Bao, W.: COVID-19 and online teaching in higher education: a case study of Peking University. Hum. Behav. Emerg. Technol. **2**, 113–115 (2020). https://doi.org/10.1002/hbe2.191
4. Basilaia, G., Dgebuadze, M., Kantaria, M., Chokhonelidze, G.: Replacing the classic learning form at universities as an immediate response to the COVID-19 virus infection in georgia. Int. J. Res. Appl. Sci. Eng. Technol. (2020). https://doi.org/10.22214/ijraset.2020.3021
5. Benseddik, M.: L'université marocaine à l'épreuve du Covid-19. AEGIS Libellio **16**, 37–44 (2020)
6. Blizak, D., Blizak, S., Bouchenak, O., Yahiaoui, K.: Students' perceptions regarding the abrupt transition to online learning during the COVID-19 pandemic: case of faculty of chemistry and hydrocarbons at the university of boumerdes—Algeria. J. Chem. Educ. **97**, 2466–2471 (2020). https://doi.org/10.1021/acs.jchemed.0c00668
7. Cadi Ayyad U UC@MOOC. http://ucamooc.uca.ma/. Accessed 9 Mar 2020
8. Cadi Ayyad University Psychological support system for students (Covid-19). https://www.uca.ma/fr/news/le-reseau-des-psychologues-solidaires-a-votre-ecoute. Accessed 2 June 2020
9. Cauchemez, S., et al.: School closures during the 2009 influenza pandemic: national and local experiences. BMC. Infect. Dis. **14**(207), 1–11 (2014). https://doi.org/10.1186/1471-2334-14-207
10. Liu, C.-H.: The comparison of learning effectiveness between traditional face-to-face learning and e-learning among goal-oriented users. In: 6th International Conference on Digital Content, Multimedia Technology and its Applications, pp 255–260 (2010)
11. Crawford, J., et al.: COVID-19: 20 countries' higher education intra-period digital pedagogy responses. J. Appl. Learn. Teach. **3**, 1–20 (2020). https://doi.org/10.37074/jalt.2020.3.1.7
12. Dhawan, S.: Online learning: a panacea in the time of COVID-19 crisis. J. Educ. Technol. Syst. **49**, 5–22 (2020). https://doi.org/10.1177/0047239520934018
13. Draissi, Z., ZhanYong, Q.: COVID-19 Outbreak Response Plan: Implementing Distance Education in Moroccan Universities. SSRN Electron. J. (2020). https://doi.org/10.2139/ssrn.3586783

Blended Learning and Transformative Processes: A Model for Didactic Development and Innovation

Loretta Fabbri, Mario Giampaolo(✉), and Martina Capaccioli

University of Siena, Siena, Italy
mario.giampaolo@unisi.it

Abstract. The Covid-19 pandemic is overwhelming the way to think and practice didactic in higher education. Academic institutions are facing the challenge of providing courses in different ways from those used before the lockdown period. In this scenario of uncertainty, blended learning seems to be a possible solution that combines the benefits of online and classroom education. Based on many studies, researchers have concluded that a mix of face-to-face and online instructional formats is the best solution for accelerating students' learning processes. This contribution describes a case study of the implementation of a didactic blended model in the bachelor and master's degrees at the University of Siena. Specifically, research objectives were (1) analyze the digital environment that characterized faculties' work before the lockdown phase, (2) describe the elements of faculties' process of didactic redesign, (3) understand their expectations, needs, attitudes, and concerns in applying technologies to teaching and learning. The analysis allows the collection of a rich amount of data that lead to the design of a blended learning model specific for the two programs in educational science.

Keywords: Blended learning · Active methodologies · Higher education

1 Introduction

The Covid-19 pandemic is overwhelming the way of think and practice didactic in higher education. Academic institutions are facing the challenge of provide courses in different ways from those used before the lockdown period. For example, all the world is astonished by the news that the University of Cambridge in England decided, for the next academic year, to carry out all the courses on-line. In this scenario of uncertainty, blended learning seems to be a possible solution that combines the benefits of online and classroom education.

Based on many studies, researchers have concluded that a mix of face-to-face and online instructional formats is the best solution for accelerating students' learning processes. However, there are still concerns related to delivering blended courses. In particular, issues such as instructional support, faculty motivation, and technology problems have been raised as complications in developing this kind of education [1]. Due to the fact that blended learning is becoming fundamental for didactic in higher education,

L. S. Agrati et al. (Eds.): HELMeTO 2020, CCIS 1344, pp. 214–225, 2021.
https://doi.org/10.1007/978-3-030-67435-9_17

faculty's accomplishments, attitudes, and expectations towards new technologies have become a key aspect of teaching. To these, students' expectation of personalization, increased retention and success rates through well- designed learning materials and processes need to be added. Faculties must not only succeed in tradition- al classrooms; they must also be fluent in Technology Enhanced Learning (TEL) [2].

This contribution describes a case study of the implementation of a didactic blended model in the bachelor and master's degree at the University of Siena. Specifically, research objectives were (1) analyze the digital environment that characterized faculties' work before the lockdown phase, (2) describe the elements of faculties' process of didactic redesign, (3) understand their expectations, needs, attitudes, and concerns in applying technologies to teaching and learning. The analysis allows the collection of a rich amount of data that lead to the design of a blended learning model specific for the two programs in educational science.

2 Method

The researchers use an embedded mixed method design (see Fig. 1) to collect both quantitative and qualitative data, merge them, and use the results to reach research objectives.

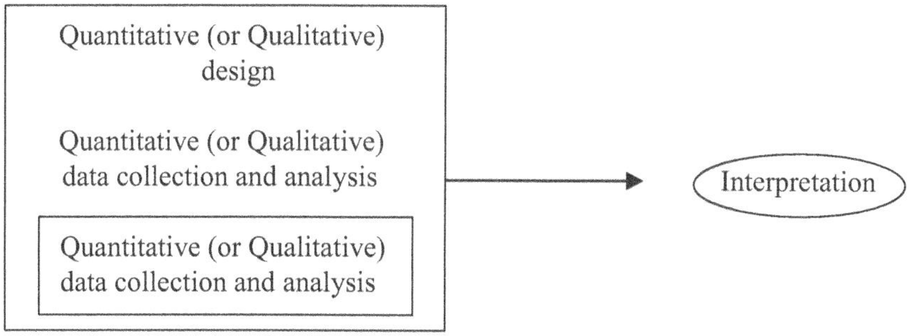

Fig. 1. The embedded mixed method design from [3]

Researchers use this design because one data collection form supplies strengths to offset the weaknesses of the other form, and also because different forms of data lead to a more complete understanding of a phenomenon.

Quantitative and qualitative data were collected using interviews with faculties and observational notes sheets to collect data during the on-line lessons and to analyze the Moodle platform (see Fig. 2).

The lesson observation and the analysis of the learning content management system allowed researchers to understand the number and the nature of activities, resources and interaction realized, while the interviews with faculties allowed to understand their expectations, needs, attitudes and concerns on the adoption of the new blended learning model.

3 Findings from Observations and Interviews

The starting point was to carry out an observation on activities and resources used by the faculties in the Moodle platform.[1] The objective was to obtain quantitative empirical data and compose a background to start research actions from.

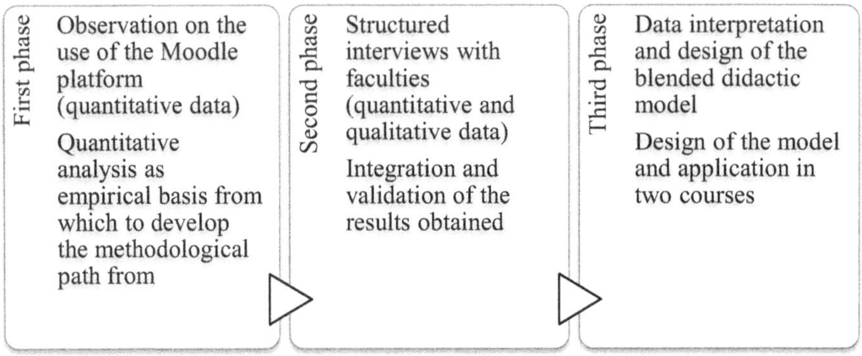

Fig. 2. The methodological process of the blended teaching model design

At the time of the first observation, dated March the 6th, 2020[2], the Department of Education, Human Sciences and Intercultural Communication the two programs refer to, 30 courses were activated within the Moodle platform, compared to the 42 total provided overall, corresponding to the 71% (N = 30) of the total. Of this 71%, 59% (N = 25)

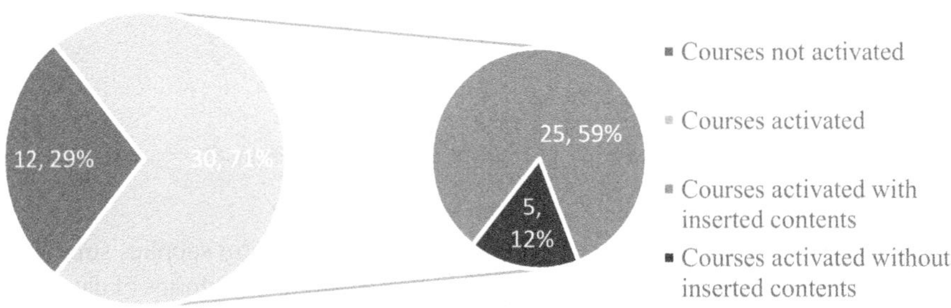

Fig. 3. Courses activated in the University Moodle platform

[1] Moodle is a virtual learning environment belonging to the family of Learning Management Systems (LMS) whose design is epistemologically based on socio-constructionist constructs. It is a web-based and open source software programmed and utilized as an e-learning tool within which it is possible to manage areas used for courses, contents, and learning. Within the platform, in fact, teachers and students can interact with each other, exchange knowledge, upload and download didactic materials and conduct learning tests [4].

[2] The face-to-face lessons have been suspended starting from March 5, 2020. The lockdown period began starting from March 10, 2020.

had contents uploaded in the platform and 12% (N = 5) had no types of contents (see Fig. 3).

Within this framework, 57% (N = 20) of the courses used their Moodle space as a repository, 23% (N = 8) used it for synchronous interaction, and 20% (N = 7) used it for asynchronous interaction (see Fig. 4).

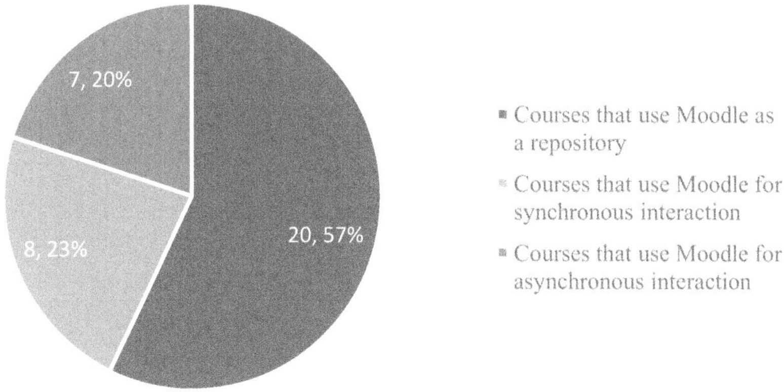

Fig. 4. Modes of use of the University Moodle platform

In terms of activities and resources offered by the online courses, it has been noted that (see Fig. 5):

- 40% (N = 10) of these offered didactic contents (slides, documents, videos, and video-lectures);
- 24% (N = 6) offered didactic contents (slides, documents, videos, and video-lectures) and allowed asynchronous interaction (learning tests and forums);
- 4% (N = 1) allowed asynchronous interaction (learning tests and forums);
- 8% (N = 2) allowed synchronous interaction (chats and videoconferences);
- 20% (N = 5) offered didactic contents (slides, documents, videos and video-lectures) and allowed synchronous interaction (chats and videoconferences);
- 4% (N = 1) offered didactic content (slides, documents, videos, and video-lectures), allowed asynchronous interaction (learning verifications and forums) and synchronous interaction (chats and videoconferences).

Nineteen days after the first observation, a second has been carried out. The goal was to monitor the use of the Moodle platform and identify which activities and resources were the most used. A first evidence found was that, of the 59 courses of the undergraduate and graduate degree programs provided, the 88% (N = 52) was opened in the Moodle platform. Overall, a clear reversal emerged in the use of the teaching solutions adopted by the teaching community: the 97% (N = 57)[3] of the courses provided, in fact, offers synchronous teaching (live videos that allow interaction between students and between

[3] Some courses combine multiple modes of use.

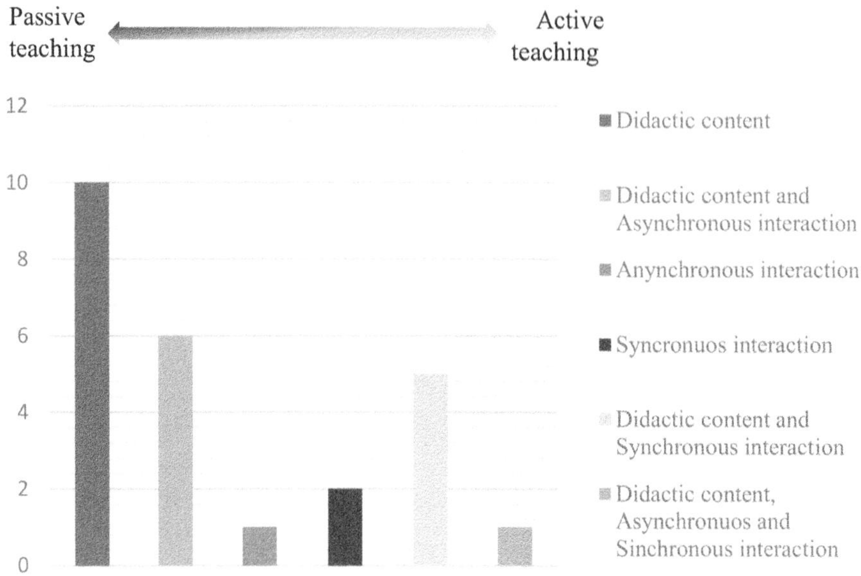

Fig. 5. Activities, resources, and tools offered by the online courses

students and professors), the 73% (N = 43) offers Moodle-based teaching and the 39% (N = 23) offers asynchronous teaching (video lectures, learning tests and forums) (see Fig. 6).

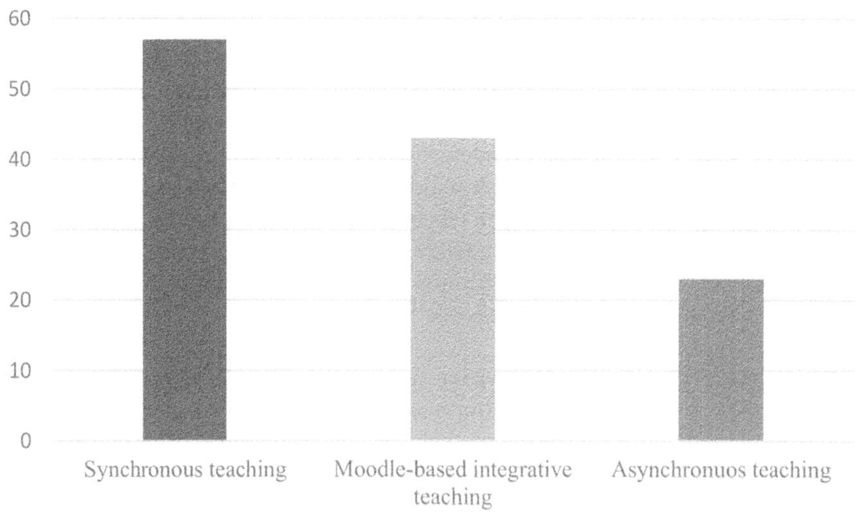

Fig. 6. Modes of use of the University Moodle platform

The panorama concerning the devices used for online teaching activities is confirmed as heterogeneous and composite (see Fig. 7):

- the 2% (N = 1) of the courses offers didactic contents (slides, documents, videos, and video-lectures);
- the 29% (N = 17) of the courses allows synchronous interaction (chats and video-conferences);
- the 46% (N = 27) of the courses offers educational contents (slides, documents, videos and video-lectures) and allows synchronous interaction (chat and videoconferences);
- the 22% (N = 14) of the courses offers educational contents (slides, documents, videos, and video lectures) and allows asynchronous interaction (learning tests and forums) and synchronous interaction (chats and videoconferences).

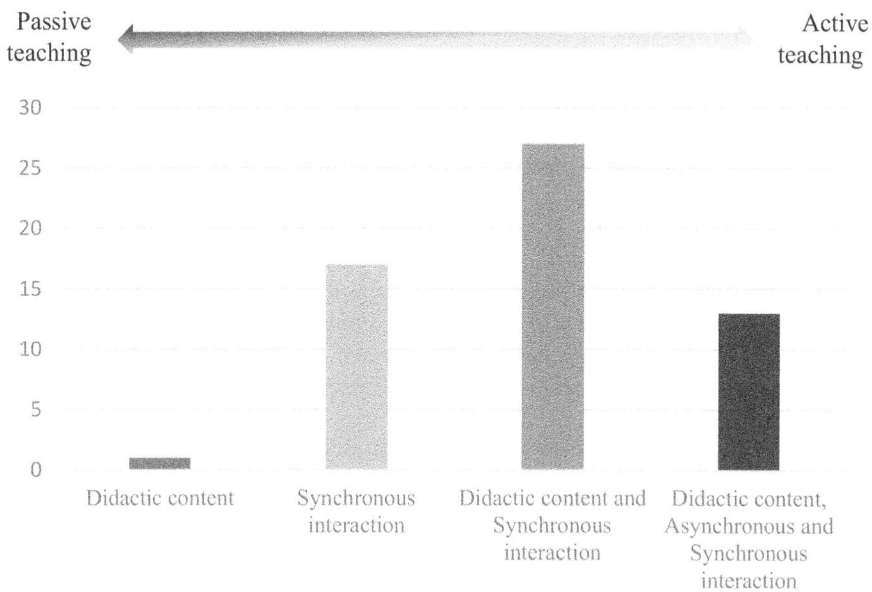

Fig. 7. Activities, resources, and tools offered by the online courses

The shift towards devices that encourages more active teaching suggests that professors, during the lockdown period, may have changed some of their working practices.

Following the two observations, structured interviews were conducted with 14 professors of the bachelor and master's degree courses. These interviews have been interpreted to analyze the viewpoints of the organizational actors involved in the transformation process of the teaching practices. A textual analysis of the content allowed to situate the changes highlighted by the previous quantitative analysis and to assign relevance to the faculty's experience.

Adapting and aligning one's teaching style to new rules, driven by technological constraints, required a cognitive effort and a reflection on one's routines, knowledge, expectations and beliefs [5]. This led to a redesign, even if partial, of the structure of the courses, and to a particular attention to the preparation of the didactic materials.

"I changed the materials [...] and the methods used (recorded lessons, videos, films, slides); the methods of assessment". (P. 2)

"Distance and invisibility don't help. This involves much more attention and effort on my part. And it is essential to look for new paths". (P. 4)

"Positive changes: [...] questioning of the teaching support material to adapt it to the new methodology (more interactive, interspersed with curiosities, videos, images so as not to weaken the attention)". (P. 7)

"The distance lessons involved specific preparation, with much more frequent use of slides and other materials". (P. 14)

The main strengths of the solutions adopted by the professors who took part in the interviews emerge from the experiences produced, thanks to experiments in the virtual classrooms: encouragement to the students' participation; facilitation of the frequency of students not attending students' frequency (working students, remote resident students, students with health problems, etc.); versatility of virtual rooms.

"Students are more inclined to participate, to ask questions and to report their experiences in the virtual classroom, there is much more participation [...]. The use of distance lessons can also be used in the future (for those who live far away, for those who cannot attend for temporary health reasons) and the lessons can also be recorded for those who work". (P. 7)

"The virtual classrooms have valuable features and allow us to share more «spaces» (we use the group chat to exchange opinions and share course contents; it allows to monitor, through real-time surveys, the students' level of lessons satisfaction and learning effectiveness)". (P. 8)

"By recording the lessons, I think I have made it easier following the interpretation and commentary of the texts in the program. Through Panopto, I have been able to integrate it with the PowerPoint presentations [...], without forgetting the opportunities students had to listen and pause at will and on the most difficult passages". (P. 12).

"More than twice as many students have used Moodle, using the resources there proposed or listening to the recorded lessons. Even when, in the last two weeks, I gave the lessons live on GMeet, I have still inserted the recordings on Moodle. Basically, the new situation has greatly reduced the difference between attending and non-attending students". (P. 14)

Finally, the conditions under which it is possible to implement learner-centered and technologically efficient distance learning are emerging from the professors' voice. Even after solving the critical issues of digital divide the constant emphasis and attention to the relational dimension [6] remains the discriminating factor for the success of online educational actions.

> *"The dialogue with the students has to be continuous. I use the method of open questions through the chat. A method that, after two weeks, is paying off. I write a word (the focus of each of my lessons is in one word) and ask them to build a «crown» of words around that word. I leave and then it's up to them. And then back to me and then it's back to them. And that's all. Now the students take intervene during the lessons without any problem. Chat is our center of gravity. That keeps us united. Final result: the construction of a mosaic".* (P. 4)

From the comparison of the empirical data obtained from the three phases of the research, an organizational learning process was progressively outlined, which involved the didactic area and the professional epistemologies of the organizational actors.

4 The Blended Model

The model we will present has been designed for a bachelor's degree program in Educational Science. The program aims to prepare professionals in the field of informal education and training and base its activities on active learning methodology and group works. Due to the pandemic crisis the program switched most of its activities on-line through the support of different systems like moodle, google meet and Panopto. It is important to note that the model is program specific and is developed for subjects like pedagogy, philosophy, psychology, sociology, etc. Despite its flexibility authors are conscious that different disciplines like French or Physics may request a different approach.

The model is based on the traditional unit of measurement of the Italian academic courses: the Credito Formativo Universitario (CFU). Normally each CFU is worth six hours of lessons and 19 h of individual studies, for a total of 25 h. To adapt each CFU to a blended didactic, the six hours of lessons are split in two hours of lessons, two hours of group work and two hours of video lessons. Courses in the two programs are normally of six and twelve CFUs that allow for a number of hours of didactic as seen below (see Fig. 8).

Video lessons are delivered through Google Meet for synchronous lessons and Panopto for asynchronous lessons. Both allow the automatic storage on the Moodle platform. Moreover, group work could be realized in two different ways:

(a) interactions between the students and the professor could happen through Forums and mailing lists used as virtual environment to post reflections, questions, and receive support from faculty and peers or as a webinar conducted by the faculty and structured as mini training path; (b) interactions among peers could happen as project work. In this case the use of forum as environment to allow students' communication and resources sharing is suggested. Faculty makes lessons in the classroom and he or she is recorded through a video camera installed in the class. Students can follow the lesson on-line, they have just to connect to a virtual room, or come to university.

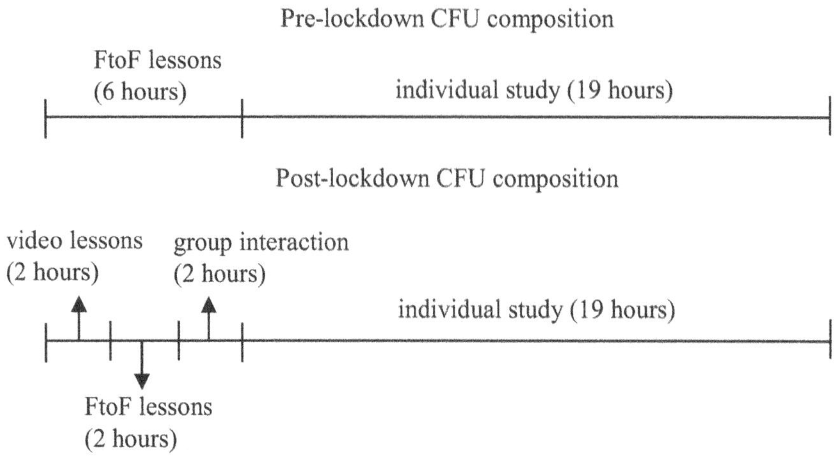

CFU composition in Pre-lockdown courses

	6 CFU courses	12 CFU courses
lessons	36 hours	72 hours
individual study	114 hours	228 hours

CFU composition in Post-lockdown courses

	6 CFU courses	12 CFU courses
video lessons	14 hours	28 hours
FtoF lessons	16 hours	32 hours
group interaction	6 hours	12 hours
individual study	114 hours	228 hours

Fig. 8. Comparison between pre-lockdown and post-lockdown courses

The presence of students at university is the second element of the model that need to be taken in consideration. Due to the normative restriction stated by the Italian government and adopted by the university governance, students could follow lessons in little groups and in prearranged rounds. Groups are created following three basic criteria. Here the aim is to allow all the students the possibility to participate in the lessons beyond their willingness. These criteria are the following: (a) the number of students that have the right to participate at the course (that is one of their mandatory courses on the study plan), the classroom capacity (due to normative restriction, classroom capacity are reduced to 1/3 of the normal) and the alphabetical order.

With this planning, could be possible to guarantee an equal presence of students in the classroom by limiting the risk of gatherings, enhance distance learning with the opportunity to participate in face-to-face lessons, and allow the delivery of more than one third of the teaching in presence (see Table 1)

Table 1. Group creation in the course of general pedagogy

Course title	General Pedagogy (module A)		
Duration	Six weeks (three lessons of two hours each week)		
Number of students	220		
Classroom capacity	30 seats (180 centimeters between students)		
Groups	Eight groups of 30 persons each		
Time schedule	**Monday**	**Tuesday**	**Wednesday**
9:00 11:00 AM	First group (N=30)	Second group (N=30)	Third group (N=30)
	Forth group (N=30)	Fifth group (N=30)	Sixth group (N=30)
	Seventh group (N=30)	Eighth group (N=30)	

During the lockdown phase, we implemented the model in two courses of the bachelor's degree program to define the principal elements that characterize faculty work in applying this model. The principal characteristic is the collaboration between the faculty, a didactic, and a technological tutor. The team meets daily on-line to design resources to be adopted during synchronous and asynchronous lessons, to design forums in which the students can post contents and faculty can comment with the support of the didactic tutor and other students. The design team projected webinars for small groups of students and an automatic evaluation system to allow students to receive feedback on the level of comprehension of the themes faced during the course.

5 Conclusive Reflections

The disorienting dilemma [5] produced by the epidemiological emergency transformed a period of high uncertainty in an opportunity for the didactic development and innovation.

What emerged from the observations of the informal conversations among professors, which took place in the period right after the closure of the University facilities, was a sense of inadequacy expressed by colleagues who needed to identify solutions capable of responding effectively to the sudden change taking place, within low-tech degree courses. Therefore, the challenge was to avoid the sense of inadequacy and rejection of new didactic practices perceived as distant from the academic tradition. At the same time, the shared will was not to reduce this opportunity to exclusively content-based online lessons.

In response to this demand, we propose the creation of micro-communities. Informal aggregations made up of organizational actors who activate a process of inquiry and co-construction of knowledge useful for organizational development [7–9]. The interest of these groups of peers will be to share a common path and try to become a learning community. These could be carried out assuming that the lockdown period, rather than an emergency, could represent an important moment of experimentation. Professors can be considered as comrades in adversity [10]. Through processes of dialogic confrontation, which will take shape within their micro-communities, they will become capable of taking charge of the problems that affect the university organization and rethink solutions that make them manageable in a perspective of growth.

The organizational development trajectories followed by these communities will develop in a non-linear way [8] and will emerge during encounters and bilateral meetings between professors. These trajectories are what Argyris and Schön [11] define espoused theories. We are speaking of that set of rules of action that formally justify the actions of individuals and frequently do not coincide with the theories-in-use, that is, with the tacit assumptions incorporated into organizational routines that effectively direct the work and behavior of organizational actors. Initially, part of the faculty while supporting the importance of implementing technology-based teaching strategies that integrate various digital tools and workspaces, will be committed to defend their positions that reflect a reductionist approach, i.e. making use of the Moodle platform alone as a repository of educational content.

Taking note of the existing will allow to contain the closed attitudes and to intervene in the transformation of the professors' meaning perspectives [5]. This will be possible by giving different times to the different types of resistance and thus allowing each professor to take part in the organizational learning process according to their own times of change [8, 9]. Encouraging different levels of participation will allow novice researchers to become the experts in possession of the skills, knowledge and experience necessary to support senior colleagues in recognizing their own difficulties and skills by providing examples, points of view and underlining new trajectories of action that would facilitate the acquisition of a more consolidated expertise.

The commitment of communities, aimed at formalizing the learning achieved, will be directed towards the institutional legitimation of the gains obtained through this high-level digital experience that will allow, on the one hand, to demonstrate that active online teaching is not only a supplement tools but can represent a progress towards the innovation of practices and, on the other hand, will allow to promote the professional development of scholars through an epistemic change of the role and identity of the university professors, who thus becomes a professional capable of managing relevant levels of technology.

References

1. Oh, E., Park, S.: How are universities involved in blended instruction? Educ. Technol. Soc. **12**(3), 327–342 (2009)
2. Kruger, J., Bliignaut, A.S.: Linking emotional intelligence to achieve technology enhanced learning in higher education. Turk. Online J. Dist. Educ. TOJDE **14**(4), 99–120 (2013)

3. Creswell, J.W.: Educational Research: Planning, Conducting, and Evaluating Quantitative Research, 4th edn. Pearson, Boston (2012)
4. Rice, W.: Moodle E-Learning Course Development. A Complete Guide to Create and Develop Engaging E-learning Courses with Moodle, 3rd edn. Packt Publishing, Birmingham (2015)
5. Mezirow, J.: Apprendimento e trasformazione. Il significato dell'esperienza e il valore della riflessione nell'apprendimento degli adulti. Raffaello Cortina Editore, Milano (2003)
6. Taylor, E.W.: Student-teacher relationships: the elephant in the classroom. In: Fedeli, M., Bierema, L. (eds.) Connecting Adult Learning and Knowledge Management, vol. 8, pp. 69–83. Springer, Heidelberg (2019). https://doi.org/10.1007/978-3-030-29872-2_4
7. Wenger, E.: Comunità di pratica. Apprendimento, significato e identità. Raffaello Cortina Editore, Milano (2006)
8. Wenger, E., McDermott, R., Snyder, W.M.: Coltivare comunità di pratica. Prospettive ed esperienze di gestione della conoscenza. Guerini e Associati, Milano (2007)
9. Fabbri, L., Romano, A.: Metodi per l'apprendimento trasformativo. Casi, modelli, teorie. Carocci Editore, Roma (2017)
10. Revans, R.W.: What is action learning? J. Manage. Dev. **1**(3), 64–75 (1982)
11. Argyris, C., Schön, D.: Apprendimento organizzativo. Teoria, metodo e pratiche. Guerini e Associati, Milano (1998)

Metamorphosis of Space into Digital Scholarship. A Research on Hybrid Mediation in a University Context

Loredana Perla(✉), Alessia Scarinci, and Ilenia Amati

University of Bari Aldo Moro, Bari, Italy
{loredana.perla,alessia.scarinci,ilenia.amati}@uniba.it

Abstract. The digitalization of the university system in Italy has proceeded "bottom-up" through the dissemination of good practices towards more and more institutionalized interventions until the spring of 2020. With the Prime Ministerial Decree (DPCM) on 9 March 2020, in fact, Italian universities were forced to suspend face to face attendance of degree courses due to the Covid-19 emergency. This made it necessary to rethink the educational space that became digital. This space requires the didactic mediation of the teacher, without which the most sophisticated offers would remain "mute". The research moves from our specific interest in identifying the main components of the imposed digital "metamorphosis" and the forms and formats of hybridization introduced in educational mediation in times of Covid-19 crisis.

The work presents the case of a "hybrid mediation" emerging in an academic context. The research project followed a phenomenological approach and a method of practical analysis with mixed methods with four different data collection actions.

Keywords: Digitalization of the university · Hybrid mediation · Third space

1 Introduction – Metamorphosis of Space in Higher Education by Effect of COVID-19

The university system in the digital age is faced with the challenge of digitization, namely the use of technologies in university management and pedagogy in order to improve and simplify processes, products and activities. EDUCAUSE's annual ECAR studies, conducted on both students and teachers in the United States, show that digitization is still in an early stage of development [1]. In particular, when referring to the digitalization of teaching and learning, despite the availability of funding, infrastructures and government strategies that manage and promote the presence of technology in educational institutions (external process), their pedagogical use is entrusted to the few academic staff within their own disciplinary fields (internal process), generating a strong contrast between what digitalization entails at an organizational and administrative level and what is required at the educational level for the improvement of teaching and learning [2]. In the Italian context, despite the great impetus received by research [3–5] and institutions

L. S. Agrati et al. (Eds.): HELMeTO 2020, CCIS 1344, pp. 226–239, 2021.
https://doi.org/10.1007/978-3-030-67435-9_18

[6], the digitalization of university teaching has so far proceeded from the ground up, thanks to the dissemination of mostly non-institutionalized good practices [7]. This trend remained constant until spring 2020, when the D.P.C.M. (Prime Ministerial Decree) of 9 March imposed on Italian universities the compulsory suspension of the attendance of degree courses due to the Covid-19 emergency, causing a strong impact on the internal and external processes of digitization of teaching and learning. During the emergency, education was the subject of national and international government initiatives, becoming itself an emergency and distance education the key to resolving the crisis [8]. The state of emergency given by the spread of Covid has resulted in a unique situation in the world of school and academia: almost 850 thousand teachers found themselves having to put into practice in a "forced" way distance learning with about 9 million students not adequately prepared to manage the tools used. Trinchero speaks of "forced distance" training because "in classical distance learning students and teachers choose to undertake a learning/teaching path remaining physically separated for some periods and meeting in presence in others. In "forced distance" training there is no choice, neither of one nor of the other" [9]. As supported by the studies conducted by Hodges et alia [10] on the impact and response to the Covid emergency, the transformation that took place in the Covid period, the emergency remote teaching, highlighted the lack of pedagogical innovation. If in the case of effective online learning the learning experiences are well planned and are based on the combination of learning design and education design skills with an impact on both the quality of education and student learning. On the other hand, in the case of emergency distance learning, these elements have been lacking. Suddenly, teachers and university students found themselves having to switch to digital pedagogies. The pandemic has placed teachers in front of the need to redefine, redesign their teaching action, considering technologies no longer as simple tools for the transmission of knowledge. The teacher must rethink and reflect on the established practices of their work and then initiate a substantial revision in the direction of improving the learning outcomes of students. The teacher must be able to combine professional, pedagogical, relational and technological skills and be able to evaluate the most suitable technological tools to be used in the different fields. This is why training must be understood as a reflective practicum as Diana Laurillard argues [11]. Professionals must be able to recursively analyze and reflect on their practices, to reflect in action. It was a time a disruption, learning by doing, and reflective practices on our own forms of teaching and learning that had to break away from the traditional transmission model and exploit the technological potential so that the new technology could "do something different from what the technology of 'learning has always done: transmitting academic knowledge to the student", as Diana Laurillard argues [11].

2 Objectives of the Study

Teachers and students found themselves co-inhabitants of an educational space to be reimagined in a short time: the digital one. Technologies, as Williamson et alia [8] point out, break through and alter "the space and time of the class" bringing it into the home environment. "We might call this the Bring Your Own School Home (BYOSH) movement. In this environment, personal screen-time is taken over at the same time as the physical spaces of the home are colonized and co-opted" [8].

This re-imagination is not at all simple because, unfortunately, space is not a category that has been placed at the center of the interest of pedagogical research [12] although new languages, new practices, new methods have been experimented for some time also in a university context (and not only in distance learning) in a learning-centered perspective [13–17]. The space, as a place where the educational process is built, could be thought of as a "living place", as emerges from the long-standing experience of the Reggio Children approach, which must be enriched every day through the selection of materials, information, practices that can motivate and intrigue [18]. The educational space is outlined as a third educator, as the quality of learning and that of the spaces go hand in hand [17, 19] and it is in the space that actions, practices and ways of use are modeled and modeled in the same contextual environment [20]. It is space, in fact, together with time, that governs practices [21] and allows the construction of training devices that mediate knowledge. And it is thanks to the devices that the incorporeal system of techniques, procedures, gestures, routines is determined: the teacher creates a "network" between these heterogeneous elements with his specific media and mediated action. Even ICTs, taken within the paradigm of media education, become conceptual artefacts [22] that bear ownership (affordances) that the media model makes "speak". Without the pedagogical mediation of the teacher, however, even the most sophisticated affordances remain "mute"[1] [12]. Hence our specific interest in investigating the metamorphosis taking place in the space of university mediation as well as being configured following the pandemic emergency, from the point of view of a theory of media education [12, 23] and following a methodological approach of practical analysis to phenomenological orientation [24–27]. A space that is defined as "third" and is currently being investigated in several fields: epistemological [20], anthropological [28], educational [29].

One other space, a social place in which to build their identity and their knowledge without being tied to a form of "learning taught", as reported by Pier Cesare Rivoltella [30].

Manuel Castells in 2004 spoke of the "revolution of space", a revolution that took place with the "internet revolution" that has expanded the global connection, amplified the dimension of flows and places, reproducing and reorganizing the structure and morphology of society in networks. Networking, affects production, sociality and cultural processes. In this sense, the educational dimension itself must abandon its traditional function of transmitting knowledge, values and meanings, and assume the logic of the network, or become a space for circulation and sharing, a place in which to connect interests, values, projects [31]. The so-called "revolution of space" [32] deserves to be explored in the context of university teaching also because of the anthropo-educational transformations that it can induce, as well as for the impacts on the quality of students' learning. These impacts need to be investigated with longitudinal and comparative research. The following investigation moves in this direction aimed, in this first step, at identifying the main constituents of the imposed digital "metamorphosis" [33] and the forms and formats of the hybridization introduced in educational mediation in times

[1] Cfr. Damiano, E.: La mediazione didattica, Franco Angeli, Milano, 2013 pp. 210–234. He reconstructs with unsurpassed clarity the reasons for the failures of all attempts to integrate technologies into face-to-face teaching: the causes lie in not solved a decisive problem in distance learning: the evaluation.

of Covid crisis. Finally, the interest of the investigation is aimed at exploring, through the theoretical sensitivity of us researchers, the concreteness of the hypothesis of the breaking point of formal training systems.

In this direction, the exploratory study aimed to answer two questions:

a) what were the ways of the flexibility of didactic mediation adopted in phase I of the Covid-19 pandemic (time, space, organization and perspectives)?
b) Which active learning mediators was it possible to use in the conditions of distance learning and with what effectiveness?
c) How was student attendance influenced by the impact of the adoption of distance learning?

3 Method

Within the exceptional phase of the COVID-19 emergency, "network" assumed an educational metaphorical sense: safeguarding the students' right to study in a constructivist learning environment. Mediation has been re-invented and forcibly rewritten through the web within a common space [34].

The work presents a case study of a post-Covid-19 university teaching redesign (OECD, 2020) that explain a "flexibility" in remote mediation, a "hybrid mediation" emerging in the academic context.

Through the 'analysis of practices' paradigm [12, 26, 35–37] the advantages and limitations inherent in this training and its educational implications were investigated.

The research design (see Fig. 1) followed a 'analysis of practices' approach from a phenomenological perspective and applying mixed-methods on quantitative and qualitative data; two levels of evidence were obtained, assumed as basis for the analysis of active-non-active mediation and for subsequent inference hybrid.

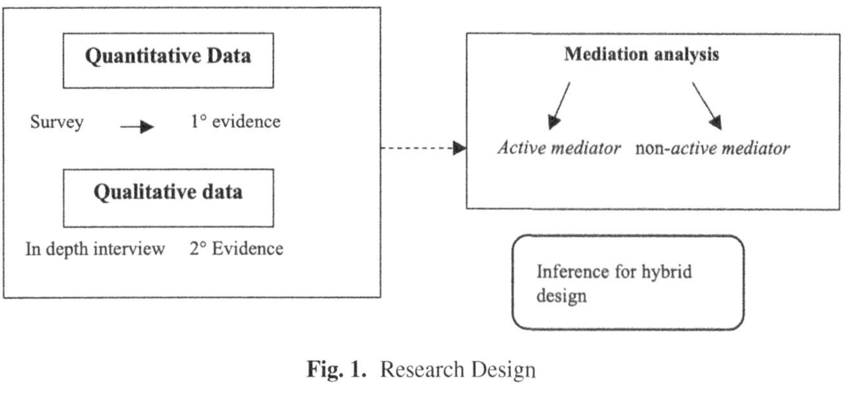

Fig. 1. Research Design

The mixed method - the collection, analysis and interpretation of data in quantitative and qualitative ways in a single study or in a series of studies investigating the same complex phenomenon [38] - responds to a paradigm of pragmatist [39] and interpretative research and an inductive approach to knowledge [40, 41].

Four different data collection actions were carried out:

1. an exploratory questionnaire for a sample of 418 students at the Courses of Education and Training Sciences and Primary Education Sciences of the University of Bari, attending remotely in the second semester of the academic year 2019–2020;
2. practical analysis of the mediatization of active learning mediators normally used in face-to-face teaching;
3. in-depth interviews with groups of students on the perception of virtual space in relation to the dimensions of motivation, organization, self-efficacy;
4. quantitative monitoring of formal and informal student interventions through a participation tracking system.

All data was collected in a Microsoft Teams environment and protected by privacy legislation (Fig. 2).

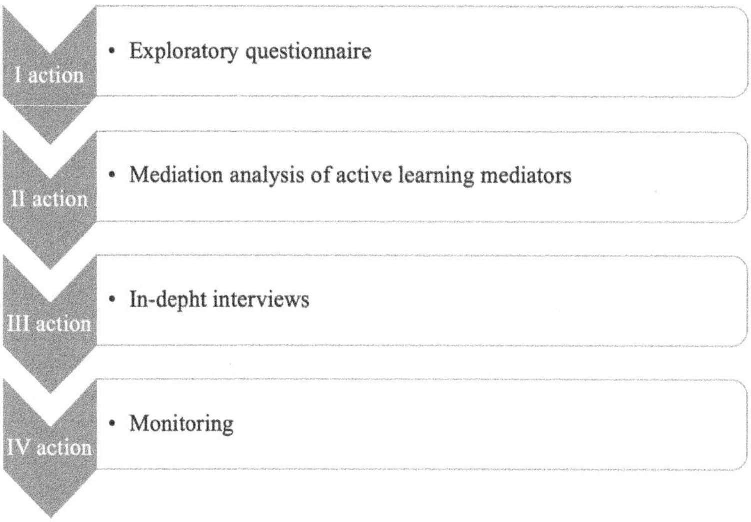

Fig. 2. Actions for collecting data

First Action:
The questionnaire revealed the perceptions of the learning experience in relation to the size of the virtual space and the mediators used. The questionnaire is made up of closed-ended questions and open-ended questions. The students were asked to express an assessment on their degree of technological competence, a useful datum to understand the perception of learning in an emergency situation such as Distance Learning (DL).

Second Action:
The second action had as object the practical analysis of the mediatization of *active learning* mediators used most of the time in face-to-face teaching.

The students were asked whether, during the courses of General Didactics and Teaching Theory and Analysis of Educational Practices followed at a distance, they had the perception that additional in-depth materials useful for learning were made available.

Third Action:

In the third section, in-depth interviews were conducted with groups of students on the perception of virtual space in relation to the dimensions of motivation, organization, self-efficacy.

The students involved were 100. The written interviews were carried out in 4 groups of 25 students. The average length of each interview was 35 min.

The students were asked to indicate at least three advantages and three disadvantages of distance learning.

Fourth Section:

The fourth section was dedicated to the quantitative monitoring of formal and informal student interventions through a participation tracking system.

4 Results

The first data analysis stated that almost all of the interviewees do not reside in Bari, that the majority are commuter students. In addition, commuters reaching the university by train or bus declare themselves very frightened at the idea of having to resume their vehicles with the new academic year – Table 1.

Table 1. General data of interviewed students

General information	
Genre	F 96,9% M 2,9% Rather not answer 0,7%
Age	18–20 years 42,8% 21–23 years 32,1% 24–25 years 4,5% >25 years 21,9%
Student with SEN	Yes 0,2% No 99,5%
Employment condition	Inactive (never worked) 44,7% Unemployed 22,5% Part-time employed 16,7% Other 13,8%
Off-site student with accommodation in Bari	Yes 10,3%
Commuter student	Yes 77,3%
In-site student	23%
How to travel to the University before the Covid-19 emergency	Train 62,2% Bus 22,5% Bicycle, car, scooter, walking 17%
Technological competences	Very good 22,7% Good 75,1% Insufficient 1,9%

This data is essential to reflect on how university teaching must be rethought. About 70% of respondents want the University to redesign a mixed mode of teaching delivery. The data therefore brought out some interesting evidence regarding the integrative and improvement potential of university teaching in blended mode.

The exploratory questionnaire analysis of the I action shows that 86.10% of respondents replied that they know how to master technologies very well and among all the students, two declare that they have insufficient technological skills (0.5%).

Almost all of the students (91.4%) declared that they followed in synchronous mode, respecting the lesson times.

The practical analysis of the mediatization of the II action highlights that 81.6% agree and recovered very often to slides, followed by articles, research reports, chapters of books and videos.

With respect to the involvement of students, the interviewees declared that 74% intervened more than in face-to-face teaching. 12.4% of students declare to intervene in equal measure both in presence and at a distance. The students were also asked whether, with respect to face-to-face teaching, if the lessons were attended more during this semester, which reasons can be attributed to the choice: 47.6% replied that they could manage time better without moving from and for the university, 24% for the greater ease in accessing virtual than physical classrooms.

Students were asked to evaluate the degree of importance of some actions carried out during the distance learning: in order to have clear the subject of the lesson (85%), to outline a topic referring to current images and examples (73%), create links between different topics (71%), receive outlines and articles (63%).

With respect to face-to-face teaching, students felt helped to think critically (97.2%), involved in lessons (95.6%), valued in learning (94.2%) and satisfied (91.4%).

The textual corpus – as transcriptions of the in-depth interviews of the III action - was then analyzed using the NVivo textual analysis software [42–44] and through the Qualitative Data Analysis (QDA) procedure, which starting from the analysis of phenomenal reality led to the emergence of a local theory (Grounded Theory) [45–51].

Four nodes were drawn from the interviews: flexibility of time, flexibility of space, organization, perspectives.

As regards the first node, flexibility of time, 88.3% of the students interviewed stated that with distance lessons they considered the saving of time used to move to and from the University very useful, 74.6% of the students declared that they had attended 100% of the lessons during the last semester and that compared to traditional teaching only 3.1% of the students declared that they had not attended. In addition, 51.2% of the interviewees stated that in the case of face-to-face teaching they could not have attended more than 50% of the lessons.

For what concern the flexibility of the space, the students were asked how they perceived the virtual classroom. 54.8% said they perceived it as an open space but with borders, while 3.8% perceived it as closed with no air.

Furthermore, from the interviews with the students, it emerges that it was easier to intervene through the chat (87%) compared to the intervention in presence, speaking during the lesson with the use of the microphone was easier than the intervention in the classroom (92%), expressing doubts through the chat was less embarrassing (89%), exposing doubts during the lesson with the use of the microphone was less embarrassing (67%), contact with teachers via email was more frequent (49%), contact with the teacher via chat was more frequent (78%).

Finally, 77.5% of students believe that both attending and non-attending students could benefit from distance learning.

From the organization node it emerges that the organization of the course was structured in an optimal way for 69.6% of the students, that the modality with which the course was structured (reception, lesson, questions) was for 80.2% of students very interesting. Specifically, the interviewees greatly appreciated the space dedicated to reception (70.6%), the space reserved for questions (76.1%), the laboratories (77.5%), evaluating the relationship established with the teacher as excellent (89%). Within the organization category, we found another node: organizational flexibility. Students were asked to evaluate teacher availability; 86.4% of the students considered it excellent and 71.8% at the end of the course, compared to the discipline, feel prepared for and ready to take the exam. 4.8% said they did not feel ready to take the exam at all, while at the end of the course 91.4% felt prepared for their future profession, unlike 1.7% who said they did not feel at all prepared. The students stated that the course (98.3%) and the labs (97.8%) left them a lot and believe that learning is definable for 75.6% as deep learning, for the 15.8% as profound learning (intense learning) and for 10% shallow learning (superficial learning).

From the perspective node, students point out that the Distance Learning DL has a lot of potential and few limits (88.3%) and 70.3% that the university should consider the use of DL even after the state of emergency Covid-19 in mode mixed.

Table 2. Synthetic codes of DL advantages and disadvantages

Advantages of DL	Disadvantages of DL
– Being able to follow the lessons from home allows you to have a comfortable and accessible location – The attendance of lessons from home leads to being less tired and the time recovered for travel and accommodation, even well in advance in the classrooms in order to find a seat, is used to study better and more – Distance learning allows new mothers, new fathers and working students to be able to connect and to be able to follow the lessons – Distance learning allows you to be more concentrated during the lessons as there is no confusion and allows you to read the slides better – Being able to follow the lessons from home allows a considerable saving of time and money	– Connection problems for the suburbs – Less frequent ways of relating to colleagues – Cooler way of relating with colleagues – Lack of socialization which occurs frequently in university classrooms – Spend many hours at the PC

The following table illustrates the advantages and disadvantages of synthetic coding (Tables 2, 3 and 4) (Fig. 3):

Table 3. Structuring of courses

General teaching			
	Hours	CFU	Hours individual study
Lesson	60	8	140
Laboratory	20	2	30
Teaching theory and analysis of educational practices			
	Hours	CFU	Hours individual study
Lesson	50	8	150
Laboratory	20	1	5

Table 4. Lesson organization

Lesson organization	
Orientation mediators: • Newspaper articles • Scientific articles • Hearing aids • Literary pieces • Visual aids	15%
Lesson: • Stimulus • Exhibition • Systematics	50%
Active learning mediators: • Occasional conversations • Purposeful conversations • Systematic conversations • Testimonials • Interviews • Exercises (role-playing activities) • Design and simulation games • Consolidation exercises • Individual work planned with structured material	30%
Closing mediators: • Systematic conversation • Control exercises • Debriefing	5%

Below are two word clouds, images made up of words, whose size varies according to the frequency with which they occur, containing precisely the most frequent words

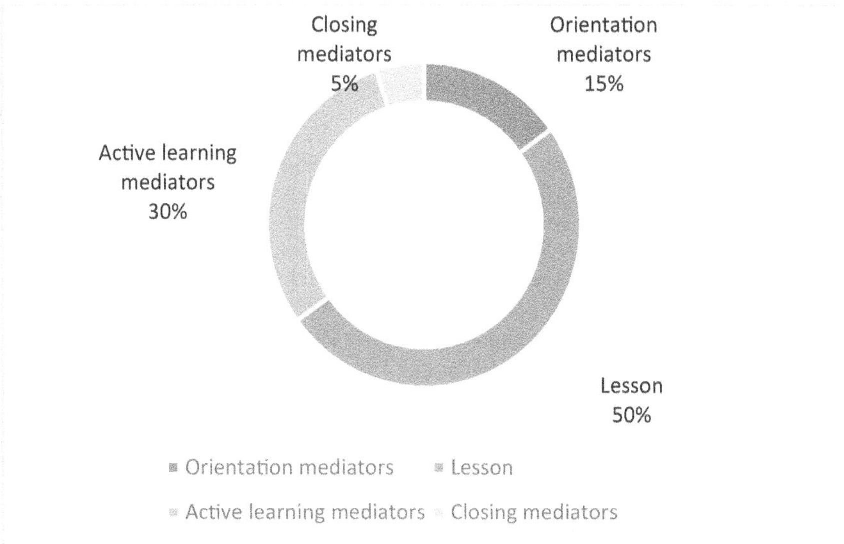

Fig. 3. Mediation figures in the lessons

in the questions in which the advantages and disadvantages of Distance Learning were investigated (Fig. 4):

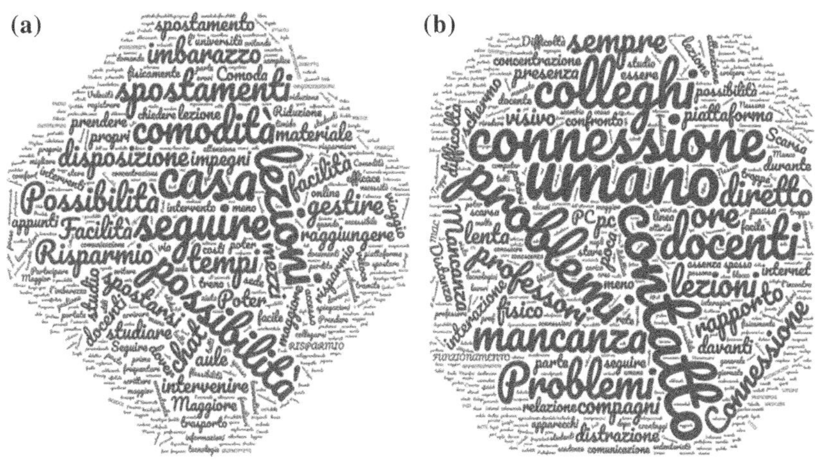

Fig. 4. a. Word cloud advantages of DL. b. Word cloud disadvantages of DL

From the quantitative monitoring of the formal and informal interventions of the students carried out with the participation tracking system, in the fourth action it emerges specifically (Table 5):

Table 5. Formal and informal participation

Formal participation	96,53%
Informal participation	78,75%
Formal participation – Synchronous lessons – Synchronous exercises – Asynchronous exercises – Synchronous laboratories – Asynchronous laboratories – Institutional mails	96,53% 98,6% 98% 97% 100% 97% 88,6%
Informal participation – Chat lesson – Chat Teams teacher – Chat Fb – FB Group Interactions	78,75% 72% 67% 84% 92%

5 Discussion and Conclusion

The survey allowed us to redesign the "teaching charter" [12] as a "mediated action with a high potential for hybridization", bringing to light the criticalities/potentialities of the pedagogical Third [52] as a space for experimentation of flexibility in teaching. One of the most relevant theoretical problems of contemporary teaching is, in fact, that of the search for tools and devices through which to induce effective, meaningful and stable learning and, in the investigation, the context of "entirely remote" has made it possible to obtain very interesting inferences for the study of mediation. Furthermore, the survey explored the impacts, in terms of student satisfaction, of the organizational restructuring of university teaching with outcomes which, we are convinced, should be taken into account in the post-Covid future in higher education systems. Italian public, traditionally reluctant to adopt e-learning formulas.

In accordance with the literature of the sector [12], mediation at the time of Covid 19 involved a strong accentuation of the dislocation of points of view with respect to interaction in the presence: from the couple, teacher and student, to actions, to mediators, cultural materials (procedural, technical, symbolic) with which the students interacted most. The field of actions has proved, once again, as a highly privileged observatory for exploring teaching.

The high level of appreciation received by the restructuring of the teaching space deserves to be emphasized: the choice of tripartite flexibility between hospitality, exhibition, activity learning and debriefing was particularly appreciated (80.2%). As well as the e-laboratories were appreciated (77.5%) which, unlike what was initially feared, it was possible to organize totally remotely by leveraging the connected 'rooms' of the platform that the groups of students could access and on the choice symbolic mediators (autobiographical and collective writings; flipped learning; tutorial approach and drill & practice) with targeted thematic focuses (Lab. 1 The knowledge of the relationship Lab. 2 Writing is ... Living Lab. 3 Me and the children at the nursery ... The practices of the relationship Lab. 4 The toolbox of the 0-3 educational relationship). The effectiveness of this choice is probably due to the fact that the students related to each other not directly but through an authentic arsenal of tools and procedures incorporated in it. The relevance of the interaction with 'cultural objects' has, therefore, overcome (and compensated for) the absence of 'flesh and blood' relationships.

A second aspect, certainly more obvious but no less important that the survey has highlighted concerns the teaching time of use of the offer. The temporal flexibility, appreciated by 88.3% of the students interviewed, allowed economic savings which, for the target of the University of Bari Aldo Moro characterized by a student population with a medium-low economic profile, constituted an element important of optimization. A second evidence supporting the optimization comes from the fact that the totally remote provision has practically reached the total number of subscribers: 51.2% of the interviewees stated that, with face-to-face teaching, they could not have attended more than 50% of the lessons.

A third and last important element for teaching purposes concerned the participatory dimension. The distance formula has allowed us to build a setting that has more 'uninhibited' the students from asking questions. This is a second element that contradicts the exact opposite prejudice of a limitation of student participation: probably in the teacher's perception there is a limit of representation of the 'ways' through which students believe they can participate in the lesson. Moreover, if 71.8% of students are self-perceived ready to take the exam immediately at the end of the course, this constitutes further evidence of the effectiveness of distance mediation, as well as the request to adopt mixed teaching also in the future (70.3%) after the state of emergency.

The exploratory study demonstrated the urgency of a reconfiguration of teaching in higher education systems. The positive aspects of collaborative approaches and the expansion of the range of tools available to students were confirmed.

But the most important element of reflection that the survey returns to us concerns the role of the teacher and we take this element as the fulcrum of a future, prospective reflection of this study. The reconfiguration in terms of centering on mediation 'tarnishes' the teaching pole in the scheme of the pedagogical Third where it appears urgent to find a theoretically legitimate and meaningful place for it. The less the teacher collaborates, the more the technologist simplifies access, the more the 'direction' of mediation becomes less and less perceptible. Research attention will be focused on the role of the teacher in the management of hybridization.

References

1. Thorin, A., Rudolph, D., Vogl, R.: Digitalization of higher education from a student's point of view. In: EUNIS (2017)
2. Tømte, C.E., Fossland, T., Aamodt, P.O., Degn, L.: Digitalisation in higher education: mapping institutional approaches for teaching and learning. Qual. High. Educ. **25**(1), 98–114 (2019)
3. Limone, P.: Ambienti di apprendimento e progettazione didattica. Proposte per un sistema educativo transmediale. Carocci, Roma (2013)
4. Rivoltella, P.C.: Media Education. La Morcelliana, Brescia (2017)

5. Gaebel, M., Kupriyanova, V., Morais, R., Colucci, E.: E-Learning in European Higher Education Institutions. European University Association (EUA), Brussels (2014)
6. Paleari, S., Corradini, F., Perali, A., Porta, F., Breno, E.: MOOCs - Massive Open On-line Courses. Prospettive e Opportunità per l'Università italiana. Fondazione CRUI (2015)
7. Ferri, P.: Università online, l'Italia tra gravi ritardi ed esamifici virtuali. In: Agenda Digitale (2017). testo disponibile sul sito: www.agendadigitale.eu/cultura-digitale
8. Williamson, B., Eynon, R., Potter, J.: Pandemic politics, pedagogies and practices: digital technologies and distance education during the coronavirus emergency. Learn. Media Technol. **45**(2), 107–114 (2020)
9. Trinchero, R.: Insegnare e valutare nella formazione a "distanza forzata". In: Scuola7 (2020). http://www.scuola7.it/2020/181/?page=1
10. Hodges, C., Moore, S., Lockee, B., Trust, T., Bond, A.: The difference between emergency remote teaching and online learning. (2020). https://er.educause.edu/articles/2020/3/the-difference-between-emergency-remote-teaching-and-online-learning
11. Laurillard, D.: Rethinking teaching for the knowledge society. EDUCAUSE Rev. **37**(1), 16–24 (2020)
12. Damiano, E.: La mediazione didattica. FrancoAngeli, Milano (2013)
13. Deschamps, J.: La Mèdiation. Un concept pour les sciences de l'information et de la communication. ISTE Editions, London (2018)
14. Felisatti, E.: PRODID: modelli, strategie e dispositivi operativi per un intervento sulla qualificazione della docenza universitaria nel contesto italiano. In: Felisatti, E., Serbati, A. (a cura di) Preparare alla professionalità docente e innovare la didattica universitaria, FrancoAngeli, Milano (2017)
15. Perla, L.: L'innovazione curricolare nella formazione del docente universitario: l'esperienza nel TLL. In: Corbo, F., Michelini, M., Uricchio, A.F. (a cura di) Innovazione didattica universitaria e strategie degli Atenei italiani. 100 contributi di 27 Università a confronto. Università degli Studi di Bari Aldo Moro (2019)
16. Perla, L., Vinci, V.: TLL (Teaching Learning Laboratory) e formazione dialettica dei docenti universitari alla didattica: primi passi verso la certificazione della competenza pedagogica in Uniba. Lifelong Lifewide Learn. **15**(32), 68–88 (2018)
17. Scarinci, A., Dipace, A.: Formazione pedagogica per l'insegnamento: il nuovo profilo professionale del docente universitario. In: Dipace, A., Tamborra, V., (a cura di) Insegnare in università. Metodi e strumenti per una didattica efficace. Franco Angeli, Milano (2019)
18. Rinaldi, C.: In dialogo con Reggio Emilia: ascoltare, ricercare e apprendere: discorsi e interventi 1984–2007. Reggio Children (2009)
19. Malaguzzi, L.: I cento linguaggi dei bambini. L'approccio di Reggio Emilia all'educazione dell'infanzia. Edizioni Junior, Bergamo (2010)
20. Ceruti, M., Lazzarini, A.: Il "terzo spazio". Per una pedagogia della complessità, "Pedagogia oggi", 1/2016, semestrale SIPED, pp. 202–213 (2016)
21. Foucault, M.: La volontà di sapere, tr. it. Feltrinelli, Milano (1996)
22. Varisco, B.M.: Valutare gli apprendimenti e le competenze. Carocci Editore, Roma (2004)
23. Perla, L.: La mediazione 'plurale' nel lavoro educativo. In: Perla, L., Riva, M.G.: L'agire educativo. Manuale per educatori socio-assistenziali. La Scuola, Brescia (2016)
24. Laneve, C.: Analisi di pratica educativa. Metodologie e risultanze della ricerca. La Scuola, Brescia (2005)
25. Perla, L.: L'intervista per dire della pratica. In: Laneve, C. (ed.) Analisi della pratica educativa. La Scuola, Brescia (2005)
26. Perla, L.: Didattica dell'implicito. Ciò che l'insegnante non sa. La Scuola, Brescia (2010)
27. Agrati, L.: Alla conquista del sapere pratico. Il laboratorio nella formazione degli insegnanti. Carocci, Roma (2008)

28. Bhabha, H.: I luoghi della cultura. Meltemi, Roma (2001)
29. Potter, J., McDougall, J.: Digital Media, Culture and Education: Theorizing Third Space Literacies. Palgrave MacMillan, London (2017)
30. Rivoltella, P.C.: New Literacies, editoriale Essere a Scuola n. 6/2020 (2020)
31. Castells, M.: La città delle reti. Marsilio, Venezia (2004)
32. Bocchi, G., Ceruti, M.: La sfida della complessità. Bruno Mondadori, Milano (2007)
33. Weller, M.: The Digital Scholar How Technology is TRANSFORMING scholarly Practice. Bloomsbury Academic, Basingstoke (2011)
34. Cope, B., Kalantzis, M.: New Learning: Elements of a Science of Education. Cambridge University Press, Cambridge (2008)
35. Altet, M.: L'évolucion des recherchers sur le processus enseignement-apprendissage et leur rôle en formation d'enseignants. Actes Colloque AIPELF, Lisbonne (1998)
36. Perla, L.: Scrittura e tirocinio universitario. Una ricerca sulla documentazione. FrancoAngeli, Milano (2012)
37. Perla, L., Agrati, L.S., Vinci, V.: The 'Sophisticated' knowledge of *e-Teacher*. Re-shape Digital Resources for Online Courses. In: Burgos, D., et al. (eds.) HELMeTO 2019. CCIS, vol. 1091, pp. 3–17. Springer, Cham (2019). https://doi.org/10.1007/978-3-030-31284-8_1
38. Leech, N., Onwuegbuzie, A.J.: A typology of mixed methods research designs. Qual. Quant. **43**(2), 265–275 (2009). https://doi.org/10.1007/s11135-007-9105-3
39. Tashakorri, A., Teddlie, C.: Handbook of Mixed Methods in Social & Behavioral Research. Sage, Thousand Oakes (2003)
40. Cameron, R.: Mixed methods research: a world of metaphors (chap. 4). In: Midgley, W., Trimmer, K., Davies, A. (eds.) Metaphors for, in and of Education Research, pp. 51–65. Newcastle upon Tyne, Cambridge (2013)
41. Cameron, R.: The emerging use of mixed methods in educational research (chap. 8). In: Baguley, M., Findlay, Y.S., Karby, M.C. (eds.) Meanings and Motivation in Education Research. Routledge, New York (2015)
42. Lewins, A., Silver, C.: Using Software in Qualitative Research: A Step by Step Guide. Sage, London (2007)
43. Pacifico, M., Coppola, L.: NVivo: una risorsa metodologica. Procedure per l'analisi dei dati qualitativi. FrancoAngeli, Milano (2010)
44. BazeKey, P., Jackson, K.: Qualitative Data Analysis with NVivo. Sage, London (2013)
45. Strauss, A., Corbin, J.: Basics of Qualitative Research: Grounded Theory Procedures and Techniques. Sage, Newbury Park (1990)
46. Charmaz, K.: Grounded theory in the 21st century. In: Denzin, N.K., Lincoln, Y.S. (eds.) Handbook of Qualitative Research, Terza edn. Sage, Thousand Oaks (2005)
47. Creswell, J.W., Plano Clark, V.L., Guttman, M., Hanson, W.: Advanced mixed methods research designs. In: Tashakkori, A., Teddlie, C., Teddlie, C.B. (eds.) Handbook of Mixed Methods in Social & Behavioral Research. Sage, Thousand Oaks (2005)
48. Creswell, J.W.: Qualitative Inquiry & Research Design. Choosing Among Five Approaches, 2nd edn. Sage, London (2007)
49. Mortari, L.: Cultura Della ricerca e pedagogia. Carocci, Roma (2007)
50. Tarozzi, M.: Che cos'è la grounded Theory. Carocci, Roma (2008)
51. Mortari, L.: Dire la pratica. Bruno Mondadori, Milano (2010)
52. Houssaye, J.: Le triangle pédagogique. Théorie et pratiques de l'éducation scolaire. Peter Lang, Verlag, Bern (2000)

Online Learning Technologies in Practice

Experimentation of Flipped Learning in a University Course on Object-Oriented Programming Paradigm

Pasquale Ardimento(✉) and Michele Scalera

Computer Science Department, University of Bari Aldo Moro, Bari, Italy
{pasquale.ardimento,michele.scalera}@uniba.it

Abstract. Several academic institutes provide students, as the first programming course, with an understanding of Object-Oriented Programming (OOP) paradigm. This requires the teacher to face several obstacles due to the necessity to explain various and deep concepts such as type, data abstraction, encapsulation and different forms of polymorphism such as overloading, coercion, sub-typing, and parameterization. This paper proposes and evaluates a teaching strategy based on a flipped classroom approach for one selected topic in a second-year programming university course, *Programming II*, held at the University of Bari and focused on the OOP paradigm. This approach lets the students learn and train on their own before coming to class. Here, they will apply the knowledge during face-to-face lessons to elaborate, reflect and compare on what has been learned. We provided a preliminary evaluation of the approach through a quasi-experiment aiming at comparing two groups of students: one instructed by a flipped classroom approach and the other one by the traditional approach. Results show that the flipped group understands better concepts and produces better source code than the traditional group.

Keywords: Flipped learning · Education · Object-Oriented programming

1 Introduction

Courses based on Object-Oriented programming paradigm are increasingly the first programming experience for many academic students. However, for such courses, the activity of teaching and knowledge transfer is characterized by facing several obstacles [1]. This involves the adoption of software development principles, practices, and tools, the application of learning analytics approaches used, for example, to improve coding abilities [2], to support students in programming task [3], to understand developer's behavior [4], but also a continuous research of new teaching strategies to improve long-term student retention. In this work, we aim to understand if a teaching strategy as the flipped classroom could improve students' performances on understanding and applying Object-Oriented concepts.

The concept of flipped classroom uses various channels of communication such as social media and the web [5] offering a teaching opportunity, which could, in turn, be a

L. S. Agrati et al. (Eds.): HELMeTO 2020, CCIS 1344, pp. 243–255, 2021.
https://doi.org/10.1007/978-3-030-67435-9_19

good compromise able to propose solutions that can involve students of all levels in a study that otherwise risks becoming anachronistic and no longer accepted by learners. In this context, it is necessary to design often iterative learning and teaching processes with continuous review [6]. The flipped classroom becomes an opportunity to actively involve students who often feel abandoned and no longer followed by academic institutions perched on the old concept of pre-schooling as the only training approach. The flipped classroom, instead, with its "preparatory phase" in which students are actively engaged in building their knowledge and skills through the use of authoritative online teaching materials validated by the teacher, becomes a framework that stimulates all students.

The face-to-face lesson, contemplated also by the flipped learning methodology but postponed to the preparatory phase, thus loses its vertical character to become an interactive moment, in the logic of the constructivist model of training [7, 8], where the teacher, after providing elementary information, such as the topic to be dealt with, will moderate the discussion basing on the material collected by the students, to generate new knowledge together with them. This phase thus becomes a discussion group, with the participation of the teacher himself, whose function, of course, is not only to answer questions on the subject, but also to support the students in their study and to unravel the doubts that may arise when reading classic textbooks, which certainly do not lose their formative value. Classic textbooks can and must be supplemented by interactive and online material chosen by the teacher to validate their authoritativeness.

The purpose of this study was to explore the flipped classroom approach as a digital pedagogy to enhance students' learning on a specific topic taught in a focused Object-Oriented course held at the University of Bari Aldo Moro. The main research questions were:

RQ1: Do the performances of the students' in understanding fundamental concepts in the context of a Programming II course increase when acquired by the flipped approach compared to the traditional approach?

RQ2: Do the performances of the students' in a programming task in the context of a Programming II course increase when acquired by the flipped approach compared to the traditional approach?

The remainder of the paper is organized as follows. In the next section, the background of the flipped classroom is described, while Sect. 3 briefly discusses the main related work. Section 4 deals with the empirical study carried out. Results and discussion are presented in Sect. 5. Finally, Sect. 6 draws the conclusions and suggests future work.

2 Background

The flipped classroom approach is a technology-enhanced pedagogy characterized by two basic teaching strategies: problem-solving and peer-assisted learning [9, 10]. The fundamental idea of the flipped classroom is that the lesson becomes homework while the time in class is used for collaborative activities, experiences, debates and workshops [11]. In this context, the teacher does not take a leadership role, but rather becomes a sort of facilitator or the director of the didactic action. During the time at home, videos and other digital resources, such as lecture slides, are widely used as contents to study, while in the classroom students experiment, collaborate and carry out laboratory activities.

To all intents and purposes "flipping" is a didactic methodology to be used in a fluid and flexible way, regardless of the discipline or type of subject. It is important that the time "gained" in class, through the use of "flipping" is optimally used. Additionally, the resources used by the student during their time at home must be effective, as well as calibrated to the level of knowledge achieved by the young person up to that point. An integrated content library with online videos screened for quality and accessibility is the best starting point to achieve a successful result. Therefore, it is also "necessary to design facilities that adapt to individual differences in terms of knowledge, training priorities and environmental factors" [12].

Nevertheless, one of the main divisions in the scientific community occurs between those advocates for structured and standardized learning environments and others that stress the importance of exploration, construction, and discovery [8].

3 Related Work

Recently, the flipped classroom approach has been applied in different subject disciplines, such as medical education [13], language education [14], and mathematics education [15]. A flipped classroom is a form of blended learning focused on student engagement and active learning "where the lecture is moved outside the classroom with the help of technology and learning activities are moved inside the classroom" [16]. It reshapes traditional face-to-face lectures into sessions consisting of active learning and problem-solving. The flipped classroom model originated in the K-12 sector but, recently, there has been a growth in the interest of the flipped classroom both in secondary education, where several studies [15, 17, 18] and in higher education institutions.

Several research studies on the flipped classroom have focused on students' academic performance and perceptions. For example, in [19] authors stated that 623 students who experienced the flipped classroom, in an environment properly set, had significant learning gains in terms of higher scores on performance in comparison to the traditional approach. They also reported that both students and teachers perceived the experience as motivational and successful. A similar comparative study was conducted by authors in [20] in a Calculus III course evaluating students' performance and students' perceptions. Results show similar performance on procedural problems and a little gain for the flipped students in the case of conceptual exam problems. Concerning students' perception, the results are mixed because flipped students reported a positive increment of communication during class while traditional students perceived more effective use of class time. A review of 2018 on flipped classroom [21] reports that the majority of research studies suggest that flipped classroom experiences do have a positive impact on the student experience and learning outcomes but that there also studies where the level of student satisfaction has decreased, or its use did not produce the expected changes in academic achievement. Moreover, even if the results obtained from these experiments are positive, they may have been influenced by the natural inclination of learners to be attracted to all that is innovative. In conclusion, while the results from this study are encouraging, this is not sufficient evidence to warrant generalization far beyond that situation. Thus, both experimental replications and further new experiments are carried out to confirm or deny the effectiveness of the flipped methodology.

4 Experiment

We carried out an empirical investigation as a quasi-experiment because it is impossible to rely on random assignments [22]. In this section, the empirical settings (goal, context, variables, research hypothesis) and the empirical design are described.

4.1 Goal

The goal of the study aims at evaluating if the Flipped approach allows students to improve their performance compared to the traditional approach. We evaluated students' performances by scoring both understanding concepts and performing programming activities. The performance focus regards how Flipped and Traditional strategies affect the capability of students to correctly understand the basic concepts and to correctly write the code to handle exceptions in Java programs.

The goals of the empirical research study are reported as follows:

- Analyze the use of two different instructional strategies to evaluate the performance of the students in understanding fundamental concepts in the context of a Programming II course.
- Analyze the use of two different instructional strategies to evaluate the performance of the students who execute a programming task in the context of a Programming II course.

4.2 Context

To explore the use of the flipped class teaching we selected the "Java Exception Handling" (JEH) topic. This topic, according to previous experience, is considered as a medium difficulty topic in the Programming II course. This course is delivered in the first semester of the second academic year of the Bachelor's degree course in Computer Science and Technology for the Production of Software at the University of Bari Aldo Moro in the academic year 2018/2019. Since we are interested in studying the effect on understanding and programming accuracy after training subjects on the proposed topic, we characterize students' profiles using both a profiling questionnaire and an "Initial Skill Assessment Test". The student profiling questionnaire served, firstly, to select only students that did not pass the Software Engineering course and, secondly, to know the average academic score of each student. The Software Engineering course is the only one, in the first two years, where knowledge of Java is required.

The "Initial Skill Assessment Test", instead, served to know which students had previous knowledge and experience on Java exceptions. These students did not partake in the study.

Therefore, using these criteria, we only selected students having a similar background on the JEH topic, and we divided them into two groups:

- FlippedGroup: students to which training was provided according to the flipped classroom;
- TraditionalGroup: students to which training was provided according to the traditional approach.

Both groups consisted of 20 students where 10 of them had academic average score (AVS) 25/30 or lower and 10 had an AVS equal to or higher than 25/30.

To full integration with e-learning web technologies each resource requires to be included in a Learning Management System (LMS). The LMS adopted is built on the Moodle learning platform supporting various strategies approaches such as blended learning, distance education, flipped classroom.

4.3 Hypothesis Formulation

The research hypotheses to be tested are:

- H01: There is no statistically significant difference in the efficacy of understanding concepts of JEH between students that have learned it using either Flipped or Traditional.
- H02: There is no statistically significant difference in the efficacy of a programming task between students that have learned JEH using either Flipped or Traditional.

It is important to highlight that, on one hand, Flipped intentionally uses time in the classroom to explore topics in greater depth and create meaningful learning opportunities while students are initially introduced to new topics outside of the classroom, whereas Traditional typically has the teacher as the primary disseminator of information during the class period. On the other hand, the Flipped approach requires students to be motivated to learn the content, the material has to be engaging and interesting. Videos should encourage students to not only watch the words but also to listen to them. For these reasons, we do not have any idea if Flipped approach improves or worsens in understanding the concept or performing the programming task when compared to the Traditional approach. Therefore, a two-sided test is required because the alternative hypotheses against which the null hypotheses (H01 and H02) are tested stipulate that the first group data distribution differs from the second group data distribution. A null hypothesis, in this case, is rejected if scores of one group are significantly larger than those of the other group. No specification is provided about the direction of this difference.

4.4 Variables Selection

There are two dependent variables: understanding accuracy and programming accuracy. To measure understanding accuracy, we asked subjects to answer a theory questionnaire of ten questions while, to measure programming accuracy, we asked subjects to insert in a little Java program the right way to throw and handle exceptions. We designed a questionnaire that satisfies the following requirements:

1. Each question was designed as a multiple-choice with four alternative answers among which one and only one is correct and all others are wrong;
2. In order to prevent that the student has no knowledge of the subject area and adopts a pure guessing strategy, we used a negative marking schema. The penalty for each wrong answer was -1;
3. No response order has been defined;
4. The average time spent per question was one minute; overall time available was ten minutes;
5. The highest score is 10, the lowest is -10.

To mitigate teacher bias, we designed the questionnaire making that test-takers are graded solely on their selections without requiring from teachers any interpretation.

Questions were defined to satisfy the following requirements:

- to match the common terminologies used in JEH;
- to describe the three exception handler components (the try, catch, finally blocks);
- to describe the technique to throw exceptions;
- to highlight critical considerations for handling exceptions in Java projects.

Concerning the programming task, we asked students to throw and catch two faults in the Object-Oriented system source code. The two exceptions were defined satisfying the following requirements:

1. the program was made up of only three classes;
2. the program requires two exceptions;
3. the exceptions are exclusively related to software requirements provided with the programming task documentation;
4. the exceptions are located in two different classes;
5. the exceptions are both "custom exceptions". These kinds of exceptions are used to add attributes and methods that are not part of a standard Java exception;
6. the program is carefully designed by the instructors;
7. the exceptions can be implemented using the time available;
8. one exception has to be caught in the method where it is thrown, the other one is thrown in a method and caught in the main class;

We measured the accuracy of programming using a score between 0 and 10, where zero means that the exception was not defined and ten that the exception was completely and correctly implemented. To evaluate solutions' accuracy and correctness, we involved three senior lecturers to mitigate the solution evaluation bias of using a single senior lecturer. Each lecturer made independent evaluations. They compared the solution with the correct and complete one defined by the teachers looking at both the answers given by students and the process they followed and the reasoning underlying the choices. The final scores were computed as the average of the scores given by the three lectures. The independent variable, that is the main factor of the experiment, is the learning strategy received before the execution of programming tasks. The two alternative treatments are as follows:

(1) Flipped, for subjects learned JEH by the flipped approach;

(2) Traditional, for subjects learned JEH by the traditional approach.

4.5 Experimental Design

To keep control and treatment groups separate, the proposed quasi-experiment is a between-subjects design. The experiment consisted of only one experimental session consisting of one questionnaire and one Java software system.

Subjects Assignment. The allotment of participants to the groups was made by satisfying the criterion that each group was composed by the same number of LAS and HAS students.

Experimental Session. The experiment is structured as a single session. In this session, the students of FlippedGroup used the Flipped approach while those of TraditionalGroup use the traditional approach. The same Java software system (JavaSystem) and questionnaire (Questionnaire) are assigned during the session ensuring that each group performs the same task having the same time (the mapping among groups, tasks, and session is reported in Fig. 1).

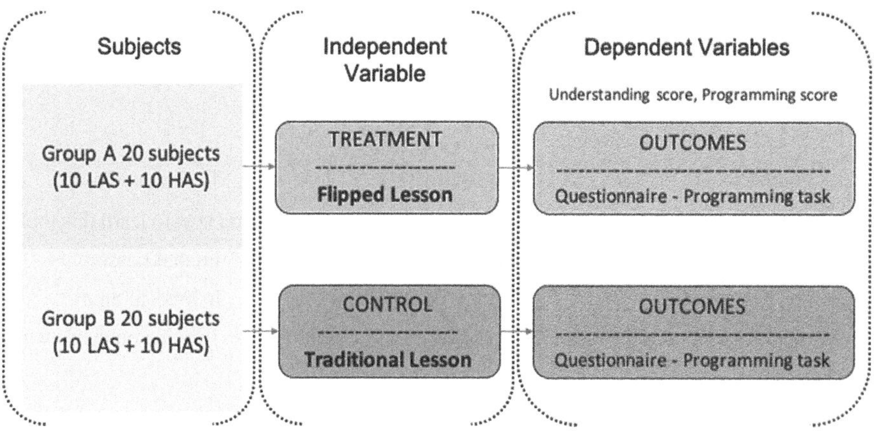

Fig. 1. The overall structure of the empirical design.

4.6 Experimental Procedure and Material

The teaching materials provided to students were:

- introduction to the concept (20 min): these lecture slides provide the basic definitions of the JEH concepts: errors and exceptions; catching and handling exception; checked and unchecked exceptions;

- explanation of JEH (60 min): these lecture slides provide details and examples for each basic concept emphasizing the activities of throwing and catching exceptions in Java;
- examples and practices on JEH (20 min): this video conveys the key evaluations to decide when and how to adopt JEH in a Java program.

To make the video attractive, we applied the following best practices: a brief video and targeted on learning goals; audio and visual elements used in combination to convey parts of an explanation; relevant ideas or concepts appropriately highlighted; a conversational, enthusiastic style to enhance engagement. Teachers advised students to repeat viewing the lecture slides and video as many times as they need to understand the concepts and practices of the JEH topic. To establish if the trial successfully carried out, we previously defined the expected learning outcomes, listed below:

- to be able to understand the concepts on JEH by answering to a theory questionnaire of ten questions;
- to be able to insert in a little Java program, made up of only three classes, the right way to throw and handle exceptions.

The two lessons (flipped and traditional) were carried out in parallel according to the scheme of Table 1 where the second and third columns list the tasks to do by, respectively, FlippedGroup and TraditionalGroup.

Table 1. Flipped class schedule

Week number	FlippedGroup	TraditionalGroup
1st lesson of the semester	A brief explanation to students on how to learn this topic	
Week n.6 1st lesson	Learn the topic on their own	Frontal Lesson
Week n.6 2nd lesson	Training on their own	Individual Study
Week n.6 3rd lesson of the week	Flipped Lesson (an activity, conducted by the teacher, of elaboration, reflection and comparison on what has been learned)	Training on their own
Week n.7 1st Lesson of the week	Questionnaire session (10 min) - Development task (20 min)	

In the first lesson of the seventh week of lessons, the students were first assigned the theory questionnaire and, then, a programming task.

The worksheets and programs were collected by the tutors for marking. The following section briefly presents the preliminary results and a discussion of them.

4.7 Analysis Method

We applied the Mann-Whitney U two-tailed test since the following hold:

- both dependent variables (understanding accuracy and programming accuracy) are measured at continuous level;
- the independent variable (the learning strategy) consists of two independent groups (FlippedGroup and TraditionalGroup);
- independence of observations, there are different participants in the two groups and each participant belongs to only one group;
- distributions of groups are not normally distributed.

We assumed a significance level of 0.05 to check the statistical significance differences of experimental results.

To evaluate the effect size of the difference we used Cliff's delta non-parametric effect size measure. Such a measure quantifies the amount of difference between two groups of observations and provides a useful complementary analysis for the corresponding hypothesis testing. Cliff's delta assumes values in the range $[-1, +1]$. Values near the lower and upper range indicate the absence of overlap between the two groups, while values near zero indicate a strong overlap between the two groups. To investigate if Flipped treatment was more or less effective to traditional training, we compared the two groups on the empirical session whose time-scheduling is in the fifth row of Table 1.

5 Results and Discussion

This section presents the empirical results and discusses the threats to the validity of the empirical study. The R environment has been used to perform the statistical analysis.

5.1 Statistical Descriptive on Understanding and Programming Performances (H01, H02)

To address the RQ1 we used the theory questionnaire which was aimed at assessing the degree of knowledge of the students. This was conducted in regard to the students' perception of having learned the concepts of the task entrusted to them. Students of the FlippedGroup gave 72% of correct answers while TraditionalGroup only 69%. Both results, obtained before the end of the course, could be considered positive and comparable to one another.

To address the RQ2, instead, we used the programming task was aimed at evaluating the accuracy of the proposed solution by the students, manually evaluated by the instructors. In the case of the FlippedGroup, 73.07% of the students performed the learning verification test with 0 errors, 19.23% made only one error while only 7.70% made multiple errors. On the other hand, the TraditionalGroup achieved worse results, where 46.15% of the students performed the learning verification test with 0 errors, 26.92% made only one error while only 30.76% made multiple errors. These results demonstrate the superior performance of the students belonging to the FlippedGroup. Moreover, in the data [23] collected it is seen that in the FlippedGroup the number of students who commit multiple errors is drastically reduced. This ultimately confirms the effectiveness of flipped learning in the classroom especially in maximizing the involvement of students.

5.2 Testing Hypothesis on Understanding and Programming Performances (H01, H02)

The row "Flipped vs. Traditional" of Table 2 shows the results of the t-test executed for the running session carried out (comparing both the understanding accuracy and programming accuracy) for groups Learning and Flipped. This table also reports, at the third and fifth columns, the effect size of the difference using Cliff's delta non-parametric effect size measure [24]. We compared the two groups to investigate if Flipped treatment was more effective than traditional training. As the table shows, the level of significance of the tests for both questionnaire and programming tasks, are over 95%. As a consequence, both the two null hypotheses can be rejected. The value of Cliff's Delta, using the standard thresholds defined for it, is medium in the case of accuracy understanding and large in the case of accuracy programming. This means that the magnitude of the difference between the two groups is higher for the programming task than the understanding task.

Table 2. Results of the *t*-Test

Comparisons	Accuracy understanding		Accuracy programming	
	p-value	Cliff's Delta	p-value	Cliff's Delta
Flipped vs. Traditional	0.04	−0.46	0.03	−0.57

5.3 Threats to Validity

Internal Validity. One possible threat was that some students could have studied the Java Exceptions attending a programming course at secondary school, signifying that the results could had been skewed. These students were filtered by using the "Initial Skill Assessment Test". Moreover, we did not inform students about the experimental hypotheses and we did not reward for participation in the experiment.

External Validity. The obtained results lack generalizability at some points. First of all, results are valid only in contexts similar to Java programming courses of computer science degrees. Even the representativeness of the materials used, all were academic exams, is not generalizable. We are also aware that different topics might have different complexity and, as a consequence, they could influence the results. It is necessary, therefore, to investigate further complexity levels beyond this medium. Finally, since the sample is not representative of all populations of students (e.g., cohorts with different educational backgrounds, different programming languages), future experimentations are necessary.

Construct Validity. The evaluation of exams was based on an evaluation process used for several years and the teaching material on the programming courses was the same for both groups. It means that the pedagogical methods used by each teacher will probably have affected the learning process effectiveness in both cases (using Flipped and not using it). To mitigate the threat that the Flipped approach could be more motivating for students, we limit the usage of Flipped only to planned session in which all the students were involved. Another threat could be related to how we measure the accuracy of programming. We relied on solutions, previously defined by authors, to objectively evaluate whether the exceptions inserted in the source code were correct.

Conclusion Validity. The conclusions are founded on an adequate statistical method fulfilling all the requirements needed to be applied. We also obtained an acceptable statistical power thanks to the number of experimental subjects that was sufficiently large.

6 Conclusion

In this paper, we presented a flipped teaching strategy for one specific Object-Oriented topic, the exceptions handling, in a second-year programming university course. The approach was evaluated comparing both the understanding and application of this concept in a programming task between two students' groups, one followed a flipped approach while the other the traditional approach. Results demonstrate that the flipped approach has the potential to improve both understanding and programming performances of students for at least a specific topic. In our future experiences, it would be interesting to investigate and analyze the flipped approach on more topics of different difficulty level and investigate the degree of satisfaction of students. These issues concern improved clarity, interest, usefulness, concreteness, simplicity, effectiveness and perception of students to have learned the concepts of the task entrusted to them, and to identify how and for what topics the knowledge can be more transferable and reusable [25].

References

1. Ardimento, P., Bernardi, M.L., Cimitile, M.: On the students' misconceptions in object-oriented language constructs. In: Burgos, D., et al. (eds.) HELMeTO 2019. CCIS, vol. 1091, pp. 97–112. Springer, Cham (2019). https://doi.org/10.1007/978-3-030-31284-8_8
2. Ardimento, P., Bernardi, M.L., Cimitile, M., Ruvo, G.D.: Learning analytics to improve coding abilities: a fuzzy-based process mining approach. In: 2019 IEEE International Conference on Fuzzy Systems (FUZZ-IEEE), New Orleans, LA, USA, pp. 1–7 (2019). https://doi.org/10.1109/fuzz-ieee.2019.8859009
3. Ardimento, P., Bernardi, M.L., Cimitile, M.: Software analytics to support students in object-oriented programming tasks: an empirical study. IEEE Access **8**, 132171–132187 (2020). https://doi.org/10.1109/ACCESS.2020.3010172

4. Ardimento, P., Bernardi, M.L., Cimitile, M., De Ruvo, G.: Mining developer's behavior from web-based IDE logs. In: 2019 IEEE 28th International Conference on Enabling Technologies: Infrastructure for Collaborative Enterprises (WETICE), Napoli, Italy, pp. 277–282 (2019). https://doi.org/10.1109/wetice.2019.00065
5. Dimauro, G., Scalera, M., Visaggio, G.: The educational cloud, problems and perspectives. Syst. Cybern. Inform. **14**(6), 40–46 (2016)
6. Scalera, M., Gentile, E., Plantamura, P., Dimauro, G.: A systematic mapping study in cloud for educational innovation. Appl. Sci. **10**(13), 4531 (2020). https://doi.org/10.3390/app10134531
7. Novak, J.D., Cañas, A.J.: Building on new constructivist ideas & CmapTools to create a new model for education. In: Concept Maps Theory, Methodology, Technology: Proceedings of the First International Conference on Concept Mapping, vol. 1, no. January, pp. 469–476 (2004)
8. Kirschner, P.A., Sweller, J., Clark, R.E.: Why minimal guidance during instruction does not work: an analysis of the failure of constructivist, discovery, problem-based, experiential, and inquiry-based teaching. Educ. Psychol. **41**(2), 75–86 (2006)
9. Abeysekera, L., Dawson, P.: Motivation and cognitive load in the flipped classroom: definition, rationale and a call for research. High. Educ. Res. Dev. **34**(1), 1–14 (2015)
10. Lo, C.K., Hew, K.F.: A comparison of flipped learning with gamification, traditional learning, and online independent study: the effects on students' mathematics achievement and cognitive engagement. Interact. Learn. Environ. **28**(4), 464–481 (2020)
11. Bergmann, J., Sams, A., Flip Your Classroom: Reach Every Student in Every Class Every Day. International Society for Technology in Education, Washington, DC (2012)
12. Ardimento, P., Boffoli, N., Convertini, V.N., Visaggio, G.: The lifelong learning in the university: learning networks and knowledge transferring. J. E-Learning Knowl. Soc. **7**(1), 21–31 (2011). https://doi.org/10.20368/1971-8829/484
13. Lin, H.C., Hwang, G.J.: Research trends of flipped classroom studies for medical courses: a review of journal publications from 2008 to 2017 based on the technology-enhanced learning model. Interact. Learn. Environ. **27**(8), 1011–1027 (2019)
14. Lin, C., Hwang, G.: A Learning analytics approach to investigating factors affecting EFL students' oral performance in a flipped classroom. J. Educ. Technol. Soc. **21**, 205–219 (2018)
15. Lo, C.K., Hew, K.F., Chen, G.: Toward a set of design principles for mathematics flipped classrooms: a synthesis of research in mathematics education. Educ. Res. Rev. **22**, 50–73 (2017)
16. Kiat, P.N., Kwong, Y.T.: The flipped classroom experience. In: 2014 IEEE 27th Conference on Software Engineering Education and Training, CSEE T 2014 - Proceedings, pp. 39–43 (2014)
17. Bhagat, K.K., Chang, C.N., Chang, C.Y.: The impact of the flipped classroom on mathematics concept learning in high school. Educ. Technol. Soc. **19**(3), 134–142 (2016)
18. Clark, K.R.: The effects of the flipped model of instruction on student engagement and performance in the secondary mathematics classroom. J. Educ. Online **12**(1), 91–115 (2015)
19. Unal, Z., Unal, A.: Comparison of student performance, student perception, and teacher satisfaction with traditional versus flipped classroom models. Int. J. Instr. **10**(4), 145–164 (2017)
20. Wasserman, N.H., Quint, C., Norris, S.A., Carr, T.: Exploring flipped classroom instruction in calculus III. Int. J. Sci. Math. Educ. **15**(3), 545–568 (2015). https://doi.org/10.1007/s10763-015-9704-8
21. Akçayır, G., Akçayır, M.: The flipped classroom: a review of its advantages and challenges. Comput. Educ. **126**, 334–345 (2018)

22. Cook, T.D., Campbell, D.T.: The causal assumptions of quasi-experimental practice - the origins of quasi-experimental practice. Synthese **68**(1), 141–180 (1986). https://doi.org/10.1007/BF00413970
23. Scalera, M., Serra, A.: Customer centric strategies for value creation: academic experimentation. J. E-Learning Knowl. Soc. **10**(2), 65–76 (2014). https://doi.org/10.20368/1971-8829/922
24. Grissom, R.J., Kim, J.J., Effect Sizes for Research: A Broad Practical Approach, 2nd edn. Lawrence Erlbaum Associates Publishers, Mahwah (2005)
25. Ardimento, P., Cimitile, M., Visaggio, G.: Distributed software development with knowledge experience packages. In: Demey, Y.T., Panetto, H. (eds.) OTM 2013. LNCS, vol. 8186, pp. 263–273. Springer, Heidelberg (2013). https://doi.org/10.1007/978-3-642-41033-8_35

Leveraging Cloud Infrastructures for Teaching Advanced Computer Engineering Classes

Experiences at the University of Pisa

Antonio Cisternino[1], Pietro Ducange[2](✉), Nicola Tonellotto[2], and Carlo Vallati[2]

[1] Department of Computer Science, University of Pisa, Pisa, Italy
a.cisternino@unipi.it
[2] Department of Information Engineering, University of Pisa, Pisa, Italy
{p.ducange,n.tonellotto,c.vallati}@unipi.it

Abstract. In the framework of Problem-Based Learning (PBL), hands-on activities play a crucial role for allowing students to acquire skills and competences. PBL is particularly suitable for teaching advanced courses including topics such as artificial intelligence, cloud computing and big data. In order to carry out practical activities, students may need specific computing and storage infrastructures, that may be not physically available in the laboratories. Thus, virtualization tools and cloud computing are often adopted for building Virtual Lab for teaching purposes.

In this work, we present our recent experiences, at the University of Pisa, in delivering two advanced courses, namely *Cloud Computing* and *Large-Scale and Multi-Structured Databases*. We discuss how we built and exploited a Virtual Lab on top of the private Cloud infrastructure of the University of Pisa as a support for the teaching-learning workflow. Moreover, we present the quantitative feedback received by the students about their experience with the Virtual Lab, showing that the learning objectives that we fixed for our courses have been fully achieved.

Keywords: Innovative Degree Programs · Cloud Computing · Distributed Databases · Virtual Lab · Problem-Based Learning

1 Introduction

Nowadays, universities offer Innovative Degree Programs, especially in technological fields such as artificial intelligence, data science and cybersecurity [8,9].

This work was supported by the Italian Ministry of Education and Research (MIUR), in the framework of the CrossLab project (Departments of Excellence).

L. S. Agrati et al. (Eds.): HELMeTO 2020, CCIS 1344, pp. 256–270, 2021.
https://doi.org/10.1007/978-3-030-67435-9_20

The curricula of such university programs include subjects requiring students to be involved in practical teaching activities and develop educational projects (usually in groups). Indeed, from a pedagogic point of view, the most effective way to get students to master IT tools and platforms is a Problem-Based Learning [2] approach based on practical activities and educational projects (preferably in a collaborative learning framework) [1]. The evolution of IT hardware with its requirements make it unsuitable for installation in classroom with instructor and students due to space, power and cooling requirements. This is the case of courses that handle subjects such as cloud and distributed computing, where an infrastructure with a large number of servers is required [10,11] to allow students to experiment with a plausible setup. These kind of problems have been reported into two recently published contributions [6,11]. The authors discussed their experiences on the transition from the use of a physical infrastructure to the exploitation of virtual resources for teaching computer networking and distributed computing courses.

Moreover, the infrastructure should be always available to students so that they can experiment through practical homework and educational projects. Finally, the ability to remotely access the infrastructure for practicing allows distance learning to support students unable to attend laboratory classes. This is what happened during the current COVID-19 pandemic emergency that required to transition from in-presence teaching to distance learning within few days [14].

In this work, we discuss our recent experience in teaching Cloud Computing and Distributed Databases courses, at the Master of Science Program in Artificial Intelligence and Data Engineering, offered for the first time in the 2019–2020 Academic Year, by the University of Pisa[1]. In order to allow students to develop hands-on activities and the education projects that we assigned to them, we have implemented a Cloud-based Virtual Lab. Students were allowed to access to a set of virtual machines (VMs), to install the required tools and frameworks, and to actually develop the assigned activities, such as client-server applications interacting with distributed databases and distributed programming exercises.

The paper is organized as follows. Section 2 discuss some recent contribution on adopting virtualization techniques and cloud computing services in the context of education. Section 3 illustrates the architecture of our Cloud-based Virtual Lab. Afterward, Sect. 4 discusses some examples of teaching workflows carried out exploiting our Virtual Lab. Section 5 reports some discussions on feedback provided by students on the Virtual Lab adoption and usage. Section 6 draws some final remarks on our teaching experiences.

2 Related Work

In the last years, a special attention has been payed in exploiting virtualization techniques and cloud-computing services as a support for teaching both traditional and innovative courses [12]. These courses include subjects such as computer networking [6], operating systems [3], cybersecurity [8,15], parallel and

[1] https://computer.ing.unipi.it/aide-lm.

distributed computing [11], big data [4] and cloud computing [5,10]. Recently, in the work published in [7], the author argues on four dimensions on which virtualization techniques and cloud computing services should be integrated into the educational framework. Specifically, he suggests that these techniques and services should be a priority for the educational institutions in terms of: i) creating a computing infrastructure based on virtualization and cloud services, ii) including virtualization and cloud computing as a teaching subjects, iii) exploiting virtualization and cloud services as tools for teaching and iv) integrating the previous concepts as a whole point of strength of the institution itself.

As regards teaching cloud computing, authors of [10], discuss their experience at the University of Zilina, in Slovakia, where they exploit a private cloud-based lab, based on OpenStack, for allowing students to carry out hands-on activities. The activities include: the installation of the virtualization platform, building VMs, creating a virtual networks with several machines and writing orchestration scripts. In a recent work published in [11], authors argue on their approach for teaching parallel and distributed computing at the Clemson University, in South Carolina, US. Specifically, authors share their experience in leveraging an US publicly available computing resource, namely CloudLab[2], as a platform to develop and host teaching materials, to allow students to carry out their practical activities and to support instructors to monitor the teaching-learning workflow. Students were first asked to take familiarity with the basics of Linux Operating Systems and of computer networking, in the virtualized framework offered by CloudLab. Then, by adopting a Problem-Based learning approach, group of students had the opportunity of building different topology of clusters on which they experimented the implementation of parallel and distributed applications. For the implementation of their application, students adopted the tools of the Hadoop environment, including Hadoop Distributed File System.

In 2019, a contribution on adopting virtualization techniques for teaching, learning, and assessing students' performance, in computer networking subjects, was presented in [6]. The author discusses how his "Networking and Telecommunications Management" course, at the University of the Pacific, in Stockton, California, has been redesigned in order to improve the low quality of the teaching-learning workflow. The author states that he achieved unsatisfactory results of teaching mainly due to the adoption of physical machines and network equipment for students hands-on activities. The new version of the course includes traditional lectures and discussion sessions that focus on theoretical and fundamental topics. Moreover, virtualization techniques are mainly used for providing students with hands-on experience in computer network management. For the practical activities, students are required to install VirtualBox[3], on the computers in a lab or on their own laptops, and then to create VMs, to install different operating systems, to organize computer networks and so on. Thanks to virtualization, many advantages are offered to the students, such as portability of their work, low cost, and freedom of experimentation.

[2] www.cloudlab.us.

[3] https://www.virtualbox.org/.

As regards teaching cybersecurity using cloud-based services, a recent contribution has been published in [8]. Authors report the results of a feasibility study that they carried out by evaluating two Cloud Service Providers (CSP), namely Google Cloud and Microsoft Azure. During summer of 2018 a group of students were involved in laboratory sessions and some practical activities were assigned to them. These activities included a number of tasks such as to connect to the cloud provider to initiate sessions, to create VMs and virtual networks and to simulate security attacks. After the lab sessions, students were interviewed face to face to evaluate the quality of their experience, in terms of usability of the services offered by the two CSPs.

Recently, a group of researchers of the eCampus University, an Italian distance learning institution, designed a virtual-lab, also based on cloud computing, for carrying out the practical activities of a sport and exercise science university program [13].

Finally, interesting suggestions can be found in [16], in which authors carry out a deep analysis of different tools for exploiting virtualization and cloud computing in higher education.

3 Cloud-Based Virtual Lab Architecture

We implemented our Virtual Lab using the private cloud infrastructure of the University of Pisa. The infrastructure runs on over 70 servers with around 3100 physical cores managed by Microsoft System Center Virtual Machine Manager[4] (SCVMM); servers run either VMware ESXi or Microsoft Hyper-V[5] to run the virtual workloads of the University. A private cloud has been allocated to support the Virtual Lab using Hyper-V servers. Using a scriptable PowerShell it is possible to manipulate VM creation, configuration, and deletion using SCVMM.

A set of tools have been implemented to automate the creation of the VMs through SCVMM. One script, in particular, is responsible for creating all the VMs for one specific class, in order to create and assign one VM for each enrolled student. The script behaves as follows: starting from the list of the students enrolled in the class, it automatically creates and configures one VM for each student; after the creation of VMs, the script automatically notify the student via emails including all the details to connect to the assigned VM. In order to keep track of the association between a VM and a student, the script automatically populate an Excel file with the IP address of each VM with the corresponding student. In this way the instructor can keep track of the assignment and connect to each VM when need to support and troubleshooting.

Each VM has a virtual network adapter connected to an overlay virtual network isolated from the internet. A virtual gateway, implemented using *pfsense*, allows the VMs to connect to Internet. A VM running OpenVPN[6] allows students to securely connect to the assigned VMs through VPN.

[4] https://docs.microsoft.com/en-us/system-center/vmm/overview.

[5] https://docs.microsoft.com/en-us/virtualization/hyper-v-on-windows/about/.

[6] https://openvpn.net/.

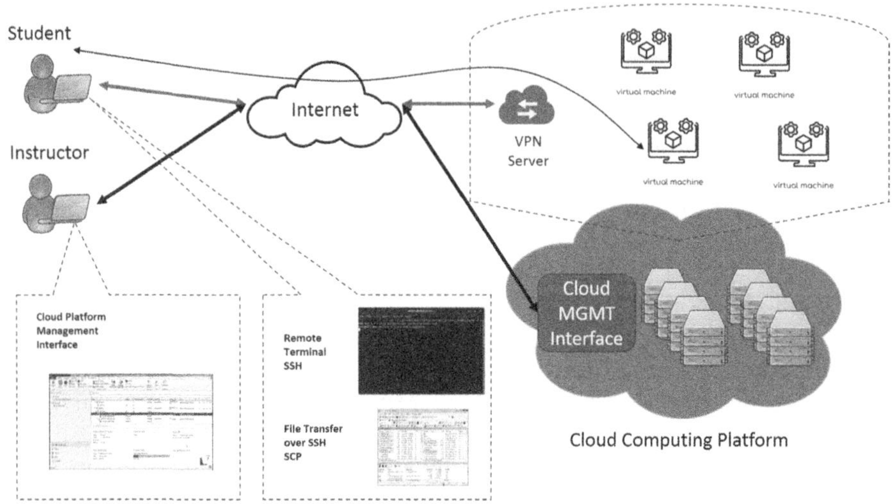

Fig. 1. Cloud-based Virtual Lab Architecture

The overall architecture of the cloud-based Virtual Lab is presented in Fig. 1. Instructors can access the management interface exposed by the cloud platform to manage the VMs for the students, also in an automated fashion by exploiting the tools we implemented. Instructors can also exploit additional functionalities offered by the cloud platform. An example is the console functionality that allows to connect to each VM. This functionality is useful to connect to a specific VM to check the progress of the students in carrying out an assignment or to troubleshoot a specific issue. On the other hand, students interacts with the VMs allocated through remote connection, e.g. a remote terminal like SSH or a file transfer. Through them they can perform any kind of assignment/exercise on the VM, from compiling and executing a program to install and configure a specific software. Exploiting the fact that VMs are all connected to the same virtual overlay network, students can also carry out group assignment in which the VMs assigned to each student can connect with other VMs assigned to other students. This is specifically useful to design assignments involving distributed software, i.e. systems made of different component running on different machines interacting through an internet/intranet connection.

4 Teaching Activities on the Virtual Lab

Once all the VMs have been allocated in the Virtual Lab, we divided students in groups of 4. Each group was required to pool together their VMs to build up a small but fully functional cluster of computers using the full management rights granted on the cluster VMs. This group organization allowed us (1) to illustrate the state-of-the art tools and frameworks in distributed environments, and (2)

Table 1. Tools adopted in the teaching activities.

Name	Description
GitHub[a]	Web platform offering distributed version control and source code management using Git
Jupyter[b]	Web-based computational environment supporting interactive data science and scientific computing
Docker[c]	Platform-as-a-service software using use OS-level virtualization to deliver software in packages (containers)
Kubernetes[d]	Container-orchestration system for automating computer application deployment, scaling, and management
MongoDB[e]	Cross-platform document-oriented database management systems supporting dataset replication and sharding
Neo4J[f]	Cross-platform graph-oriented database management systems supporting transactions and advanced queries in graphs
HDFS[g]	Distributed, scalable, and portable file system for the Hadoop framework
YARN[h]	Resource management handling distributed applications for the Hadoop framework
Hadoop[i]	Software framework for distributed processing of big data using the MapReduce programming model
Spark[j]	Distributed general-purpose cluster-computing framework using the MapReduce programming model

[a]https://github.com/.
[b]https://jupyter.org/.
[c]https://www.docker.com/.
[d]https://kubernetes.io/.
[e]https://www.mongodb.com/.
[f]https://neo4j.com/.
[g]https://hadoop.apache.org/docs/current/hadoop-project-dist/hadoop-hdfs/HdfsDesign.html.
[h]https://hadoop.apache.org/docs/current/hadoop-yarn/hadoop-yarn-site/YARN.html.
[i]https://hadoop.apache.org/.
[j]https://spark.apache.org/.

to design practical activities involving the installation, setup, configuration and use of these tools and frameworks on the virtual cluster.

We organized the practical activities into two main categories, namely *tools setup* and *distributed programming* activities. The learning objectives of the tools setup activities are to allow students to setup and to correctly configure complex software stacks in distributed environments. In addition, we enabled students to experience the tools on distributed runtime support environments. The tools adopted in our courses are reported in Table 1.

Manual setup and configuration allow students to face the real system administration problems and challenges that these tools present, having to understand the different abstractions in complex configurations each one introduces. Once the learning objectives are achieved, it is possible to leverage one of the many management software to automatically configure these systems being aware about the performed operations. This approach is two-fold: firstly, the students will manually configure the different tools to understand their deployment and configuration potentialities, then the automatic configuration will help them to reproduce with almost no effort the settings required to perform the following distributed programming activities.

The main learning goal of the distributed programming activities is to let students learn how to design and develop programs suitable to interact with or run onto state-of-the-art platforms for cloud and distributed computing and storage.

The practical activities requires a careful preparation setup. Besides the preparation of lecture notes and slides describing the architecture, implementation, usage and application programming interfaces (APIs) of the selected tools, the instructor must devote time to setup, test and debug the steps to perform the activities on a specific Virtual Lab. After the preparation steps, the administration of these practical activities requires a mix of face-to-face teaching, using slides and electronic notes, with supervised and unsupervised hands-on sessions.

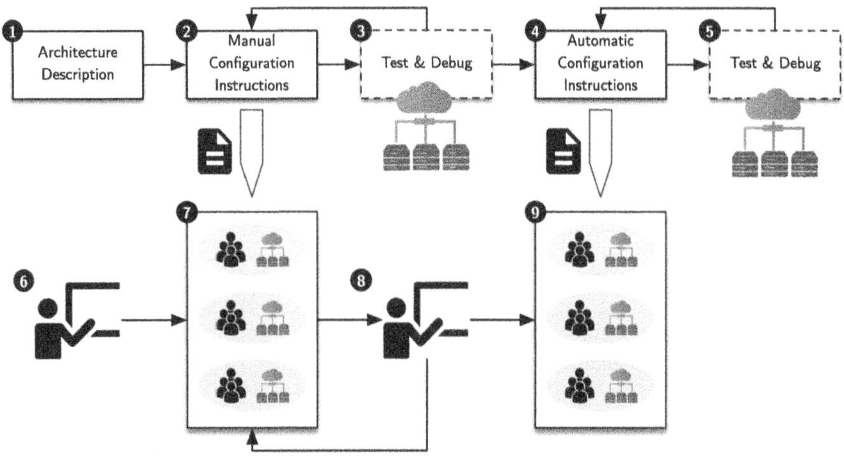

Fig. 2. The workflow of the tools setup activities.

The workflow of the tools setup activities is illustrated in Fig. 2, and the steps are described below:

1. The instructor prepares the slides and/or lecture notes describing the architecture and implementation of the selected tool.

2. The instructor prepares the manual tool configuration instructions to be carried out by the student groups. These instructions must provide a step-wise approach to the setup and configuration of the tool, illustrating the different options and specific details of each tool's underlying infrastructure; the instructions are uploaded on `GitHub`.
3. The instructor tests and debugs the prepared instructions on the dedicated Virtual Lab, refining and correcting the configuration instructions prepared in the previous step.
4. The instructor prepares the automatic tool configuration instructions to configure the selected tool with minimal user interaction. Once the students have carried out the manual configuration setup, it is important to provide automatic configuration procedures to avoid spending additional time to configure from scratch the tool in case of faults, reboots or migrations of the Virtual Lab underlying resources. The instructions are uploaded on `GitHub`.
5. The instructor tests and debugs the prepared instruction on the dedicated Virtual Lab, refining and correcting the configuration instruction prepared in the previous step.
6. The instructor presents the architecture and the implementation design of a selected tools. Students download the instructions of the practical activities and the instructors discusses with the electronic hands-on notes the main activities to be carried out during the unsupervised practical sessions.
7. In an unsupervised way, the student groups focus on reproducing the instructions and commands specified in the electronic notes, at their own pace.
8. After a given amount of time, the instructor supervises the groups and provides feedback and help on the main problems the students could have encountered during the unsupervised practical sessions.
9. At the end, the students are allowed to download the automatic configuration instructions from `GitHub` to avoid the manual setup in case of persistent errors or availability issues of the Cloud platform.

Since the setup, configuration and administration of software tools often require commands to be issues at the command line, it is important to provide students with clear, concise and easy "cut-and-paste" notes to speed up the most difficult configuration commands and to avoid errors.

The workflow of the distributed programming activities is summarized in Fig. 3, and the steps are described below:

1. The instructor prepares the slides and/or lecture notes describing the constructs and APIs of a selected programming environment.
2. The instructor prepares the description of the programming exercises to be carried out by the student groups during the unsupervised practical session, uploaded on `GitHub`.
3. The instructor implements the solutions of the proposed exercises, and uploads them on `GitHub`.
4. The instructor tests and debugs the solutions on the dedicated Virtual Lab, refining and correcting them; the solutions are uploaded on `GitHub`.

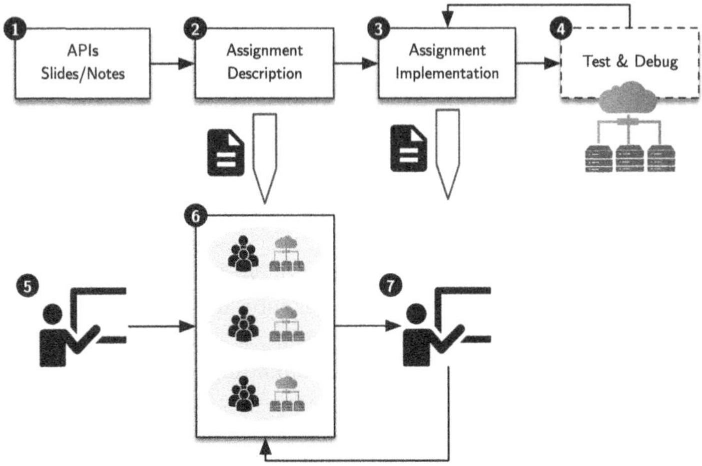

Fig. 3. The workflow of the distributed programming activities.

5. The instructor presents the constructs and APIs of the selected programming environment. Then, he/she provides and discusses the exercises to be carried out during the unsupervised practical sessions.
6. In an unsupervised way, the student groups focus on solving the programming assignments.
7. After a given amount of time, the instructor supervises the groups and provides feedback and help the on main problems the students could have encountered during the unsupervised practical sessions. The groups are now allowed to download and test a proposed solution to the programming exercises hosted on `GitHub`.

It is worth noticing that, in both workflows discussed above, students are not enabled to view the automatic configurations and the proposed solutions before finishing the assignments.

Since groups and students in the same groups have different learning paces, it is important that the instructors provide and discuss the exercises by providing a priori the solutions of the programming assignments. In doing so, groups and/or students within groups can perform during the practical session different activities, depending on their own learning pace, such as discussing and analysing the source code of the provided solution, compiling, testing and adapting the provided solution, and/or developing their own solution and comparing the results with the given one.

Once the student groups successfully master different tools and programming environment through the provided exercises, they are requested to implement a final project. As regards the Cloud Computing course, the project focuses on developing a specific distributed algorithm on the top of MapReduce, and providing a demo of its implementation on the group's Virtual Lab; in the last edition of the course, students have been requested to implement a version of the kNN algorithm, namely a simple supervised machine learning algorithm for classification task, in MapReduce, on both the Hadoop and Spark platforms. As regards the Large-Scale and Multi-Structured Databases, students have been requested to design and implement a Java application which interacts with both Document-Based and Graph-Based databases, taking appropriately into consideration data replica, sharding and consistency. Students were required to deploy and run the application on a virtual cluster built on the Virtual Lab.

5 Discussions

The Virtual Lab that we briefly described in this work was adopted for carrying out the teaching activities of two courses, namely *Large-Scale and Multi-Structured Databases* and *Cloud Computing*, delivered by the University of Pisa. The first course was delivered in presence mode, from September to December 2019. As regards the second course, due to the emergency of the COVID-19 pandemic, most of the lectures have been held in on-line mode. Around 100 students were enrolled to both courses and 25 working groups were created. The practical classes were attended by 40–70 students. As for the resources occupied by the VMs, we have allocated about 2TB of RAM, 200 Computing Cores and 9TB of hard disks. The ability to allocate resources on the University on private cloud allowed us to allocate enough resources that in a public cloud setup would have been impractical and expensive, and it has been a key to the Virtual Lab delivery.

Overall, students appreciated the acquisition of skills using the Virtual Lab and the instructors collected a number of positive feedbacks during classes. However, some problems on the cloud infrastructure occurred especially during the March–May 2020 period and students experienced some difficulties for connecting to their VMs. These problems were probably due to the network congestion related with the COVID-19 emergency. With this first edition of the course we validated that it is practical to let students experience setup and configuration of complex and distributed software platforms, thus we intend to continue developing and improving this format in the future editions of the courses.

In order to collect a detailed feedback and highlight issues and drawbacks with our approach, a feedback form was provided to the students on July 2020, at the end of both the courses. The main goals of the questionnaire are summarized in the following:

1. To assess the overall experience from the point of view of the students;
2. To measure the overall usability of the platform and of the tools adopted;
3. To measure the extent of the connectivity issues experienced during the period March–May 2020.

In order to assess the overall experience, a set of three questions were included in the questionnaire for students. The first two questions focused on evaluating the overall experience of using the platform in two different phases of the labs, namely class exercises and final project, respectively. The third question focused

2020), 15 groups concluded their projects and a total of 55 students passed the exam with average mark higher than 28 points (30 points is the highest mark). Then, after the second exam period (June–July 2020), 14 more groups concluded their projects and the number of students that passed the exam reached a number equal to 82, with average mark higher than 28.5 points. Finally, as regards Cloud Computing course, after the first exam period (June–July 2020), 16 groups concluded their projects and a total of 52 students passed the exam with average mark higher than 28.5 points.

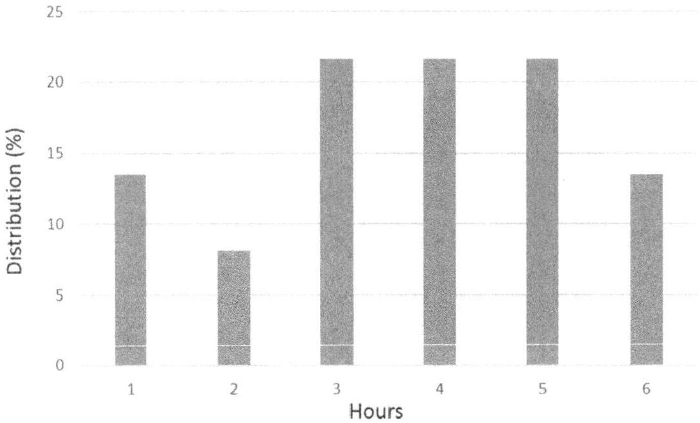

Fig. 7. Session duration.

6 Conclusions

In this work, we have discussed and shared our experience in delivering two advanced courses, in the framework of an innovative Master Degree in Artificial Intelligence and Data Engineering, offered by the University of Pisa. Specifically, their subjects are Cloud Computing and Distributed Databases. The two courses have been approached by the instructors following a Problem-Based learning approach. Indeed, students have been required to carry out hands-on activities for acquiring skills for designing, implementing and experimenting applications in a distributed fashion. Moreover, students have been organized in small groups for developing a final project as part of the exam.

We have mainly discussed our experience in building and exploiting, as a support of the teaching-learning workflow, a Virtual Lab, that has been built on the private cloud infrastructure of the University of Pisa. The Virtual Lab has been used by the instructors for delivering the practical class and by the students for carrying out assigned activities and for developing the final projects. Indeed, thanks to the Virtual Lab, both instructors and students were able to build and use clusters of virtual machines on which distributed application and storage systems were installed and run.

We have shown the results of a campaign that collected student opinions about their experience with the Virtual Lab. To this aim, we submitted a simple questionnaire to each student, adopting an online feedback form. Results have shown that, even though connectivity issues were experimented, students appreciated both the Virtual Lab and the teaching approach adopted by the instructors. Moreover, by analyzing the records of winter and summer exam periods, more than 80% of the students passed the Large-Scale and Multi-Structured Databases exam. As regards the Cloud Computing course, more than 50% of students passed the exam, but we have to consider that student still have the winter period for taking the examination. Finally, the average mark achieved by the students is higher than 28.5 over 30.

By analyzing the students feedback and the results achieved by the students at the exam, from the instructors point of view, we can remark that the learning objectives that we fixed for our courses have been fully achieved. A great effort from the technical point of view has been made for the development and the maintenance of the Virtual Lab. However, there are still some problems on which we are working with the technicians of the University of Pisa, in order to have a more stable and efficient virtualization system. Moreover, the Virtual Lab described in this work will be tested in the next academic year also by instructors of other innovative courses. A more in-deep analysis of the validity of our methodological approach, supported by the novel technological infrastructure, will be carried out, in order to overcame the limitations of the current analysis. These limitations are strictly related with the reduced number of students and courses involved in the usage of the proposed virtual-lab. Moreover, a control group was missing in our analysis because both courses involved in the experimentation were at their first edition.

References

1. Admiraal, W., et al.: Students as future workers: cross-border multidisciplinary learning labs in higher education. Int. J. Technol. Educ. Sci. **3**(2), 85–94 (2019)
2. Chis, A.E., Moldovan, A.N., Murphy, L., Pathak, P., Muntean, C.H.: Investigating flipped classroom and problem-based learning in a programming module for computing conversion course. Educ. Technol. Soc. **21**, 232–247 (2018)
3. Dobrilovic, D., Stojanov, Z.: Using virtualization software in operating systems course. In: 2006 International Conference on Information Technology: Research and Education, pp. 222–226. IEEE (2006)
4. Eckroth, J.: Teaching big data with a virtual cluster. In: Proceedings of the 47th ACM Technical Symposium on Computing Science Education, pp. 175–180 (2016)
5. Gillam, L., Li, B., O'Loughlin, J.: Teaching clouds: lessons taught and lessons learnt. In: Cloud Computing for Teaching and Learning: Strategies for Design and Implementation, pp. 82–94. IGI Global (2012)
6. Huang, A.: Teaching, learning, and assessment with virtualization technology. J. Educ. Technol. Syst. **47**(4), 523–538 (2019)
7. Klement, M.: Models of integration of virtualization in education: virtualization technology and possibilities of its use in education. Comput. Educ. **105**, 31–43 (2017)

8. Kolhar, M., Alameen, A.: Before teaching cybersecurity in the university: usability analysis of the cloud platform with learner's perspective. TEM J. **8**(3), 733 (2019)
9. Li, Y., Wang, X., Xin, D.: An inquiry into AI university curriculum and market demand: facts, fits, and future trends. In: Proceedings of the 2019 on Computers and People Research Conference, pp. 139–142 (2019)
10. Moravčík, M., Segeč, P., Uramová, J., Kontšek, M.: Teaching cloud computing in cloud computing. In: 2017 15th International Conference on Emerging eLearning Technologies and Applications (ICETA), pp. 1–6. IEEE (2017)
11. Ngo, L.B., Denton, J.: Using CloudLab as a scalable platform for teaching cluster computing. J. Comput. Sci. **10**(1), 100–106 (2019)
12. O'Donnell, E., O'Donnell, L.: A review of virtualisation and cloud computing for higher education. In: Encyclopedia of Information Science and Technology, 3rd edn., pp. 7487–7496. IGI Global (2015)
13. Picerno, P., Pecori, R., Raviolo, P., Ducange, P.: Smartphones and exergame controllers as BYOD solutions for the e-tivities of an online sport and exercise sciences university program. In: Burgos, D., et al. (eds.) HELMeTO 2019. CCIS, vol. 1091, pp. 217–227. Springer, Cham (2019). https://doi.org/10.1007/978-3-030-31284-8_17
14. Rapanta, C., Botturi, L., Goodyear, P., Guàrdia, L., Koole, M.: Online university teaching during and after the Covid-19 crisis: refocusing teacher presence and learning activity. Postdigit. Sci. Educ. **2**, 923–945 (2020). https://doi.org/10.1007/s42438-020-00155-y
15. Salah, K., Hammoud, M., Zeadally, S.: Teaching cybersecurity using the cloud. IEEE Trans. Learn. Technol. **8**(4), 383–392 (2015)
16. Segeč, P., Moravčík, M., Kontšek, M., Papán, J., Uramová, J., Yeremenko, O.: Network virtualization tools-analysis and application in higher education. In: 2019 17th International Conference on Emerging eLearning Technologies and Applications (ICETA), pp. 699–708. IEEE (2019)

Presente Digitale: An Online Education System for Teachers

Michela Fazzolari[1(✉)], Stefania Fabbri[1], Ilaria Matteucci[1], Marinella Petrocchi[1,2], and Anna Vaccarelli[1]

[1] Institute of Informatics and Telematics - National Research Council, Pisa, Italy
{m.fazzolari,s.fabbri,i.matteucci,m.petrocchi,a.vaccarelli}@iit.cnr.it
[2] IMT School for Advanced Studies, Lucca, Italy

Abstract. In this paper, we introduce the rationale, goals, and structure of Presente Digitale, an ambitious Italian project for the realization of an online education system on Digital Culture. Presente Digitale is dedicated to teachers and their students. Its aim is to offer paths of reflection closely linked to the digital world, which can respond to the current needs of schools and society about Digital Culture and helps in effectively convey this knowledge. This will give young people the opportunity to integrate their prior knowledge with a 'teacher's points of view', and, mostly important, to be able to take a safe and solid path when approaching the labour market. The courses are free of charge and available online, making the participation really flexible.

Keywords: Digital Culture · Online education systems · Cybersecurity · Presente Digitale

1 Introduction

Digital Culture is both a common term and an urgency felt by the representatives of different categories of people: citizens, workers, students, each with their own needs and peculiarities. According to [11], *Digital Culture* is a wide concept conveying the idea that technology and Internet significantly affect the way we interact, behave, think and communicate.

From the many statistics published at Italian and European level, it is evident that *digital skills* [1] are now necessary for any job and are a crucial for finding one. Furthermore, there are often not enough professionals specialised in *soft-skills* on the labour market. Providing the foundations of Digital Culture and skills, not only related to technical aspects but extended to cultural ones, is crucial to create the awareness needed to use the digital tools available today.

Work partially supported by TOFFEe (Tools for Fighting FakEs), an integrated activity project funded by IMT School for Advanced Studies Lucca; and by Registro.it, the registry office for the '.it' domain.

L. S. Agrati et al. (Eds.): HELMeTO 2020, CCIS 1344, pp. 271–285, 2021.
https://doi.org/10.1007/978-3-030-67435-9_21

In the last few months, many initiatives have been launched in Italy by public and private entities to promote Digital Culture in the various fields, but one of the main starting point can only be the School.

In fact, the challenge is the ability to introduce these skills into the labour market, with the aim of producing a radical upheaval by exploiting the potential of digital applications. In this regard, it is undeniable that the attitude to change can be found in young people, namely students.

Digital skills create opportunities for new careers, catalogued by the European Commission and defined in the UNI 11506:2017 standard. In Italy, AGID (AGency for Digital Italy) has developed guidelines for the quality of digital skills in ICT professions (inspired by European documents) identifying 6 different areas of expertise and 23 new professional profiles. We must provide Italian students with these opportunities in order to help them enter the labour market.

The Italian Ministry of Education, University and Research (MIUR)[1] is currently paying attention to this need and is launching initiatives to spread the use and culture of digital technology in schools.

In fact, the National Plan for Digital Education (PNSD) [4], states that 'it is time to invest in an organic innovation design in Italian schools, with coherent programmes and actions including access, learning environments, devices, platforms, digital administration, research, training and of course didactics, methodology and competences'.

A weakness of this process is the poor digital culture of most teachers, who struggle to keep up with the change. Therefore, the first step to foster the spread of Digital Culture in Schools is to provide teachers with suitable cultural tools and help them to transfer the new skills acquired in teaching, giving them training on Digital Culture issues.

To this aim, online training is increasingly taking hold: many subjects provide quality courses, mainly upon payment, on various topics, including the use of technologies in teaching, but not on Digital Culture. A notable exception is Ireland: the local Department has launched a website dedicated to teacher training, namely http://www.pdsttechnologyineducation.ie/en/, whose claim is 'Promoting and supporting the integration of ICT in Education'. This portal offers online training courses on ICT, explanations on the use of technology and targeted educational paths and publishes best practices.

And this is the aim of the project described in this work, *Presente Digitale*[2]: to create, in Italy, a portal for free online training for teachers focused on Digital Culture issues, but which also offers lines of thought to be proposed in classes and additional materials for teachers and students.

The manuscript is organised as follows. Section 2 provides an overview of online courses dedicated to teachers in Italy and abroad. Section 3 presents the project *Presente Digitale*, with its objectives, targets and partners involved. Section 4 is dedicated to the course programme and provides, as an example, a detailed description of the Cybersecurity course. Finally, the conclusions in

[1] https://www.miur.gov.it.

[2] Italian translation of 'Digital Today'.

Sect. 5 summarise the content of the manuscript and provide food for thought for the future.

2 Online Learning Courses

The educational offer of online courses dedicated to teachers is very rich and extends to many topics. The current health situation, linked to the Coronavirus pandemic, has further increased the offer, especially of free (short) courses: being unable to organise on-site courses, some organisations have offered free of charge material to support the teachers that were involved in distance learning during the lockdown.

Most of the online courses available concern teaching subjects, with ideas for in-depth study and non-traditional teaching; others deal with more transversal topics related to teaching methods, even the most innovative ones that make use of technology. For example, Erickson offers a course oriented to innovative and inclusive teaching[3] and one dedicated to raise awareness on the use of the Internet among adolescents[4].

Recently, a new provision of the Italian Ministry of Education, made Civic Education compulsory in all schools. Therefore, online training courses in this subject have flourished, both because it has been reintroduced after many years with renewed content and because the Ministry's provision requires teachers to attend these courses.

In Italy, in general, teachers are obliged to attend refresher courses to obtain a minimum number of annual training credits. They have a small budget from the Ministry to pay for these courses. For this reason, almost all the courses offered are subject to payment and are registered with the Ministry of Education, so that credits can be given to the teachers who attend them.

Even abroad the offer of courses for teachers is very wide, but it maintains the same characteristics as the Italian one with respect to the topics. At the end of the course, a certificate or certification is issued, according to the various national standards.

For example, the online learning platform Coursera[5] offers massive open online courses (MOOC) from various subjects and organisations all over the world, including courses on distance learning[6].

However, even in such a wide offer, we have noticed the lack of basic training on the use of networks, not necessarily (or not only) as a tool for teaching but as a resource. As mentioned above, many training courses focus on how to deal with ICT-supported didactics, and often concern the use of tablets or interactive whiteboards in classrooms, but do not focus on their operation. See, for example,

---

[3] https://www.erickson.it/it/esperto-in-didattica-innovativa-e-inclusiva-22-09-2020 (accessed 2020-09-09).

[4] https://www.erickson.it/it/sensibilizzare-gli-adolescenti-alluso-di-internet-corso-introduttivo (accessed 2020-09-09).

[5] https://www.coursera.org/.

[6] https://www.coursera.org/learn/teach-online (accessed 2020-09-09).

the platform docenti.it[7], which, among the training courses, offers a 200-hours specialized course on the educational use of the tablets, or the Mnemosine institution[8], which among the training courses for teachers[9], proposes a course geared to teaching with digital tools.

One of the teachers' issues is the lack of knowledge on the Internet, its mechanisms and the technologies connected to it (web, social, chat, smartphones, etc.) compared to their students. This causes problems, both because they lose authority in these fields and because they are unable to guide their students and provide them with the educational and cultural support they need to use the Internet in an informed and safe way.

Some institutions offer vertical courses on the Internet and on computer science, such as coding[10] and cyberbullying[11], and, compared with the time when our project started, today there is also a course on IoT[12].

Also abroad there are vertical courses on computer science and Internet but at (almost) university level (for example Future Learn offers courses on networking[13], encryption and cryptography[14], and computer systems[15]). Among the foreign experiences, the Merlot[16] portal is also interesting, as it gathers a huge international community of users who share free online courses.

The project *Presente Digitale* aims to fill this gap and offer basic training on Internet issues through courses recognised by the Ministry, but totally free of charge. Moreover, as we will see later on, the training offer proposed by *Presente Digitale* ranges over various topics of interest related to the Internet, its history, its security, networking aspects, and so on. All the themes are addressed considering that the contents are directed to the teachers, but also themselves can exploit such materials to convey knowledge to their students.

3 The Project

The project *Presente Digitale* envisages the creation of an online education system for free online training, which also offers paths of reflection closely linked to

[7] https://www.docenti.it.

[8] https://www.formazionedocenti.it/.

[9] https://www.formazionedocenti.it/corsi-di-formazione-per-i-docenti/ (accessed 2020-09-09).

[10] https://formazione.deascuola.it/offerta-formativa/evento/coding-e-apprendimento-creativo/ (accessed 2020-09-09).

[11] https://formazione.deascuola.it/offerta-formativa/evento/cyberbullismo-ed-educazione-al-digitale/ (accessed 2020-09-09).

[12] https://www.imparadigitale.it/shop/corsi-on-line/tecnologie-corsi-on-line/introduzione-a-internet-delle-cose-db11/ (accessed 2020-09-09).

[13] https://www.futurelearn.com/courses/introduction-to-networking (accessed 2020-09-09).

[14] https://www.futurelearn.com/courses/encryption-and-cryptography (accessed 2020-09-09).

[15] https://www.futurelearn.com/courses/computer-systems (accessed 2020-09-09).

[16] https://www.merlot.org/merlot/.

the digital world and which can respond to the current needs of School and Society, addressing specific issues in the classroom and offering in-depth materials for teachers and students.

The material that will be offered will:

- Foster the Digital Culture of teachers;
- Provide some cultural and methodological tools to master the digital world.

The material will be made available under a license that will ensure its full use for educational purposes (Open Educational Resources). The key topics of the training will be: History and Functionalities of the Network, Digital Identity, Social Networks, Intellectual Property, Digital Communication, Digital Marketing, Big Data and Internet of Things, Internet for Learning and Teaching, Computational Thinking and Programming, Cybersecurity, Privacy Protection.

Thus, the themes will be closely related to Digital Culture and the Internet. Each theme will be organised in modules and dealt with at two levels:

- Basic level: video lectures with in-depth analysis and optional exercises.
- In-depth level: networked assisted activities, exercises and tests to obtain training credits.

The contents will be organised and delivered in such a way as to comply with the requirements of the Italian Ministry of Education (MIUR) for teacher training. The courses have the aim of providing teachers with appropriate cultural tools to address the themes of the Internet in the classroom and to become a guide and reference for students in their *online life*, being able to perform their educational function in this field as well. The training course will offer ideas for developing guided reflections on the themes of web and Digital Culture in the classroom, combining students' great confidence in technology with the experience and cultural mediation of the teacher.

3.1 Objectives

The project aims to meet the training needs of teachers on Digital Culture issues.

In teacher training, computer literacy has acquired a central role; in fact, as reiterated in the aforementioned PNSD 'Teacher training must be centred on educational innovation, taking into account digital technologies as a support for the implementation of new educational paradigms and the operational planning of activities. We must move from the school of transmission to the school of learning'.

According to the OECD-Talis 2018 report [3] which involved teachers from 48 countries and individual regions, ICT stands out among the topics on which Italian teachers would like to have more training: only 36% feel prepared, against 43% of the OECD average, despite the fact that 47% of teachers use computers and software in the classroom (however below the OECD average, equal to 53%), but they still have poor or inadequate technologies (Fig. 1).

If we analyse the type of activities carried out at school with digital technologies (Fig. 2), we note that these technologies are mainly used for consulting

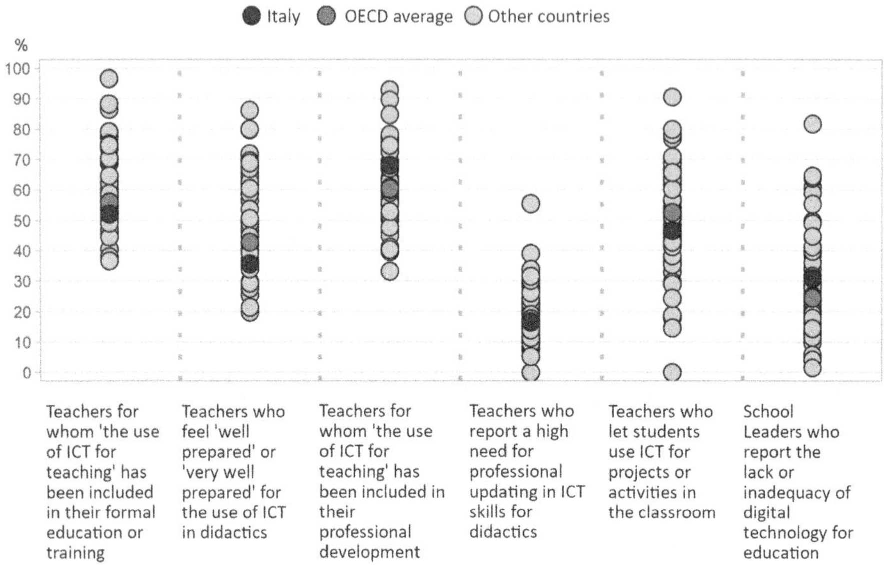

Fig. 1. ICT in teaching. Note: Only countries with available data are shown. Source: OECD, TALIS 2018 Database, Tables I.3.17, I.3.21, I.3.1, I.3.5, I.3.9 and I.3.13.

sources and content (most teachers do it in 47.3% of schools) or are used for presentations (29.3%) or as an evaluation tool (28.9%). According to AGCOM[17] 'this evidence suggests that the willingness of the teaching staff to use digital is too often limited to each class, leaving little room for the use of innovative technologies aimed at opening up classes, exchange and transversal collaboration between teachers and students, both between classes in the same institute and between classes in different institutes'.

The Digital School Observatory considers these data rather alarming, 'especially when contextualised with the identikit of the children attending schools today, the so-called Generation Z. These students were born in the digital age, with high knowledge on PCs and smartphones, but no thanks to school: 47% of students have learned almost nothing about new technologies in school. This is also because, in 2 out of 3 cases, the school has never bothered to organise specific courses aimed at improving students' knowledge about, for example, coding, programs, operating systems and 3D printers. Nor on security and appropriate online behaviour, given that 40% (48% in the Southern Italy) have never had the opportunity to take classes on the risks of the Net'.

At European level, as the European Commission's *Education and Training Monitoring Report (2019)* [2] explains, there are the same problems: in addition to the lack of equipment (or its malfunctioning), which hinders the use of technologies in schools, teachers also indicate the absence of teaching models on how to use ICT, and their insufficient personal skills (according to the Commission's

[17] https://www.agcom.it.

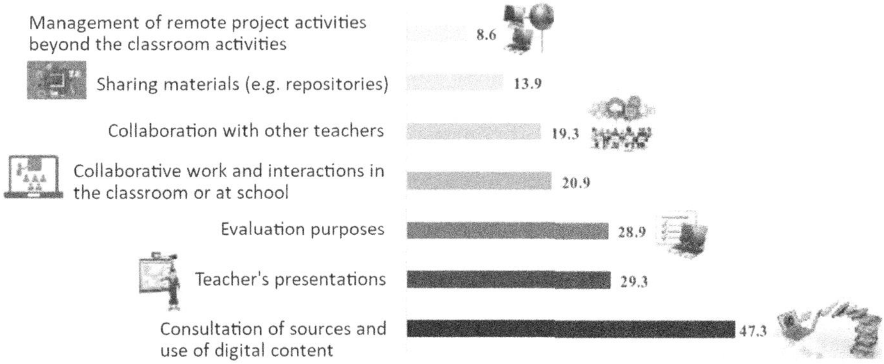

Fig. 2. Type of activities carried out at school with digital technologies. Source: AGCOM elaborations on MIUR data.

report, in the European Union 39.4% of teachers said they were well prepared in the use of technologies for teaching).

Therefore, there seems to be a gap in the preparation of teachers in relation to the *digital*: the lack of knowledge on technologies, the lack of Internet surfing and, therefore, the incapacity of interpreting the relationships and behaviours that are established there, make the teacher inadequate to play the role of educator for their students on this mostly unknown terrain.

The project is therefore a cultural action for teachers, a starting point for the learning of tools, technologies and the daily use of digital technology, to be put at the service of school activities. The final objective is to enable teachers to use the skills acquired in their daily relationship with students, transmitting awareness and mastery of digital to the new generations, making them able to respond to the challenges of a rapidly changing world, which increasingly requires mental agility, transversal skills and an active role for young people. As educators, they cannot ignore the fact that it is necessary to move competently, not only from a technical point of view, in order not to live as outcasts. To do so, it is necessary to have a Digital Culture.

The online courses that will be available on the platform cover the various aspects (architecture, technical aspects, privacy, security, etc.) of Digital Culture and offer teachers tools and skills to deal with these issues in the classroom with greater security and awareness, adding teaching and adult experience to the mere knowledge which students partly have.

This process may favour the transfer of the elements of Digital Culture to the students, not necessarily through *standard* educational paths but through reflections on life on the Internet, which for the *millennials* is as obvious as the *real* one, guided by the teacher, or by incorporating digital culture as a *hidden* message in the educational contents.

3.2 Target

The digital skills required by teachers (and the training courses addressed to them) exclusively concern the use of technology in teaching, but not the knowledge of the digital world, made of course of technology, but also of theory, relationships and behaviour. Those who have these skills consider them a personal, rather than a professional, baggage. And yet, in every school, those who have this background become a point of reference for colleagues who find it hard to keep up with technological innovation.

However, and noticeably, teachers can authoritatively transfer knowledge and skills only if they master the subject. It is, therefore, important that teachers move with ease in the world of the Internet (and the technologies and tools connected to it), in order to be able to guide their students in this field too.

This need, keenly felt as digital, is transversal to every other teaching subject and therefore affects every teacher, not only those involved in STEMs (Science, Technology, Engineering and Mathematics), and is also transversal to every school level, from primary to secondary, since, nowadays, even the youngest children are familiar with the Internet and technology.

As we have analysed in the previous section, statistics describe a digital shortcoming within the teaching staff and it is thus necessary to fill this gap. For these considerations, we believe that the main target group is teachers of all school levels. In fact, basic content and more specialised content, from which teachers can choose, will be available. Initially, we will propose some paths of reflection aimed at high school teachers, because the discussion on these issues with adolescents aged between 13 and 18 is particularly challenging and demanding and cannot be superficially approached. Moreover, this priority derives from the fact that high school students are the ones who most urgently need to acquire tools and skills on these issues so that they can better orient themselves in the choice of a possible university faculty or work sector.

Subsequently, in the development of the platform, we will propose pathways oriented to middle school teachers and finally to primary school teachers. As a secondary target we will identify students and, in this case too, priority will be given to high school students, because they are the protagonists of work experience at the end of their school career. Identifying this target is possible because courses are not oriented towards teaching, but towards the acquisition of skills and cultural deepening of digital issues. The material we will provide will therefore be suitable to train this young audience as well.

3.3 Partners

The project involves two institutes of the National Research Council of Italy, the Institute of Informatics and Telematics (IIT-CNR) in Pisa and the Institute for Educational Technologies (ITD-CNR) in Genoa. Both institutes have been providing training to teachers and students of the Italian school on many Digital Culture issues for many years. Research and training activities are provided for by the Statute of the CNR and are decided by the individual Institutes according to their own skills.

Namely, the IIT-CNR[18] provides experience and skills in the network and digital sector, which derive from its specific research activities and the presence in the Institute of Registro.it[19], the registry of .it domains that the Institute has managed since its establishment in 1987.

The ITD-CNR[20] currently is the only Italian public scientific institute entirely dedicated to research on educational technologies. This strong characterisation on a specific research sector is one of the strengths of the Institute, and it has made it a centre of competence and a reference point both in Italy and Europe. ITD-CNR provides experience and expertise in the field of teaching, tools and methodologies dedicated to it.

Researchers, technologists and technicians from the two Institutes participate in the project.

The IIT-CNR also provides technical skills for the design, implementation and management of the IT platform, while ITD-CNR is involved in the design phase, thanks to the experience gained in the implementation of other training platforms (see e.g. sd2.itd.cnr.it/training).

4 Educational Programme

Some of the existing training e-portals for teachers offer courses on the use of digital technology in teaching, but none of them is focused on Digital Culture. Instead, the innovation of *Presente Digitale* lies on the topics, closely linked to Digital Culture and the net. The main addressed topics are the followings:

- Cybersecurity.
- Internet for educational purposes (e.g., Open Educational Resources, Massive Open Online Courses).
- Computational thinking and computer programming.
- Privacy protection in the age of the Internet of Things, Big Data and Artificial Intelligence.

Teaching is realized via Moodle[21], a free and open-source Learning Management System (LMS) that can be used i) to organize learning courses in a highly customizable way and ii) to publish teaching materials in a safe and protected environment, accessible only to registered users. It will be possible to use each course in two different ways:

- Free fruition (time-independent, without the issue of credits): the courses are based on video lectures, in-depth articles, reference materials.

[18] https://www.iit.cnr.it.
[19] http://registro.it.
[20] https://www.itd.cnr.it.
[21] https://moodle.org.

- Assisted/guided use (time-dependent, with the issue of credits): the courses are based on video lectures, reference materials, tutoring activities (exercises, online workshops), webinars, evaluation tests and a final test to obtain training credits. This type of fruition implies the attribution of 'training credits' and therefore an evaluation of the achievement of the training objectives.

At the current status of the project, two courses have been finalized, namely the Cybersecurity course and the course of Educational use of Internet Resources. These courses, however, are not still available for delivery, as they are in the testing phase. In fact, all courses are first delivered to a small sample of people, to assess their impact, results and appreciation, and then they will be made available to everyone.

4.1 Courses Design

When dealing with the design of online training courses, we actually refer to a variety of design activities:

- The entire educational path.
- The individual training modules.
- Teaching materials (e-content).
- Online activities (e-tivity).
- Evaluation tools.

Due to the complexity of this process, it is convenient to split it into two phases, *macro-design* and *micro-design*, respectively.

The objective of the macro-design phase is the overall design of the training course. In this phase, the general aims, the main topics to be addressed, the type of teaching approach (on-site, distance, blended), a first hypothesis of its possible modularization and the related timing of delivery and/or use are defined. Therefore, at this stage, an overview of the course is drafted, based on which the micro-design phase will be then developed.

During this phase it is necessary to consider some key elements, such as the audience, the project constraints, the macro-objectives to be achieved, the specific topics to cover, the general evaluation criteria, etc. Once these elements have been defined, it is possible to outline a first hypothesis of course modularization, in which, generally, each single module is matched to one of the disciplinary macro-topics.

Once the macro-design phase is finished, we can deal with each single part of the course (modules and topics), detailing and modelling it according to the specific educational objectives that we intend to achieve. Basically, we move on to the micro-design phase, in which we define in detail and develop everything that characterizes the course, from the specific educational objectives, to the related study materials, teaching activities and evaluation methods.

This is the most complex and substantial phase of the entire design process; thus, it may be useful to divide it into two sub-phases, which are referred to as educational micro-design and e-content/e-tivity micro-design. The educational micro-design implies the detailed definition of the structure of each single module, while e-content/e-tivity micro-design consists in the definition of the didactic materials and of the collaborative online interaction, respectively.

4.2 Example Course: Cybersecurity

One of the first courses available in *Presente Digitale* is the Cybersecurity course, which has been designed, developed and teached by researchers of IIT-CNR, in particular by representatives of the Trustworthy and Secure Future Internet team. Nowadays, the term Cybersecurity is widely used to identify several facets related to information security. In fact, Cybersecurity is intended as the set of means and technologies aimed at protecting information systems [9]. The aim of the course is to introduce Cybersecurity definitions and concepts, by describing some methods for the protection of computer systems and data and by showing their applications in specific scenarios. This course presents:

- An overview of Cybersecurity concepts.
- Information protection techniques, such as pills of cryptography [10].
- Techniques for accessing and using online resources and information in a safe and private way [12].
- Cloud and mobile security issues and known techniques for their solutions [13].
- Techniques to test the security of a system through penetration testing, with practical examples from the automotive world [6].
- Methods for the analysis of risks in a cyber-system [5].
- Attacks on material and moral goods of the individual, due to a malicious use of social networks (e.g.., fake news and hate speech) [7,8].

The course features video lectures of about 6–12 min, readings, documentary research, discussion groups. During the course, self-evaluation tests are proposed. The duration is estimated in 25 h, spread over five weeks, divided as follows: 6 h of traditional teaching, 10 h of educational activities, 9 h of individual study.

At the beginning and at the end of the course, two questionnaires will be proposed to the participants, in order to explore the expectations and the evaluation of the course, respectively. A final examination is foreseen for the assignment of credits, and it will include both multiple-choice questions and open questions.

Figure 3 shows a screenshot taken from the Moodle platform, which highlights the dashboard of a user. From this page it is possible to access the subscribed courses.

The course has been organized in 5 different modules, and each module includes 7–10 activities. Each module generally follows the same structure: in particular, it begins with a brief introductory video lecture, which lasts a couple of minutes and includes an overview of the topics covered in the module, the presentation of the key concepts, and the activities that will be addressed. Likewise, each module ends with a concluding video lecture, which summarizes the topics covered and gives a very short preview of the contents of the next module.

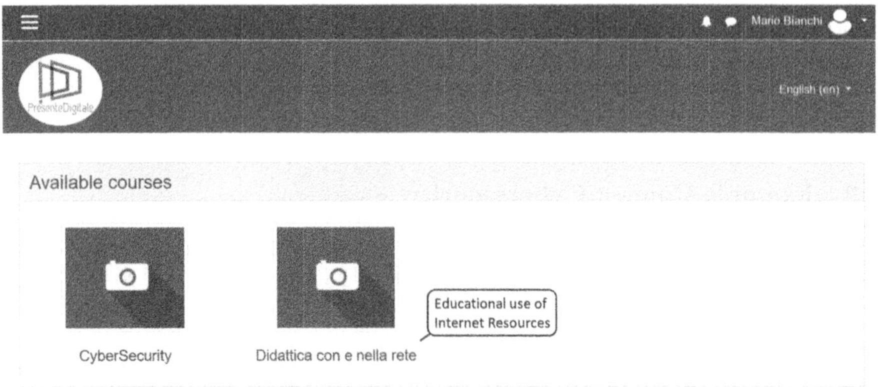

Fig. 3. *Presente Digitale*: the Moodle dashboard of the user.

The remaining activities are also implemented by video lectures, and they are supported by a set of learning resources, assessment exercises and tests. Learning resources are provided in the form of video lectures, video-clips, text and multimedia documents, tutorials, self-evaluation tests, and various resources available on the cloud. An example screenshot is provided in Fig. 4, which shows the presentation of Module 4 of the course: Vulnerability Analysis and Risk Management.

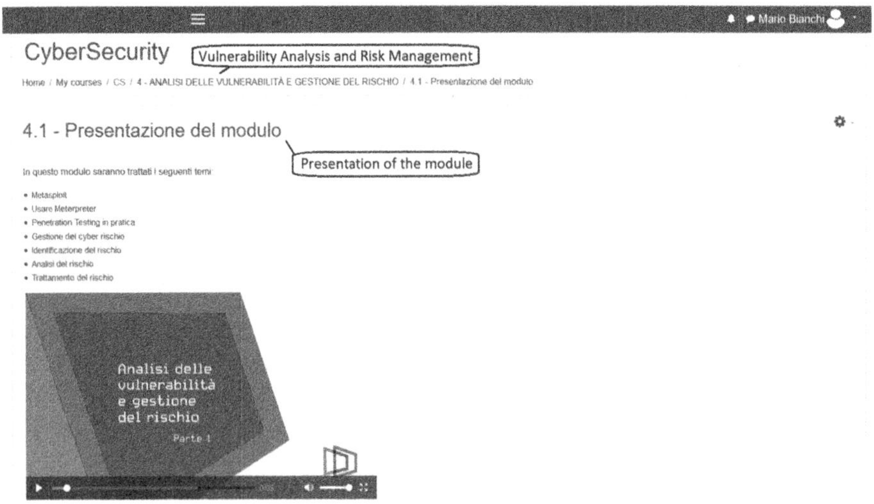

Fig. 4. *Presente Digitale*: introduction to a module of the course.

As assessment instruments, Moodle workshops will be available for peer-review activities, along with self-assessment activities for peer discussion through forums, and a FAQ service.

The macro-design scheme of the course is reported in Table 1. For the reader's convenience, it has been translated in English, while the original scheme has been developed in Italian, due to the nature of the project.

Table 1. Macro-design scheme of the Cybersecurity course.

Module 1	**Introduction to Cybersecurity**
	Activity 1: Introduction to the module
	Activity 2: Introduction to information security
	Activity 3: Cyber threats
	Activity 4: Cybersecurity properties
	Activity 5: Individual study and documentary research
	Activity 6: Exercise
	Activity 7: Recap and preview
Module 2	**Cryptography and communication protocols**
	Activity 1: Introduction to the module
	Activity 2: Cryptography: introduction and historical notes
	Activity 3: Symmetric key encryption
	Activity 4: Asymmetric key encryption
	Activity 5: Protocols for confidentiality
	Activity 6: Authentication protocols
	Activity 7: Individual study and documentary research
	Activity 8: Exercise
	Activity 9: Recap and preview
Module 3	**Access Control and Usage Control**
	Activity 1: Introduction to the module
	Activity 2: Access control
	Activity 3: Usage control
	Activity 4: Writing Access and Usage Control policies
	Activity 5: Application scenarios
	Activity 6: Individual study and documentary research
	Activity 7: Exercise
	Activity 8: Recap and preview
Module 4	**Vulnerability Analysis and Risk Management**
	Activity 1: Introduction to the module
	Activity 2: Metasploit
	Activity 3: Using Meterpreter
	Activity 4: Penetration Testing in practice
	Activity 5: Cyber Risk Management
	Activity 6: Risk identification
	Activity 7: Risk analysis
	Activity 8: Risk treatment
	Activity 9: Exercise
	Activity 10: Recap and preview
Module 5	**Security Applications**
	Activity 1: Introduction to the module
	Activity 2: Security in cloud systems (part 1)
	Activity 3: Security in cloud systems (part 2)
	Activity 4: Security in mobile systems (part 1)
	Activity 5: Security in mobile systems (part 2)
	Activity 6: Security in Social Media: introduction and examples
	Activity 7: Security in Social Media: countermeasures
	Activity 8: Exercise
	Activity 9: Course conclusion

5 Conclusions and Future Perspectives

Ensuring the possibility to do online training is one of the greatest modern challenges to spread the use and culture of digital in schools. Moreover, as recent events have shown, having suitable, flexible and easily accessible tools for all possible users is a real need for modern education.

In this paper, we have described *Presente Digitale*, an ambitious Italian project for the creation of an online education system on Digital Culture, dedicated first of all to teachers and secondly to their students, and which allows them to receive free online training on Digital Culture issues. The courses currently planned deal with topics related to the Internet and ICT, such as network history, information and device security, data privacy on the Internet and artificial intelligence, and so forth.

The project was created to fill teachers' gaps on digital issues and to ensure that they can effectively transmit this knowledge to their students. This will give young people the opportunity to integrate their previous knowledge with the 'teacher's point of view' and, above all, to have a more conscious approach to the labour market.

The project is still under development, since the finalized courses are still in the testing phase, at the end of which they will be made available. Future developments will certainly include the integration of further courses related to the Digital world. Future perspectives include the possibility of integrating techniques to analyse the data gathered from the Moodle platform, both to assess users satisfaction and to monitor the commitment and engagement of participants during lessons.

References

1. Digital Skills & Jobs. https://ec.europa.eu/digital-single-market/en/policies/digital-skills. Accessed 12 June 2020
2. Education and Training Monitor EU analysis. https://ec.europa.eu/education/resources-and-tools/document-library/education-and-training-monitor-eu-analysis-volume-1-2019. Accessed 09 Sept 2020
3. OECD-Talis 2018 Report. https://www.oecd.org/education/talis/TALIS2018_CN_ITA_it.pdf. Accessed 09 Sept 2020
4. Piano nazionale scuola digitale. https://www.miur.gov.it/scuola-digitale. Accessed 12 June 2020. (In Italian)
5. Amutio, M., Candau, J., Mañas, J.: MAGERIT–version 3.0: methodology for information systems risk analysis and management. Ministry of Finance and Public Administration, Madrid, Spain (2014)
6. Bella, G., Biondi, P., Costantino, G., Matteucci, I.: Are you secure in your car? (poster). In: 12th Conference on Security and Privacy in Wireless and Mobile Networks, WiSec, pp. 308–309 (2019)
7. Caldarelli, G., De Nicola, R., Del Vigna, F., Petrocchi, M., Saracco, F.: The role of bot squads in the political propaganda on Twitter. Commun. Phys. **3**(1), 1–15 (2020)

8. Del Vigna, F., Cimino, A., Dell'Orletta, F., Petrocchi, M., Tesconi, M.: Hate me, hate me not: hate speech detection on Facebook. In: First Italian Conference on Cybersecurity (ITASEC 2017), Venice, Italy, 17–20 January 2017, pp. 86–95 (2017)
9. Jang-Jaccard, J., Nepal, S.: A survey of emerging threats in cybersecurity. J. Comput. Syst. Sci. **80**(5), 973–993 (2014)
10. Katz, J., Lindell, Y.: Introduction to Modern Cryptography. CRC Press, Boca Raton (2014)
11. Miller, V.: Understanding Digital Culture. SAGE Publications, Thousand Oaks (2020)
12. Sandhu, R.S., Samarati, P.: Access control: principle and practice. IEEE Commun. Mag. **32**(9), 40–48 (1994)
13. Suo, H., Liu, Z., Wan, J., Zhou, K.: Security and privacy in mobile cloud computing. In: 9th Wireless Communications and Mobile Computing Conference (IWCMC), pp. 655–659. IEEE (2013)

Online Learning Strategies and Resources: e-Tutoring, Communities, Webinar and Tools

E-Tutoring in Higher Education: A Case Study

Paolo Raviolo(✉), Salvatore Messina, Irene Mauro, and Marco Rondonotti

eCampus University, Novedrate, CO, Italy
paolo.raviolo@uniecampus.it

Abstract. The present work is focused on the key skills' analysis of the e-tutor in Ecampus online University on the bases of the reference models described in literature. The analysis is based on a validated questionnaire translated in Italian and submitted to a sample of 220 ToL of the university. The specific objective was: (a) map the tasks, roles and duties of e-tutors; (b) validate a survey tool that on a quantitative basis that can detect the e-tutor skills; (c) improve the TOL and TD skills of the eCampus university, thanks to the data collected. The results show how the role of e-tutor in this University is hybrid, it does not imply a specific disciplinary competence but presupposes a pedagogical background linked to the actual design of the student's learning experience within the online university. The development of these skills rely largely on day by day practice, through a more or less implicit process of reflection and, implicitly, the reference to an informal community that offers guidance and support to novices.

Keywords: e-tutoring · Higher education

1 Context of the Research

According to the available public data (data.ustat.miur.it) published by the Ministry for University and Research (MIUR), students enrolled in an online degree course in the academic year 2018–2019 (most recent data available) were more than 113 thousand, approximately 6.6% of the total number of university students in Italy. The data extracted from the Degree Course Quality indicators made available by Cineca (www.cineca.it) for Quality Assurance Assessment and updated in June 2020, tell us that there are more than 17,000 enrolled in the Degree Courses of the Ecampus Telematic University.

The present work is focused on the key skills' analysis of the e-tutor in one of the 11 Italian online universities, eCampus University, which is one of the biggest online universities in Italy with more than 25000 students and 54 degree courses. The eCampus Telematic University offers 49 degree courses, of which 31 three-year courses and 18 master's courses, as well as 5 innovative degree courses. The degree courses are divided into 5 faculties: Economics, Law, Engineering, Humanities and Psychology [1].

The setting of the Telematic University is characterized by a precise classification of didactic contents: in fact they are organized into "didattica erogativa" and "didattica interattiva".

L. S. Agrati et al. (Eds.): HELMeTO 2020, CCIS 1344, pp. 289–299, 2021.
https://doi.org/10.1007/978-3-030-67435-9_22

The first level, didattica erogativa (DE), is the complex of contents similar to frontal teaching in the classroom, focused on the presentation/illustration of the contents by the teacher: audio-video recordings, web conferences, courses or similar events.

A second level is based instead on interactive teaching (didattica interattiva-DI), or the complex of:

- Teacher's presence, usually through demonstrations or additional explanations in FAQ, mailing lists or Web forums (demonstrations or operational suggestions on problem-solving, exercises etc.).
- Short interventions by the participants (for example in a discussion or a group: web forums, blogs, wikis).
- Structured e-tivities (individual or in a group) through reports, exercises, case studies, problem-solving, web searches, projects, production of artifacts created by students, with related feedback.
- Evaluation forms such as surveys or tests.

The tutorial function plays an essential role in education based on online distance learning (ODL), as well as in education in general, including adult education.

In fact, knowledge is built in a context showing significant analogies with lifelong learning [2], in which the relationship between learner-tutor-teacher becomes fundamental. The e-tutor is therefore understood as the one who «interacts directly with learners to support their learning process when they are separated from the tutor in time and place for some or all of these direct interactions» [3].

At eCampus Telematic University, the tutor plays a key role in building/creating/developing the student's learning path, especially considering that the total number of students enrolled at eCampus Telematic University is approximately 25.000, distributed among the 54 degree courses on the educational offer.

Of the total number of students, many have a previous record, and some of their credits are often recognized, but each one's new academic record needs to be further personalized. The enrollment procedures and schedules are different from traditional universities. Students can enroll anytime during the academic year and start attending their degree courses.

This is one of the reasons why e-tutors must have specific skills in order to manage a personalized approach to each student, building together a specific study course which is suitable for their needs.

Considering the number of students and of teaching courses, the University provides the presence of two types of tutors to support students and teachers, the so-called online tutors (TOL) and the disciplinary tutors (TD).

A specific number of students is assigned to each TOL, whose task is to follow the students' entire study course, monitoring, accompanying and supporting them in planning their studies, exam enrollment and interaction with teachers and University.

The e-tutors have both orientation and monitoring functions and technical support functions (introduction and familiarization of the student with the technological environment, access registration, saving, storage of materials, ongoing technical assistance).

He contributes to the continuous improvement of teaching quality as well as of the service offered to students during their studies.

The TD is a qualified expert in the discipline who supports and adds his own functions to those of the teacher in charge of teaching, contributes to the continuous improvement of the quality of teaching, of the service offered to students and of student learning, in order to guarantee high qualitative standards and reduce dropout rates, improve the average length of studies and contain the number of out-of-course students.

The TDs collaborate with the professors of the SSD they belong to for the correct preparation of teaching materials and contribute to the performance of Interactive Didactic (DI) activities and related to learning in situation; in particular, they carry out teaching activities in virtual classrooms or in any case through the use of the University platform and favor the proper performance and monitoring of the distance learning activities. Furthermore, they support students in understanding the contents and in the development of papers and exercises, encouraging and supporting forms of online collaboration based on synchronous and asynchronous tools.

2 Objectives and Methods

The university context presented, and also the analysis of the literature on the figure of the e-tutor, allows us to attempt a first mapping of e-tutoring skills in the eCampus Telematic University with respect to reference models [3–6], referred to the specificity of Higher Education. It is assumed that understanding the importance of the roles of the e-tutor and identifying their skills is fundamental for the success of e-learning solutions [7] in order to ensure an effective teaching-learning process.

With the research we want in particular to pursue three aims:

a) map the tasks, roles and duties of TOLs and TDs, in order to understand the different levels of skills that will occupy different areas of e-tutoring [4] required of the two categories of tutors present in eCampus university;
b) validate a survey tool that on a quantitative basis that can evaluate the skills of the various tutor roles useful at national and international level;
c) improve the TOL and TD skills of the eCampus university, thanks to the data collected.

The choice is to proceed using an approach attributable to mixed methods [8]. To pursue the aims just mentioned, the following tools have therefore been prepared:

1) a survey of TOL skills through the validation and adaptation in Italian of the tool prepared by De Metz and Bezuidenhout [9] to collect data;
2) analysis of the job description assigned to TDs and TOLs;
3) focus group and interview for the detection of professional skills of TD and TOL.

In this research we will focus on the analysis of the data obtained from the administration of the questionnaire conceived by De Metz and Bezuidenhout [9], a tool that investigates the perceptions of competence of the e-tutor in higher education contexts

[10]. The main purpose and results of this study are referred to the perceptions of e-tutors about their roles and the competences possessed. More specifically, how e-tutors perceived their job roles in terms of time, importance and workload; what specific skills e-tutors need to fulfill their role in universities and to what extent e-tutors perceive they have the necessary skills to successfully fulfill these central and peripheral roles. These objectives are strictly connected to the areas present in the questionnaire. The tool is made up of 28 items, almost all corresponding to closed responses on a likert scale with 5 responses. The survey is structured in five areas: on: (a) demographic information; (b) perception of e-tutors' general work roles, (c) concepts of effective tutoring, and (d) perceptions of e-tutor's central and peripheral roles and competencies. In Area B of the questionnaire were included some questions which examine the importance and utility of tutoring's role to provide guide and support to the students in the academic fields. These above-mentioned characteristics relate to the e-tutors' perception compared to their positions and the importance of their role for other members of the university. In Area C of the questionnaire there are the most relevant e-tutors activities. To define the different roles that e-tutors can play in the academic contexts were used the classifications, which is composed of three levels [11]: 1) cognitive, to support and develop learning process through course materials and learning object; 2) affective, to create a calm setting that supports each student to improve their feelings of self-worth; 3) systemic, to realize strong administrative procedures and ensure school information management system as clear as possible. We referred to eight significant roles which e-tutor can play [12]: technologist; manager/administrator; advisor/counsellor; assessor; content facilitator; researcher; and designer. The best representation of these roles defines eleven main roles of blended learning that e-tutor can play [3].

Three open-ended questions were also included in the questionnaire to enable a deeper level of information sharing and analysis. Interviewees were asked to discuss what factors impacted their effectiveness as an e-tutor and which were the difficulties preventing them from being an effective e-tutor, and if they had any other comments on their e-tutoring experience at the eCampus Telematic University.

This questionnaire was translated and adapted into Italian by our research team and administered to a sample of 220 TOL of the eCampus telematic university, not corresponding to the total number of TOLs used by the university to support all students, but it is of the TOL inside the University which follow on average a few students (25 students); the other TOLs carry out this activity at affiliated training agencies, organized independently.

3 Results

1. The Sample

The questionnaire was distributed through the *QuestionPro* online platform to the entire group of 220 TOLs of eCampus. Our sample consists of the 130 interviewees who completed the compilation correctly. Of these, the substantial majority are female (78%, while only 22% are male) and the average age corresponds to 39 years. As regards the degree of education, 69% declare that they have a master's degree, 23% a three-year or single-cycle degree, 6% have obtained a Master's degree (1st or 2nd level), while only 2% have a doctorate of research. The sample seems to be equally distributed even though there is a slight decrease in the engineering department: in fact 22% holds the role of e-tutor for the law department, 21% for psychology, 20% for literature, 18% for economics, while 15% for engineering.

2. Perceived Importance of the Duties Required by the Job Position

Interviewees show a high level of attachment to the role and university institution they represent. In response to the question «How important is e-tutor's work for you», 68% of the sample assigns the maximum value of 5 (on a scale of 1 to 5) and 26% chooses the value of 4, signaling attachment to the role 67% say that it is important to represent the University, showing the awareness of how the role is decisive both for the affiliation of students to the university and for their success in the academic career: «The first moment of meeting with the student is fundamental to create a feeling and an important didactic link» (cod_93902[1]).

An interesting fact emerges from the item that asks TOLs to express themselves in relation to their attachment to the University organization. The average value chosen in response to the question «How would you define your relationship with the University» is 4.08 (value expressed on a scale from 1 to 5); 39% of the sample assigns the maximum value indicating that they live a «Very good» relationship, and 35% chooses the value of 4. This data seems to be in contrast with what emerges from the answers to the questions «To what extent do you think that University does appreciate your work as an e-tutor?» and To what extent do you think the university is attentive to your needs?»; compared to the first question only 17% choose value 5, 35% choose value 4, 25% choose 3, 18% choose 2, and 5% choose the minimum value. The values are lowered again slightly for the second question, since only 12% choose the value 5, 32% choose the value 4, 37% the 3, 15% the 2, and 4% choose the value minimum.

With respect to the three questions, therefore, we can say that we pass from an average value of 4.08 to those of 3.39 and 3.36; even if it remains overall not sufficient, there is a significant decrease. The data seems to suggest that TOLs appreciate the quality of the relationships that are established with colleagues, but that at the same time they struggle to see their role recognized within the organization. In fact, if there is no lack of statements that emphasize the presence of a «*dynamic and stimulating work environment and cooperation between colleagues*» (code_90368) as a value, there are also those that do not hide the problems: «*For our professionalism, commitment and importance we should be gratified and loyal at work level in a more stable way*» (code_95705). The overall picture remains that of professionals aware of their abilities, despite knowing that: «*Teamwork in the office and in eCampus in general, with the secretariat, the technicians, the area managers is fundamental every day and in perspective to always improve in future: if I work well it is not only because I am good, but also thanks to those who work with me and vice versa*» (cod_28419).

It has been asked to the e-tutors to express themselves in relation to the roles that see them most demanding in carrying out their work; interviewees declare that they are

[1] This section contains the identification codes that the *QuestionPro* platform automatically assigns to interviewees.

particularly so by assignments that ask to be «Pastoral» towards students. The technical, informative and administrative role follows, again highlighting how TOLs spend many resources in providing concrete support for the most bureaucratic and organizational issues. The «Pedagogical», «Social» and «Managerial» roles remain in the background (Fig. 2).

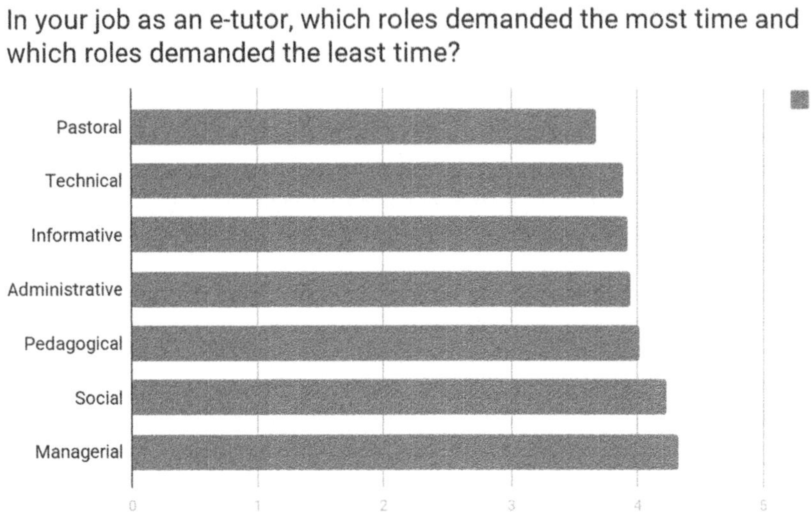

Fig. 1. Questionnaire: item n.9

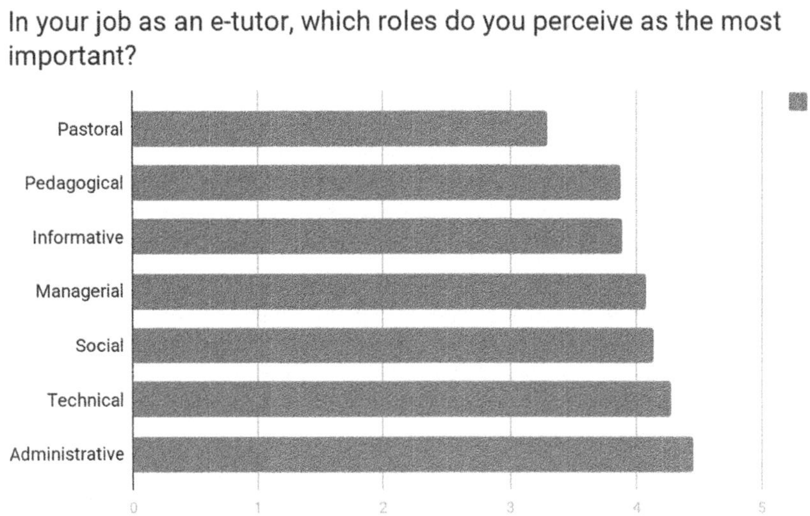

Fig. 2. Questionnaire: item n.10

The following table instead highlights how interviewees perceive the importance of the tasks involved in their work (Fig. 2).

Being «Pastoral» remains in first place, showing once again how TOLs interpret coaching for students, as is also apparent from the words of an interviewee: *«I try to be available when students contact me»* (cod_49397). This data is confirmed in the choices of interviewees relating to the specific item «I am always available when students want help»; always moving on a scale from 1 to 5, the full majority (67%) chooses the maximum value, and a substantial part (28%) chooses the value 4. The remaining 5% is distributed over the other three possible options, but none of the TOL responds by attributing the minimum value.

The relational dimension is also present in the second choice, that of the «Pedagogical» role; the «Managerial» roles goes from last to fourth place. TOLs have the availability and the desire to get involved at this level, since they perceive their contribution as relevant: *«It would be good to have feedback from us, because we are the first contact which interact with students, before making organizational decisions»* (cod_25973). Therefore, the discrepancy between what TOLs feel called to do and what they feel as functional to the success of their professional commitment seems significant.

3. Perceived Competence

From the data collected through the battery of items dedicated to the perception of competence of TOLs in relation to the required tasks, it appears that on average interviewees feel that they have a level of competence rather relevant for their duties. An element of complexity seems to be the fact that *«not all subjects are covered, therefore, in order to guarantee the service, it is pushed to cover lessons in subjects that are not completely mastered ... making the tutor uncomfortable and reducing the effectiveness for the student»* (cod_24405). The university's attention to the academic path of TOL is also emphasized by those who say that *«[...] initial training should be more dictated on the disciplinary sector and divided by skills»* (cod_95862).

A significant element is the fact that the three roles towards which interviewees declare greater competence are precisely on the transversal ones; in fact, the most frequently chosen options are: «I provide timely feedback»; «I provide students with advice on an individual basis»; «I see my role as an e-tutor as a friend until the end of the course, walking with the student-participants and learning with them». It is relevant how the TOL's taking charge of students is seen as an important dimension, which also leads to the generation of friendships.

As regards, instead, the roles for which the respondents perceive they do not have the appropriate skills are the specific ones, for which an activation from a cognitive/didactic point of view is also required: «I am involved in the creation of new relevant knowledge»; «I manage communication and create communities, in online discussions»; «Project useful learning activities (pre-course activities)».

From this point of view, TOLs do not feel they have the necessary skills to support students in reflecting on learning activities and on the results obtained.

As the graphic below shows, to express the degree of agreement on «I encourage discussion among students», on a scale of 1 to 5, only 19% of interviewees attributes the maximum value of 5, 31% chooses the value 4, 29% gives the value 3, 18% chooses the value 2, and 3% the 1. Even if the values are positive, in reality the average value remains among the lowest of the whole battery of questions in the item. The data collected suggest that the interviewees' work does not support the exchange of information between students, especially those related to disciplinary knowledge; it seems that TOLs do not perceive the role as an opportunity offered to students for the development of collaborative learning. The role of the e-tutor in collaborative contexts is very important because it is a key figure for synchronous and asynchronous communication between teachers and the group of students. This type of mediation requires having the necessary skills to organize and monitor the normal course of teaching activities. In addition, the lack of aptitude towards enhancing collaboration within a group of students in carrying out a task, also affects the ability to feel part of the university community (Fig. 3).

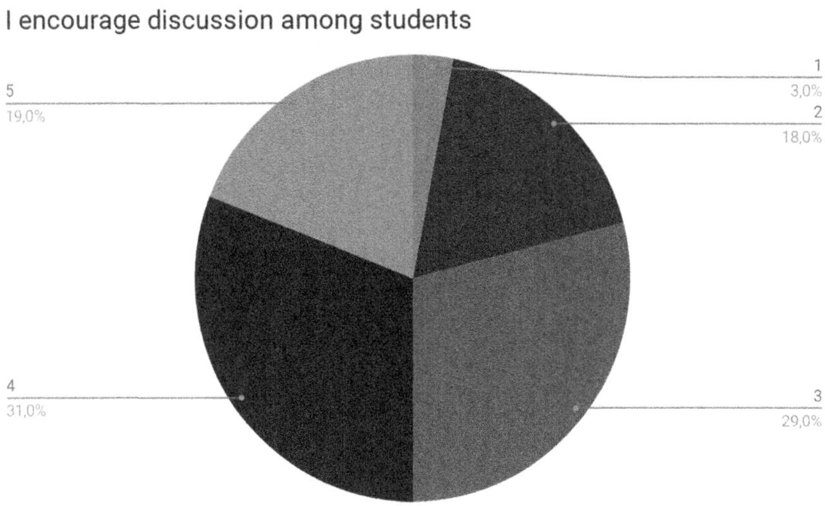

Fig. 3. Questionnaire: item n.12

The attitude of interviewees, however, remains available in getting involved in professional growth paths: *«[...] constant updates should be done in a better and more complete way»* (cod_92688).

4. Factors that Influence the Effectiveness of the E-Tutor

The factors which are indicated by the sample as important for the effectiveness of their work, can be basically divided into two groups.

The first highlights in particular the professionalism that implies the quality of the preparation provided by the initial training course; the reference to the skills acquired through work experience seems particularly interesting: it highlights the fact that they register reflexivity as not only effective but also practiced. Another fact that often returns is that of continuing education: TOLs not only perceive the importance of continuous updating but also show interest and proactiveness in performing their role in the best possible way.

In addition to 39% which indicates professionalism, there is a fact that amazes for its relevance: with the same percentage, empathy is indicated as an element of effectiveness of one's work at the university. The data is significant as it is not only an indicator of the skills necessary for the counseling offered to the student (that is to say what is the basis of the possibility of establishing an «affective-emotional attachment to me»), but also in terms of affiliation with the institution: *«We are the main interface of the University with users: over the years it has been created an excellent attraction for friends and relatives of my students who have signed up asking to be followed specifically by me»* (cod_93902).

5. Difficulties that Prevent You from Being an Effective E-Tutor
The 49.5% of respondents also wanted to report some critical issues that tend to compromise the effectiveness of the work of TOLs. If 30.5% refers to problems relating to the IT infrastructure made available (underlining, for example, how *«the equipment at the workplace is insufficient»* (cod_88457) and the presence of *«technical problems that frequently prevent the linear use of the platform, in the manner we illustrated at the time of presentation»* (cod_25973)), 45.8% report the presence of difficulties attributable to the organization of the university. For the most part, these are obstacles dictated by bureaucratic complexity, the slowness of communication by the university and the lack of direct connection with the teachers; the impression is that there are too many gears to move to solve a problem. This forces us to ask for the intervention of other professionals of the university (such as the secretariat), already totally overburdened with other tasks; the result is that it is not possible to interact quickly and correctly either internally at the university or with students. Finally, a significant number of interviewees emphasize the request to follow an excessive number of people.

Overall, however, the attitude with which these reports are made maintains great confidence in the university, as shown by these two comments relating to the research of our team: *«I am very happy that this questionnaire has arrived: it is as if we were finally leaving from the gray area»* (cod_93902), *«I hope in a moment of sharing with the TOLs the study and the results that will emerge»* (cod_67387) this means not only that the movement of the university towards them is understood and appreciated but there is all the willingness to collaborate to overcome the main difficulties. A decisive attitude, that of TOLs, which challenges and deserves to be strongly taken into consideration.

4 Conclusions

E-tutors in higher education play a key role in facilitating the learning process for students. They provide a crucial support to student-academic organization interaction in order to ensure their educational success. Their main role is focused on preventing the student from feeling isolated and with the aim of bridging the gap between students, student and teacher, student and university [10, 13, 14]. Ideally the e-tutor system should provide a sense of community, where students can meet and feel part of a larger academic community. This aspect is fundamental to minimize the feeling of detachment that is common among students who attend online universities.

In the case examined, the Ecampus University, e-tutors perceive their role as central to the university and see it above all as a role of guidance, guidance and facilitation for students. The key skills of e-tutors in this context are mainly on the technical infrastructure, on the organization of the university and on the social dimension that are important to manage effectively the relationship with students. The role of tutors in this university is not designed to provide for a specific disciplinary support to students, even if each tutor operates mainly on a faculty, they do not necessarily have an academic background on topics relevant for the faculty degree courses.

Initial training and ongoing training, alongside continuous reflection on one's professional experience, emerge as important elements for fulfilling the role of e-tutor in a satisfactory way. On the other hand, many e-tutors highlight the lack of disciplinary skills as an obstacle to the optimal performance of their role, this can probably be related to a non-optimal information to students and tutors themselves about the actual role of e-tutors in this organization, or even to the actual non-optimal coverage of disciplinary tutoring roles in the organizational model of the university.

The organizational complexity and technical problems of the IT infrastructure often emerge among the elements that obstacle the performance of an effective online tutoring role, even if it is precisely in these cases that the tutor's role of facilitator has the opportunity to be deployed in a particularly effective way.

Overall, the e-tutoring model promoted by the university focuses on the transversal dimension linked to the use of the technological infrastructure and the organization and administrative processes of the university. On the other hand, while the strictly pedagogical dimension remains in the background, it is precisely the tutors who contribute substantially to the deployment of the real student's learning experience, supporting students in the construction of the study plan, suggesting the chronological articulation of courses and exams, offering support to complete the e-activities and in the final exam preparation.

It is therefore a hybrid role, which does not imply a specific disciplinary competence but presupposes a pedagogical background linked to the actual design of the student's learning experience within the online university. The development of these skills in this context rely largely on day by day practice, through a more or less implicit process of reflection and, implicitly, the reference to an informal community that offers guidance and support to novices.

Probably a further phase of the research could proceed on two directions: (1) a further in-depth study on the existence and nature of an existing community among online tutors will be able to provide a further level of detail on the specific skills of these professional figures and on the methods and practices that develop and sediment them; (2) e recognition of the space of disciplinary competences as a common ground among e-tutors, academic tutors and teachers, to better understand whether there are overlapping spaces or spaces not covered by their respective roles.

Note about the author: Irene Mauro: Context of the research; Salvatore Messina: Objectives and methods; Paolo Raviolo: Conclusions; Marco Rondonotti: Results.

References

1. Raviolo, P.: Online higher education teaching practices. In: IC4E Tokyo 2019 Proceedings, pp. 79–84. ACM, Tokyo (2019)
2. Greco, G.: L'apprendimento nell'era della connettività: una riflessione sociologica al confine tra comunicazione ed educazione. In: Scarcelli, C.M., Stella, R. (eds.) Digital literacy e

giovani. Strumenti per comprendere, misurare e intervenire, pp. 21–31, Franco Angeli, Milano (2017)
3. Denis, B., Watland, P., Pirotte, S., Verday, N.: Roles and competencies of the e-tutor. In: Networked Learning 2004: A Research Based Conference on Networked Learning and Lifelong Learning: Proceedings of the Fourth International Conference, pp. 150–157. Lancaster Press, Lancaster (2004)
4. Salmon, G.: E-Moderating: The Key to Teaching and Learning Online. Psychology Press, England (2003)
5. Kemshal-Bell, G.: The Online Teacher. TAFE NSW Information Technology, New South Wales (2001)
6. Berge, Z.L.: Facilitating computer conferencing: recommendations from the field. Educ. Technol. **35**(1), 22–30 (1995)
7. McPherson, M., Nunes, M.B.: The role of tutors as an integral part of online learning support. Eur. J. Open Distance E-learn. **7**(1) (2004)
8. Creswell, J., Plano Clark, V.: Designing and Conducting Mixed Methods Research. SAGE Publications, Thousand Oaks (2017)
9. De Metz, N., Bezuidenhout, A.: An importance–competence analysis of the roles and competencies of e-tutors at an open distance learning institution. Australas. J. Educ. Technol. **34**(5), 27–43 (2018)
10. Gow, L., Kember, D.: Conceptions of teaching and their relationship to student learning. Br. J. Educ. Psychol. **63**, 20–33 (1993)
11. Tait, A.: Planning student support for open and distance learning. Open Learn. **15**(3), 287–299 (2000)
12. Goodyear, P., Salmon, G., Spector, M.J., Steeples, C., Tickner, S.: Competences for online teaching: a special report. Educ. Technol. Res. Dev. **49**(1), 65–72 (2001)
13. Chang, C., Shen, H., Liu, E.Z.: University faculties' perspectives on the roles of e-instructors and their online instruction practice. Int. Rev. Res. Open Distance Learn. **15**(3), 72–92 (2014)
14. Horner, G., Gouws, P.: E-tutoring support for undergraduate students learning computer programming at the University of South Africa. In: Computer Science Education Research Conference 2016, Pretoria, South Africa (2016)

The Strategic Role of the E-Tutor in New Learning Contexts

Simona Ferrari(✉) and Serena Triacca

Catholic University of the Sacred Heart, Milan, Italy
{simona.ferrari,serena.triacca}@unicatt.it

Abstract. Digital media have opened up new opportunities to review e-learning. The three ages of media describe a shift from technology for distance education, to technology-supported groups and, currently, technology for Community development. Reflecting on the profile of the e-tutor in the third phase of e-learning, our research was guided by three key-questions: what functions does the e-tutor fulfill? What tools does the e-tutor need? What actions should the e-tutor take care of, in term of communication? The research plan, carried out on 9 online courses, is based on quanti-qualitative method (a pre-course survey, a post-course survey, learning analytics, content analysis of tutor's interactions and self-report). The results highlight the strategic role of the e-tutor in new contexts of learning.

Keywords: E-tutor · E-learning · Online community

1 Introduction

E-tutor had always represented the bridge between institutional training programs and individual needs, between staff and participants and between teachers and learners, interacting «directly with learners to support their learning process when they are separated from the tutor in time and place for some or all of these direct interactions» [1]. It has been a multi-face profession as the terms used in literature to refer to: online tutor, online moderator [2], e-moderator [3], distance education tutor, e-instructors [4], online teachers [5], online instructors [6], e-tutor [1].

Literary review highlights e-tutoring as a «central instructional strategy, integrated fully in everyday learning and teaching in institutions» [7]. As de Metz showed, he is «strategically important for the perception of the quality and attractiveness of the university but conversely can also be a vulnerable link in the university's educational chain» [8]. This is the reason why identifying tutoring skills is necessary for the success of e-learning [9]: these don't deal with subject matter expertise and technical skills but

---

This article has been developed jointly by the authors. Simona Ferrari wrote the sections: *1. Introduction*, *2. A Nested Method*, *3.2. The Shape of Tutorship in Different Learning Contexts*. Serena Triacca wrote the sections: *1.1. Research Contexts*, *3.1. The Essential Role of the E-tutor*, *3.3. E-tutor's Kit: Monitoring the Asynchronous Communication*. Section *4. Conclusions* has been written jointly.

L. S. Agrati et al. (Eds.): HELMeTO 2020, CCIS 1344, pp. 300–314, 2021.
https://doi.org/10.1007/978-3-030-67435-9_23

require pedagogical, information, and communication skills to manage and facilitate online learning.

More than 20 years ago, Ryan et al. [10] and Lentell [11] advised that the role of e-tutors is not *stabile*, but it is changing. According to them, this change is necessary nowadays. Digital media have opened up new opportunities to review e-learning [12]. The three ages of media describe a shift from «technology for distance education», to «technology-supported groups» and, currently, «technology for Community development» [13].

Reflecting on the profile of the e-tutor in the third phase of e-learning, our research was guided by three key-questions:

- What functions does the e-tutor fulfill?
- What tools does the e-tutor need?
- What communication actions should the e-tutor take care of?

1.1 Research Contexts

In this contribution we analyze the role of the e-tutor in nine different courses offered by Catholic University of Milan (Italy), that refer to three main contexts (Table 1).

Table 1. Contexts and courses

Context	Course name	N. of participants
1. Third mission, MOOC	1. *Virtually* (4 editions)	2321
	2. *3-6-9-12: growing up with digital screens* (3 editions)	3154
	3. *Digital education* (1 edition)	4877
	4. *Peer&Media education* (3 editions)	1608
	5. *Community tutor* (3 editions)	969
	6. *Spectrum of cyberbullying behaviors* (5 edition)	5878
2. Higher education, blended learning	1. *Business management and consulting (*Master's degree)	405
3. Third mission, E-learning	1. *Teaching with episodes of situated learning – beginner* (2 editions)	89
	2. *Teaching with episodes of situated learning – advanced* (1 edition)	25

According to Tuunainen [14], the Third Mission encompasses a wide range of activities involving the generation, the use, the application and the exploitation of knowledge and other university capabilities outside academic environments, in order to promote technology transfer and innovation, social engagement and continuing education.

Since the academic year 2014/15, CREMIT (Research Centre about Media Education, Innovation and Technology), in collaboration with ILAB (Centre for innovation and development of educational and technological activities), decided to experiment with MOOCs as a new environment for Media Education training.

MOOCs took place in Blackboard Open Education, an affordable platform based on the same virtual learning environment (VLE) adopted by Catholic University since 2001 (Blackboard Academic Suite). Blackboard Open Education offers essential technological functionalities: learning unit easy to set up; good tracking tools; badges; adaptive release to make different paths for the users.

Six different MOOCs, representing a complete path in media education, both for the topics discussed and for the design choices, has been offered:

- *"Virtually"* [15], *"3-6-9-12: growing up with digital screens"* [16] and *"Digital education"* for building an educational framework;
- *"Peer&Media education"* [17] and *"Community tutor"* [13] for providing methodological perspectives;
- *"Spectrum of cyberbullying behaviors"* for presenting cyber-stupidity as a framework to understand digital phenomena.

MOOCs represent a "light" training model to reach many adults (parents, educators, health workers, teachers, university students, police and services etc.) increasing their digital literacy and not just their digital practices [18]. The main features are the easy enrollment, the choice of gamification, the accurate balance of number and length of video-lessons and the in-depth analysis of the time needed for the activities. This "lightness", engaging and motivating participants, is a sort of "passage" running to a more institutional training system, both to university courses and to in-service training for teachers and professionals.

The Faculty of Economics designed an innovative Master's Degree to better support working students: this was an opportunity to develop a blended solution in the academic year 2016/17. The features of the blended model are a mix of synchronous (webinars and live feed-backs to solve problems or doubts related to contents or activities) and asynchronous online activities (video lessons, forums) and intensive training in the classroom (biweekly), individual and group assessment, e-tutoring [19].

In order to satisfy the several training requests regarding the method of Episodes of Situated Learning [20] by teachers of all levels, in the academic year 2018/19, an e-learning course for beginners was developed and delivered in two editions [21]. In the academic year 2019/20 an advanced course was designed to guide the mastery of the ESL method.

In the courses mentioned above, e-tutors carry out a variety of tasks concerning at least five clear functions [22]:

- technological: it is essential to set up and manage the online environment and to guarantee the first access, solving technical issues to decrease the levels of anxiety of the participants towards technological tools. The e-tutor can also act as a facilitator, in order to promote a conscious and critical use of technology;

- organizational: this function is connected to the course and activities design and management of space, time and training contract;
- social: the e-tutor takes care of the social environment, creating the conditions for facilitating socialization among the participants, enlivening the discussion boards and observing the trend of the online messaging;
- conceptual: this pedagogical function is essential for supporting the learning process and furthering the knowledge building of the community. The discussion boards are the privileged place where this function can manifest mostly, even if several participants favor one-to-one correspondence with the e-tutor;
- evaluative: this function is provided for in all phases of the training course. The e-tutor tests and monitors technology before and during the course time; he gives feedback to participants on content and activities; it gives feed-back to staff, even through data analysis.

Finally, the peculiarities of the contexts that differently solicits the e-tutor in carrying out his functions must be underlined (Table 2).

Table 2. The peculiarities of the three contexts

	MOOC	Blended learning	E-learning
Class size	Large class size per edition (300–5000)	High number of active students at once (100)	Small class size per edition (30)
E-tutor	Subject matter expert	Not a subject matter expert	Subject matter expert
Evaluation	Not an e-tutor's responsibility	E-tutor's responsibility	Not an e-tutor's responsibility
Assessment	E-tutor's responsibility	Not an e-tutor's responsibility	E-tutor's responsibility
VLE	One for each edition	Student Community, 27 courses of the graduate program[a]	One for each edition

[a]E-tutor updates and oversees the Student Community, a dedicated environment which joins all the students. Students are also enrolled in specific courses, depending on their own study plan.

2 A Nested Method

The research plan is based on quanti-qualitative method:

- a pre-course survey which includes questions about demographic information, previous experiences and motivations of students attending the course. We selected the items referred to student's expectations toward e-tutors;

The main expectations of the participants of MOOCs relate to the exploration of topics of personal interest (71%) and the download of useful contents for educational or professional activities (46%). Discussing topics with colleagues and e-tutors is not a priority (26%). Participants of MOOCs expect the e-tutor to perform mainly a conceptual ("Clarifying any doubts regarding the contents", 41%), organizational ("Send course and content updates", 39%) and technological function ("Help desk", 24%).

Among the distinctive elements of the blended course, students consider extremely important to deepen useful topics for the profession both theoretically and hands-on (69%), the opportunity to organize study and attendance according to one's personal and work commitments (64%), the webinars' recordings (62%) and teaching materials in different formats (57%). The most appreciated features are the possibility of using online materials and managing activities asynchronously, as highlighted in a recent meta-analysis [28]. Only 33% of participants consider taking advantage of the e-tutor support an extremely relevant element. Furthermore, students expect the e-tutor to perform mainly an organizational and technological function.

The main expectations of the participants of the e-learning courses concern the design of an Episode of Situated Learning, thanks to the guidance of the e-tutor (45%) and the study of the ESL method (32%). Participants expect the e-tutor to perform mainly a conceptual function ("Being guided in the design activity", 32%; "Clarifying any doubts regarding the contents", 29%).

Data comparison between pre-course, in which students underrate the relevance of e-tutor, and post-course survey (high percentage of satisfaction) highlights the importance of his presence.

As seen in Table 4, satisfaction in all the courses is distributed on the higher values of the scale (a six-point Likert scale, from 1 = totally dissatisfied to 6 = totally satisfied).

Table 4. Customer satisfaction

Customer satisfaction		MOOC	Blended learning	E-learning
Overall	Totally satisfied	49%	26%	59%
	Very satisfied	37%	56%	32%
E-tutoring	Totally satisfied	30%	37%	80%
	Very satisfied	32%	45%	14%

The percentage of completion of the courses represents a further element of satisfaction: 63% participants of MOOCs, 56% students of the Master's Degree[2] and 93% participants of the e-learning courses complete the course and obtain the final degree.

According to the e-moderation model [3] and constructivism, we imagined that e-tutor had to fade away during the course: as noted in the qualitative comments of the post-course survey and in the self-report of the e-tutors, the feed-back of the participants was, on the contrary, that they'd liked him/her to be present during the whole learning process in the three contexts. This result was unexpected in MOOC.

[2] The percentage of graduates is calculated taking as a basis the number of students who currently have completed the two-year period (n. 303).

3.2 The Shape of Tutorship in Different Learning Contexts

An important outcome of our research is the task analysis in the three different e-learning models.

Data from the self-report describe the self-perception of the own tutorship. Each tutor was asked to self-evaluate through a 1–6 scale the activation of a list of different behavior during the course. These behaviors are the "translation" of e-tutor's tasks and different tasks are traced to the correspondent function. In Table 5 we present the average score of each task in the three contexts and the general value.

In this contribution we cannot detail each element, we just underline that:

- more differences among context impact on: time and deadline adjustment, data management, community's organization and management, motivation and engagement support, promoted output (digital artifacts) both internally and externally, troubleshooting and content clarification, finding additional contents, testing and monitoring technology, assessment and feedback on content and activities, data analysis. This depends on tutor's job description;
- technical support varies according to target's digital competences and previous experience of e-learning;
- giving information about the course, followed by course design and launching, guiding, prompting and regulating communication are the most frequent tasks. Less in the Blended Learning context, were the Project Manager is included in the staff as course designer;
- low activation in activities' design and support and personalization of group learning as training contract management in the E-learning context.

This outcome was discussed with e-tutors. It was used to analyse the self-description of tutorship and reflect on it looking at the course design and at the job description (individual level) and to reflect on unexpected results as lack of competences or professional needs and to plan formative sessions (group level).

Recovering Denis [1], to questioning this data we can see that:

- troubleshooting and content clarification are central tasks in e-learning because e-tutor is also a content expert, closer to an e-teacher; it is peripheral in blended learning because e-tutor is asked to be closer to e-moderator;
- finding additional contents is central in blended learning due to his strategic role in supporting group work and method of study of the students;
- assessment and feedback on content and activities are requested by staff and not as a duty toward students;
- time and deadline adjustment are not requested in e-learning context because it is an "intensive course". Also Community's organization and management are not an expected task due to the small groups that tutor have to tutee;
- in MOOCs a peripheral roles deal with identification of technological solutions to meet needs, data management, activity design, support and personalization of group learning, troubleshooting and content clarification, finding additional content, supervision and monitoring the course, assessment and feedback on content and activities,

Table 5. Results from the self-report (mean)

Functions	Tasks	MOOC	Blended learning	E-learning	General
Technological	Course design (1.1, 1.2)[a]	5,6	5,0	4,3	4,6
	Technical support (1.5)	4,6	4,0	3,3	4,1
	Identification of technological solutions to meet needs (1.4)	2,8	3,0	4,0	3,2
	Data management (1.3)	2,0	4,5	1,7	2,4
Organizational	Time and deadline adjustment (2.4, 2.5)	5,4	1,0	1,7	3,5
	Activities' design (2.1)	2,0	1,0	2,3	1,9
	Training contract management (2.2)	3,4	3,0	1,0	2,6
	Community's organization and management (2.7)	3,6	5,5	2,0	3,5
	Giving information about the course (2.3)	4,8	5,5	4,0	4,7
	Support and personalization of group learning (2.6)	1,0	1,0	1,0	1,0
Social	Launching, guiding, prompting and regulating communication (3.1, 3.2, 3.3, 3.4, 3.6, 3.9)	4,3	4,9	5,0	4,6
	Motivation and engagement support (3.5, 3.7, 3.8, 3.10, 3.11, 3.12, 3.13, 3.14, 3.15)	3,8	3,9	5,5	4,3
	Promote output (digital artifacts) both internally and externally (3.16, 3.17)	2,1	1,0	3,8	2,4

(continued)

Table 5. *(continued)*

Functions	Tasks	MOOC	Blended learning	E-learning	General
Conceptual	Troubleshooting and content clarification (4.1, 4.2)	2,5	1,0	5,8	3,2
	Finding additional contents (4.3)	2,6	4,0	5,0	3,6
	Offering media-educational food for thought (4.4)	2,6	2,0	3,3	2,7
Evaluative	Testing and monitoring technology (5.1, 5.2, 5.3)	3,1	5,2	1,9	3,2
	Supervision and monitoring the course (5.4, 5.5, 5.6, 5.7, 5.9)	2,6	4,5	3,8	3,4
	Assessment and feedback on content and activities (5.8, 5.11)	1,6	1	5,7	2,8
	Giving feedback to staff (5.12)	3,8	4,5	4,7	4,2
	Data analysis (5.10)	1,8	4,5	1,7	2,3

[a]Numbers in parentheses represent the item number of the behavior categorized and present in the self-report.

data analysis. This tutorship depends on a job description that requires to be a content expert;

- on the contrary, in Blended context where the focus of e-tutor action is not on the content but on the learning process, we found identification of technological solutions to meet needs, time and deadline adjustment, activities' design, training contract management, support and personalization of group learning, troubleshooting and content clarification, assessment and feedback on content and activities as peripheral;
- in e-learning context, data management, time and deadline adjustment, activities' design, training contract management, community's organization and management are not central but ask for a professional development in managing community of practice, in supporting and personalizing group learning, in testing and monitoring technology, in data analysis.

Analyzing the data over time from 2006 [27] to nowadays, we can evidence that:

- technological function becomes relevant due to learning analytics and the evolution of Learning Management Systems. It's necessary to reflect on the relationship between informal learning and digital media;
- organizational and social functions should face with digital communication (horizontal dimension, peering, importance of the community, micro-leaning, co-creation of content and new-visibility);
- conceptual function should integrate finding additional contents and offers media-educational food for thought. Information Literacy and Media Literacy should be part of tutorship;
- e-valuation [29] asks e-tutor to be able to observe a community at work, to provide feedback, to test tools, to read, understand and use Learning Analytics.

Data show a change in tutorship functions and their development during the course concerning different contexts. The cycle of tutorship functions developed in 2006 [27] is still valid for blended and e-learning courses but not for MOOC due to community's dimension. This element needs to be investigated further (Fig. 1).

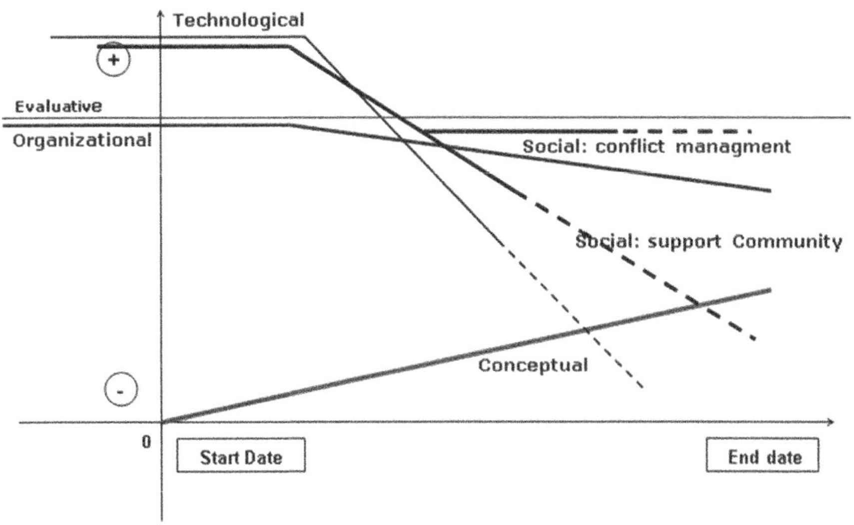

Fig. 1. Cycle of tutorship functions [22]

The other set of data that help to analyse "tutorshape" came from discussion board analysis.

As the Table 6 shows, we need to move from a tutorship guided by e-tivity to activity, where communication strategy is based on promoting and supporting engagement and bridging.

Table 6. Results from discussion board analysis (percentage)

	Access and Motivation		Online Socialisation		Information Exchange		Knowledge Construction		Development	
	Setting up system and accessing	Welcoming and Encouraging	Sending and Receiving Messages	Familiarizing and providing bridges between cultural, social and learning environments	Searching personalizing software	Facilitating task and supporting use of learning materials	Conferencing	Facilitating process	Providing links outside closed conferences	Supporting responding
3-6-9-12	24,89	50,67	2,22	2,67	0,00	8,89	0,00	2,67	0,00	0,89
P&M	26,09	61,96	3,26	3,26	0,00	5,43	0,00	0,00	0,00	0,00
Cyber	26,37	53,85	3,30	3,30	0,00	0,00	0,00	0,00	0,00	0,00
EAS 1	1,94	19,61	2,91	2,72	0,00	0,19	0,00	71,07	0,00	0,00
Edudig	47,62	38,69	2,98	2,38	0,00	7,14	0,00	1,19	0,00	0,00

3.3 E-Tutor's Kit: Monitoring the Asynchronous Communication

This final section contains some reflections gained during the experimentation of a specific monitoring tool throughout the first year of activation of the Master's Degree "Business management and consulting".

As seen in Sect. 2, a monitoring grid of incoming and outgoing email between e-tutor and students was implemented. Thanks to a prompt data entry work, the visualization of messages distribution, through pre-set tables and graphics, allowed the acknowledgment of particular courses, themes or situations that act as "points of accumulation" of interest and attention. The number of emails sent by each student was also counted. These data (especially if very low or very high, i.e. no email received or high number of emails received) and the tracking of the platform allowed the e-tutor to act more effectively its evaluative function.

This tool supported in fact the e-tutor's autonomy in evidence-based decision making, helping him to formulate new announcements or clearer messages towards the individual, the small group or the Community, to create supplemental materials (tutorials, guidelines), organize Webinar on specific issues or contact a specific student by phone. Furthermore, it is useful for those situations that fall outside the e-tutor's area of competence and need to be reported to the staff.

At the same time, during the development of the course and in line with the course work plan, the e-tutor builded up a tool kit made of scripts, i.e. templates of messages useful in the different stages of training, guidelines, tutorial, FAQs. Several scripts can be defined before the courses start; many others, however, must be imagined as the exchange of messages with the participants becomes more frequent and intense. The scripts must be results of self-reflection on the personal communicative style.

Certainly, as you can imagine, a significant variable is represented by the e-tutor's experience and skills. The e-tutor must take care of his tool kit, updating it constantly, experience after experience.

While in the e-learning courses the "beating heart" of learning were the forums, in which all the members participated, in the MOOCs many contacts took place privately via email. We are planning to propose this tool also to the e-tutors of the MOOCs, to support reflexivity and a more systematic approach to communication.

4 Conclusions

Considering this background, we are glad to define some elements on which we believe it is important to focus, for institutions implied in education and for research:

- the e-tutor as a professional figure and his/her training: it is of fundamental importance to prepare specific training courses with particular attention to methods and tools for managing communication, teaching and learning mediated by digital tools [30]. The construction of skills could be supported by forms of mentorship making it possible to model practices and stimulate reflexivity [31, 32]; no less important is the management of the tutorship in a team in order to actively exchange spaces between peers by co-building toolkits with colleagues;
- technological development: Learning Analytics are usually functional to the evaluation process or to guide the teaching function. It is necessary to invest in the development of a dashboard that supports the work of the e-tutors (thanks to the adoption of a visual format, and to the alert settings, to the possibility of passing from the macro dimension to a micro dimension) and that it is customizable in relation to the training contexts;
- research: if on the one hand it is necessary to invest to find new indicators useful for the development of the dashboard, another interesting research area is represented by the investigation on the methods of interaction between intelligent agents (chatbots) with human communication. We can say that the five functions of e-tutoring take place on two levels, one of a management-informative nature and one critical-reflective. If the first level could be managed by intelligent systems powered by the tutor, the second necessarily requires the e-tutor to take charge. At the moment, the AI systems are not able to put in place the relational quality of the human being, his ability to decode and interpret messages.

References

1. Denis, B., Watland, P., Pirotte, S., Verday, N.: Roles and competencies of the e-tutor. In: Proceedings of the Networked Learning Conference (NLC 2004), Lancaster, UK (2004)
2. Spector, J.M., De la Teja, I.: Competencies for online teaching (2001). http://files.eric.ed.gov/fulltext/ED456841.pdf
3. Salmon, G.: E-Moderating: The Key to Teaching and Learning Online. Routledge, New York (2011)
4. Chang, C., Shen, H., Liu, E.Z.: University faculties' perspectives on the roles of e-instructors and their online instruction practice. Int. Rev. Res. Open Distance Learn. **15**(3), 72–92 (2014)
5. Goodyear, P., Salmon, G., Spector, J., Steeples, C., Tickner, S.: Competencies for online teaching. Educ. Technol. Res. Dev. **49**, 65–72 (2001)
6. Savory, J.R.: Be vocal: characteristics of successful online instructors. J. Interact. Online Learn. **4**(2), 141–152 (2005)
7. Donnelly, R., McSweeney, F.: Applied E-Learning and E-Teaching in Higher Education. Information Science Reference, New York (2008)
8. De Metz, N., Bezuidenhout, A.: An importance–competence analysis of the roles and competencies of e-tutors at an open distance learning institution. Australas. J. Educ. Technol. **34**(5), 27–43 (2017). https://doi.org/10.14742/ajet.3364
9. McPherson, M., Nunes, M.B.: The role of tutors as an integral part of online learning support (2004). http://www.eurodl.org/materials/contrib/2004/Maggie_MsP.html
10. Ryan, S., Scott, B., Freeman, H., Patel, D.: The Virtual University: The Internet and Resource-Based Learning. Kogan Page, London (2000)
11. Lentell, H.: The importance of the tutor in open and distance learning. In: Tait, A., Mills, R. (eds.) Rethinking Learner Support In Distance Education, pp. 64–76. RoutledgeFalmer, London (2003)
12. Ferrari, S.: Mediamorfosi dell'e-Learning. In: Rivoltella, P.C., Rossi, P. (eds.) Tecnologie per l'educazione, pp. 95–109. Pearson Italia, Torino (2019)
13. Rivoltella, P.C.: Tecnologie di comunità. ELS La Scuola, Brescia (2017)
14. Tuunainen, J.: Hybrid practices? Contributions to the debate on the mutation of science and university. High. Educ. **50**(2), 275–298 (2005)
15. Rivoltella, P.C.: Le virtù del digitale. Per un'etica dei media. Morcelliana, Brescia (2015)
16. Tisseron, S.: 3-6-9-12. Apprivoiser les écrans et grandir. Edition éres, Toulouse (2016)
17. Rivoltella, P.C., Ottolini, G.M. (eds.): Il tunnel e il kayak. Teoria e metodo della Peer & Media Education. Franco Angeli, Milano (2014)
18. McAuley, A., Stewart, B., Siemens, G., Cormier, D.: The MOOC model for digital practice (2010). https://tinyurl.com/y7yl2n9y
19. Triacca, S., Bodega, D., Rivoltella, P.C.: Blended solution and higher education. The case of the Catholic University: e-tutoring for personalization. Educ. Sci. Soc. **9**(2), 198–210 (2019)
20. Rivoltella, P.C.: Fare didattica con gli EAS. Episodi di Apprendimento Situato. La Scuola, Brescia (2013)
21. Triacca, S., Petti, L., Rivoltella, P.C.: Designing and re-designing the e-learning course «Teaching with Episodes of Situated Learning». Res. Educ. Media **11**(2), 95–100 (2019)
22. Rizzi, C., Tassalini, E.: Funzioni. In: Rivoltella, P.C. (ed.) E-Tutor. Profilo, metodi, strumenti, pp. 33–50. Carocci, Roma (2006)
23. Salmon, G.: E-Tivities: The Key to Active Online Learning. Routledge, London (2002)
24. Mentis, M., Ryba, K., Annan, J.: Creating authentic online communities of professional practice. E-J. Instr. Sci. Technol. **5**(1), 1–15 (2002)
25. Scaife, J.: Scaife Supervising The Reflective Practitioner: An Essential Guide to Theory and Practice. Routledge, London (2010)

26. Creswell, J.: Research Design: Qualitative, Quantitative and Mixed Methods Approaches. Sage Publications, London (2003)
27. Rivoltella, P.C. (ed.): E-Tutor. Profilo, metodi, strumenti. Carocci, Roma (2006)
28. Ryan, D., Risquez, A.: 'Lessons Learnt': the student view in the #VLEIreland project. Ir. J. Technol. Enhanc. Learn. **3**(2), 1–10 (2018). https://doi.org/10.22554/ijtel.v3i2.40
29. Ferrari, S., Garavaglia, A.: Dall'Evaluation all'E-valuation. E-Learn. Knowl. Manag. **3**, 42–46 (2004)
30. Rivoltella, P.C., Cattaneo, A. (eds.): Tecnologie, formazione, professioni. Idee e tecniche per l'innovazione. Unicopli, Milano (2010)
31. Schön, D.A.: Il professionista riflessivo. Edizioni Dedalo, Bari (1993)
32. Johns, C. (ed.): Becoming a Reflective Practitioner. Wiley-Blackwell, Hoboken (2017)

Improving Student Progression in Distance Learning Using Synchronous Webinars

Georgina Stebbings(✉), Chris Mackintosh, Adrian Burden, and Dave Sims

Department of Sport and Exercise Sciences,
Manchester Metropolitan University, Manchester, UK
g.stebbings@mmu.ac.uk

Abstract. Webinars facilitate synchronous communication and are an opportunity for social interaction and collaborative learning between students on distance learning programmes.

We surveyed 30 distance learning students and 19 tutors about their experiences of webinar delivery, in addition to analyzing unit performance pre- (2016–2018) and post- (2018–2020) webinar integration for one Level 4 distance-learning unit in sport and exercise science.

Of the students who responded, 93% reported attending webinars as part of their programme, while 51% of tutors reported delivering a webinar as part of their teaching. Comparisons of unit performance pre- and post-webinar integration revealed an increase in unit attainment and reduction in the number of first time fails. Both students and tutors rated the addition of webinars to the distance-learning programme positively, with students rating the educational and technological quality of the webinars higher than tutors.

In conclusion, utilizing webinars to facilitate social interaction and collaborative learning on distance learning programmes contributed to improved student attainment and progression.

1 Introduction

Distance learning typically assumes a constructivist approach to learning, whereby individuals actively construct their own knowledge through consultation and engagement with learning resources. Such learning resources are predominantly delivered, or hosted, online through computer-mediated communication (CMC) systems, eBooks, or a combination of these and other sources [1, 2]. Delivery and/or engagement with these resources can occur synchronously, where students engage in real-time; asynchronously, where students engage at a time convenient to them; or a combination of both of these in a blended approach [3].

In accordance with social constructivism, both social interaction and collaboration with more knowledgeable others are necessary for effective learning [4, 5]. During synchronous distance learning, opportunities for collaborative learning and interaction between tutors and students are frequent, only if implemented appropriately through the use of available CMCs, such as live chat forums, online activities and video calls [2, 6]. If collaborative learning is to be successful, however, students need to feel part

L. S. Agrati et al. (Eds.): HELMeTO 2020, CCIS 1344, pp. 315–323, 2021.
https://doi.org/10.1007/978-3-030-67435-9_24

of a wider learning community and overcome the feelings of isolation that 22–68% of distance-learning students fear [7, 8]. Feelings of isolation significantly contribute to the lower rate of student progression and retention observed across distance learning programmes, which continues to be an important challenge facing institutions offering these programmes, primarily due to the associated high dropout rates [9, 10].

Overcoming feelings of isolation and establishing a sense of community can be difficult for asynchronous distance learning, as the pace at which individuals learn, and the timing of their engagement with online discussion forums and activities, is wholly independent of others [11]. Nonetheless, as distance learning is becoming increasingly popular and attracting a variety of students from diverse backgrounds, all with different learning styles and communication preferences, it is important to accommodate these differences by providing various synchronous and asynchronous opportunities for collaborative learning wherever possible [12]. In some instances of cohort-based distance learning, such as those recently adopted by many higher education institutions in response to the challenges posed by the COVID-19 pandemic, opportunities for both synchronous and asynchronous engagement are apparent. Evidence exists to suggest that opportunities for both synchronous and asynchronous engagement contribute to reducing feelings of isolation for traditional full-time students [13], but it remains unclear if this approach may benefit distance learning students in the same way. In comparison to traditional full-time students, those completing distance learning programmes are typically mature, having had a considerable absence from learning, are less technology/computer literate and often face family, financial and/or other barriers to learning [14]. Consequently, distance learning students' motivation to learn tends to be intrinsic, compared to traditional full-time students who are extrinsically motivated [11]. Nonetheless, incorporating opportunities for both synchronous and asynchronous engagement in distance learning may help overcome feelings of isolation, which in turn could benefit student progression and retention.

Webinars are seminars delivered via the worldwide web and are a convenient, accessible and cost-effective tool to facilitate synchronous student-tutor and student-student interaction. Previous research has demonstrated that students enjoy participating in webinars and doing so strengthened their social presence [2], which is shown to increase the likelihood of future participation in online learning communities [15]. Participation in webinars affords students an opportunity to develop their learning beyond what might otherwise be achieved from learning alone, via interactions with more knowledgeable others according to the 'Zone of Proximal Development' [5, 16]. Thus, in cohort-based distance learning, where synchronous opportunities to interact with knowledgeable others exist, but may be limited, utilizing webinars to facilitate student learning may contribute to enhanced intrinsic motivation to learn and improved student attainment. In traditional settings, webinar-based learning is associated with trivial improvements in educational attainment compared to face-to-face delivery [17, 18], meaning, webinars are just as effective as face-to-face delivery for traditional full-time students. It remains unclear, however, to what extent webinar integration into distance learning might improve attainment. Furthermore, it is possible that webinars may also contribute to improved student progression in distance learning through a combination of enhanced attainment, strengthened social presence and sense of community.

The aims of this study, therefore, were to assess the impact of webinar-based learning on unit attainment and student progression in distance learning at Level 4 of a sport and exercise science undergraduate UK degree, and to gain insight into the enabling factors that may contribute to any improvements in unit attainment and progression.

2 Method

The local Ethics committee of Manchester Metropolitan University granted ethical approval for this study, which was conducted with undergraduate students in sport and exercise science, who were typically mature and working full time. The study utilized two different methodological approaches to address our research questions. Firstly, a quantitative analysis of unit performance data was undertaken for a single Level 4 undergraduate unit. Analysis was completed over a 4-year period (September 2016–April 2020), which included two years prior to webinar integration (Pre) and two years post webinar integration (Post). Webinars were delivered by the same tutor throughout the 4-year period using Adobe Connect (v11, Adobe Inc., San Jose, California, USA), which allowed multi-level interaction and synchronous communication between students and the tutor. Unit performance data included attainment and progression, as well as the number of webinars that were delivered, how often these were viewed and by what proportion of the student cohort.

For the second approach, an online survey was developed (Jisc Online Surveys) that comprised a maximum of 25 questions (minimum of 21 questions). Due to differences in webinar engagement, respondents were not required to answer all survey questions. Questions included those requiring responses to a 5-point and 10-point Likert scale, plus two open-ended questions asking participants to comment on their experiences or perceptions of webinar engagement. Thus, both quantitative and qualitative data were obtained. A link to the survey was emailed to 150 potential respondents, from which 50 responded and 49 gave their consent to take part. Of the respondents, 30 were students (mean [standard deviation] age 33 [9] years) and 19 were tutors (age 37 [8] years, with 11 [8] years teaching experience). Data from the online survey were exported from the Jisc online platform for subsequent analysis.

Data were analyzed using Microsoft Excel and SPSS (v25, IBM Statistics). Unit performance was compared pre- and post-webinar integration using Fisher's exact test or one-tailed independent t-tests, where appropriate, and reported as mean (standard deviation [SD]). Where sample size was too small to conduct inferential statistical analysis, as in the case of minimum and maximum attainment, descriptive statistics are reported. Quantitative survey questions were reported separately for tutor and student groups as median (interquartile range [IQR]). Responses to open-ended questions were subject to a simple thematic analysis and were reported according to their relative frequency to provide a deeper insight into the experiences and perceptions of webinar-based learning. Alpha for all inferential tests was accepted as <0.05.

3 Results

On average, 48% (6%) of students engaged synchronously with the webinars. Asynchronous engagement, via viewing recordings of the original webinars, was also evident with an average of 80 (3) views per webinar (range 54–156 views), completed by 44% (11%) of the student cohort at a rate of 7 (3) views per webinar, per student.

Comparison of unit performance pre- and post-webinar integration revealed a significant 8% increase in mean unit attainment ($P = 0.03$), despite no notable improvement in maximum attainment (2%, see Fig. 1). A significant reduction in the number of first time fails ($P = 0.02$) was also apparent, with minimum attainment notably higher post-webinar integration (41%, see Fig. 1). Ultimately, student progression post-webinar integration increased 11% ($P = 0.04$) compared to pre-webinar integration.

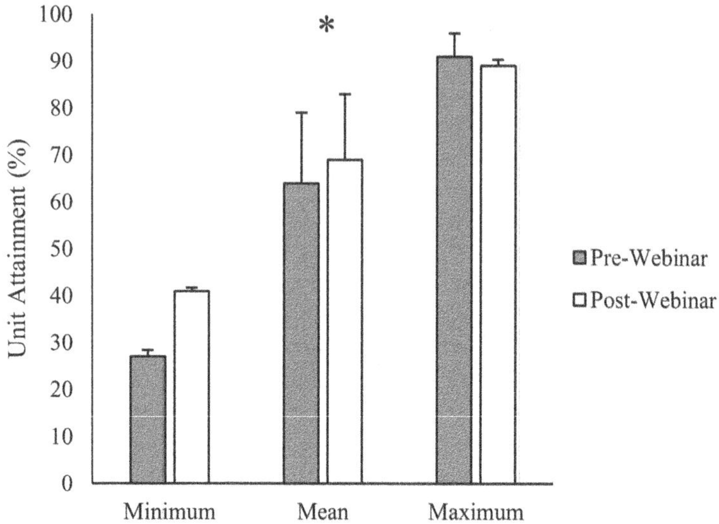

Fig. 1. Comparison of unit attainment between pre- and post-webinar integration. Data are mean (SD). * denotes $P = 0.03$.

Of the survey respondents, 93% of students reported attending webinars as part of their programme, whilst 51% of tutors reported delivering a webinar as part of their teaching. Both students and tutors rated the addition of webinars to the distance-learning programme positively on a 10-point Likert scale (median [IQR] = 9 [2] & 8 [2]), with students also rating the educational (8 [3] & 7 [1]) and technological (8 [2] & 6 [2]) quality of the webinars higher than tutors (see Fig. 2).

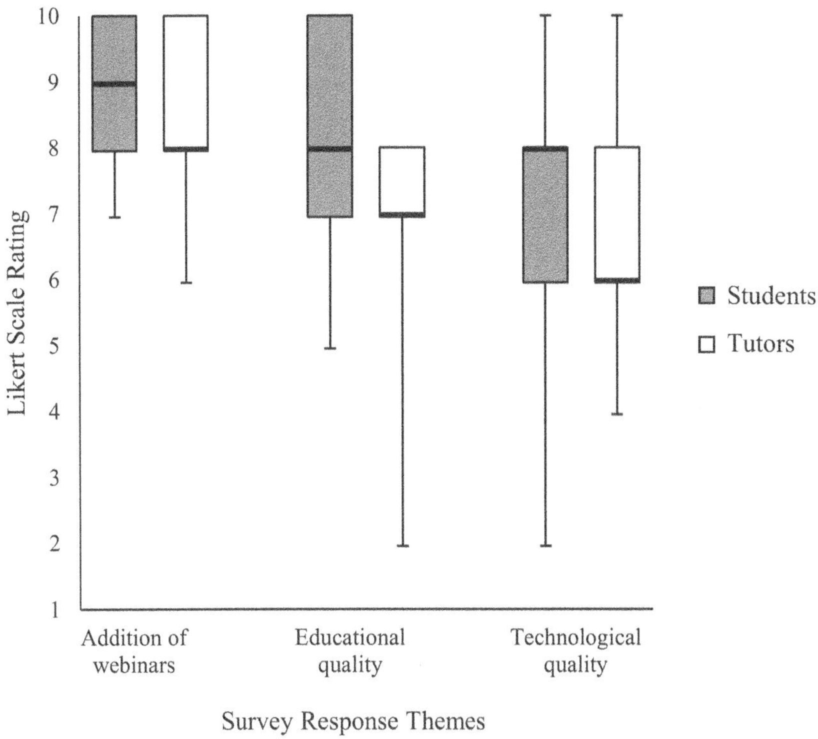

Fig. 2. Quantitative survey responses from students and tutors regarding their experiences and perceptions of webinars. Data are median (thick black line), upper and lower quartiles as the box and minimum and maximum values represented by whiskers; maximum values are represented by the upper quartile where no whiskers are shown.

In response to the open-ended questions, both students and tutors reported finding webinars useful for facilitating student understanding (60% & 26%) and enjoyed the opportunity for social interaction (37% & 42%; see Fig. 3). Technical issues, including poor sound quality and inexperience with webinar platforms were reported most frequently as the biggest challenges by students (23%) and tutors (26%; see Fig. 3). Notably, training was listed as the primary factor (60%) that would encourage those tutors yet to deliver a webinar to do so in future.

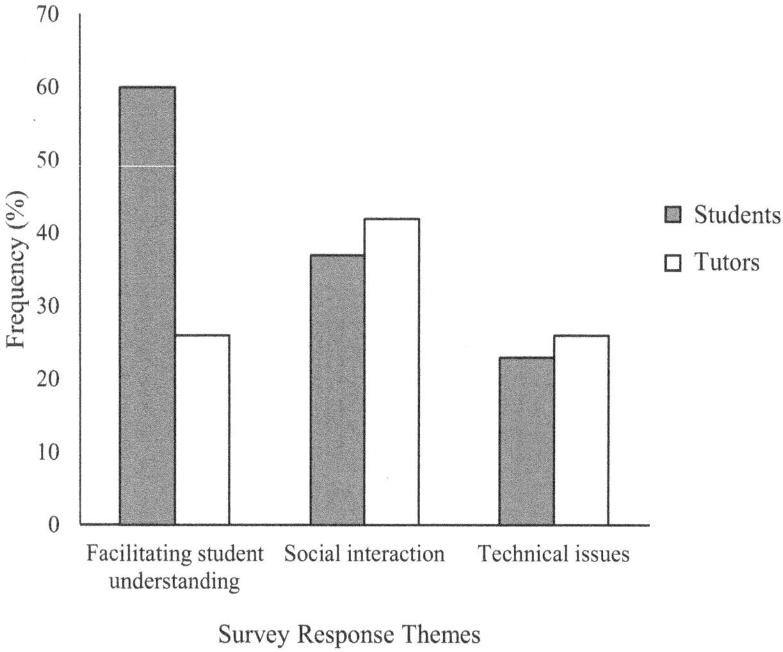

Fig. 3. Qualitative survey responses from tutors and students regarding their experiences and perceptions of webinars.

4 Discussion

The aims of this study were to assess the effectiveness of webinar integration for improving unit attainment and student progression and to gain insight into the factors that may contribute to improvements for distance learning students in sport and exercise science. Post-webinar integration, we observed an increase in mean unit attainment and student progression. In addition, tutors and students both highlighted the opportunity for social interaction and effective facilitation of learning as primary factors for engaging with webinars.

Poor student progression and retention is widely reported across distance learning in comparison to traditional face-to-face delivery [8, 11], which has been attributed to reduced motivation to learn, amongst other factors [8, 11]. Whilst distance-learning students are typically intrinsically motivated to learn, scheduling synchronous webinars may aid both intrinsic and extrinsic motivation [11, 19]. Through social and cognitive engagement with peers, students are held accountable for their attendance (extrinsic) and benefit from opportunities for intellectual discussions and collaboration with peers (intrinsic) [20], which are likely to contribute to enhanced understanding and, ultimately, attainment. Encouraging student-student interaction during webinars will likely also help to strengthen social presence and reduce feelings of isolation, which have been considered a threat to learning by 22–68% of distance learning students [7, 8]. Use of webinars to reduce the threat of isolation may have helped to explain the 8% increase in mean attainment and 11% increase in student progression in the current study. As we did not directly assess social presence or isolation, however, future research should seek to investigate the impact of webinars on these factors for distance learning.

Interestingly, it appears that those students most at risk of failure in the current study benefitted most from the inclusion of webinars. Indeed, the observed increase in minimum attainment and reduction in the number of fails, rather than an increase in maximum attainment, contributed to the overall increase in mean unit attainment and improved student progression. Collaborative learning during the webinars used in the current study was facilitated by the same experienced tutor and it seems plausible that through interactions with more knowledgeable peers and tutor, the least capable students are better able to develop the higher order learning skills necessary to progress through our distance learning programme post-webinar integration than pre-webinar integration [21]. In accordance with the notion of the 'Zone of Proximal Development,' social interaction and collaboration with more knowledgeable others is essential for cognitive development [5]. Using webinars as a strategy for collaborative learning affords students an opportunity to develop higher order learning skills through experiencing multiple perspectives and explaining, debating and critically analyzing information [21].

Effective webinar-based learning, however, is largely dependent on session design, manageable group sizes, network infrastructure and ability to use appropriate online platforms [3]. This emphasizes the need for appropriate staff training to maximize the benefits of webinar-based learning. Current integration of webinars on our distance learning programme is low (5 of 15 units). Based on survey responses, lack of integration is attributed to a lack of tutor training deterring tutor engagement, and is an important consideration for any education provider planning to offer distance learning in future. Nonetheless, survey responses highlighted social interaction and facilitation of learning as primary factors for student engagement in webinars. Thus, as the webinar experiences of tutors and students was overwhelmingly positive, and appears to have contributed to an increase in mean unit attainment, integrating webinars into distance learning, particularly in sport and exercise sciences, appears justified. Future research, however, should investigate if our findings for Level 4 students are replicated across Levels 5, 6 and 7.

Considering the adoption of online and eLearning tools has been accelerated as a consequence of the COVID-19 pandemic, the results of this study are likely to have relevance beyond distance learning. Our findings identify webinars as a potential tool for traditional campus-based programmes, who are now likely using online or blended delivery to support students at risk of failure in future. It is important, however, to acknowledge the characteristic differences between traditional full-time students and distance learners and recognize that our observations from typical distance learning students may not be generalizable to traditional full-time students and warrants further research.

In conclusion, integration of webinar-based learning into our sport and exercise science distance-learning undergraduate programme improved unit attainment and student progression at Level 4 and was perceived positively by both tutors and students. Prior to integrating webinars into higher education programmes requires adequate tutor training, however, without which many tutors are reluctant to adopt this tool as part of distance learning delivery. Future research should seek to confirm our observations at Level 5, 6 and 7.

References

1. Kerr, E.B., Hiltz, S.R.: Computer-Mediated Communication Systems: Status and Evaluation, pp. 2–3. Academic Press, New York (1982)
2. Wang, S.-K., Hsu, H.-Y.: Use of webinar tool (Elluminate) to support training: the effects of webinar-learning implementation from student-trainers' perspective. J. Interact. Online Learn. **7**, 175–194 (2008)
3. Romiszowski, A., Mason, R.: Computer-mediated communication. In: Jonassen, D.H. (ed.) Handbook of Research for Educational Communications and Technology, 2nd edn., pp. 397–431. Simon & Schuster Macmillan, New York (2004)
4. Weller, M.: Delivering Learning on the Net: The Why What and How of Online Education. Routledge Falmer, London (2002)
5. Vygotsky, L.S.: Mind and Society: The Development of Higher Mental Processes. Harvard University Press, Cambridge (1978)
6. Gillet-Swan, J.: The challenges of online learning: supporting and engaging the isolated learner. J. Learn. Des. **10**(1), 20–30 (2017)
7. Park, C.: The Taught Postgraduate Student Experience: Overview of a Higher Education Academy Survey. The Higher Education Academy, York (2008)
8. Rush, P.: Isolation and connection: the experience of distance education. Distance Medit. Knowl. **30**(2) (2015). https://doi.org/10.4000/dms.2509
9. Hartley, S., Gill, D., Walters, K., Bryant, P., Carter, F.: Twelve tips for potential distance students. Med. Teach. **23**(1), 12–15 (2001)
10. Simpson, O.: Student retention in distance education: are we failing our students? J. Open Distance e-Learn. **28**(2), 105–119 (2013)
11. Croft, N., Dalton, A., Grant, M.: Overcoming isolation in distance learning: building a learning community through time and space. J. Educ. Built Environ. **5**(1), 27–64 (2010)
12. Curtis, D.D., Lawson, M.J.: Exploring collaborative online learning. J. Asynchronous Learn. Netw. **5**(1), 21–34 (2001)
13. Gomez, E., Azadi, J., Magid, D.: Innovation born in isolation: rapid transformation of an in-person medical student radiology elective to a remote learning experience during the COVID-19 pandemic. Acad. Radiol. **27**(9), 1285–1290 (2020)
14. Kahu, E.R., Stephens, C.V., Leach, L., Zepke, N.: The engagement of mature distance students. High. Educ. Res. Dev. **32**(5), 791–804 (2013)
15. Kear, K., Chetwynd, F., Jeffries, H.: Social presence in online learning communities: the role of personal profiles. Res. Learn. Technol. **22**, 19710 (2014)
16. Louvigné, S., Uto, M., Kato, Y., Ishii, T.: Social constructivist approach of motivation: social media messages recommendation system. Behaviormetrika **45**(1), 133–155 (2017)
17. Gegenfurtner, A., Ebner, C.: Webinars in higher education and professional training: a meta-analysis and systematic review of randomized controlled trials. Educ. Res. Rev. **28**, 1–19 (2019)

18. Ebner, C., Gegenfurtner, A.: Learning and satisfaction in webinar, online, and face-to-face instruction: a meta-analysis. Front. Educ. **4**(92), 1–11 (2019)
19. Whiting, M.J., Liu, J., Rovai, A.P.: Distinguishing sense of community and motivation characteristics between online and traditional college students. Q. Rev. Distance Educ. **9**(3), 285–295 (2008)
20. Blumenfeld, P.C., Kempler, T.M., Krajcik, J.S.: Motivation and cognitive engagement in learning environments. In: Sawyer, R.K. (ed.) The Cambridge Handbook of the Learning Sciences, pp. 475–488. Cambridge University Press, Cambridge (2006)
21. So, H.-J., Brush, T.A.: Student perceptions of collaborative learning, social presence and satisfaction in a blended learning environment: relationships and critical factors. Comput. Educ. **51**, 318–336 (2008)

2. The differential effects of online/Distance learning and Presential/Traditional classroom instruction on interest of students in undergraduate degree Introductory Biology Course.
3. The differences between male and female students' achievement in undergraduate degree Introductory Biology Course.
4. The differences between male and female students' in undergraduate degree Introductory Biology Course.
5. The interaction effect of method and gender on achievements of students.
6. The interaction effect of method and gender on interest of students.

Four research questions aligned to the specific purposes were answered using Mean and Standard Deviation. Two null hypotheses on interaction effects of gender and method of instruction were tested using ANCOVA at 0.05 level of significance.

2 Literature Review

Recent studies on student's engagement and technology have reported the importance of computers and information technologies on promoting students learning outcomes [5, 9]. The use of Information, Communication Technologies (ICT) enable learners think critically and reflectively during instructions. This subsequently stimulates higher order thinking in the Blooms taxonomy of education objectives such as analysis, synthesis, judgment, and application of knowledge especially when both synchronous and asynchronous instructional modes are used [10, 11]. The ease of communication between participants, increased participation in the discussion, anonymity of participants, transparency, ability to recruit diverse population who are ICT compliant in a class, are some of the advantages of Distance learning [12]. These advantages make Distance Learning a gender friendly teaching strategy, suitable for teaching male and female students in Science based disciplines for enhanced learning outcomes irrespective of gender [13]. Gender differences in science in favor of males, have been attributed by many researchers to factors such as female students' lack of exposure to science-related activities outside the classroom [14], gender biases of teachers with respect to strategies in asking questions and delivering answers, cultural influences from home, school and society, differences in spatial abilities, cognitive abilities, and mathematics background [14, 15]. This study is apt because females are significantly under-represented in ICT, accounting for only 3% of ICT graduates globally as reported by [9]. Distance/Online learning is important because it has been found that ICT will be used as a working tool in all facets of Science, Technology, Engineering and Mathematics (STEM) education and careers [12]. It has also been reported that by 2020, 98% STEM related jobs will require ICT skills and that there will be one million vacant posts in computing because of lack of skilled personnel [3].

The point most cited as a disadvantage of DL is the lack of physical contacts between students and the difficulty in resolving queries arising from instructions [4, 6]. That students cannot develop the socialization and interpersonal skills in online learning, as it appears on traditional learning methods as found by [4, 17] may be due to students' and teachers previous experiences with DL prior to beginning their online learning. The fact that students thought there were less support and interaction in DL may be due to lesson formats and the profiles of students and lecturers who are not used to taking DL classes. Also, [3] found that it is only less than 2 out of 10 students who showed lack of satisfaction with their participation in a virtual course. The few numbers expressing dissatisfaction is in tandem with the finding by [13] that audio visual technological aids integration in science teaching and learning process boost students' interest irrespective of their gender. This is because by active engagement of students, they construct their own knowledge as learning shifts from teacher dominance to learner centered activities.

A systematic review and analysis conducted by [18] focused on distance learning instruction, reported that it was evident that student's performance was better when learning was either a combination of an online environment and offline modules than traditional face-to-face conditions. When exploring what the differences are between distance learning and Presential face-to-face educational programs for students, research conducted by [17] suggests that the interactions between the instructor and students are ultimately what impacts learning. No significant difference was found when quizzes were administered online, and non-interactive video were available for students. However, simulations that prompt learners' responses and reflections yielded positive outcomes. Just as in traditional face-to-face classrooms, when the instructional content limits the response requirements and does not tap into higher order thinking skills, the output produced by the students are limited and not challenged. In an online (synchronous or asynchronous), or in a face-to-face setting, the greatest outcomes can be reached when students are provided with an opportunity to interact and think critically particularly regarding student access and availability. The purchase, development, and implementation of online learning tools which include, a learning management system (LMS), as well as content storage and retrieval systems, email communication, document drop boxes, grade inquiries, discussion boars, learning objects and contents, as well as online testing capabilities make the appearance of an online program intimidating to construct. However, these features are both attractive and welcome challenges for today's students, lecturers and even the Education Ministries of countries that embrace/accept the opportunity to work with technology to create a flexible mode of delivery.

The introduction and implementation of online components into course delivery benefits both the schools and the learner because of reduced costs, greater flexibility and convenience as emphasized by [19]. One factor that may explain the best performance in the distance mode is the greater obligation to pay attention to the contents. It is not easy to find out if a student in the Presential/traditional classroom setting is paying attention to the contents that are salient in instruction or not.

3 Methods and Materials

One hundred and fifty (150) undergraduate degree students in their first year of Science Education in 2019/2020 academic year constituted the sample. Participants were volunteers from Biology, Chemistry, Physics and Mathematics special areas who were offering Basic Biology for Science Education students (Course code: SED 111). On request by authors that are the regular classroom lecturers of the course, participants were recruited for the study. The consent for carrying out this research was given by the appropriate authority of the University, a committee domiciled in the faculty of Education and the study assigned number FECOO189. Questionnaire was applied to students at the beginning of the semester before lockdown, for collection of the demographic profiles of the students, during the first lecture in which the course was introduced. Participants consisted of two groups namely: those leaving school for interstate travels to join their families in stay safe practice and those on campus either as indigenes of Nsukka or having their parents or caregivers within Nsukka town. These two sets were assigned to groups 1 and 2. Group 1 consisted of 24 males and 51 females exposed to Distance learning while group 2 was made up of 22 males and 53 females who were exposed to instructions in a Presential classroom setting with keen safety consciousness against Covid-19 spread. The experimental group were exposed to both synchronous and asynchronous modes while the control were exposed to face to face classroom lectures with technological aids integration during the lesson. For the Distance learning group, the virtual environment used was Blackboard collaborate. Blackboard Collaborate is a secure online classroom meeting space where lecturers and students virtually connect with video, audio, screen sharing, and whiteboards, discussion of assignments and submission of assignments and feedback via WhatsApp and e-mail.

Week 1 lesson 1 was face to face instruction in which DL students were provided with the online link, presentation of the course unit objectives, how to be a virtual student, features of Blackboard App and hints on effective utilization of synchronous and asynchronous modes for online learning. Week 2 was used for pretest in both groups. Formative evaluation questions were given online in synchronous mode. The difference between the two instructional groups was on teaching strategies. Face to face start up lecture in week 1 for DL group gave the learners the opportunity to meet each other and their instructor one on one for the study. The study duration was 6 weeks. Week 6 was used for administration of achievement and interest scale posttests for both groups. In the DL group, the asynchronous mode throughout the 4 weeks of experiment always succeeded the synchronous mode with teacher's present. Students were expected to log onto the provided link for accessing the course contents individually from their homes and read the week's course material, download resources such as lecture transcripts and follow instructions to complete tasks in asynchronous mode. Assignments emphasized practical applications that involved tasks submission online. Students communicated and interacted with the instructor and with each other by e-mail and WhatsApp; posted their comments regularly in asynchronous online forum, commented on and generated ideas with other students while the instructor coordinated the procedure. In both the Distance Learning and the Presential modalities, the specific objectives and the instructional contents were the same.

For group 2 students exposed to Presential (face to face) classroom, lectures were supported with audio visual technological aids such as students' laptops and smart phones. These were used in driving home some abstract points in the physiological processes of what happen in coition and ejaculation during intercourse in humans. As lectures progressed, students were provided with the link for login to you tube downloads of male and female reproductive systems. As the explanations of the physiological processes went on, students visualized the processes and as teacher interrogated their understanding of these processes using probing questions, students attempted answers to the functions of parts such as the ovary, spermatozoon, fallopian tube and the uterus. The teacher's role during the instruction was more of guidance oriented in groups 1 and 2. Students raised questions for clarification of issues on slides presented. In the 6th week, students were provided the same tests as posttest to ascertain the degree of change in behavior as a result of treatments given that lasted for 4 weeks. Students scripts were collected, graded and analysis of data ran using Mean and Standard deviation in answering the four research questions. The two null hypotheses were tested using ANCOVA at 0.05 level of significance.

4 Results

Research results are as presented below using histograms.

Research Question One: What is the effect of Distance learning and Presential classroom instructions on students' achievement in undergraduate introductory Biology course?

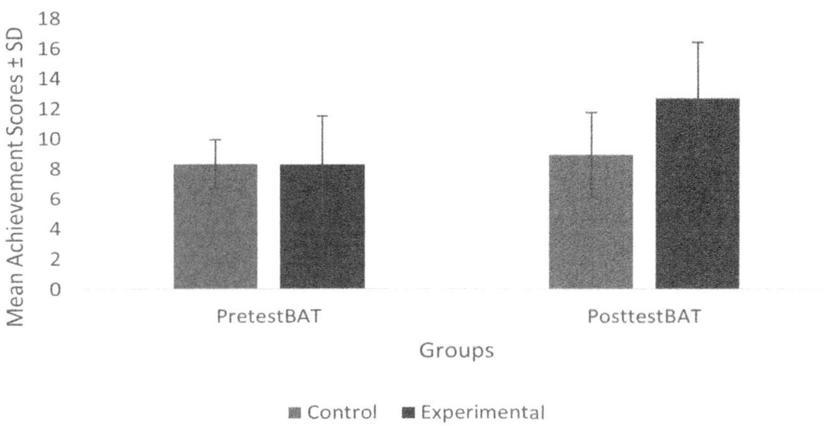

Fig. 1. Differential effects of Distance Learning and Presential classroom instructions on students' achievement in undergraduate introductory Biology course

Figure 1 above show the same Biology Achievement Test (BAT) take off mean scores in both experimental and control groups (pretest). Students exposed to Distance Learning instruction had significant higher mean score in posttest BAT than those exposed to presential classroom instruction.

Research Question Two: What is the effect of Distance Learning and Presential classroom instructions on students' interest in undergraduate introductory Biology course?

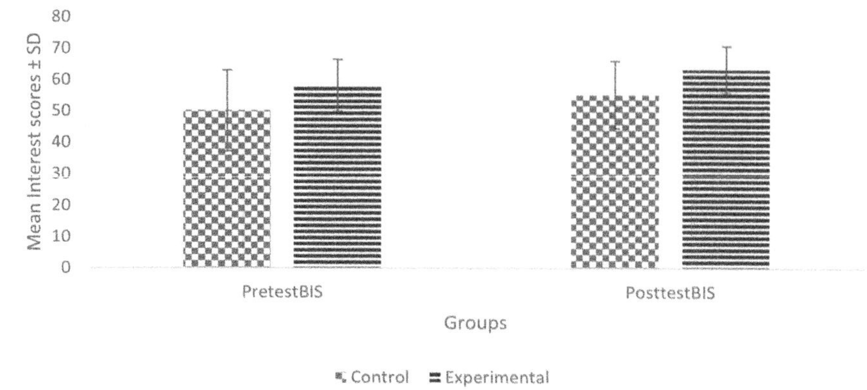

Fig. 2. Mean differential effects of Distance Learning and Presential classroom instruction on students' interest in undergraduate introductory Biology course.

Figure 2 above show that students exposed to Distance Learning instruction had significant higher posttest mean interest score than those exposed to presential classroom instruction. Pretest BIS score for Experimental group was also higher than that of control group. Since extraneous variable of subjects interaction was controlled by having the introduction of the purpose of study done for control group at a different confine when the experimental group students had left campus; the superiority seen in pretest interest score in favor of group 1 may have arisen from their exposure to hints of online learning in the study which may have tuned them up for the instructions.

Research Question Three: What is the influence of gender on achievement scores of students in undergraduate introductory Biology course?

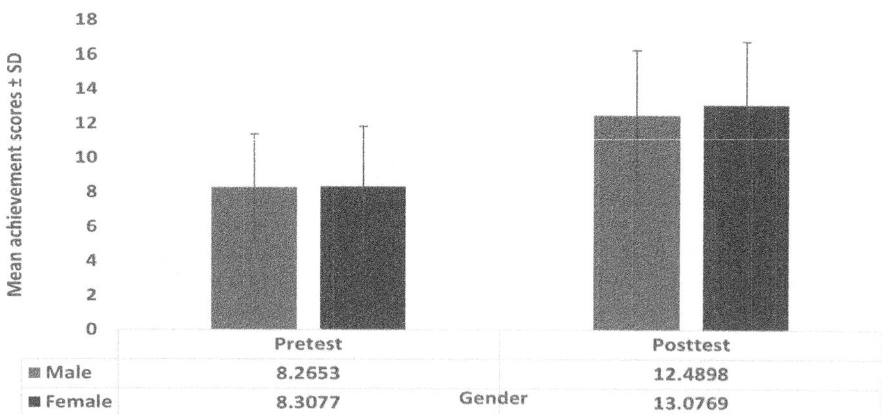

Fig. 3. Differential effects of experiment on males and females' achievement scores in undergraduate degree Introductory Biology course.

Figure 3 above show no difference in pretest achievement mean scores (8.26 and 8.30) for males and females.

It also shows no significant difference between the posttest mean achievement scores of males (12.48) and females (13.09) exposed to Experiment.

Research Question Four: What is the influence of gender on students' mean interest scores when exposed to Distance Learning?

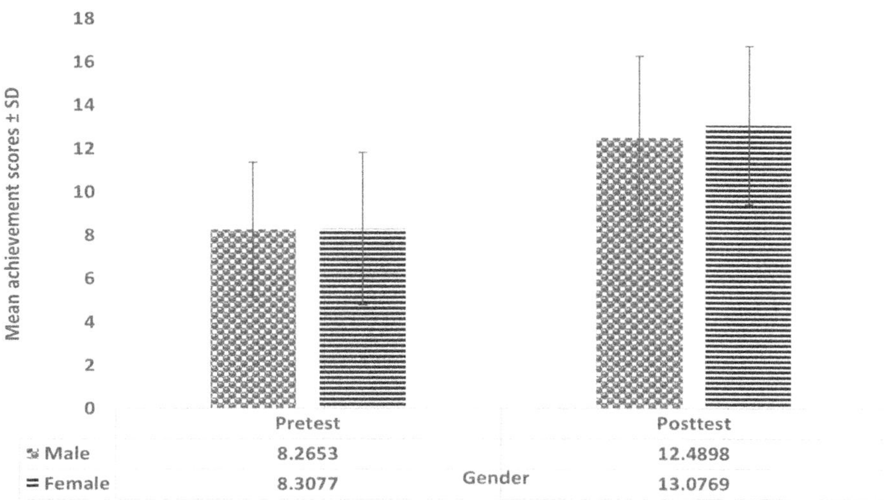

Fig. 4. Differential effects of experiment on interest scores of males and females in undergraduate degree Introductory Biology course.

In Fig. 4 above there is no significant difference between the Pretest and Posttest mean interest scores of male and female students exposed to Experiment. There is similarity in take-off interest sores (pretest). The slight difference by gender in Posttest was not substantial.

Hypothesis One: Hypothesis one was a test of ANCOVA that probes interaction effects between experiment and gender on students' Posttest achievement scores. Figure 5 explains if such interactions were found.

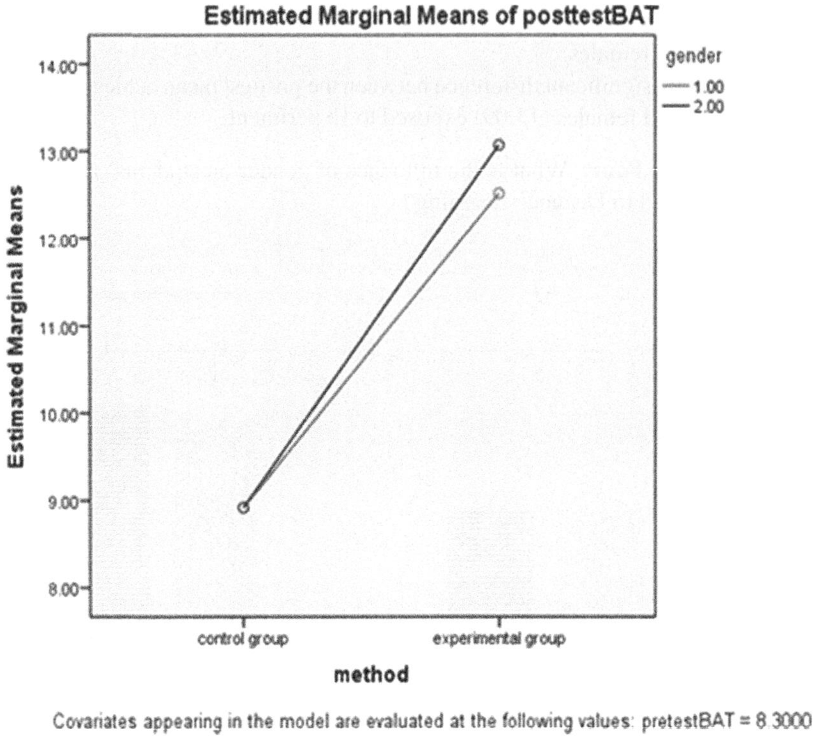

Fig. 5. ANCOVA on interactions between Experiment and gender on students' achievement scores.

On Fig. 5 above, no interaction between experiment and gender was found. The two graph lines of males and females on Fig. 5 do not intersect. Instead, the lines move nearer the control. The tilting portray that a slight interaction was found within control group. Such was not found in the experimental group. The null hypothesis set ab initio was accepted.

Hypothesis Two: There is no significant interaction effects of methods and gender on students' Posttest interest scores.

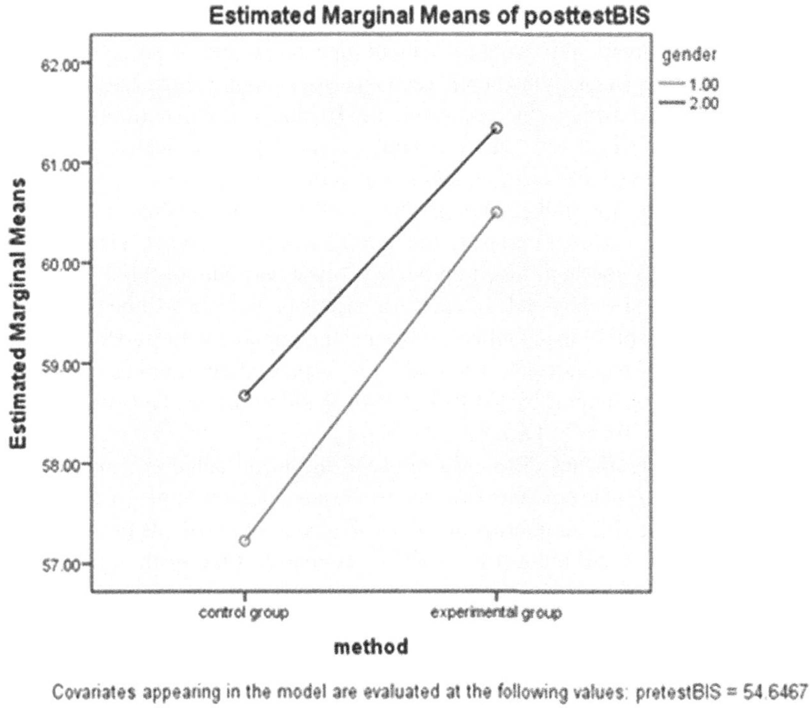

Fig. 6. ANCOVA on interactions between Experiment and gender on students' Interest scores.

On Fig. 6 above, no interaction between experiment and gender was found. The two graph lines of males and females on Fig. 6 do not intersect at all both in the control and experimental group. As such the hypothesis of no significant interactionwas accepted.

4.1 Summary of Major Findings

1. Students exposed to Distance learning instruction had higher mean achievement and interest scores than those exposed to presential instruction.
2. There is no significant difference between the mean achievement and interest scores of male and female students exposed to Distance learning instruction.
3. The interaction effect of method and gender on students' achievement and interest were not significant.

4.2 Discussions

The discussion of findings was done based on the three major findings and points above.

The results of the study show that students exposed to Distance learning had higher mean achievement and interest scores than those exposed to presential classroom instruction. The superiority of DL over Presential face to face classroom in achievement and interest in this study was as a result of great opportunity the DL students had over the face to face (Presential) classroom modality. Online learning exposure enabled the experimental group, pay attention to contents without time constraints as posed by Presential classroom, autonomy in resolving controversial issues encountered during synchronous mode was guaranteed using asynchronous mode. By this, learning shifted from teacher dominance to learner centered activities built upon world wide web-based information search that resolved all 'seaming less controversial' and or not easy to understand contents/issues. Also, the higher interest shown by DL even in Pretest over Presential classroom was because of exposure to modalities of being a virtual student, lesson objectives etc. which got them tuned up before pretest was administered. This finding agrees with those of [18] that student's performance is higher when some portion, or all their schooling takes place in an online environment compared with students who are in traditional face-to-face conditions. The finding of higher interest amongst DL students is in tandem with the finding by [3] that statistical difference exists between DL and Traditional groups in favor of DL.

There was no significant difference between the mean achievement and interest scores of male and female students exposed to Distance Learning instruction. In addition, there was no significant interaction effect of gender and methods of instruction on students' achievement and interest in SED 111 course. But the method of instruction exerted influence on the achievement and interest of students on the course. This was a result of the great obligation upon every learner in the DL group, to pay attention to details irrespective of their gender. The finding agrees with Sivapunniam as cited by [12] that students (females) who have been distracted or deterred from learning due to their traditional home and school environment are offered a welcomed break from the monotony of traditional classroom instruction and have the opportunity to make choices about their learning in online environment. By this the cord of superiority of males over females in science learning outcomes was weakened and broken in the course studied.

The findings of the study authenticate social constructivist learning theory propounded by [20] that learning is a socially mediated exercise where a learner constructs knowledge based on interactions with the social (Online) environment. That knowledge formed by a learner is influenced by environment (context) and prior knowledge held by the learner. Therefore, according to social constructivist learning, teachers should provide learners with an opportunity to negotiate meaning and to collaborate with peers and adults who are experts including teachers in knowledge construction.

5 Conclusion

Successful living in a dynamic and ever evolving world demands that our education system must keep pace with trends of scientific and technological development. Education stakeholders especially of Higher institutions of learning must break off from "almost on hold mood and dormant system" that the Pandemic (Covid 19) has relegated us to, especially the developing countries such as Nigeria. Distance Education is here to stay with us and therefore "a must embrace" by institutions of Higher learning. The superiority of Online/Distance learning over Presential/Traditional classroom in students' achievement and interest in their introductory Biology course reveal the importance of DL and students' great potential and capabilities of succeeding in a globalized world.

Since DL has proved in this study, an excellent educational practice for our 21st century dynamic world, institutions of higher Education stakeholders in all nations of the world should welcome and prioritize the implementation of Online/DL as a major education development challenge. Grassroot preparedness should start with Administrators of institutions of higher education, Lecturers and students, Curriculum planners, Education policy makers, Education ministries and Government. These stakeholders should play their roles in providing enabling environment for DL to thrive. Administrators of higher Education should contribute their quota by sponsoring their lecturers to international conferences and workshops for learning new ways of teaching sciences using new technologies. Lecturers and students should be monitored regularly on extent of integration of DL in courses implementation. Incentives/rewards should be given to lecturers whose practices/ applications of technological tools and DL in science teaching are remarkably different from others. In online/DL, students should be given opportunities to negotiate meanings, construct their knowledge as they collaborate with specialists who are global experts in their learning domains. Seminars involving faculty members on effective application of online/DL should be organized regularly in institutions of higher learning.

Education policy makers and ministries should make policies with favorable dispositions that project online/DL growth in their countries. There should be proper integration of online/ DL in the programs of Education science faculties by curriculum planners and developers around the world. Government of every country has great role to play to ensure that institutions of higher education strive and thrive in a competitive globalized world through prioritizing education budgets and funding of online/Distance Learning.

References

1. Middleton, A.J.: How effective is distance education? Int. J. Instr. Media **24**, 133 (1997)
2. Shachar, M., Neumann, Y.: Twenty years of research on the academic performance differences between traditional and distance learning: summative meta-analysis and trend examination. MERLOT J. Online Learn. Teach. **6** (2010)
3. Francescucci, A., Foster, M.: The VIRI (Virtual, Interactive, Real-Time, Instructor-Led) classroom: the impact of blended synchronous online courses on student performance engagement, and satisfaction, Canadian. J. High. Educ. **43**, 78–91 (2013)
4. Gossenheimer, A.N., Bem, T., Carneiro, M.L.F., de Castro, M.S.: Impact of distance education on academic performance in a pharmaceutical care course. PloS One **12** (2017)
5. Chen, P.-S.D., Lambert, A.D., Guidry, K.R.: Engaging online learners: the impact of Web-based learning technology on college student engagement. Comput. Educ. **54**, 1222–1232 (2010)
6. Hu, S., Kuh, G.D.: Computing Experience and Good Practices in Undergraduate Education: Does the Degree of Campus Wiredness Matter? (2001)
7. Laird, T.F.N., Kuh, G.D.: Student experiences with information technology and their relationship to other aspects of student engagement. Res. High. Educ. **46**, 211–233 (2005)
8. Robinson, C.C., Hullinger, H.: New benchmarks in higher education: student engagement in online learning. J. Educ. Bus. **84**, 101–109 (2008)
9. Korobova, N., Starobin, S.S.: A comparative study of student engagement, satisfaction, and academic success among international and American students. J. Int. Students **5**, 72–85 (2015)

10. Duderstadt, J.J., Atkins, D.E., Van Houweling, D.E., Van Houweling, D.: Higher Education in the Digital Age: Technology Issues and Strategies for American Colleges and Universities. Greenwood Publishing Group (2002)
11. Thurmond, V., Wambach, K.: Understanding interactions in distance education: a review of the literature. Int. J. Instr. Technol. Distance Learn. **1**, np (2004)
12. Larwin, K.H., Erickson, M.J., Given, E.: The potential impact of online/distance education for K-12 special education students: a meta-analytic investigation. In: Presentation at the Conference on Higher Education Pedagogy, Blacksburg, VA (2015)
13. Ibe, E., Abamuche, J.: Effects of audiovisual technological aids on students' achievement and interest in secondary school biology in Nigeria. Heliyon **5**, e01812 (2019)
14. Galdi, S., Cadinu, M., Tomasetto, C.: The roots of stereotype threats: when automatic association disrupt girls maths performance. Child Dev. **85**, 250–263 (2014)
15. Dimitrov, D.M.: Gender differences in science achievement: differential effect of ability, response format, and strands of learning outcomes. Sch. Sci. Math. **99**, 445–450 (1999)
16. Lizzio, A., Wilson, K., Simons, R.: University students' perceptions of the learning environment and academic outcomes: implications for theory and practice. Stud. High. Educ. **27**, 27–52 (2002)
17. Zhang, D., Zhou, L., Briggs, R.O., Nunamaker, Jr. J.F.: Instructional video in e-learning: assessing the impact of interactive video on learning effectiveness. Inf. Manag. **43**, 15–27 (2006)
18. Means, B., Toyama, Y., Murphy, R., Bakia, M., Jones, K.: Evaluation of evidence-based practices in online learning: a meta-analysis and review of online learning studies (2009)
19. Sadaghiani, H.R.: Using multimedia learning modules in a hybrid-online course in electricity and magnetism. Phys. Rev. Spec. Top.-Phys. Educ. Res. **7**, 010102 (2011)
20. Vygotsky, L.: Socio-cultural Theory. Mind in Society (1978)

The Flipped Inclusion Model: Eco-Sustainable and Inclusive Accessibility in the Era Covid-19

De Giuseppe Tonia(✉), Annalisa Ianniello, and Felice Corona

University of Salerno, 84084 Salerno, Italy
tonia.degiuseppe@springer.com

Abstract. Information and Communication Technologies (ICT), supported by the transnational interconnection of Web 4.0 constitute the main development driver to provide education of fair and inclusive quality, aimed at promoting the realization of systemic change for the Qualitative Well-being of humanity.

Flipped Inclusion's model, tested at the University of Salerno, aims to impinge on cognitive and attribution styles, on the creation of ecological-inclusive profiles in pursuit of the Sustainable Development Goals outlined by the 2030 Agenda. Flipped Inclusion is configured as a democratic model of existential planning metadisciplinary - for the development of a new ecological, active and responsible welfare, starting from the constitution of a *way of life* capable of connecting individuality and sociality, in light of the complex changes in the contingent liquidity socio-political-economic. The longitudinal-multi-perspective pilot study carried out between 2014 and 2017, in formal (academic courses, school) and informal spaces of University of Salerno, involved 1822 students. From the qualitative-quantitative research data it emerges that: the flipped inclusion model has favored the promotion of an inclusive context, through a modification of their own style of prosocial attribution. In the second phase of the experimentation of the model, from 2017 and currently in progress, and that is placed also in the historical epidemiological period from COVID-19, and in line with the implementing provisions of the Prime Ministerial Decree of 4 March 2020, is investigating the comparative use of different Open and Distance Learning accessibility tools with e-learning platforms in a perspective of expanding the sample and fields of investigation in compliance with the modular logic of Flipped Inclusion.

Keywords: Flipped inclusion · Complex blended learning · Education for Sustainable Development (ESD) · Era Covid-19

1 Introduction

Universal access to knowledge, an intangible resource for economic growth, innovation and socio-cultural progress, is configured as a universal human right, in compliance

D. G. Tonia—She has curated main focus the research and she wrote the paragraph 2) Method.
I. Annalisa—She wrote the paragraph 3) Results of the pilot study and new lines of research.
F. Corona—He curated scientific coordination and he wrote paragraph: 1) Introduction; 4) Conclusions.

L. S. Agrati et al. (Eds.): HELMeTO 2020, CCIS 1344, pp. 337–351, 2021.
https://doi.org/10.1007/978-3-030-67435-9_26

with the essential principles of: 1) cultural diversity; 2) freedom of expression; 3) equal access to education; 4) and information [1]. The establishment of a fair knowledge society, prerequisite for the full development of the person, from knowing how to act sustainably [1], proactively, and prosocially-inclusive, requires the conscious management of "tools that facilitate access to resources and services, promote exchanges and encourage remote collaboration" [2] (p. 1). Not surprisingly, Information and Communication Technologies (ICT), supported by the transnational interconnection of Web 4.0, within the Framework of Action of Agenda 2030 [3], constitute the main development driver to provide education of fair and inclusive quality [3], aimed at promoting the realization of systemic change [1] for the Qualitative Well-being of humanity. In this sense, pedagogical epistemology, within the context of the relational ethics paradigm, is called to build (*bildung*) sustainable communities of knowledge citizenship [4] within a lifelong learning perspective, through the promotion of knowledge management, inclusive-integrated multidimensional approaches of ecological-relational re-qualification. This educational imperative reflects the need to invest in processes of cognitive autonomy, self-reflection, and critical analysis [5] for the creation of sustainable citizens [4], inhabitants of the hyper-complex, postmodern, socio-systemic society. In this regard, the need for syntropic-collaborative partnership, "on in- definite and global spacetime arcs" [6] (p. 32) constitutes the hard core on which to rest the interdependent balance ecology-economy-social equity [3], and re-orient the processes to the inclusive principles of Education for Sustainable Development (ESD). It's about of de-building, through the conscious use of cross-media-transformative tools, the heterotopia of nonplaces [7], s-confined neutralized spaces that reify the identity essence of *homo clausus* [8], undermine the ontological security and affect planetary socio-cultural asymmetries.

2 Method

In line with this theoretical premise, for the development of ecological subjectivities [4], the existential project model Flipped Inclusion [9], tested at the University of Salerno, in line with the implementing provisions of the Prime Ministerial Decree of 4 March 2020, invests in simplexity [10] and non-linear [11] distance learning-planning. Through the application of the inter and trans-disciplinary pedagogical-transformational architecture in Moodle, an open source platform, Flipped Inclusion aims to impinge on cognitive and attribution styles, on the creation of ecological-inclusive profiles in pursuit of the Sustainable Development Goals [1] outlined by the 2030 Agenda [3]. In particular, it intends to train pro-socially relational-cooperative-communicative individuals to: 1) promote the well-being of all at all ages (Objective 3); 2) ensuring quality inclusive and equitable education (Goal 4); 3) promote sustained, inclusive and sustainable economic growth (Goal 8); 4) reduce inequalities (Goal 10) [3].

Flipped Inclusion [12] is configured as a democratic model of existential planning [13] -metadisciplinary - for the development of a new ecological, active and responsible welfare, starting from the constitution of a *way of life* [13] capable of connecting individuality and sociality, in light of the complex changes in the contingent liquidity [14] socio-political-economic. It invests in the constitution of civic identities 1) literate to- wards sustainability, 2) from cultural and social skills, 3) from inclusive, creative-independent thinking 4), predisposed to the art of sharing [13] through operational procedures of computational logic.

In Flipped Inclusion the work process is organized in a deconstructive perspective [15], divided in 4 macro-phases that are transformative in nature, the modules follow a top down and bottom-up approach through the didactic transposition of Frame Analysis [16] and the ecological-systemic perspective [17]: starting from "an exploratory investigation (phase 1- Explore), the aim is to discover (phase 2- Idea) and design products and processes for solving the problem (phase 3 - Project) to be applied experimentally in the field (Phase 4 - Experiment)" [18] (p. 164). It invests "in a procedure that circumscribes stimuli of interest (Key), specifies a frame of observation (frame), which tends to identify a problem/challenge to be analyzed (framing) and to seek structural methodological resolutions for specific interventions (framework)" [18] (p. 164).

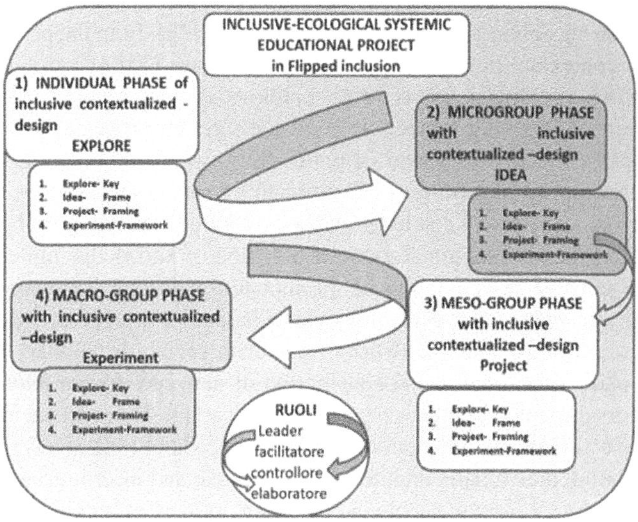

Fig. 1. Project work [12] (p. 68)

In this sense, the focus is on the design, initially individual and subsequently co-built, of self-consistent, modular, searchable, reusable and interoperable Learning Objects (LO), consisting of digital assets of text, video and images:

1) adaptable to the individual (pedagogical purpose), for the composition of minimum teaching units whose assembly, aimed at the eco-sustainable educational project, allows the construction of personalized didactic paths;
2) dynamically generated rather than pre-assembled (technological purpose), for the formation of inclusive digital-intelligent agents;
3) agile and accessible (economic purpose), to build a socially useful and profitable market of ecological values [19].

The learning units/resources (LO), invested with the quality of the Flipped Inclusion educational approach, are systemically elaborated [17] in 4 stages: "1) individual, to responsibly explore methods of action; 2) micro group, to proactively design through forms of interaction; 3) in meso group, to design collaborative forms of proactive co-responsibility; 4) and macro group work, to experiment forms of co-responsible, proactive and prosocial cooperation" [20] (p. 9). Through the use of Moodle, an e-learning environment of dynamic-constructivist learning, the aim is to facilitate an interactive situated procedure to stimulate authentic participation processes, functional to the training of insiders of the eco-sustainable quality, for the development of communities of practice in practice [21].

The delineation of the Learning Objects follows the cyclical-algorithmic sequential recursion that characterizes the EIPE pedagogical-problematic matrix of the Flipped Inclusion model, acronym of:

1) *Explore* - the meanings of sustainable development [22], from the perspective of the reflective-contextual investigation (Inquiry Learning) [23] of a critical (practical-not idealist), ecological (ecocentric), ontological (incorporated) [24] approach. The design of Learning Objects is activated through processes of identification and semantic selection of a word-stimulus (Key), which emerged from systematic *response prompting procedures* [25], resonating with the socio-ecological problems of eco-egoic society of knowledge. This exploratory analysis (Problem Finding-Setting-Analysis) is functional to the acquisition of knowledge aimed at the conscious sustainable re-generation of the human-intellectual heritage. It invests in thought conceived as an investigation, which defines knowledge as a process located in the action, to promote a network of personal, social, disciplinary and methodological skills functional to the constitution of new eco- logical *tables of values*, of a universal-axiological that respects natural capital. By experimenting with the validity of eco-inclusive exploratory paths and procedures (reflexively managed), the aim is to build, individually and in micro-meso-exo and macro- group, educational elements in digital format, usable in e-learning, in view of training in reflexivity of principles and practices of sustainable development.
2) *Idea* - creative and divergent paths [26] of ecological, social and economic reconciliation [27], of conscious critique of education for unsustainability [22], through the conceptual circumscription (Frame) of the psycho-social problem investigated (Key). The discovery learning [26] applied to the construction of Learning Objects co-dis- cussed in Moodle stimulates the potential for lifelong learning [28], for the development of intuitive-deductive significance (people) who are co-responsible for the eco conservative-balance. Through the psycho-pedagogical-constructivist methodology of discovery learning, the aim is to stimulate (Fading) the discovery of new models of action that support the socio-environmental compatibility of development. In an active way, for insight, the discovery of past, present and future ecological scenarios is promoted, between similarities and differences, to invest in processes of motivation for sustainable change for the psycho-physical well-being of the community. It invests in the development of lateral thinking skills [29] (Shaping) for the generation of ideas that preserve the stock of exhaustible energy resources,

for the management of a negative environmental impact, to safeguard the process of environmental renewal.

3) *Project* - the transition towards a sustainable Europe by 2030 [1], through the delineation of Learning Objects qualified for the development of an Environmental Philosophy [22] aimed at inclusive-ecological transformation of cognitive-behavioral styles. Through mastery learning strategies [30], to the "keyword (key) that has become a concept (Frame) is added the challenge-problem (Framing) on which the solution re- search is intended" [18] (p. 178). In context of the formation of an "intersubjective dialectic in which anti-dogmatic rationality (decision making) is never separated from ethics" [31] (p. 25).
   It invests in the design of qualitative actions, in the re-construction of systems of representation of the world to describe and explain the phenomena of reality, in the acquisition of new systems of meaning to orient oneself. The aim is to promote a transdisciplinary-incremental path for delineating ecological problems and intercurrent connection relationships, with a view to constraction responsible behavioral chains (Chaining), capable of not altering the ecosystem-natural balance. It is a question of designing, in steps of increasing complexity, an educational heritage consisting of knowledge and know-how, capable of adapting to new contexts, of mastering knowledge and skills of sustainable development, for the education of inclusive-proactive citizens.
4) Experiment - in Moodle the solution (problem solving) of alternative [22], systemic, flexible and reversible pedagogical proposals, "aimed at satisfying the needs of the pre- sent generation without compromising future generations" [32] (p. 2). In this phase, the learning experience (Framework) [33] becomes a patrimony of self-consistent knowledge, the principle of further evolutions, for the micro-meso-exo and macro systemic-group interconnection [17] of the co-designed Learning Object. The co-creation and co-discussion of artifacts (LO) in Moodle, in promoting processes of Self-help [34], of positive-motivational reinforcement, aims to experience inclusive development cooperation [1] communities [35] - interdependent.
   Through the democratic comparison of personal-individual performances with the teacher and with peers (Modeling), the aim is to promote forms of guided participation, hyper-collaboration, to enhance self-correction skills and of self-regulation and generate new experiential solutions, choosing divergent paths [18] to autonomously solve problems of eco-sustainable development (Fig. 2).

In this sense, it invests in the ESD [3] in Networked Collaborative Learning (NCL) [36], for the transformation of schemes and perspectives of meaning, also through socio-hermeneutic functions of the suite of training tools available in Moodle [37], for the use of:

1) *chats* and *forum*, places for meeting, elaboration and sharing of inclusive-ecological meanings, functional to the implementation of psychosocial relationships to the co-creation of communicative-participatory processes. The aim is to build communities in communication (group-chat), through the activation of synchronous textual-virtual discussions, instant conversational exchanges, since "messages in textual form imply a rigorous organization of thought and coherence of messages, which

interaction agent-agent/agent-environment, for the shared co-design of learning objects aimed at the ecological transformation of people, performances, knowledge and skills. The use of Moodle, linked to connectivist pedagogies facilitating virtual-inter- personal communication and collaborative learning [36] invests in the construction of a cultural heritage of experiences, for the establishment of a social sense of individual skills and of more effective, self-assessing, self-directed learners.

Also in e-learning, Flipped Inclusion make use of a constant evaluation (monitoring) and self-evaluation (processing) control of the Learning Objects produced, of the micro-meso and macro eco-inclusive contextualized designs "intentionally designed to guide and develop learning (individual, collaborative, organizational) with effects on the educational, economic and social system" [46] (p. 52). It invests in an evaluation as a dialogic construction with a hermeneutic character, a central element of the training process capable of re-evaluating the active nature of the teaching-learning process, which becomes a significant construction for those who develop it (learners/participants). In Flipped Inclusion, assessment becomes in itself a responsible relational-training process [46], which defines forms of ecological literacy [4]. The learners fill in the synoptic-project sheets of the innovative-participatory pedagogical approach, organized according to standard evaluation rubrics by role, objective and phases [18]: 1) rubric a knowledge and skills; 2) rubric b- communication skills; 3) rubric c- cognitive and metacognitive skills; 4) rubric d- social and pro-social competences [18]. In this way, the aim is to promote reflection processes on the eco-sustainable training experience, to bring the learning process back to a social event, and not just an individual one, to favor the epistemological anthropological, natural and cultural.

The didactic investment in the construct-phenomenological-transformative approaches of the Flipped Inclusion model [9] is rooted in the value attributed to self-managed and co-managed empowered learning. Through co-produced and co-regulated self-determination approaches, we make use of a design structure (EIPE) in continuous, recursive and modular reorganization of the computational system, aimed at overcoming the sequential accumulation of linear approaches.

3 Results of the Pilot Study and New Lines of Research

The longitudinal-multi-perspective pilot study carried out between 2014 and 2017, in formal (academic courses, school) and informal spaces (University of Salerno - Department of human-philosophical sciences and training, Department of Medicine and Surgery), involved 1822 students (1772 academics and 50 of compulsory school), with a simple random sampling of 911 participants [18].

Interpretative-descriptive-transformative, multi-method research was developed through the application of action-research and experimental research [40]. The research data was collected through the integration of qualitative and quantitative research tools and methodologies.

The quantitative analysis was carried out by:

1) the tabulation of data relating to the comparative analysis of structured evaluation sheets (monitoring) by levels (individual, micro-meso and macro group phase) and self-evaluation (processing) by role;

2) re-test after 3 years from the application of the Flipped Inclusion model to a sample of 80 participants (students and interns), for which a synchronic comparison of the same by course and by phases of the paths was carried out.
3) the administration of the Toronto Empaty Questionnaire to a sample of 20 respondents (students and interns), multidimensional scale (measurement of 4 factors: 1. Self-confidence, 2. Balance; 3. Sensitivity; 4. Non-conformity) of the likert type, with 16 items, to evaluate the level of empathy (as an emotional process) personal, functional to the decoding of social cognition and to the evaluation of the promotion of prosocial behavior [47] (Fig. 3).

The Toronto Empathy Questionnaire

Please read each statement below carefully and rate how frequently you feel or act in the manner described. Circle your answer on the response form. There are no right or wrong answers or trick questions. Please answer each question as honestly as you can.		NEVER	RARELY	SOMETIMES	OFTEN	ALWAYS
1.	When someone else is feeling excited, I tend to get excited too	0	1	2	3	4
2.	Other people's misfortunes do not disturb me a great deal	0	1	2	3	4
3.	It upsets me to see someone being treated disrespectfully	0	1	2	3	4
4.	I remain unaffected when someone close to me is happy	0	1	2	3	4
5.	I enjoy making other people feel better	0	1	2	3	4
6.	I have tender, concerned feelings for people less fortunate than me	0	1	2	3	4
7.	When a friend starts to talk about his\her problems, I try to steer the conversation towards something else	0	1	2	3	4
8.	I can tell when others are sad even when they do not say anything	0	1	2	3	4
9.	I find that I am "in tune" with other people's moods	0	1	2	3	4
10.	I do not feel sympathy for people who cause their own serious illnesses	0	1	2	3	4
11.	I become irritated when someone cries	0	1	2	3	4
12.	I am not really interested in how other people feel	0	1	2	3	4
13.	I get a strong urge to help when I see someone who is upset	0	1	2	3	4
14.	When I see someone treated unfairly, I do not feel very much pity for them	0	1	2	3	4
15.	I find it silly for people to cry out of happiness	0	1	2	3	4
16.	When I see someone being taken advantage of, I feel kind of protective towards him\her	0	1	2	3	4

Add each item results and divide total by 4 to find determine your score:

Higher scores indicate high levels of self-reported empathy while scores below 45 are indicative of below average empathy levels

Scoring: Item responses are scored according to the following scale for positively worded items 1, 3, 5, 6, 8, 9, 13, 16. Never = 0; Rarely = 1, Sometimes = 2, Often = 3, Always = 4. The following negatively worded items are reverse scored: 2, 4, 7, 10, 11, 12, 14, 15. Scores are summed to derive total for the Toronto Empathy Questionnaire, which can range from 0 to 64. Males' general score for this measure ranges from 43.46 to 44.45, while females tend to score within the range of 44.62 to 48.93. Gender differences as measured by this questionnaire are reported as being moderate

Fig. 3. The Toronto Empathy Questionnaire [47].

The qualitative research was conducted through interpretative and factual sociological-phenomenological practices [20]: 1) focus group; 2) participatory observation (individual and of micro-meso- and macro-groups); 3) descriptive evaluations of the Learning Objects produced.

From the administration of the post-test carried out three years after the experimentation on the sample of students who participated in the research, it emerges that:

79% of students regularly attended the course in Flipped Inclusion; 46% of participants found a change in their learning style (knowledge and skills), 45% on communication style, 58% an impact on style cooperative and 59% on the relational style. For 6% of the sample, the Flipped Inclusion model did not affect their communication style [20] (Fig. 4).

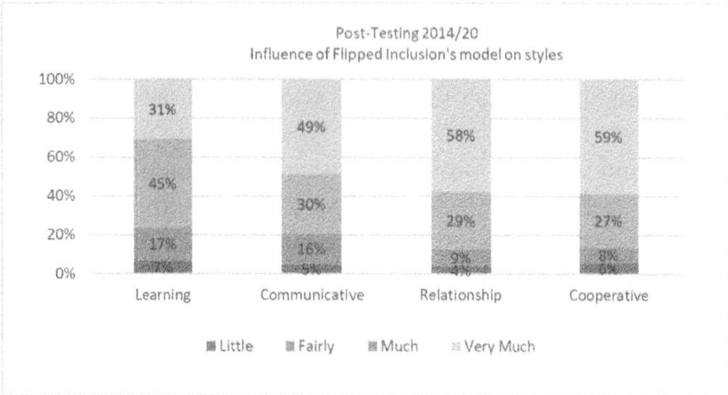

Fig. 4. Data- learning, communicative, relational, cooperative styles [20]

There is a significant prevalence of a positive trend regarding the predisposition of participants to active listening (55%), to accepting the rules (54%), to resolving conflicts (51%) and understanding the needs of others (55%). The lowest percentage of the sample (4%) is recorded in the capacity of active listening (Fig. 5).

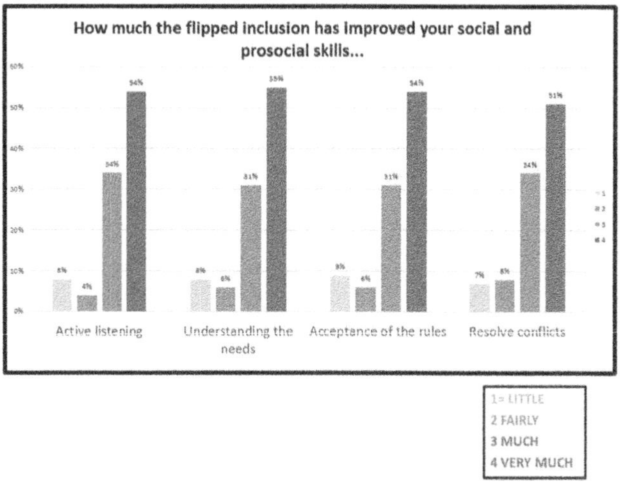

Fig. 5. Item analysis—prosocial skills [12] (p. 80)

From the post-test it also emerges that 45% of the sample of students perceived a personal change in the prosocial-inclusive profile (Fig. 6 and Fig. 7).

61% of the sample believe that the flipped inclusion model has favored the promotion of an inclusive context, through a modification of their own style of prosocial attribution.

"The probabilistic value of the conclusions, which characterize the experimental educational research, taking into account the impossibility of reaching the definition of causal inferences, with the exposure of the evaluation of the result to the risks of imprecision and indeterminacy, both for the innumerable intervening variables, both

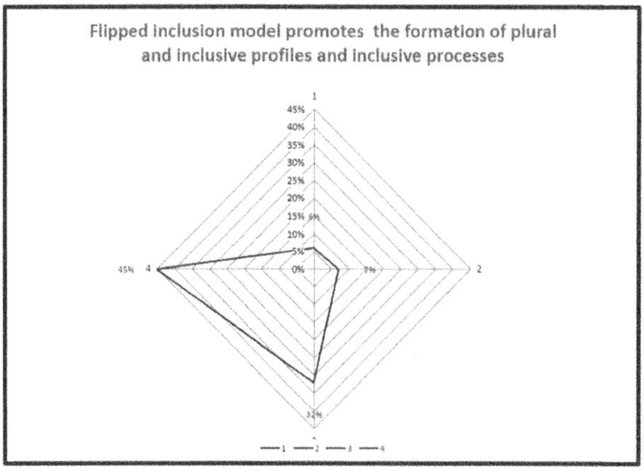

Fig. 6. Percentage data - Promotion of inclusive profiles and processes [12] (p. 81)

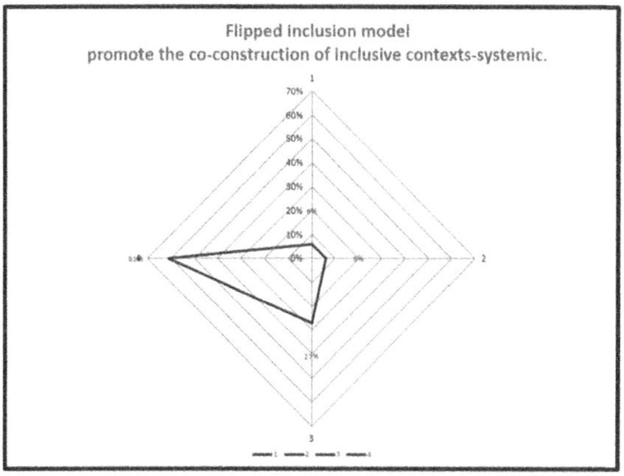

Fig. 7. Percentage data - Promotion of inclusive contexts [20]

due to the impossibility of a rigorous control of unpredictable dynamic phenomenal events, it has only partially allowed to reach a first evaluation of the significance of the research results. Further in-depth studies with rigorous control measures are therefore necessary" [18] (p. 210).

PHASE 2) - New Research Perspectives

The second phase of the experimentation of the model, from 2017 and currently in progress, is placed also in the historical epidemiological period from COVID- SARS19 and constitutes a strategic representative example of the immersive educational need with emergency connotations, which also highlights new ways to guaran- tee, 1) equal opportunities, 2) right to study, 3) participation, 4) inclusion [1].

The new explorative-descriptive-transformative study is investigating the comparative use of different Open and Distance Learning accessibility tools with e-learning platforms [37] in a perspective of expanding the sample and fields of investigation in compliance with the modular logic of Flipped Inclusion [40].

In adaptive, self-developed and self-organized, responsive and co-accessible spaces, cooperative dynamics are highlighted, in a profitable alternation of negotiation- creation and sharing that blurs geographical limits and boundaries of the self, in the awareness that education (also for sustainable development) is always, first of all, a communicative process [13]. In declining the concept of inclusion in web-based learning, from an ecological-systemic perspective [17] in the didactic logic of flipped learning [11], the Flipped Inclusion project architecture is connected to the enterprise education to produce aware-competent human resources, supporters of the pursuit of the objectives of Education for Sustainable Development (ESS) [3].

With the new descriptive-transformative research, therefore, we are proceeding according to the quantitative collection of the first phase of experimentation and with the same detection tools, assisted by the systematic traceability of the platforms. The investment in the web-based context of the flipped inclusion model is aimed at promoting forms of selective-participatory co-responsibility of segments and vector elements present in the network [35], to be applied for the promotional purpose of inclusive cross-media environments/places in which to experience positive proactive and prosocial relationships [42].

The accessibility of the training content, in order to represent a prerequisite of inclusiveness, requires flexibility management relating to: 1) training objectives; 2) educational paths; 3) evaluation criteria; 4) verification tools. In this regard, in the new experimentation of the Flipped Inclusion model, the production and evaluation of the accessibility of content follows ISO/IEC 40500: 2012 [49] criteria of: 1) perceptibility (web content and user interface); 2) Usability; 3. Understanding, such as readability, identification-prevention of errors); 4. Robustness as a compatibility optimization [49]. Just like in presence and in blended learning mode, the activities of micro-meso-exo-macro systemic [17] and collaborative problem solving [36] are proposed through the different platforms, used not only to activate mixed forms of communication, but also for the collective-resolutive identification of the specific analysis of a social problem, in the evaluation of the process [46] of co-creation of co-constructed works.

4 Conclusions

The scientific evidence (Fig. 1) shows the influence of the Flipped Inclusion model on cognitive and attribution styles (learning, communicative, relational, cooperative), and on the formation of inclusive-prosocial individual and collective profiles - presupposition to reconvert the lifestyles of the citizens of knowledge, beings in praxis capable of transforming the world [50] with a view to eco-sustainable development [22]. The use of e-learning ecologies broadens the boundaries between formal and informal education, facilitates the eco-sustainable, spiritual and cultural improvement of personalities by producing new forms of organization of knowledge, no longer a product of singular entities but a distributed phenomenon (collective intelligence).

[42] in chaotic and complex virtual spaces, which underline the non-linear nature of learning. Flipped Inclusion, an existential design model [40], intends to evoke the founding value of an education with multi-dimensional socio-anthropic-educational traits. It is

a matter of fostering awareness of the strategic value of the new didactics of individual and collective corporeality anchored to generative processes of prosociality, in which everyone feels the active protagonist of learning processes, of eco-inclusive behavior models [27], such as to facilitate the civil commitment and democratic-collective action [51] and favor proactive inclusion affecting public, economic and social policies (Advocacy).

References

1. UNESCO Education for Sustainable Development Goals: learning objectives. https://unesdoc.unesco.org/ark:/48223/pf0000247444. Accessed 12 June 2020
2. Commissione delle Comunità Europee. https://www.europa.eu.int/comm/elearning. Accessed 12 June 2020
3. ONU Transforming our world: the 2030 Agenda for Sustainable Development. https://www.un.org/ga/search/view_doc.asp?symbol=A/RES/70/1&Lang=E. Accessed 12 June 2020
4. Corcoran, P.B., Weakland, J.P., Wals, A.E.J.: Envisioning Futures for Environmental and Sustainability Education. Wageningen Academic Publishers, Netherlands (2017)
5. Paul, R., Elder, L.: The Nature and Functions of Critical and Creating Thinking. The Foundation for Critical Thinking. Dillon Beach, CA (2004)
6. Giddens, A.: Le conseguenze della modernità. Fiducia e rischio, sicurezza e pericolo. Il Mulino, Bologna (1994)
7. Augé, M.: Non luoghi. Introduzione a un'antropologia della surmodernità. Elèuthera, Milano (2009)
8. Elias, N.: La società degli individui. Il Mulino, Bologna (1990)
9. De Giuseppe, T., Ianniello, A., Corona, F.: Flipped inclusion, between didactic research and university teaching for lifelong learning. In: Proceedings of International Conference on Digital Pedagogies (ICDP), pp. 1–8. Elsevier, Amsterdam (2019)
10. Sibilio, M.: La didattica semplessa. Liguori, Napoli (2014)
11. Bergmann, J., Sams, A.: Flip YOUR Classroom Reach Every Student in Every Class Every Day. International Society for Technology in Education, Washington (2012)
12. De Giuseppe, T., Corona, F.: Flipped inclusion between educational emergencies and transformative socio-semiotic didactics. In: Delello, J. (ed.) Disruptive and Emerging Technology Trends Across Education and the Workplace, pp. 52–89. IGI Global, Pennsylvania (2020)
13. Dewey, J.: Democracy and Education: An Introduction to the Philosophy of Education. Macmillan, New York (1916)
14. Zygmunt, B.: Liquid Modernity. Polity, Cambridge (2000)
15. Derrida, J.: De la grammatologie. Minuit, Paris (1967)
16. Goffman, E.: Frame Analysis. Armando Editore, Roma (1974)
17. Bronfenbrenner, U.: Ecologia dello sviluppo umano. Il Mulino, Bologna (2002)
18. De Giuseppe, T.: Flipped inclusion. L'impianto teoretico tra bisogni emergenti e prospettive epistemologiche. Aracne, Roma (2018)
19. Gibbons, A.S., Nelson, J., Richards, R.: The nature and origin of instructional objects. In: Wiley, D.A. (ed.) The Instructional Use of Learning Objects, pp. 25–59. Agency for Instructional Technology and Association for Educational Communications and Technology, Bloomington (2002)
20. De Giuseppe, T., Ianniello, A., Corona, F.: Transformativity of the flipped inclusion model, between anthropocentric ergonomics of social capital, and ecological-systemic empowerment. Information **11**(8), 1–35 (2020)
21. Lipari, D., Valentini, P.: Comunità di pratica in pratica. Palinsesto, Roma (2013)
22. Huckle, J., Sterling, S.: Education for sustainability. Earthscan, London (1996)

23. Kuhn, T.S.: La struttura delle rivoluzioni scientifiche. Einaudi, Torino (1962)
24. Payne, P.G.: Environmental education in curriculum theory. J Environ. Educ. **37**(2), 25–35 (2006)
25. Morse, T.E., Schuster, J.W.: Simultaneous prompting: a review of the literature. Educ. Train. Dev. Disabil. **39**(2), 153–168 (2004)
26. Bruner, J.: The Process of Education. University Press, Cambridge (1961)
27. Dale, A., Newman, L.: Sustainable development, education and literacy. Int. J. Sustain. High. Educ. **6**(4), 351–362 (2005)
28. Dorier, J.-L., García, F.J.: Challenges and opportunities for the implementation of inquiry-based learning in day-to-day teaching. ZDM Math. Educ. **45**(6), 837–849 (2013). https://doi.org/10.1007/s11858-013-0512-8
29. De Bono, E.: Lateral Thinking: Creativity Step by Step. Harper & Row, New York (1970)
30. Bloom, B.S.: Stability and Change in Human Characteristics. Wiley, Hoboken (1964)
31. Luppi, E.: Progettazione e valutazione di un percorso formativo basato sui Learning Object per chi educa allo sviluppo sostenibile. J. Theor. Res. Educ. **8**(1), 21–46 (2013)
32. Hurlem, B.G.: Our Common Future. World Commission on Environment and development. Oxford University Press, Oxford (1987)
33. Kolb, D.A.: Experiential Learning. Prentice Hall, Upper Saddle River (1984)
34. Knowles, M.S.: Self-directed learning. Strumenti e strategie per promuoverlo. FrancoAngeli, Milano (2014)
35. Wenger, E.: Communities of Practice: Learning, Meaning and Identity. Cambridge University Press, New York (1998)
36. Trentin, G.: Networked Collaborative Learning. Social Interaction and Active Learning. Chandos Publishing, Oxford (2010)
37. Beatty, B., Ulasewicz, C.: Online teaching and learning in transition: faculty perspectives on moving from blackboard to the moodle learning management system. TechTrends **50**(4), 36–45 (2006)
38. Benigno, V., Trentin, G.: La valutazione nella formazione a distanza. In: Trentin, G. (ed.) Telematica e formazione a distanza. Il caso Polaris, pp. 207–227. Franco Angeli, Milano (1999)
39. Cerini, G., Spinosi, M.: Voci della scuola Duemilaquattro. Le novità del sistema educativo. Una guida per orientarsi. Tecnodid, Napoli (2003)
40. De Giuseppe, T., Ianniello, A., Podovsovnik, E., Corona, F.: The educational research flipped inclusion between social metamorphosis and technocratic hybridizations. In: Podovsovnik, E. (ed.) Examining the Roles of Teachers and Students in Mastering New Technologie, pp. 27–57. IGI Global, Pennsylvania (2020)
41. Probst, G.: Selbstorganisation - Ordnungsprozesse in sozialen Systemen aus ganzheitlicher Sicht. Verlag Paul Parey, Berlin (1987)
42. Beni, G., Wang, J.: Swarm intelligence in cellular robotic systems. In: Dario, P., Sandini, G., Aebischer, P. (eds.) Robots and Biological Systems: Towards a New Bionics?. NATO ASI Series, vol. 102, pp. 703–712. Springer, Heidelberg (1993). https://doi.org/10.1007/978-3-642-58069-7_38
43. Berti, E.: Aristotele. Laterza, Roma (2017)
44. Stigmergia e impression management. https://www.studiotpp.com/wp-content/up-loads/2018/06/Stigmergia-e-Impression-Managment.pdf
45. Binda, L.: La comunicazione economico-finanziaria e le nuove tecnologie. FrancoAngeli, Milano (2008)
46. Galliani, L.: Web ontology della valutazione educativa. Pensa Multimedia, Lecce (2009)
47. Spreng, R.N., McKinnon, M.C., Mar, R.A., Levine, B.: The Toronto Empathy Questionnaire: scale development and initial validation of a factor-analytic solution to multiple empathy measures. J. Pers. Assmt **91**(1), 62–71 (2009)

48. Corona, F., De Giuseppe, T.: La didattica flipped for inclusion. In: Limone, P.P., Parmigiani, D. (eds.) Modelli pedagogici e pratiche didattiche per la formazione iniziale e in servizio degli insegnanti, pp. 132–154. Progedit, Bari (2017)
49. Web Content Accessibility Guidelines (WCAG) 2.0. https://www.w3.org/TR/2008/REC-WCAG20-20081211. Accessed 26 May 2020
50. Freire, P.: La pedagogia degli oppressi. EGA, Torino (2002)
51. Obar, J.A., et al.: Advocacy 2.0: an analysis of how advocacy groups in the united states perceive and use social media as tools for facilitating civic engagement and collective action. J. Inf. Policy **2**(1), 1–25 (2012)

Author Index

Abamuche, Joy 324
Agrati, Laura Sara 170
Ait Si Ahmad, Hana 199
Amati, Ilenia 226
Aneke, Joseph 324
Ardimento, Pasquale 243

Bak, Gerda 158
Berrada, Khalid 199
Bonavolontà, Valerio 151
Bruschi, Barbara 187
Burden, Adrian 315

Capaccioli, Martina 214
Casalino, Gabriella 3
Castellano, Giovanna 3
Cataldi, Stefania 151
Cisternino, Antonio 256
Corazza, Laura 100
Corona, Felice 337

D'Errico, Francesca 17
Daniel, John 141
De Carolis, Berardina 17
Di Pietro, Anastasia 28
Dipace, Anna 28
Ducange, Pietro 256

El Kharki, Khadija 199
Eradze, Maka 28

Fabbri, Loretta 214
Fabbri, Stefania 271
Fazlagic, Bojan 28
Fazzolari, Michela 271
Ferrari, Simona 300
Fischetti, Francesco 151
Frisch, Muriel 73

Giampaolo, Mario 214

Hirasawa, Shigeichi 40
Hunvik, Sølve Robert Bø 56

Ianniello, Annalisa 337
Ibe, Ebere 324
Ishida, Takashi 40

Karkina, Svetlana V. 86
Kővári, Edit 158

Limone, Pierpaolo 115
Lindseth, Frank 56

Macauda, Anita 100
Macchiarulo, Nicola 17
Maci, Davide 151
Mackintosh, Chris 315
Marchisio, Marina 187
Matteucci, Ilaria 271
Mauro, Irene 289
Mena Marcos, Juan J. 86
Messina, Salvatore 289
Mort, Neil 141

Nakazawa, Makoto 40
Ndi, Simon-Joseph 73
Nicolini, Simona 100

Paciello, Marinella 17
Palestra, Giuseppe 17
Panciroli, Chiara 100
Paragot, Jean-Marc 73
Perla, Loredana 226
Petrocchi, Marinella 271
Pfeffer-Meyer, Victoria 73
Piccinno, Marco 126

Raviolo, Paolo 289
Rondonotti, Marco 289

Sacchet, Matteo 187
Saito, Tomohiko 40
Scalera, Michele 243
Scarinci, Alessia 226
Sims, Dave 315
Stebbings, Georgina 315

Tonellotto, Nicola 256
Tonia, De Giuseppe 337
Toto, Giusi Antonia 115
Triacca, Serena 300

Umezawa, Katsuyuki 40

Vaccarelli, Anna 271
Valeeva, Roza A. 86
Vallati, Carlo 256
Vessio, Gennaro 3
Vinci, Viviana 170

The manufacturer's authorised representative in the EU is Springer Nature Customer Service Centre GmbH, Europaplatz 3, 69115 Heidelberg, Germany. If you have any concerns regarding our products, please contact ProductSafety@springernature.com

Printed and bound by CPI Group (UK) Ltd, Croydon, CR0 4YY
28/09/2026
02224082-0003